BEST LITTLE STORIES

from the Life and Times of

WINSTON CHURCHILL

Other Books by C. Brian Kelly

BEST LITTLE IRONIES, ODDITIES & MYSTERIES OF THE CIVIL WAR
with "Mary Todd Lincoln: Troubled First Lady" by Ingrid Smyer

BEST LITTLE STORIES FROM THE AMERICAN REVOLUTION
with "Select Founding Mothers" by Ingrid Smyer

BEST LITTLE STORIES FROM THE CIVIL WAR
with "Varina: Forgotten First Lady" by Ingrid Smyer

BEST LITTLE STORIES FROM THE WHITE HOUSE
with "First Ladies in Review" by Ingrid Smyer

BEST LITTLE STORIES FROM THE WILD WEST
with "Fascinating Women of the West" by Ingrid Smyer

BEST LITTLE STORIES FROM VIRGINIA
with "The Women Who Counted" by Ingrid Smyer

BEST LITTLE STORIES FROM WORLD WAR II

BEST LITTLE STORIES OF THE BLUE AND THE GRAY
with "Generals' Wives" by Ingrid Smyer

BEST LITTLE STORIES

from the Life and Times of

WINSTON CHURCHILL

C. Brian Kelly

with "His American Mother Jennie" by Ingrid Smyer

CUMBERLAND HOUSE
NASHVILLE, TENNESSEE

Best Little Stories from the Life and Times of Winston Churchill
Published by Cumberland House Publishing Inc.
431 Harding Industrial Drive
Nashville, Tennessee 37211

Copyright © 2008 by C. Brian Kelly and Ingrid Smyer-Kelly

Quotations from Winston Churchill are reproduced herein with permission of Curtis Brown Ltd. of London on behalf of The Estate of Winston Churchill. Copyright Winston S. Churchill. Quotations from Lady Mary Soames's book *Clementine Churchill* are reproduced herein with permission of Curtis Brown Ltd. of London on behalf of The Lady Soames. Copyright Lady Mary Soames.

Spellings in quotations from British sources have been standardized for the reader's benefit.

Cover design by Gore Studio Inc., Nashville, Tennessee

Library of Congress Cataloging-in-Publication Data
Kelly, C. Brian.
  Best little stories from the life and times of Winston Churchill / C. Brian Kelly ; with "His
    American mother Jennie" by Ingrid Smyer.
      p. cm.
  Includes bibliographical references and index.
  ISBN-13: 978-1-58182-634-0 (pbk. : alk. paper)
  ISBN-10: 1-58182-634-6 (pbk. : alk. paper)
    1. Churchill, Winston, Sir, 1874–1965. 2. Churchill, Winston, Sir, 1874–1965—Anecdotes.
  3. Prime ministers—Great Britain—Biography. 4. Statesmen—Great Britain—Biography.
  5. Churchill, Randolph Spencer, Lady, 1854–1921. I. Smyer-Kelly, Ingrid, 1927– His American Mother Jennie. II. Title. III. Title: His American Mother Jennie.
  DA566.9.C5K45 2008
  941.084092—dc22
    [B]   2008027010

Printed in Canada

1 2 3 4 5 6 7 8 9 10—10 09 08

To Harald, Freddie, and Lester

Contents

Part 2: Political Ascendancy

Part 3: Betwixt and Between

Part 4: Battle for Survival

Part 5: Final Glimpses

Introduction

It was just a century ago that a brash and fast-rising young political star in England first gained a seat in the British cabinet, with many more high government posts to come . . . with an unrivaled accumulation of honors and other achievements (the Nobel prize for literature, for instance) yet to come as well. Eliminate his role as Britain's great World War II prime minister, and Winston Spencer Churchill—soldier, journalist, author, politician, and statesman—would be considered an extraordinary and historically important figure in British history anyway. Add his determined leadership during World War II, and you have the man that most Britons consider the greatest Englishman of all time, according to a nationwide BBC poll taken not so many years ago.

Altogether he served in eight cabinet posts before he became the nation's wartime prime minister. Once a young man in a hurry, he then, *after* hitting age sixty-five, served twice as prime minister, those two tenures coming a decade apart. By the time he left No. 10 Downing Street a second time in 1955, he also had served fifty-five years in Parliament, albeit not continuously.

Throw aside his World War II leadership, and he still remains the man who made sure the British would have their workday tea breaks and, in warfare, the world's first tank. He was the man who had the fleet ready and mobilized for World War I. He was the great orator who famously sent the English language to war against Adolf Hitler during World War II . . . despite a lifelong speech defect. He was the Englishman of stubborn, bulldog visage who, together with American president Franklin Delano Roosevelt, forged the grand alliance of Allies that defeated the worldwide Axis powers in the same war. And, not so incidentally, thanks to his colorful American mother, Jennie Jerome (see pages 355–402), he was, himself, half American.

Amazingly—especially for a man who expected to die young, like his aristocrat father—his public service began with his days as a young cavalry officer under Queen Victoria in the nineteenth century and stretched into the second half of the twentieth century with his two terms as prime minister and many years in Parliament. A frail child, only a so-so student in school, and a Sandhurst Military College graduate, he was already internationally famous when he first took a seat in Parliament in 1901 under Victoria's son, King Edward VII, at age twenty-six.

From that point on, his contributions to British society, and especially the British military, were without parallel. "He was closely involved in the early development of aviation, learning to fly before the First World War, and establishing the Royal Naval Air Service," noted Churchill's leading biographer, Sir Martin Gilbert, in *Churchill: A Life*. "He was closely involved in the inception of the tank. He was a pioneer in the development of anti-aircraft defense and in the evolution of aerial warfare."

Gilbert observed that Churchill from his early years always "had an uncanny understanding and vision of the future unfolding of events." Further, he held "a strong faith in his own ability to contribute to the survival of civilization, and the improvement of the material well-being of mankind." In addition, "His military training, and his natural inventiveness, gave him great insight into the nature of war and society."

Personal courage? Proven "on the battlefields of the Empire at the turn of the century, on the western front in 1916, or in Athens in 1944 [see pages 274–79]." At the same time, Churchill held "a deep understanding of the horrors of war and the devastation of battle."

On another level, it also took personal courage—and uncommon fortitude—to continue to speak out in the 1930s again and again in the face of stubborn indifference, even humiliating dismissal, both in and out of Parliament, about the dangers posed by a fast-rearming Nazi Germany. On a related point, noted biographer Gilbert, "He foresaw the building of weapons of mass destruction, and in his last speech to Parliament proposed using the existence of the hydrogen bomb, and its deterrent power, as the basis for world disarmament."

Meanwhile, often forgotten in the wake of his World War II leadership, is the fact he first made his mark politically as a "radical" and social reformer, despite his aristocratic background. While he had been born in a palace, lawmaker Churchill teamed up with the Welsh firebrand David Lloyd George early in the twentieth century to set Britain on the path to becoming a welfare state that provided a government share of pensions for widows and orphans, help in finding jobs, restrictions on allowable working hours, and unemployment insurance, among other new measures. Also stemming from his wide-ranging interests and boundless energy were significant advances in prison reform, a new governmental role in arbitration of labor disputes, and better working conditions for factory workers.

He favored a national health service and, long before the slogan became known in America, called for a war on poverty.

Not only was Parliament, with its legislative function, a vehicle for his many aims, but so were the various government posts he held over the years, beginning with his appointment as under secretary of state for the colonies in 1905 as a rising political star at the age of only thirty-one. Next named to the Privy Council (albeit without ministerial portfolio), he then, in 1908, achieved cabinet status as president of the board of trade (somewhat similar to the U.S. secretary of commerce). Just down the road was appointment as secretary of the home office, quickly followed—just in time for World War I—by his move to the time-honored post of first lord of the admiralty (basically, civilian head of the Royal Navy). Still "in government" after taking blame for the Dardanelles-Gallipoli military disaster, a chastened Churchill briefly contented himself with the largely empty title of chancellor of the Duchy of Lancaster before finding really meaningful work again as minister of munitions under Prime Minister David Lloyd George for the latter part of the war.

With the fighting over as of late 1918, Churchill next, in 1919, accepted the double-barreled post of secretary of state for war and air. Still another shuffle saw him take over the cabinet-level office of colonial secretary in 1921, but that post fell by the wayside when, still recouping from an appendix operation, he was defeated in his 1922 reelection bid (for Parliament) at Dundee, Scotland.

After winning election to Parliament from Epping, just outside London proper, however, Churchill took on his late father's old post as chancellor of the exchequer under Prime Minister Stanley Baldwin. Among other perks, that meant moving into No. 11 Downing Street, next door to the prime minister's traditional home at Number 10—and sharing a back garden with Number 10. The 1928 elections sent both Churchill and Baldwin packing, literally . . . although Winston, while no longer a cabinet minister, did hold on to his parliamentary seat.

Except as a parliamentarian, he would not be back in government until once again appointed first lord of the admiralty on the eve of yet another worldwide conflict, World War II. That, in 1939, was when the word went out to the Royal Navy's far-flung ships at sea: "Winston's back."

Just months later, in May 1940, who should be moving into No. 10 Downing Street but the latest prime minister of England, Winston Spencer Churchill. (Actually, with London suffering under the Blitz and Number 10 itself taking damage from German bombers, Churchill and his wife, Clementine, spent many days and nights elsewhere.)

His Conservative Party then lost the 1945 general election, and Churchill once more was relegated to a parliamentary seat only. But then, looming large yet again and by now in his midseventies, in 1951 he was returned to No. 10 Downing Street for a second time in his long governmental career.

Whatever Winston Churchill's role, in or out of high government position, back bench or majority party seat in Parliament, biographer Martin Gilbert observed, "Churchill was a persistent advocate of conciliation, even of coalition; he shunned the paths of division and unnecessary confrontation. In international affairs he consistently sought the settlement of the grievances of those who had been defeated, and the building of meaningful associations for the reconciliation of former enemies." In addition, "It was he who first used the word 'summit' for a meeting of the leaders of the Western and Communist worlds, and did his utmost to set up such meetings to end the dangerous confrontations of the Cold War." Meanwhile, among the international agreements he negotiated over the years, "with patience and understanding, were the constitutional settlements in South Africa and Ireland, and the war debt repayment schemes after the First World War I."

A public figure almost from puberty, Churchill was a master of many talents. Always the "advocate of bold, farsighted courses," he had as "one of his greatest gifts, seen in several thousand public speeches, as well as heard in his many broadcasts," the ability "to use his exceptional mastery of words, and love of language, to convey detailed arguments and essential truths; to inform, to convince, to inspire."

On a personal level, Gilbert wrote of his former boss, "He was a man of great humor and warmth, of magnanimity," and in political philosophy "a consistent and life-long liberal in outlook." He was a man often sought out by "successive Prime Ministers for his skill as a conciliator." At the same time, "His dislike of unfairness, of victimization and of bullying—whether at home or abroad—was the foundation-stone of much of his thinking."

In sum, Gilbert noted: "Churchill's public work touched every aspect of British domestic and foreign policy, from the struggle for social reform before the First World War to the search for a summit conference after the Second. It involved Britain's relations with France, Germany, the United States, and the Soviet Union, each at their most tested time."

All true, but certainly Churchill still is best known today for that dramatic period of world history when he first took the reins of political leadership, when he first became prime minister and answered the need of his nation during World War II. As Gilbert expressed it: "His finest hour was the leadership of Britain when it was most isolated, most threatened and most weak; when his own courage, determination and belief in democracy became at one with the nation."

For all his worldliness, though, his many accomplishments, his giant strides across the twentieth century, Winston Churchill apparently was the lonely man in a crowd, to judge by his own comments over the years in letters to his wife (and as duly reported by their daughter Mary in her biography of her mother, *Clementine Churchill.*)

Writing his wife-to-be in April 1908, as newly appointed president of the board of trade but after losing a by-election for Parliament from northwest Manchester, Winston said: "Write to me again. I am a solitary creature in the midst of crowds." Not so incidentally, he would go on to win a seat in Parliament from Dundee, Scotland, within weeks; Dundee remained his constituency for the next twelve years.

Years later, from the fateful Big Three Conference at Yalta in early 1945, he wrote: "I miss you very much. I am lonely amid this throng." And, in still another epistle to his beloved, an interesting admission by Churchill also well worth history's attention: "I am so devoured by egoism that I would like to have another soul in another world and meet you in another setting, and pay you all the love and honor of the great romances." This letter came from Churchill when he was in the front-line trenches of World War I, between his appointments as first lord of the admiralty and minister of munitions.

A great man with great flaws, but still great nonetheless, Churchill was very human. He may have leaned on alcohol a bit more than his doctor would have liked, and he certainly chewed, if not smoked, cigars incessantly. He took up painting, and became quite an artist, to overcome his "Black Dog" bouts of depression . . . but always his basic credo was, no matter what the obstacle or adversity, "Never give up."

Meanwhile, daughter Mary (Lady Mary Soames) once said of her parents in an interview, Winston and Clementine weren't *social*. "Their world was a trade world," she told Graham Turner of the *Daily Telegraph* after turning eighty in 2002. "One lived one's life by the sitting and rising of the House of Commons. They weren't part of society—their friends came mainly from politics. Ascot, Goodwood, the London season meant nothing at all to them. And they despised café society."

Mary, happily married to Christopher Soames, a post–World War II British ambassador to France, raised five children and was widely hailed for her biography of her mother. Mary's siblings, though, came to sad ends. Diana committed suicide; both Randolph and Sarah went through divorces and died young.

Religion? "They weren't churchgoers," said Mary about her parents, "though my father supported the whole idea and my mother was certainly a believer. As a matter of fact she did become a churchgoer in the last years of her life. She loved going with all of us every week when she stayed with us after Papa died."

It was in January 1965 when that day came, when Winston Churchill, always a believer in his own destiny, died at the age of ninety exactly on the seventieth anniversary of his father's death as if somehow . . . well, *planned*.

But meanwhile, what a story he wrote! And his American mother too!

—C. Brian Kelly, Ingrid Smyer-Kelly
Charlottesville, Virginia, June 2008

BEST LITTLE STORIES

from the Life and Times of

WINSTON CHURCHILL

★ PART 1 ★
Listen, Listen to His Story

My Dear Mamma

Precocious from the start, determined to have his way, he also was a loving and endearing child. In one of his earliest surviving letters, written from Blenheim Palace soon after Christmas 1881, just a month after he turned seven, he wrote: "My Dear Mamma: I hope you are quite well. I thank you very very much for the beautiful presents those Soldiers and Flags and Castle they are so nice it was so kind of you and dear Papa I send you my love and a great many kisses Your loving Winston."

There, you could well argue, was his life's story: soldiers, flags, and castles. All begun with the American mother and blue-blood father whom he venerated.

Impetuous Start

He was born on November 30, 1874, less than ten years after the American Civil War, in a monumental ancestral palace that rose like a mirage from the gently swelling English countryside next door to the Cotswolds. His birth in a first-floor cloakroom there at the height of the Victorian age was a bit early, they say—seven and a half months after his mother, American-born Jennie Jerome, married his father, British-born-and-raised Lord Randolph Churchill. Attending a ball when labor pains seized Jennie, the new parents had to borrow a local resident's baby clothes for their newborn, because they were visiting from London and little Winston Leonard Spencer Churchill had arrived so unexpectedly.

Somebody, it would appear from the babe's apparently normal birth with no hospital stay or time spent on machines for "preemies," had been a bit impetuous. Otherwise, what to make of it? "Many authors dwell on the question of whether he was conceived out of wedlock," conceded Churchill granddaughter Celia Sandys, author of five books on Winston. "Personally, I think it matters not at all but, although I lean toward that theory, I cannot understand why Jennie, an extremely intelligent girl who could certainly count up to nine, would have placed herself in the unpleasant position of giving birth surrounded by her Marlborough in-laws whom she disliked intensely." After all, the ball she and husband Randolph were attending did take place at Blenheim Palace, Randolph's ancestral home built in the eighteenth century by the famed Duke of Marlborough.

Additional note: The timing of the infant Winston's arrival of course was awkward fare for his biographers too. Here's how one of them, Henry Pelling, dealt with the situation in his *Winston Churchill*: "As the weight at birth does not seem to have been recorded, or if recorded has not been revealed . . . we must suspend judgment on whether this was simply the first instance of Winston's impetuosity or whether it also involved yet another example of Lord Randolph's." *FYI also*: Even while naming the grownup Winston Churchill its Man of the Year for 1940, *Time* magazine felt constrained to call him, "This seven-month child of a British peer and an American heiress," but did not explain the "seven-month" reference.

His Mother and His Nanny

Precocious, impetuous, whatever . . . the young Winston was destined, like many a child of his age and aristocratic social set, to be raised by servants, at some distance from his parents—in his case, by beloved nanny Elizabeth Ann Everest, also called "Woomany" or "Woom." As he once, himself, wrote about his mother, the beauteous Jennie: "She shone for me like the Evening Star. I loved her dearly— but at a distance." It was his nanny Elizabeth Everest, he said, "who looked after me and tended all my wants. It was to her I poured out my many troubles."

Listen, Listen to His Story

Not only did the infant Winston Churchill begin life in baby clothes borrowed from a solicitor's wife in the village of Woodstock, hard by Blenheim Palace, he soon would become an often-troublesome child destined to be notably frail, to be marked by a speech impediment, to struggle in school, to survive a near-death bout with pneumonia, to suffer at least three concussions from blows to the head . . . destined even to survive a minor stabbing by a schoolmate armed with a penknife, and all before he entered his teen years.

And yet, as his granddaughter Celia Sandys wrote in *The Young Churchill*, "If the child born at Blenheim palace a hundred and twenty years ago [that is, 1874] had not, against all the odds, survived his early years, the world we live in today [1994] would be a very different place."

Or, as his nephew Peregrine Churchill wrote (in the same book): "If you know a lonely child who has poetry in its heart but a tongue distorting the words it tries to utter, whose muscles refuse to obey and fingers drop what it would grasp, whose infantile achievements wither from lack of encouragement; let it listen to the story of young Winston's boyhood and learn to believe there is always hope, and never, never give up."

Kicked That Hat to Pieces

Among his many troubles as a child, other than surprisingly frail health for such a robust-looking man who lived to be ninety, was his early schooling. He wasn't quite eight years old when he was enrolled at St. George's near Ascot, a boarding school where the boys were often flogged—little Winston included—for breaking the rules. One child later recalled the headmaster's floggings produced a "mass of blood" on the victim's bottom.

Here, though, we see a key to Winston's developing character. Another alumnus recalled, "[Winston] had been flogged for taking sugar from the pantry, and so far from being penitent, he had taken the headmaster's sacred straw hat from where it hung over the door and kicked it to pieces. His sojourn at the school had been one long feud with authority."

But another aspect of his personality also was emerging. He was, said a third alumnus, "a red haired and restless boy, rather small for his age, who through his exhibitionism and quarrelsome attitude got on everyone's nerves."

And true, even as an adult he frequently would get on people's nerves.

Boarding School Travails

When young Winston was sent off to boarding school at not quite eight years in age, "He thus found himself suddenly translated into a bewildering and hostile society very different from home, at the modest little house No. 2 St. James Place [London], with his baby brother [Jack] and attentive nurse," commented nephew Peregrine Churchill. Also left behind were the mother he adored and the aristocratic father he admired as well as, quartered in his nursery, nearly one thousand toy soldiers the child dearly loved as well.

In exchange for life in a "cozy little nursery," he now "had to learn how to survive against the ailments fickle Nature had unreasonably given him at birth; and then the tyranny of schoolmasters who would have him learn, with threat of the birch, subjects in which he had no interest or understanding."

He was at this time, in 1882, already the survivor of a concussion suffered from a fall from a donkey. More generally, wrote granddaughter Celia Sandys, the youthful Winston was an "impish, lonely and sickly little boy who, by his own tenacious attitude to life, lived to fulfill his youthful dreams and fantasies." Thus, it positively was, from the start, in his nature to fight back . . . in his own inimitable way of course.

His career at St. George's School, Ascot, began badly from the first moments after his mother dropped him off. "When the last sound of my mother's departing wheels had died away," a grownup Churchill wrote some years later, "the Headmaster invited me to hand over any money I had in my possession. I produced my three half-crowns, which were duly entered in a book."

Then, too, that same "gloomy evening," Winston later wrote in his sometimes embellished autobiography, *My Early Life*, he grappled with the first declension of the Latin word for table: *mensa*. Grappled with an "aching" and even rebellious heart at that. What was the point, he wondered. *Mensa* meant "a table." *Mensa* also meant "O table." *Mensam* also meant "table." *Mensae* meant "of a table" or "to or for a table." And *mensa* again could mean "by, with, or from a table." To young Winston, it all appeared "absolute rigmarole." Having memorized it anyway, he asked the master what it all meant.

Mensa means a table, he was told. Well, in that case, what about "O table?" That you would use "in speaking to a table."

Speaking to a table? "But I never do," Winston blurted, quite honestly amazed.

For that he was threatened with severe punishment for impertinence.

"Such was my introduction to the classics from which, I have been told, many of our cleverest men have derived so much solace and profit," he wrote.

Corporal punishment at the school was very real and no joke, however. Widely dreaded, it once was described by student Roger Fry as a "swishing" that was given with the master's "full strength" and that quickly drew blood on the "wretched boy's bottom."

Such was the punishment that Winston was known to defy on occasion. "Dreadful legends were told about Winston Churchill," said Maurice Baring, the student who related the straw hat story. "His naughtiness appeared to have surpassed anything."

Ever the Handful

Born in Blenheim Palace, Winston did not actually live there as a child, although he came to know it well from many visits with his paternal grandparents, the seventh Duke and Duchess of Marlborough, who did live there. In fact, young Winston spent so much time at Blenheim that he was noted at St. Georges for "spicy expressions" he picked up in the palace stables, according to classmate Harry Kessler.

Stables or no stables, for a child, the huge, sprawling palace was a wonderland to wander, inside and out. A royal gift to John Churchill, the first Duke of Marlborough, England's great hero of the battle of Blenheim, Bavaria, in the War of the Spanish Succession, the palace named Blenheim was seventeen years in the making (1705–22). "Kings and princes from across Europe had to confess that even their palaces could not compare with the stately home of the Spencer Churchills, Dukes of Marlborough," wrote Keith Roberts in his short biography, *Churchill.*

Indeed, Blenheim's interior of great halls and grand apartments simply went on and on, one after another. Built as a series of squares with an inner court, large outside plaza, and a large Italian garden, Blenheim also offered an adventurous child a large lake, hills, forests, and more gardens to explore, among other features to be found in the great estate's parklike grounds. Among them even today are Blenheim's Pleasure Gardens, which include a fascinating Marlborough Maze along with a Butterfly House and an adjoining exhibition of tools and machines needed to operate the estate from its beginnings to the 1960s.

"His family, although welcome at Blenheim, had no country house of their own," wrote granddaughter Celia. "Thus, Winston and [his baby brother] Jack spent a great deal of time [there] under the disciplinarian eye of their grandmother the Duchess." Since Winston's father was a younger son, he was not first in line to inherit. In fact, once he married his American bride, he "was to be constantly preoccupied with his lack of money," as would Winston himself as an adult.

Further constraining Lord Randolph's options was the tradition among the British aristocracy that "precluded sons from salaried employment except in the armed forces or the Church." Like his own father, Winston's father took a third route—politics. But that, too, had a drawback. He would serve in Parliament, yes, but . . . no pay. And so, he "was forced to rely on an allowance" from his father, who as a duke was one of only twenty such titleholders in all of England.

Lady Randolph (as Jennie Churchill was known), unsurprisingly, did not like being "beholden" to her in-laws. She in fact kept her visits to Blenheim to a minimum, and once wrote her mother that her mother-in-law, the Duchess of Marlborough, "hates me simply for what I am—perhaps a little prettier and more attractive than her daughters." And quite true, Jennie was known far and wide as a great beauty.

Meanwhile, when Winston was a tyke of two, a falling out between Lord Randolph and his good friend the Prince of Wales, the future king of England— "with whom there was even talk of a possible duel"—was responsible for the couple's exile from London society for a two-year stay in Dublin, Ireland. Lord Randolph would be serving there as secretary to his politician father, the duke, who had been appointed viceroy of Ireland.

While in Ireland, Randolph, still holding the traditional Marlborough seat in Parliament from the small town of Woodstock, returned on occasion to the House of Commons to make a speech—with the result, ironically, that even in social exile he began climbing the ladder of political ascendancy. During this period also, noted Roberts in his biography, "the first steps were being taken to end the Churchills' banishment from court circles," even though it would be some months before "Randolph and the Prince of Wales sat down at table together again." Soon coming, in fact, would be the family's return from Ireland in 1884 and young Lord Randolph's plum appointment as secretary of state for India.

For little Winston and his even younger brother, the combination of aristocratic custom, the demands of high society, and Lord Randolph's enlarging political career all frequently conspired to leave the children in the care of servants. While the Churchill boys had their devoted nanny, their parents, typical of their social circle, tended to be distant figures, virtually all of Churchill's biographers like to point out. Celia Sandys's book on Winston's early life, on the other hand, noted that his mother, at least, did spend many recreational hours with him— playing, walking, reading.

Meanwhile, when it became obvious that St. George's was not the place for young Winston, his parents placed him in a small, free-spirited school at Brighton where, in his own words, "there was an element of kindness and sympathy which I had found completely lacking in my first [schooling] experiences. . . . At this school I was allowed to learn things which interested me: French, History, lots of Poetry by heart, and above all Riding and Swimming."

But the child still was a handful, whether at home or at school, it seems. After Winston's father left home for a tour of India in December 1884, his mother plaintively wrote that she could not "undertake to manage" Winston over Christmas without the help of his nanny, Elizabeth Everest. Then, as an afterthought, she added, "I am afraid even she can't do it."

It was here, at the school in Brighton, and this very month, that Winston had a run-in with a student who stabbed him in the chest—ever so slightly—with a penknife a teacher had loaned them during a drawing examination. The affair was quickly forgotten, however, and Winston returned to school after the Christmas holiday without further incident. He then wrote his mother, with obvious tongue in cheek: "You must be happy without me. No screaming from Jack or complaint. It must be heaven on earth."

Soon after that, he was off to see a specialist on deafness, giddiness, and noises in the head—"the first indication," noted Celia Sandys, "that it was acknowledged that Winston had a problem with his ears and therefore probably his balance." She added, "This, combined with a speech defect, was a challenge he had to overcome throughout his life and was undoubtedly the reason that so many seemingly minor childhood scrapes became full-scale incidents."

Early in 1885, Jennie wrote to her husband that Winston looked very pale and delicate when she visited the school to see him in a play. One of the two headmistresses told her "she thought he was far from strong." To which, Jennie added, "What a care the boy is!"

Actually, Lord Randolph himself was not in the best of health at this time. One reason for his sailing to India prior to entering the government as secretary of state for India, wrote Sandys, was "to restore his failing health on the long [roundtrip] sea voyages."

Additional note: Even more than Blenheim, its adjoining village of Woodstock was steeped in English history. Queen Elizabeth I, only a young princess at the time, had been imprisoned here. James I also hunted here. Much earlier, Richard the Lion Hearted and the Black Prince both were born here, and here also Henry II kept his mistress, Rosamond "the Fair Rosamond" Clifford.

The history of Woodstock, the storybook-looking little village next to Churchill's birthplace of Blenheim Palace, "begins with the history of Britain," noted Peregrine Churchill and coauthor Julian Mitchell in their book *Jennie*. A Roman road, "still visible, paved with cobblestones," runs through its nearby park. "In Saxon times," Peregrine and Mitchell added, "the kingdoms of Wessex and Mercia met nearby. The country was heavily wooded, and there was probably a royal hunting lodge in the valley of the little river Glyme, where the forest began."

Later, a royal manor was established at Woodstock, and its visitors included "all the great names of the succeeding thousand years of British history." Thus, Alfred the Great and Ethelred the Unready hunted here. Henry I maintained a menagerie here with exotic animals such as lions, bears, and camels, while his son Henry II and Thomas Beckett (subsequently murdered by Henry's henchmen) had their "first great quarrel here."

Henry II kept Rosamond in a "bower" here, but only until his queen, Eleanor of Aquitaine, reacted, it seems. "Legend says that Eleanor poisoned the well, and Rosamond went to an early grave in nearby Godstow Nunnery."

Later, the sixteenth-century Princess Elizabeth "was imprisoned in the gatehouse of the Manor by her [half] sister Bloody Mary." And "James I hunted the deer every year: there is a tradition that his son Charles I was himself hunted through the park by Oliver Cromwell and the Roundheads. But after the Restoration in 1660, the Royal Manor fell into disuse until it was granted to John Churchill, first Duke of Marlborough."

John Churchill was, of course, the person who leveled the old manor and built the grandiose Blenheim Palace within sight of the ancient village of Woodstock . . . which, in the meantime, had become a Parliamentary constituency. Here, Winston's father campaigned for Parliament; here, his mother Jennie, long before campaigning elsewhere for Winston, campaigned for Lord Randolph as well.

Organized Wars

As noted in the book *Churchill at War* by British historian Geoffrey Best, Winston's younger cousin Clare Frewen recalled that Winston had a playroom containing a plank table sporting "thousands of lead soldiers arranged for battle." She added, "He organized wars."

That certainly sounds like the larger-than-life Winston Churchill soon to storm the British public . . . and the world. It also sounds like the Winston Churchill as sometimes depicted by his critics.

Said cousin Clare, "The lead battalions were maneuvered into battle, peas and pebbles committed great casualties, forts were stormed, cavalry charged, bridges were destroyed—real water tanks engulfed the advancing foe." A most impressive show, she added, and further, it was "played with an interest that was no ordinary child's game."

Nor did the games end in the playroom. At a small summer rental in the country, sixteen-year-old Winston and younger brother Jack assembled a log house, dug a ditch around it, filled the ditch with water, and constructed a drawbridge "that really could pull up and down," Frewen related. She was then about seven years old, but she clearly remembered: "Here again war proceeded. The fort was stormed. I was hurriedly removed from the scene of action as soon as mud and stones began to fly."

Historian Best added that the "piece de resistance of the defense was a giant catapult firing unripe apples." But he also warned against making too much of the youthful Winston's play with toy soldiers. Not every boy who plays with toy soldiers and fights imaginary battles "goes on to attain military distinction." And so, "In seeking the sources of Winston's later talents for war it is unwise to make too much of his boyhood enthusiasms."

In point of fact, Geoffrey Best also noted that at his three schools—before Sandhurst, England's West Point—"Churchill was the subject of a good deal of complaint, but rarely for quarreling with other boys or for fighting. He was on the small side, often unwell, and as likely to be the victim of aggression as its agent."

Meanwhile, as the next academic step for Winston after his school at Brighton, only the best of England's so-called public schools would do for a child of blue-blooded Lord Randolph. Thus, Eton, situated in the Thames Valley, was considered but rejected—family doctor Robson Roose objected that the low-lying valley's fogs would not be good for Winston's health. That consideration, for one, made Harrow, founded in 1572 and situated atop a hill in Middlesex, the better choice.

But now, a small, as-yet unresolved controversy. When Winston took the entrance exam, accompanied by the Brighton school's Charlotte Thompson, reported Geoffrey J. Fletcher in the winter 2006–7 issue of the American-based Churchill Centre's *Finest Hour* quarterly publication, questions arose over Winston's knowledge of Latin. "Charlotte reported to his mother that he had suffered from severe nervous excitement and had told her that he had never translated Latin into English."

This was very odd since "he had spent a full year translating Caesar and Virgil." Oddly, too, in his own *My Early Life*, Winston himself claimed that he failed to answer anything in the exam's Latin section.

Perhaps, speculated Fletcher, Harrow's headmaster, the Reverend James Edward Cowell Welldon, who knew of the youngster's "latent" knowledge of Latin, may have decided on that basis to overlook the exam problem. Whatever the case, Welldon was accused of "gross favoritism" at the time, noted Fletcher. "Perhaps the truth was that Lord Randolph being at the summit of national politics, Welldon preferred to avoid the embarrassment of rejecting his son. Yet Harrow historians have declared that not even Lord Randolph's son could have been admitted at that time knowing no Latin." And so, stalemate on that issue.

As for the young student's other school subjects, they tended to suit the man who emerged in later life as the Winston Churchill known to us all today. "His strong subjects were History, Geography and English Literature; the essay topic he chose in one of the Sandhurst entrance exams was 'The American Civil War' and he received higher marks for English History than anyone else," noted Geoffrey Best in *Churchill and War.*

From Harrow, young Churchill moved on to the Royal Military College (later, Academy) at Sandhurst in 1893—although he had to take the entrance exam three times. After Winston served his time at Harrow in the officers training corps, an army career seemed a natural next step for someone of his "birth and parentage," and at Harrow he had proved himself a good shot with the army's regulation Martini-Henry rifle. "The rifles kick a good deal," he wrote home from Harrow, "it is awfully jolly."

Predicted His Own Future

While at Harrow, a "public school" in England but actually, by American terms, a private boarding school, young Winston Churchill allegedly predicted his future with uncanny accuracy. And perhaps, considering his sometimes overweening self-confidence, it's possible that he did.

The story comes from Sir Murland Evans, an older schoolmate at Harrow. The two boys, about fifteen or sixteen in age, were casually talking one day when Churchill's oddly prophetic predictions came up . . . spontaneously and out of the blue. "It was a summer's evening in one of those dreadful basement rooms in the Headmaster's House, a Sunday evening to be exact, after chapel evensong," recalled Sir Murland. They began to talk about their respective futures.

"Will you go into the army?" asked Evans.

Probably, said the young Churchill.

And then into politics? Following your father's footsteps?

"I don't know, but it is more than likely because, you see, I am not afraid to speak in public."

As is well known, Churchill did go into the army. He served briefly as a journalist, and he used the fame gathered in both pursuits to propel himself into politics, the consuming interest of his adult life. And . . . as one secret to all his success, he certainly had no fear of speaking in public. He repeatedly proved, even to his own detriment, totally unafraid to say whatever was on his mind. All of which, for a bright, even precocious young English lad of his particular background, was fairly predictable, true. But more, much more, stuck in Sir Murland's memory.

When Winston mentioned that he had dreams about where he eventually would be in life, his classmate asked, "Where is that?"

"Well," came Winston's surprising reply, "I can see vast changes coming over a now peaceful world; great upheavals, terrible struggles, wars such as one cannot imagine; and I tell you London will be in danger—London will be attacked and I shall be very prominent in the defense of London."

Taken aback, the young Evans said: "How can you talk like that? We are forever safe from invasion, since the days of Napoleon." True enough at the time, but Winston was thinking far ahead, and in fact, he said so: "I see farther ahead than you do. I see into the future. This country will be subjected somehow to a tremendous invasion, by what means I do not know, but I tell you I shall be in command of the defenses of London and I shall save London and England from disaster."

As events turned out, of course, on the very day that Churchill accepted appointment as prime minister, May 10, 1940, London, all of England, even the British Empire itself was at an hour of extreme peril. At dawn that very day, his own grandson and namesake Winston Churchill has noted, Hitler "launched his blitzkrieg against Holland, Belgium, Luxembourg and France." The Nazi predator and that other predator, the Soviet Union, already had dismembered Poland.

As Churchill's grandson also noted: "Viewed objectively, Britain's position was hopeless. Hitler had amassed a huge war-machine, out-producing Britain in almost every field of military production by a factor of two or even three to one. Europe was at his mercy. Soviet Russia was his ally. Only 21 miles of English Channel stood between him and his next intended conquest. The mood at home was divided."

Divided? The teenaged Churchill of Harrow days apparently didn't predict this aspect of Britain's great danger, but it indeed was a fact. His grandson summed up: "Even after Churchill became prime minister there were many Members of Parliament and even a handful of Ministers, who favored a 'negotiated settlement' with Hitler." It would have been "dressed up as a peace Agreement," but it really would have been "surrender, with the dismantling of both the Royal Navy and Royal Air Force." Such a result would have been double disaster. "Hitler would have been free to turn East with all his might to defeat Stalin's Russia. Then he would have turned West once again and all the apparatus of the Nazi domination—concentration camps and death camps—would have been established in England's green and pleasant land."

Certainly, the young Churchill did not, could not, foresee all such possibilities as a student back in the 1890s, but he clearly sensed he would play a critical role in the future of his island nation. As his grandson noted: "Of all the remarkable qualities of Winston Churchill there is none more amazing then his unshakable belief in his destiny."

Additional note: When Sir Murland heard that Churchill's late son Randolph planned to write an official biography of his father, the latter's old schoolmate came forward with his startling recollection. In 1999 Randolph's son (Winston's grandson) recalled the story in a speech and an article in which he joined those advocating his grandfather as "Man of the Millennium," the one-thousand-year period about to end that year.

Parental Empathy Lacking

All those years that young Winston either endured or enjoyed his various schools, his mother and father had their busy lives. "Winston passed his first eighteen months at Harrow without so much as a single visit from his father," noted Robert H. Pilpel in *Churchill in America*. "Dearest Winston," wrote the teenager's mother one time, "I am sending this by Everest who is going to see how you are getting on. I would go down to you—but I have so many things to arrange for the Ascot party next week that I can't manage it."

Elizabeth Ann Everest, or "Woomany," his old childhood nanny, thankfully was still in the employ of the family. As noted before, Winston himself wrote that his mother was the "Evening Star" in his life. He loved her "dearly—but at a distance." Whereas, Woomany "was my confidante. . . . It was to her I poured out my many troubles."

Indeed, it had been Everest who found, and reported, the flogging scars on young Winston's buttocks when he was at St. George's. "Those scars along with a general physical collapse led to his finally being withdrawn from St. George's and placed under the more benign supervision of [the] two spinsters who ran . . . [his] small school in Brighton," wrote Pilpel.

If Brighton and then Harrow were major improvements in Winston's school life, his mother and father remained distant, especially his father. "You never came to see me on Sunday when you were in Brighton," is one lament addressed to "My dear Papa" shortly before Winston's twelfth birthday, now preserved for posterity among his childhood letters. And another, from a few months later, cited in Pilpel's book: "I wish you could come to the distribution of prizes at the end of this term, but I suppose it is impossible."

Not long after, coming across Winston and younger brother Jack playing with their toy soldiers at home one day, Lord Randolph did take a moment to ask thirteen-year-old Winston if, after going on to Harrow, he would like to enter the army, Pilpel recalled. Winston, by his own account, thought at the time "it would be splendid to command an Army," so he quickly said yes, "and immediately I was taken at my word."

At last, here was vindication . . . of a sort. "I thought my father had discerned in me the qualities of military genius." Not quite, it turned out. "But I was told later that he had only come to the conclusion that I was not clever enough to go to the Bar [that is, become a lawyer]."

After his first eighteen months at Harrow passed with no visit by Lord Randolph, Winston still was trying. In the summer of 1889, Harrow's "Speech day" was looming, and Winston "begged" his father to visit. "I shall be awfully disappointed if you don't come," he plainly stated in "a long letter of entreaty." The youngster also asked his mother to use her influence on her politically active husband.

But still Lord Randolph did not make the short trip to Harrow, noted Pilpel, adding that Winston's parents not only "neglected" him but "they rarely missed an opportunity to berate him or compare him unfavorably with his brother." For instance, in the letter announcing she was busy with plans for the Ascot party, Winston's mother also said that his latest school report card was "a very bad one." Not only that, "You work in such a fitful inharmonious way that you are bound to come out last." And worse, as any child psychologist would agree, "There is Jack on the other hand—who comes out at the head of his class every week—despite his bad eye."

Still to come, however, was an absolutely shattering missive, this time from father to son and on the heels of Winston's triumph in finally winning admission to Sandhurst after two failing attempts. In the first place, his latest score in the entrance examination was only good enough to qualify Winston for the cavalry, rather than the infantry cadetships. In that failure, wrote Winston's father, "is demonstrated beyond refutation your slovenly happy-go-lucky harum-scarum style of work for which you have always been distinguished at your different schools."

And as if that were not enough chastisement for the young man to ponder: "Do not think I am going to take the trouble of writing to you long letters after every folly & failure you commit and undergo. I shall not write again on these matters & you need not trouble to write any answer to this part of my letter, because I no longer attach the slightest weight to anything you may say about your own acquirements and exploits."

Perhaps worst of all was the admonition: "If you cannot prevent yourself from leading the idle useless unprofitable life you have had during your school days & later months, you will become a mere social wastrel, one of the hundreds of public school failures, and you will degenerate into a shabby unhappy & futile existence."

Such words, coming from the person who, by his own account, had "the greatest and most profound influence" on Winston's early life, had to be crushing. "To me he seemed to own the key to everything or almost everything worth having," Winston himself wrote.

Remarkably, though, Churchill did not allow such parental disapproval to prevent him from achieving success far beyond his father's wildest dreams for either of his two sons. Perhaps, as many have surmised, the young Winston was spurred on by such criticism to prove himself despite it. Then, too, since his father was diagnosed as suffering from the embarrassing disease syphilis (although Winston apparently didn't know it) and then had his political career cut short by an early death, it also has been surmised that perhaps the young Winston started his own political career to "make up" for his father.

No Half Measures Here!

Even as a very young man, Winston Churchill never was one to stop at half measures. Soon after entering Sandhurst, he dropped a gold watch his father had given him into a pool formed by a stream. Keep in mind the absolute awe in which this sensitive young man held his aloof father—member of Parliament, government minister, descendant of the famous Duke of Marlborough, and occasional friend of the Prince of Wales, the future king of England.

Obviously frantic at the thought of losing the watch, young Winston quickly stripped off his clothes and dived in after it. Not just any gold watch, this one bore the family arms in enamel on the back, and he already had irritated his father by dropping it on the pavement and denting it.

Now, it had disappeared. Poking about the uneven bottom in the cold, murky water, Churchill could stay in for only about ten minutes. He then had the pool dredged . . . and still no watch. So he hired twenty-three soldiers to dig out a new course for the stream, borrowed the college fire engine, and had the pool pumped dry.

That did it—he found the watch, but then came a further patch of bad luck. As reported by biographer Sir Martin Gilbert, he sent it at once to his father's watchmaker in London for cleaning and repairs. By chance, Lord Randolph visited the watchmaker that very week . . . and of course he was told about the latest damages to the watch. Furious at the news, he wrote a searing letter to his eighteen-year-old son that, he told his wife, Winston "won't forget."

Additional note: Such angry outbursts by Winston's father happened more and more frequently. Not only did he seldom visit Winston at his various schools, he seemed to delight in writing castigating letters to him . . . all this to a son who worshiped his father.

What young Winston did not know at the time was that his father was gradually falling under the dark influence of the ugly illness diagnosed by the doctors of the day as syphilis . . . but to give Lord Randolph the benefit of the doubt, his affliction may have been a brain tumor or similar disease instead. In either case, the unfortunate Lord Randolph slowly became more and more irrational, resigned in a huff from his cabinet post as chancellor of the exchequer under Lord Salisbury as prime minister, carried on more and more incoherently in Parliament, and finally, after a short spell in a straitjacket while traveling abroad, died at the age of forty-five.

Close Calls for Winston

In the meantime, Winston himself had come close to death more than once up to that time. In March 1886, at the age of eleven, he came down with a dangerous case of pneumonia. It was so alarming that the family doctor stayed overnight with the boy for a few days and fought fevers that went as high as 104. Winston's recovery took weeks. Now attending the school in Brighton that he enjoyed so much, he didn't return to classes until July of that year.

His illness came at a busy time in his father's political career—just before Lord Randolph was appointed chancellor of the exchequer at the youthful age of thirty-seven, much to his son's great pride and awakening interest in matters political.

Another of the many times that young Winston came close to death he was all of eighteen and taking part with younger brother Jack and a cousin in a high-spirited chase at a country estate in Bournemouth shortly after the new year's holiday of 1893. Running away from the other two youngsters, Winston leaped into the upper branches of a fir tree from a bridge over a ravine, but he failed to find a good hold and fell twenty-nine feet onto the hard ground below. He was unconscious for three days; he took weeks to recover.

Badly bumped and bruised of course, he was sore all over . . . but especially in one thigh. That was just one year before x-rays came into use. Seventy years later, in 1963, when x-rays were routine, it was discovered he had fractured his thighbone as a result of that 1893 tumble.

☆ ☆ ☆

Still another time, just shortly afterward, that the world might have been deprived of his further services, Winston and Jack came close to drowning in a Swiss lake, according to Winston's later writings. On holiday in Switzerland in 1894, the two brothers had taken out a rowboat, stopped, and jumped in for a swim.

But just then a breeze came along and, catching the boat's sail-like red awning, started to carry it out of reach.

A good swimmer, Winston went after it . . . to no avail. It just blew farther away. "Up to this point," he recalled, "no idea of danger crossed my mind." After all, as he noted, the sun still "played upon the sparkling blue waters; the wonderful panorama of mountains and valleys, the gay hotels and villas still smiled."

With the boat eluding his grasp each time he swam near, however, the boys' situation began to look serious. "But now I saw death as near I believe as I have ever seen him," wrote Winston in the sometimes overly dramatic style he favored as a young man. "He was swimming in the water at our side, whispering from time to time in the rising wind which continued to carry the boat away from us at about the same speed we could swim."

Finally, with a supreme effort, Winston of course caught the boat, and the brothers returned safely ashore. Jack, though, poor unsuspecting Jack, "though tired, had not apparently realized the dull yellow glare of mortal peril that had so suddenly played around us."

A Staggering Blow

The very next year, 1895, two devastating events took place in Winston Churchill's life—just after his graduation from Sandhurst in December 1894, ranked 20th in a class of 130. Not so incidentally, he left Sandhurst still favoring the cavalry rather than the infantry, much to his father's disapproval, which had been strongly expressed as usual. Then, in January 1895, that same distant and critical father, whom Winston had venerated so much, died.

"All my dreams of comradeship with him, of entering Parliament at his side and in his support, were ended," Winston wrote. "There remained for me only to pursue his aims and vindicate his memory."

As mentioned before, the doctors attending Lord Randolph blamed the embarrassing venereal disease syphilis for the illness that led to his irrationality, physical frailty, and death, but it's not clear just when Winston learned of that diagnosis. What is known is that he interpreted his father's early death and that of his father's older brother, the latest Duke of Marlborough, as meaning that the family genes also could mark him for an early death. This apparently was one reason why Winston always seemed to be a young man in a hurry as he vaulted through the first third of his life . . . truly rushing through his early adult years while also managing to distinguish himself simultaneously in three different careers: the military, journalism, and politics. Each vocation by itself would have been enough for most men, but not so with Winston. And it was typical of him that for a time he made them all interchangeable. Even as a young cavalry officer, he wrote for newspapers. And while writing for the newspapers or on leave from his military duties, he made public speeches on the issues that interested him . . . all the while making his own political plans.

Interestingly enough, a key to this frenzy was the fact that, after Lord Randolph's death, Winston and his mother became a close-knit team dedicated to the goal of achieving success—Winston's success—with his mother often interceding among the high and mighty of her social circle on behalf of her precocious son . . . who ironically would live to be ninety and die, to the very day of the month, on the seventieth anniversary of his father's death.

Still Another Blow

Another blow for Winston in 1895 came with the death of his nanny, Elizabeth Everest. "She had been my dearest and most intimate friend during the whole of the twenty years I had lived," Winston sorrowfully recalled. Naturally, she hadn't been his nanny all twenty years, but there's a story in that. Just a week before his seventeenth birthday in 1891, Winston found out that his parents planned to dispense with her services, since eleven-year-old Jack really didn't need a nanny anymore. Winston objected strenuously, while the faithful Mrs. Everest only protested, "Please don't tell Jackie about my going." It then was arranged that she would work for Lord Randolph's mother, the boys' grandmother . . . and there they would still see her as often as they liked.

But that was not quite the end of the story.

Two years later, Winston learned that Everest was to be dismissed from that job . . . by letter. He again protested, warning that for her, an old woman by now, to be "packed away" like this, after nearly twenty years with the family, would "possibly, if not probably break her down altogether." Still, she was dismissed by letter.

Winston kept up with her anyway, even to her final hours in July 1895, even to finding her a nurse and a doctor for those final hours . . . even to making her funeral arrangements. Chances are, too, some historians say, he had in mind her plight when, with David Lloyd George years later, he helped develop social legislation providing a safety net for older people in need like his beloved Mrs. Everest.

To Hold Thousands in Thrall

Although Winston Churchill first visited America just before his twenty-first birthday, in November 1895, he was on his way to Cuba to observe and write newspaper articles about the rebels fighting their Spanish overlords, a dispute soon to escalate into the 1898 Spanish-American War. His stopover in New York City turned out to be as memorable and significant as his days spent with the Spanish troops chasing rebels in Cuba. First and foremost, it marked his first meeting with Bourke Cockran, the U.S. Congressman from New York who was both an alleged lover and indisputably a lifelong friend of Winston's mother.

As probably the single-most-important outcome of the young Englishman' s first visit to America, this same Irish-born American politician became the great Winston Churchill's model orator. An aging Churchill told Adlai Stevenson: "It was an American who inspired me and taught me how to use every note of the human voice like an organ. He was my model. I learned from him how to hold thousands in thrall."

When Winston landed in New York on November 9, he went directly to Cockran's apartment at Fifth Avenue and Fifty-eighth Street—at the bottom of Central Park and close to the site of the famous Plaza Hotel. His mother had arranged for him to stay with her friend Cockran. Writing her the very next day, Winston said, "Mr. Cockran is one of the most charming hosts and interesting men I have met."

An emigrant from Ireland at the age of seventeen, the New York attorney, now about forty years in age, lived in a "flat," as Winston called it, that was "beautifully furnished and fitted with every convenience." In the days ahead, even as a young blade of twenty, Winston was lavishly entertained by his host, meeting all kinds of the right people, socially and politically, along with relatives of his mother. There would be a tour of West Point and a visit to a U.S. warship, but no one could even guess how else Winston spent a good part of his time in New York City.

Try sitting on the bench next to a judge presiding over a murder trial.

Or visiting firehouses to see how firemen reacted to fire alarms.

"On the alarm bell sounding," Winston wrote to his brother, Jack, "the horses at once rushed into the shafts—the harnesses fell onto them—the men slid half dressed down a pole from their sleeping room and in 5½ seconds the engine was galloping down the street to the scene of the fire. An extraordinary feat which seems incredible—unless you have seen it."

The visitor from England was also greatly taken by the murder trial he was allowed to follow from the judge's bench. "There is a great criminal trial going on now, of a man who shot a fellow who had seduced his sister," Winston told Jack. "I met the judge at dinner the other night and he suggested my coming to hear the case," he explained, adding that to sit on the bench and watch the case unfold was "quite a strange experience and one which would be impossible in England." It hardly needs saying that such an arrangement would not be a standard practice in America, either, especially with the judge, according to Winston, "discussing the evidence as it was given with me and generally making himself socially agreeable." Noted the visitor, "All the while, a pale miserable man was fighting for his life." As events turned out, the accused was acquitted on grounds of insanity.

Winston, in the meantime, despite his Sandhurst background, was "horrified" by some of the regulations he learned of at West Point. Among these was the stricture allowing the cadets only two months' leave during their first two years at the academy. "In fact," he wrote, "they have far less liberty than any private school boys in our country."

As for America, his mother's homeland, and Americans in general, Winston was both enthralled and appalled. "This is a very great country," he told Jack at one point. "Not pretty or romantic but great and utilitarian." Then, too, "there seems to be no such thing as reverence or tradition. Everything is eminently practical and things are judged from a matter of fact standpoint. Take for instance the Court House. No robes or wigs or uniformed ushers. Nothing but a lot of men in black coats and tweed suits. Judge prisoner jury counsel & warders all indiscriminately mixed. But they manage to hang a man all the same, and that after all is the great thing."

Even at such tender age, Winston Churchill obviously held strong opinions. Indeed, there was more to his observations. The "essence of American journalism," he opined, "is vulgarity divested of truth." If that seems a bit harsh, he did add, "I think, mind you, that vulgarity is a sign of strength." In fact, he went on to say, "A great, crude, strong, young people are the Americans—like a boisterous healthy boy among enervated but well bred ladies and gentleman."

In sum, even though there were charming, refined, and cultured people here, "Picture to yourself the American people as a great lusty youth who treads on all your sensibilities—perpetuates every possible horror of ill manners—whom neither age nor just tradition inspire with reverence—but who moves about his affairs with a good-hearted freshness which may well be the envy of older nations of the earth."

Additional note: Since Cuba also was a destination for Winston in his first foray into the New World, he went to Spain's island colony off the Florida coast, and there experienced a baptism of gunfire that sent bullets whistling just inches from him. "There is nothing so exhilarating as to be shot at without result," he observed. In the years ahead, he was destined to be *exhilarated* that same way many times.

His Bad Arm

In 1897 came Winston's first posting abroad as a cavalry officer, requiring travel in which he reportedly suffered a significant but little-known injury on the way to his duty post at Bangalore, India. As his skiff came alongside the Sassoon Dock in Bombay, for his first step onto Indian soil after the voyage from England, he later asserted, the water was surging around the small craft.

"We came alongside of a great stone wall with dripping steps and iron rings for handholds," he wrote in *My Early Life*. As the little boat bobbed up and down, he reached out for a ring, grabbed it . . . and, wouldn't you know, just then the skiff "swung away, giving my right shoulder a sharp and peculiar wrench." That unfortunate wrench probably was a tear of the capsular attachments of the shoulder joint, according to Dr. John V. Banta, a professor of orthopedics at the University of Connecticut Medical School.

Writing in the *Finest Hour*, the quarterly publication of the American-based Churchill Centre, Banta noted that although the shoulder did not "go out" at the very moment of the injury, Winston later noted "its persistent instability," with actual dislocations taking place at various moments . . . such as slipping on a staircase, reaching for a book on a high shelf, or simply sleeping with his arm under a pillow.

Imagine, then, what a handicap this was to him when he was playing polo . . . as Winston did up to his early fifties. He later said the injury might "cripple me at polo . . . prevent me from ever playing tennis and [prove] a grave embarrassment in moments of peril, violence and effort." A year after the injury, he completely dislocated the shoulder when he slipped on some steps just before the inter-regimental polo tournament held in Meerut, India.

To continue playing polo, Churchill learned to strap his right elbow to his side . . . and at Meerut, his regimental team won the tournament. He himself scored two goals.

But imagine what a handicap this would be in a life-and-death cavalry charge into a mass of fanatical Arab dervishes in which he could not wield a sword in hand-to-hand fighting . . . as was the case for Supernumerary Lieutenant Winston Churchill of the 21st Lancers in 1898 at Omdurman in the Sudan.

"On account of my shoulder," he wrote, "I had always decided that if I were in-volved in hand-to-hand fighting I must use a pistol and not a sword." Thus, when the woefully outnumbered 21st Lancers charged into the massed dervishes at Om-durman, Churchill sheathed his sword ("not the easiest thing to do at a gallop," he noted wryly) and wielded a semiautomatic Mauser pistol, which held a ten-round clip. A real "ripper," he called the weapon. As is well known, Winston survived Om-durman without a significant scratch, but several dervishes he encountered did not. Clearly, it was a testament to his courage that he took part in this and many other battlefield scrapes in spite of the handicapping injury to his sword arm.

Additional note: Meanwhile, Winston sprained both ankles and dislocated his right shoulder when he fell down some stairs on February 9, 1899, *after* Omdur-man and shortly before another inter-regimental polo tournament in India. "My arm is weak and stiff & may come out again at any moment," he wrote to his mother. He played anyway, right arm strapped to his side, and scored three goals as his team won in the finals with a total of four.

Military Adventures Found

His shoulder injury also would have been a high-risk handicap two years before Omdurman, when he traveled to the northwest frontier above India and below

Afghanistan as a correspondent reporting home to England on British attempts to subdue the region's rebellious tribesmen and, oddly, also as an officer temporarily attached to the Malakan Field Force. In this double guise he reported home to the *Daily Telegraph* in the form of letters from the front, thanks to the arrangement made by his mother, and he himself fought the fierce tribesmen alongside his fellow British officers.

As is clear from his own comments, the young cavalry officer, would-be journalist, and aspiring politician was delighted to be going into a zone of great personal danger. The greater the danger, in fact, the greater his chances of personal glory . . . and likely political success. Of this he made no bones.

Winston very much hoped the newspaper would use his name, he confided to his mother, "as otherwise I get no credit for the letters." He added, "It may help me politically to come before the public in this way."

Thus he was furious, wrote Geoffrey Best in *Churchill and War*, "when the *Daily Telegraph* put not his name but his initials in the byline . . . he was angry again when the terms his long-suffering mother fixed with the paper on his behalf were only £5 per letter instead of the £10 that he thought the acceptable minimum."

Meanwhile, ever the juggler of several interests at once, in order to attend the small war on the roof of India, he wangled a month's leave from his regular posting in Bangalore. He then appeared on the scene of operations in the northwest initially armed with only with the faintest of blessings from the British commander on the scene, Gen. Sir Bindon Blood, a social acquaintance who had promised back in England to give Winston an assignment only when there was a vacancy in the officer ranks—meaning when some unfortunate was killed or too badly wounded for duty. As events turned out, Winston was given such an assignment soon after his arrival, and he acquitted himself well in one skirmish after another. He even earned the honor of being mentioned in dispatches for his "courage and resolution " before his stay ended after about four weeks, during which time he saw action at least fifteen times (by his own count).

Without a doubt, as this episode in his life came to an end, no one could ever accuse Winston Churchill of shirking or hanging back in battle . . . quite the opposite, he repeatedly sought out the hottest spot on the field and conducted himself as if protected by an invisible shield. In three actions (*he* reported, unsurprisingly) he bravely rode his gray horse up and down the skirmish line while others took cover.

Sir Bindon himself commented that Lieutenant Churchill was "working away equal to two ordinary subalterns." As the campaign continued, the general speculated that, given a chance, the young man might earn the Victoria Cross, Britain's highest military award for bravery.

In sum, it can be assumed that Winston returned to his comparatively dull Bangalore duties quite pleased with himself. After all, he wrote to his mother later that year, "I am more ambitious for a reputation for personal courage than anything else in the world." He told brother Jack the same thing . . . but coupled the thought with the surprising statement that "in many ways" he was a coward, "particularly at school."

And what to make of this calculating scenario he also committed to paper in a letter to his mother that fall on the northwestern frontier? Ordered under enemy pressure to hurry over to another unit with a message to come help out, Winston, in his own words, "half turned to go on this errand, when a happy thought struck me. I saw in imagination the company overwhelmed and wiped out, and myself, an Orderly Officer to the Divisional General, arriving the sole survivor, breathless." Just in case something like that did happen, Winston told his colonel, "I must have that order in writing, Sir." In response, "the colonel looked surprised, fumbled in his tunic, produced his pocket book and began to write."

What about his thoughts on the possibility of being cut down by the bullets flying about the battlefield? To his mother he commented, "I am so conceited, I do not think the gods would create so potent a being for so prosaic an ending." It should be no surprise to learn that he turned his adventures on the northwest frontier into a successful book: *The Story of the Malakand Field Force.*

During his time in India, not so incidentally, Winston not only did a lot of self-educating by comprehensive reading in classical history and philosophy in books his mother sent from England, he also produced a somewhat autobiographical novel, *Savrola*, which is considered fairly forgettable as literature but of some historical interest in view of the man he later became.

Added Adventure Assured

The next great adventure for young Churchill was Field Marshal H. Herbert Kitchener's campaign in the Sudan, where the fanatical Mahdi who had trapped and killed Gen. Charles George "Chinese" Gordon at Khartoum in 1885 had

been followed by another fanatical leader known as the Khalifa. In 1898, Kitchener inched forward alongside the Nile with an army of twenty-five thousand
men, building a railroad across 385 miles of desert as a line of supply for the ponderous drive toward Khartoum.

The climax was the storied battle of Omdurman, which Winston described as
"the last in the long chain of those spectacular conflicts whose vivid and majestic
splendor has done so much to invest war with glamour." Here, too, Churchill's own
21st Lancers also contributed the last regimental cavalry charge of the British army.

Not totally an imperialist even in Victorian days, Winston wrote that viewing
the corpses of the slain dervishes three days later was quite a different proposition.
"All was filthy corruption," he noted. "Yet these were as brave men as ever walked
the earth." In fact, he added, their claim beyond the grave to a "valiant" death was
just as good as that of any Englishman.

But . . . how had this mere lieutenant of the 4th Hussars based in India managed to attach himself to a highly publicized campaign in the Sudan while his
own Hussars stayed back in India? He of course had pressed his mother in England to intercede on his behalf with "all the people you know." When that produced no concrete result, Winston wrote a personal letter to the prime minister,
Lord Salisbury, another highly placed family friend and one who had liked the
Malakand Field Force book.

Bold as usual, Winston told the PM he would like to go on the Sudan campaign because (1) the capture of Khartoum would be a historic event and (2) "because I can . . . write a book about it which from a monetary, as well as from other
points of view, will be useful to me."

As events turned out, he was posted to the 21st Lancers as a supernumerary
lieutenant, he finagled another leave from his duty post at Bangalore, he arranged
to write about the Sudan campaign for the *London Morning Post*, he performed
well in the battle of Omdurman and its famous cavalry charge, he wrote well-
received newspaper stories, and he derived another book from the entire affair—
the two-volume *River War*, which was published in 1899.

Clearly enough, a young man only in his early twenties, Winston was on a
roll—and he was coming to the attention of the British public. As a mere subaltern, moreover, he had the audacity to be critical of Kitchener in the *River War*
book. Yet, all that Winston had achieved so far was nothing compared with what
came next: his capture and audacious nine-day escape saga that occurred during
England's second war with the Boers of South Africa.

First, though, the fabled "potent being" saw political destiny slip away—for
the moment—when he impulsively ran for a seat in Parliament that opened up in

a special election in the factory town of Oldham. When one Conservative from Oldham died and the second Conservative serving that constituency retired, the Tories asked Winston to join their ticket, since under British rules members of Parliament did not need to live in the district they represented. He did run, but the Liberals won both newly opened seats. Thus Winston's parliamentary aspirations appeared a bit dim.

Additional note: Despite the defeat, Winston had a good time, it seems. "I shall never forget the succession of great halls packed with excited people," he wrote to his first love, Pamela Plowden, daughter of a British officer stationed in India. He was enthralled with "speech after speech, meeting after meeting—three even four in one night—intermittent flashes of Heat & Light & enthusiasm—with cold air and the rattle of a carriage in between: A great experience. And I improve every time"

"Astonishing Din"

Hardly had Winston Churchill brushed himself off from that initial somewhat bruising political encounter of July 1899 than opportunity knocked anew in September with an agreement from the *Morning Post* allowing him to cover the suddenly renewed Boer War in South Africa at the incredible salary of £250 a month, a princely sum even by today's standards.

Here, some would argue, was the real emergence of Winston Churchill, that child of destiny! For now, as chapter 1 of his *Great Boer War Adventure*, came the tale of the great train ambush. It began just two weeks after his arrival in Natal, at the end of October 1899 . . . it began as war correspondent Winston Churchill, still armed with the Mauser pistol used at Omdurman, climbed aboard an armored British military train on a routine-sounding patrol under the command of an old friend from the northwest frontier, Capt. Aylmer Haldane.

As luck (and good Boer tactics) would have it, the train was ambushed by Boers who fired on it with three field pieces and blocked the tracks behind with a huge boulder. Running backward to escape the artillery shells, the train collided with the boulder, three cars were derailed, and the rest of the train—now under fire—was blocked by the wreckage.

Correspondent Churchill, offering to help, took over the crew trying to clear enough room on the tracks for the engine, the rest of the train, and the troops to retreat. Luckily, it turned out, he left his trusty Mauser pistol in the engine cab and thus was not armed when captured an hour or so later. For much of that time, while Haldane and his men engaged the Boers, Winston and his crew were under steady fire as they struggled to clear the tracks. Wrote Haldane afterward: "I would point out that while engaged on the work of saving the engine, for which he [Winston] was mainly responsible, he was frequently exposed to the full fire of the enemy. I cannot speak too highly of his gallant conduct."

Indeed, as Winston himself wrote from captivity two weeks later to his family's longtime acquaintance, the Prince of Wales, "When you reflect that the range was only 900 & 1,300 yards, you may imagine the pounding we had and what an astonishing din the great projectiles exploding and crashing among the iron trucks [railroad cars] made."

Meanwhile, Haldane noted that he had "formally" placed war correspondent Churchill back "on duty" for the task of clearing the tracks, meaning that, when he was captured, Churchill was back in his military guise . . . although he protested to the Boers that as a newspaperman he was a noncombatant who should *not* be detained. As usual, he juggled his roles. Thanks to his efforts, in any case, the engine and some British troops did escape, while fifty others, Haldane among them, were captured.

Winston at that point was alone some distance down the tracks, but a single Boer horseman caught up and took him prisoner at gunpoint. Winston could have avoided capture because, moments before, he had been aboard the newly freed engine and tender and on the way to safety with twenty wounded men, the engineer, and assorted others . . . but he chose to jump off and start back on foot to the ambush site to help the men left behind, especially Haldane.

Winston and Haldane landed in the State Model Schools Prison in the Boer capital of Pretoria . . . where, together with another man, they hatched an escape plan that called for them to go over a back wall when the sentries weren't looking.

Soldier-journalist Churchill at first had hopes his claim to be nothing more than a journalist would result in release for him at least, but the Boers knew better. If nothing else, pistol or no pistol found on his person, his exploit in freeing the engine, which they badly wanted for their own use, was widely reported in the newspapers of the day. Thus, in the second week of December, Winston was told in no uncertain terms that his chances of release were dim. That very night, December 12, 1899, he went over the wall.

Terror Confronted

The escape plan hatched by Winston, Aylmer Haldane, and a sergeant major named Brockie called for all three to go over the wall one after the other, but the sentries apparently changed position about the time Winston managed to scramble over—his two companions were unable to follow him.

Left totally on his own in somebody's back garden in Pretoria, nearly three hundred miles from safety in neutral Portuguese East Africa, Winston was, for once, he later acknowledged, nearly paralyzed with fear. The plan had been to go over the wall, drop into the back garden on the far side and, well, that was the extent of it.

"There our plan came to an end," Winston later wrote. "Everything after this was vague and uncertain. How to get out of the garden, how to pass unnoticed through the streets, how to evade the patrols that surrounded the town, and above all how to cover the 280 miles to the Portuguese frontiers, were questions which would arise at a later stage."

Perhaps that's one reason why he had spent some of the time waiting to go over the prison wall in what he described as "positive terror." To this he added, "Nothing, since my schooldays, has ever disturbed me so much as this."

The night of the escape, however, he steeled himself and made his bold bid when a sentry turned his back to talk to another. Winston darted out from a hiding place inside the prison, a former school, and "ran to the wall, seized the top with my hands and drew myself up." But now his fears almost stopped him. "Twice I let myself down in sickly hesitation, and then with a third resolve scrambled up."

Lying flat on top of the wall, Winston looked back. Not fifteen yards away, the two sentries were busy talking. Silently, Winston lowered himself into the garden beyond and crouched among some bushes to await his companions.

Minutes later, a man emerged from the nearest house . . . to which the garden apparently belonged. In the dark, he seemed to be staring for long moments at the young journalist's hiding place in the bushes. "I cannot describe the surge of panic which nearly overwhelmed me," Winston recalled. "I dared not stir an inch. My heart beat so violently that I felt sick. But amid a tumult of emotion, reason, seated firmly on her throne, whispered, 'Trust to the dark background.'"

He did, and in moments a second man emerged from the house, and the two walked off together. By his account, Winston waited an hour for his companions to join him, but nothing happened. Finally, crawling back to the prison wall, he heard two prisoners on the other side talking so-called nonsense but also using his name.

Risking a cough, he let them know of his presence. They understood the message and relayed word that the sentries appeared suspicious, the escape attempt was off for the night—could he get back into the prison compound? Go back? No way! Quite suddenly, all was different. "Now all my fears fell from me at once. To go back was impossible. I said to the officers, 'I shall go on alone.'"

That is exactly what he did. Boldly walking through the town, passing among the Boer merchants and others strolling the streets, he reached the Delagoa railroad tracks just past a station, waited a short time, and boarded an outbound freight "with difficulty" while it was moving slowly. He hid for the night under some sacks of coal and jumped off the train the next morning to take shelter in a small wood, in company, he later wrote in the *Morning Post*, "with a huge vulture, who displayed a lively interest in me."(In another account of his escape he noted the vulture's "hideous and ominous gurglings from time to time.")

Later it was suggested that he had abandoned Haldane and Brockie that previous night. In *In the Footsteps of Churchill: A Study in Character*, Richard Holmes notes "in 1912 [Winston] successfully sued *Blackwood's* magazine which had repeatedly attacked him on the score." Holmes goes on to say, "It is impossible to prove the case beyond reasonable doubt. However, while I do not believe that Winston deliberately abandoned Haldane and Brockie, I cannot imagine him waiting too long on the far side of that wall."

Interestingly, too, on December 21 Churchill wrote in the *London Morning Post* that he had successfully completed a nine-day escape, during which he followed the rail line for five nights, hid and rested by day, and finally hopped another train for a ride of another two and a half days, all the while hidden under sacks, before finally reaching Lourenco Marques in neutral Portuguese East Africa (Mozambique today). This was stunning news for the British public, to hear this way from a man who had disappeared days before, deep in enemy territory, with everyone on the lookout for him, and a £25 reward offered for him, dead or alive. Winston was instantly famous . . . in a surprisingly difficult war not going well, he was a national hero.

Actually, his newspaper account was not quite true. The real story, kept quiet for the moment, was that after leaving his hiding place with the vulture and waiting in vain for another train on his second night at large, still many miles short of Portuguese East Africa's closest border, Winston came across a coal mine manager's house and knocked on the door. Happily for the desperate Winston, the manager was an Englishman, John Howard, who allegedly said: "Thank God you have come here! It is the only house for twenty miles where you would not have been handed over, but we are all British here, and we will see you through."

Howard and engineer Dan Dewsnap—who hailed from Oldham—hid Winston in the coal mine amid a colony of white rats. "As he was being hidden," reported Martin Gilbert in *Churchill: A Life*, Dewsnap "pressed his hands with the words, 'They'll vote for you next time.'"

After three days of hiding in the dark underground stables of the pit ponies, Winston fell ill. A doctor was added to the escape conspiracy, and he said that Winston had become "very nervy" and must be brought to the surface. He then was locked in a surface storeroom and, on the evening of December 19, was hidden among bales of wool in a railcar soon hooked up to a train headed for the Portuguese territory. By late afternoon on December 21, after a search of the railcar failed to unearth him, Winston stepped off in the freight yards at Lourenco Marques as a free man again.

Additional note: For an exacting picture of what Winston Churchill the future politician and statesman looked like at age twenty-five, the Boers' wanted poster issued on the heels of his escape suffices very well. "About 5 ft, 8 inches tall," it said, "average build, walks with a slight stoop, pale appearance, red brown hair, almost invisible small moustache, speaks through the nose, cannot pronounce the letter 's,' cannot speak Dutch, has last been seen in a brown suit of clothes."

Another description comes from Christine Lewis, an American girl whom Winston met en route from India to England by ship in the spring of 1899. "The gangplank was about to be raised," she wrote, "when down the wharf ran a freckled, red-haired young man in a rumpled suit, carrying an immense tin cake box. Although he had nearly missed the boat, he seemed utterly unruffled and, seating himself by the rail . . . he carefully examined the other passengers." Later she was placed opposite him at lunch. "Hardly had he been seated when he bent across the table and said, 'You are American, aren't you? . . . I love Americans. My mother is an American.'"

No Rest for the Eager

After his escape from the Boers, did this same slightly stooped, sometimes lisping figure go home to England and peace and quiet, perhaps even to a backwater political sinecure based on his newfound fame? No, not at all. The forgotten part of his story, a Hollywood tale if there ever was one, is that he now rushed back to the fighting scene . . . and there escaped perhaps his closest brush with death yet.

The added irony here is that brother Jack, an officer fighting the Boers by now, had just arrived on the scene aboard their mother's hospital ship, the *Maine*. He entered combat with Winston and promptly was wounded in the leg. (Yes, their mother's hospital ship was the *Maine*! And yes, Jennie was there too . . . the entire family never did things by a partial measure.)

And here, observed Winston, was "an instance of Fortune's caprice." For here, he explained: "There was a very hot fire, bullets hitting the ground or whizzing by in dozens. Jack, whose luck was fresh, was lying down. I was walking about without any cover—I who have tempted Fortune so often. Jack was hit."

Jack returned to Durban and brief treatment as Jennie's first patient on the hospital ship she helped to organize and equip, largely through a fund-raising campaign among American sources . . . and then had named for the American battleship blown up in Havana harbor in February 1898. Not badly hurt after all, Jack soon returned to the South African campaign and did his bit in the fairly normal fashion that apparently was his destiny in life.

Winston, typically for him—and far from the normal subaltern's activities—carried on as a correspondent for the *Morning Post* while accepting a lieutenancy in the South African Light Horse as the regiment's assistant adjutant. Typically, too, he was in, at, or near one scrape after another. In one case, a feather was clipped off his hat by a stray bullet. In another, he emerged unscathed from a burst of shrapnel that wounded eight other men. He was with the British relief column that broke the Boers' siege of Ladysmith, and then he joined Ian Hamilton's march through the Orange Free State to Pretoria. For that advance, he attached himself at one point to Angus McNeill's Scouts, commanded by an old friend from schooldays at Harrow . . . and once again almost lost his life.

In this case, the scouts were advancing on a hill when the Boers arrived on the crest and fired down on the approaching British. As the scouts turned for cover, Winston, dismounted for the moment, reached for his horse, placed his foot in a stirrup, and started to swing up into the saddle . . . but the horse shied and the saddle slipped under the animal's belly. Thoroughly spooked, the horse galloped off.

So here was Winston on foot and alone again, just as he had been at the train ambush. Once more he was seemingly at the mercy of the Boers, with no cover in sight for a mile. Since he had a newly acquired Mauser pistol with him as "one consolation," he wrote later, "I could not be hunted down unarmed in the open as I had before. But a disabling wound was the brightest prospect." As he turned and ran, he thought, "Here at last I take it."

But out of nowhere appeared a lone scout on a horse, and he obligingly swung Winston up behind him when the young soldier and journalist shouted, "Give me a stirrup." They galloped off, Boer bullets singing about their ears.

While he was hanging on to the horse's mane, Churchill noticed it was thick with blood. The horse evidently had been hit. "My poor horse, oh, my poor horse—shot with an explosive bullet," the scout cried.

"Never mind," said the pragmatic Winston. "You've saved my life."

He would never forget his rescuer's reply. "Ah, but it's the horse I'm thinking about."

Additional note: Winston thought the trooper who saved him should be cited for his bravery, but his recommendation was not acted upon. Six years later, however, as undersecretary of state for the colonies, Winston made sure that this man, Charles Roberts, received a Distinguished Conduct Medal for his brave action.

Meanwhile, in the best of the adventure-writer tradition, who should be with the British troopers who liberated his old prison in Pretoria not long after, but former prisoner Winston Churchill. Who should give a cheer and a salute of his hat as the prisoners came pouring into the yard to greet their liberators, but former prisoner Winston Churchill. And who already had wired the prison superintendent,

Louis de Souza, a telegram saying, "Escape not due to any fault of your guards," but former prisoner Winston Churchill.

Mother at War Too

When Lady Randolph heard about her frequently surprising son's capture and, a month later, his successful escape odyssey, the word came from his newspaper, the *London Morning Post*. "I regret to inform you Mr. Winston Churchill has been captured by the Boers," said the telegram she received in the middle of the night on November 17, 1899, from the newspaper's editor. "He fought gallantly after an armored train in which he was traveling was trapped."

Jennie Jerome Churchill had been visiting friends "in the country" and had planned to attend a "great fete at Claridge's Hotel" the next day on behalf of the hospital ship *Maine*, which she was just then organizing to care for wounded British soldiers of the Boer War.

A second telegram, this time from subeditor Oliver Borthwick, "a great personal friend of ours" (and son of newspaper owner Lord Gleneck), provided more detail. "No mention of his being wounded," Borthwick reported. "He not only displayed great personal bravery, carrying the wounded to safety, but by his coolness and bravery encouraged the others."

In *Reminiscences of Lady Randolph Churchill*, Jennie recalled, "My feelings may be imagined, and I passed some terribly anxious moments," but still, she had to go ahead with her hospital-ship project, just then nearing fruition. "Had it not been for the absorbing occupation of the *Maine*, I cannot think how I could have got through that time of suspense," she added.

As it was, she soon sent a cable to President William McKinley with a request for an American flag for the ship. She also enlisted a highly placed intermediary to ask Queen Victoria for a Union Jack. As events turned out, the McKinley administration, well aware of the strong pro-Boer sentiment among many Americans, declined to send a flag, but Queen Victoria said yes. In fact, the Duke of Connaught, Jennie's intermediary (also the mother of the Prince of Wales), informed her by letter on December 4, "I am happy to tell you that the Queen has consented to present a Union Jack to the Hospital Ship *Maine* as a mark of her appreciation of the generosity of those American ladies who have so nobly come forward, and have at such great expense equipped a hospital ship for wounded British officers and men."

Some days later, the "huge Union Jack, embellished in the center with the red cross on a white ground," was hoisted ceremoniously aboard the ship with "a number of distinguished people" on hand. Jennie kept "a judicious silence" about McKinley's refusal and supplied a U.S. flag herself. On December 23 the ship sailed for South Africa . . . with an extremely happy Jennie on board. "Although the morning broke dark and foggy," she also wrote, "I started with a light heart, as I had heard the day before that my son Winston, after escaping from Pretoria, where he had been a prisoner after the armor train disaster at Chieveley, was safe at Lourenzo Marquez [Lourenco Marques]."

As before, she had received word on Winston's latest adventure from his newspaper, the *Morning Post*. This time via the still relatively new telephone device. "All I could hear was 'Hurrah! Hurrah!' shouted by different voices, as one after another seized the instrument in their kind wish to congratulate me."

With various adventures of her own, Jennie would be staying in South Africa for many weeks. Her son Jack briefly would be a patient aboard her ship, thanks to a minor gunshot wound to the leg, and she would have brief visits with Winston as well. One highlight would be to pass the scene where Winston's train had been ambushed by Boers. "Sure enough," she wrote, "there was the train, lying on its side, a mangled and battered thing, and within a few yards a grave with a cross—three sentries mounting guard—marking the place where the poor fellows killed in it were buried." At Chieveley also, she saw a large British railroad cannon named, she was told, for her. Sure enough, the name "Lady Randolph Churchill" was painted on it in bold white letters.

Not Done Yet

Winston himself did not bother to mention his last great adventure of the Boer War in his memoirs, but Gen. Ian Hamilton did . . . forty-four years after the fact. That, reported biographer Martin Gilbert, was when Hamilton "published a full account of what he called Churchill's 'conspicuous gallantry (the phrase often used in recommendations for the VC [Victoria Cross]) for which he has never received full credit."

In the battle of Diamond Hill on June 11, 1900, the British column led by Hamilton had paused below the crest of a high mound held by Boers. The key to victory would be to storm that summit, "but nobody knew it," Hamilton wrote, "until Winston, who had been attached to my column by the High Command, somehow managed to give me the slip and climb this mountain, most of it being dead ground to the Boers lining the crestline, as they had to keep their heads down owing to our heavy gunfire."

Before anyone realized Winston's whereabouts or what he was up to, he had settled into a niche hardly a pistol shot below the Boers—"no mean feat of arms in broad daylight"—and had begun signaling "if I remember right, with his handkerchief on a stick, that if I could only manage to gallop up at the head of my mounted infantry, we ought to be able to rush this summit." All the while merely a half dozen Boers could have run just twenty yards past the brow of the hill and "knocked him off his perch with a volley of stones."

Meanwhile, thus advised to rush the crest, Hamilton did—"the battle, which ensured that the Boers could not recapture Pretoria, was in Hamilton's opinion 'the turning point of the war,'" Gilbert observed of this long-unsung example of Winston's initiative and courage.

In his own account of his last days in South Africa, now that the war was all but over, Winston related that he boarded a train that ran from Pretoria to Cape Town at the bottom of the continent for his sea voyage home, but a hundred miles south of Johannesburg, just below Kopjes Station, the train unaccountably stopped. When he stepped out to see what was going on, "to his horror, a Boer shell burst almost at his feet, 'with a startling bang,'" he reported. Winston saw that the wooden trestle just ahead was on fire. "The train was crowded with soldiers being sent south, or home," added Gilbert. Winston also quickly saw that no one was in command and troops were beginning to detrain and mill about in confusion . . . no officers in sight.

"Churchill now took charge. Fearing an ambush like that of the armored train . . . he ran along the track to the engine, 'climbed into the cab and ordered the engine-driver to blow his whistle to make the men get back into the train, and steam back instantly to Kopjes Station.'"

All this was done, fortunately, and Churchill had a last glimpse of "dark figures" in the dry waterbed under the burning trestle. He shot at them and they scattered without shooting back.

Later, at Kopjes Station, it was learned that the train just ahead of Winston's was under attack by a large Boer guerrilla force—more than fifty soldiers aboard the train were killed or wounded, and now the rail line to Cape Town was cut. That being the case, "Churchill borrowed a horse to continue his journey homeward."

Additional note: As he was ending his South African adventures, Winston's dispatches to the *Morning Post* had earned him "the highest sum yet paid to a journalist for such work," Gilbert reported. In addition, his latest book, *London to Ladysmith via Pretoria*, based of course on his Boer War adventures (and laced with his own trenchant observations), was doing very well, with eleven thousand copies sold in less than six weeks.

Back to Oldham

Next for the intrepid young journalist-soldier would be politics . . . another try at the brass ring from none other than Oldham, the same cotton-manufacturing town where he had lost his first bid for a seat in Parliament. Now, too, it wouldn't hurt that Oldham's own Daniel Dewsnap had been instrumental in effecting Winston's escape from the Boers by hiding the fugitive in a coal mine and smuggling him aboard a train that carried him to freedom.

Speaking at the town's Theatre Royal after returning to England, the now nationally famous Churchill cited Dewsnap's generous role in his great escape from the Boers much to the delight of the local audience. And who so helpfully should be in the audience but Dewsnap's wife! Thus, in October 1900, Conservative Party contender Winston Churchill not only sought election again to Parliament from the Liberal-leaning town of Oldham, but this time he won. Although his margin of victory was only 230 votes, his long-sought political career at last was under way—and he still was only twenty-five.

Meanwhile, on top of his newspaper and book proceeds, a lecture tour in England, Canada, and America also contributed to the Churchill pocketbook. Yet he enjoyed only mixed results in America, where popular feeling leaned toward the rebellious Boers rather than the British. Winston's travel to America in late 1900 and early 1901, incidentally, would be just the second of sixteen visits he would make over his lifetime to the land of his mother's birth.

Future as PM Predicted

Fresh both from his election to Parliament from Oldham on October 1, 1900, and a highly successful lecture tour in England, Winston Churchill embarked for America in December for more lectures—which meant he was back in touch with his mother's Irish-born friend Bourke Cockran.

Noting his victory as a parliamentary candidate, Winston proudly announced he also had emerged as "one of the two or three most popular speakers" in the overall parliamentary campaigning . . . not just for himself but for other candidates as well. Thus, Winston proudly said, he had been "engaged on a fighting tour, of the kind you know—great audiences (five or six thousand people) twice and even three times a day, bands, crowds and enthusiasm of all kinds."

His subsequent tour in America, however, turned out quite differently. In the first place, Churchill's U.S. agent, James Pond, proved to be embarrassingly overzealous in advertising that the visiting speaker from England was the hero of five wars, the author of six books (instead of five), and should be considered "the future Prime Minister of England."

Then, too, American audiences were markedly thin and less than enthused on behalf of the British in the war with the Boers in South Africa. Even so, at a gathering in the grand ballroom at the Waldorf Astoria Hotel arranged by Cockran, Churchill was introduced by none other than Mark Twain, who helpfully announced, "Mr. Churchill by his father is an Englishman, by his mother he is an American, no doubt a blend that makes the perfect man."

In another talk that same day, Winston himself raised the editorial eyebrow of the *New York Times* with the apparently unthinking remark that America and Britain were linked by the common desire for a daily bath . . . with the implication that the rest of the world might not appreciate the virtues of bathing.

Another highlight of Churchill's second visit to the United States was his meeting the *American* Winston Churchill, a well-known novelist of the day. According to Winston's granddaughter Celia Sandys, the American Winston gave a dinner for the British Winston when the latter visited Boston. Such was the confusion between the two Winstons, she told an audience in Richmond, Virginia, in November 2007, that her grandfather received the dinner bill and his American host received the other's mail that was forwarded from England.

As a prelude to their meeting, she explained, her grandfather some months earlier had mistakenly thought the congratulations he was receiving for his fiction writing "arose from the serialization of his [first and only] novel, *Savrola*, in *Macmillan's* magazine prior to its publication in New York and London." Not quite the case, though. "Once he realized there was another Winston Churchill, he wrote to his American namesake proposing that he would always sign himself Winston Spencer Churchill. He hoped this would avoid confusion and 'commend itself to Mr. Winston Churchill.' It did, and when he arrived in Boston one of his first visitors was the other Winston Churchill."

The *Boston Herald*, Celia reported, noted that her grandfather's lecture the evening of his dinner with the other Winston drew one of the largest crowds ever seen at the city's Tremont Hall. His talk there, the newspaper observed, stirred "a running fire of laughter and applause."

Other sources report that while the two Winstons strolled across the Boston Common to the Charles River, the British Winston said to his American counterpart, "Why don't you go into politics? I mean to be Prime Minister of England: it would be a great lark if you were President of the United States at the same time."

So there, if the story is true, you have it: even before first taking a seat in Parliament, Winston said it aloud . . . he intended to be prime minister.

As for his American counterpart, he did win election to the New Hampshire legislature two years later, but he lost a bid for governor in 1906 and dropped out of politics.

Additional note: Meanwhile, after a Christmas break, Churchill journeyed to Canada, where he found audiences more appreciative of his British point of view, but where he had a very public scrap with his agent Pond. After they patched things up, Churchill moved on to Michigan and Chicago, where, among other statements, he repeated his odd axiom that "the symbol of Anglo-Saxon unity [meaning American and British] is the bathtub and the toothbrush."

Further lecture commitments took him to Winnipeg, Milwaukee, and

Minneapolis before his return to New York and a final lecture in Carnegie Hall the night of January 31, 1901. By his own later tally, after three months of public speaking in England and two months in Canada and the United States, he had "spoken for an hour or more every night except Sundays, and often twice a day." His travel all that time, he said, had been unceasing—usually at night and by a schedule that meant "rarely sleeping twice in the same bed." And this had followed "a year of marching and fighting with rarely a roof or a bed at all."

Nonetheless, in America and Canada he earned an astounding amount—the modern equivalent of $160,000 or more. Although exhausted, Winston could now return to England happy on that score.

Unsurprisingly, he spent his last day in New York with his good friend and mentor Bourke Cockran, who saw him off aboard the steamship *Etruria* for the voyage home. As Martin Gilbert noted in *Churchill and America*, "It was to be 28 years before he returned to the United States."

When Egos Collide

Just after arriving in America for his second visit to his mother's homeland, this time for the lecture tour based upon his Boer War experiences and sudden fame in England, Winston met Theodore Roosevelt, who took an instant and lasting dislike to the young and newly elected Member of Parliament. No one really knows why.

TR's dislike for Winston apparently began when they dined together at the gubernatorial mansion in Albany, New York. This was in December 1900, right after Governor Roosevelt had won election to the vice presidency as William McKinley's running mate in the presidential sweepstakes of that year. As events turned out, just months later, TR would become president on the heels of McKinley's assassination in September 1901.

"There is no record of whether this Albany dinner went badly," wrote Parliamentarian Roy Jenkins in his massive Churchill biography of 2001, "but it certainly did nothing to prevent the development of a deep and surprising Theodore Roosevelt animus against Churchill."

A case in point is TR's remark in a letter to Theodore Roosevelt Jr. in 1908, long after TR had won the presidency in his own right in 1904. In the letter, the elder Roosevelt said, "Yes, that is an interesting book of Winston Churchill's about his father, but I can't help feeling about both of them that the older one was a rather cheap character, and the younger one is a rather cheap character." The reference was to Winston's perhaps overly long, two-volume biography of his father, Lord Randolph, whose governmental and political career, while meteoric, was fairly brief. Then, too, in a letter that same year to Senator Henry Cabot Lodge of Massachusetts, TR flat-out said, "I dislike the father and I dislike the son."

This posed a bit of a problem when Winston sent President Roosevelt a copy of a new book . . . by Winston himself, it so happened. TR turned to his ambassador to the Court of St. James, Whitelaw Reid, for advice. The book had come by way of Ambassador Reid, in fact. So TR told Reid, "I do not like Winston Churchill, but I suppose I ought to write to him." And he did write a short thank-you note, conveyed by the ambassador.

Asked years later why her father felt that way about Winston, TR's feisty daughter Alice summed it up in six words: "Because they were so much alike."

★ PART 2 ★
Political Ascendancy

Maiden Speech Watched

Election to Parliament meant an entirely new life for the young subaltern-newspaperman-book author. And that new life, after his actual seating in the House of Commons, would not really begin until he had delivered a maiden speech to the House.

When he did take his seat on February 14, 1901, the Boer War still wore on in South Africa, Queen Victoria had just died, and her son had taken the throne as Edward VII. With the Victorian Age giving way to the much shorter-lived Edwardian, it was an auspicious moment for one to begin a parliamentary career.

For many a newcomer, though, starting out in that storied, historic body could be an experience likely to intimidate. But not for Winston, spurred as he was (wrote his son Randolph) "by a burning sense of personal destiny as vivid as that of the young Bonaparte [Napoleon]."

At this point, young Winston was a bachelor (he never was noted as a ladies' man), was still turning to his mother for advice and useful contacts . . . but for once, thanks to his accumulating lecture and writing fees, he was able to send money to her, instead of the other way around. Here's what son Randolph also wrote in the second volume of his father's official biography: "He owed little to anyone save his name and his family tradition; he had been a true soldier of fortune who had made his way to the front with his own sword and pen." As a result: "He had gathered a modest fortune of £10,000 by unremitting toil. On this he could hope to support himself as a bachelor for the next four to five years."

Thus, on the day he was seated in Parliament (a nonpaying position until 1911), Winston was able to send his mother a check for £300 with a note graciously acknowledging, "In a certain sense it·belongs to you, for I could never have earned it had you not transmitted to me the wit and energy which are necessary."

The widowed Jennie Churchill by this time was herself only forty-seven years old and was married again—to George Cornwallis-West, a handsome subaltern in the Scots Guards who was only days older than Winston. Regardless of the awkward situations this posed for all concerned—or perhaps because of that—Winston felt moved by year's end to give up the annual £500 allowance his mother had been paying him and Jack.

Meanwhile, as newly crowned Edward VII opened Winston's first parliamentary session that February 14, the young newcomer to the House of Commons needed little tutelage in its sometimes arcane ways, most of them basically unchanged from the days of his father, Lord Randolph. As a student of his father's career, Winston had learned the customs of the legislative chamber, had read all of his father's speeches, and actually had memorized many of them.

He knew the insider's jargon too. References to "upstairs" meant committees, "another place" meant the House of Lords, "my right honorable friend" referred to leaders of his own party, and "the right honorable gentleman" to leaders of the other party. In addition, his son Randolph noted, Winston was well aware that speeches should not simply be read and that the person giving the speech always addressed the Speaker of the House.

As an astute student of parliamentary affairs, Winston also would have known "that the Mace on the table was the symbol of the King in Parliament, which is where the legality of the state is vested: but that when money matters are discussed, the Mace is put under the table, the Speaker leaves and the House goes into Committee under a Chairman so as to emphasize the Commons power over the purse."

For all his knowledge, family tradition, and sparkling accomplishments as a young man, Winston still faced a crucial day on February 18, 1901—a crucial evening, really, since it was shortly after 10:30 p.m. when he rose to meet his first challenge as a Member of Parliament: the maiden speech.

"The word had gone round the dining room and smoking room that he intended to speak," wrote Randolph. The House began to fill soon after dinner, only to be treated first, it so happened, to a "swashbuckling" speech by David Lloyd George, the future World War I prime minister who just now "was emerging with a growing reputation after more than ten years in the House."

Jennie (Churchill) Cornwallis-West of course was seated in the ladies gallery, along with four paternal aunts of young Winston. Among other leading lights on hand, either as spectators or on parliamentary business of their own were the next prime minister of England, Arthur Balfour; Mr. and Mrs. Joseph Chamberlain, parents of future Prime Minister Neville "Peace in Our Time" Chamberlain; and the soon-to-be prime minister, Herbert H. Asquith. In all, commented

Winston's former newspaper, the *London Morning Post*, "He had an audience to listen to his maiden speech which very few new members have commanded." Added the *Yorkshire Post*: "And in that packed assembly, everybody a critic, watching to see what sort of a start he would make in politics, Winston Churchill made his debut."

The consensus later was that it went well, even very well, although some of the press reaction was predictably political, either pro- or anti-Conservative Party. At least two of the so-called radical papers of the day noted that he spoke with a lisp—and it is true, Winston Churchill, whom we note today for his great oratory, always did have trouble getting his tongue around the letter *S*. As for his own reaction, Winston told a well-wisher, "It was a terrible, thrilling yet delicious experience."

To be sure, this was not a major policy speech. That would come later . . . many of them. And in just three years, in 1904, Winston would set his country's political circles agog with his crossing of the House floor from the Tory side to that of the Liberals, a truly flamboyant switch of parties.

For now, though, he had managed to get through his maiden speech with generally good ratings, despite the somewhat surprising focus of his speech: to suggest that the Boers, his own personal enemies, should be treated with fairness and generosity in their pending defeat. He also paid passing but heartfelt homage to his late father's days in the chamber.

Until Now

Until now, Winston Churchill's life story had been simple and straightforward, his son Randolph later wrote. "The story told itself."

But now—in the second year of the twentieth century—Winston, only twenty-six years old, already was "world famous and well-equipped to tread the stage which his father had quit a decade before." Now, too, his stage "will become richly peopled; new issues and controversies, often of great complexity, will emerge." More specifically: "He will cross the floor of the House of Commons, he will write his father's life, he will get married and become a father."

In the political realm, added Randolph, the second volume of his projected multivolume biography of his father (*Winston S. Churchill: Young Statesman, 1901–1914*) covers "not only Churchill's abandonment of the Tories for the Liberal Party; it also deals with the considerable social revolution with which he and [David] Lloyd George were principally concerned, which involved as its political climax the clipping of the powers of the House of Lords in the Parliament Act." After that, Churchill "quits these fields for war preparation at the Admiralty." In all, up to 1914, "Churchill will be seen to have played a leading role in all the exciting and indeed frenzied events which marked the first six years of [Prime Minister Herbert H.] Asquith's famous administration."

As Randolph also might have mentioned in his short preface, during this period also Winston would become fascinated by a new-fangled machine, the airplane—he would take flying lessons, he would create the air arm of the Royal Navy, he would predict the arming of these flying machines as weapons of war. He also would be lucky to survive a crash.

Helpful Prompting Needed

Just before Winston Churchill rose to deliver his maiden speech in the House of Commons that February night in England, there had been a little unexpected hitch in his plans. He was all set to begin with carefully chosen opening words when, as often is the case in the House, the unanticipated took place and threatened to throw him off course before he could utter a word.

His future Liberal Party associate David Lloyd George rose to announce he would not yet seek a vote on an amendment he had submitted earlier. He then took the opportunity to launch into an attack on the military operations against the Boers in South Africa, especially those of Col. Herbert Kitchener of Sudan fame. Here was trouble. Now, Winston would have to adapt his opening to a changed context, even if the subject still were the Boer War.

Luckily for him—"Manna [from Heaven] could not have been more welcome in the Wilderness," he later acknowledged—his seatmate, Thomas Gibson Bowles, whispered a quick suggestion for a new opening line: "Instead of making his violent speech without moving his moderate amendment, he had better have moved his moderate amendment without making his violent speech."

Helpfully prompted in this way, Winston rose and said: "When we compare the moderation of the amendment with the very bitter speech which the honorable member has just delivered, it is difficult to avoid the conclusion that the moderation of the amendment was the moderation of the honorable member's friends and leaders, and that the bitterness of the speech was all his own." Next, in acknowledgment of the suggestion by Bowles: "It has been suggested to me that it might perhaps have been better, upon the whole, if the honorable member instead of making his speech without moving his amendment, had moved his amendment without making his speech."

From there, with this smooth rendition of the Bowles suggestion, Winston Churchill, still a young man in a hurry, was off to the races—the political races he always had wanted.

Additional note: While Winston in time learned to deal with the chamber's rough-and-tumble debating ways, the fast riposte didn't come to him right away . . . and there did come one blatantly obvious lapse, one truly frightening moment early in his career as a widely noted orator. This was the time he simply, in the midst of a fairly routine House oration, forgot where he was, groped for the right words, then sat down, speechless, with his face buried in his arms.

It happened on April 22, 1904, just a month before he crossed over to the Liberal benches. Winston was forty-five minutes into a speech, apparently operating as usual without notes, when amnesia struck. He couldn't remember what he had planned to say next. For a wonderfully erudite man—so careful and meticulous in his planning that during World War II he, on average, spent an hour of preparation for every minute of speech-making time—this was a startling lapse.

As the more knowledgeable of Winston's onlookers knew, however, the painful hiatus not only was embarrassing, but it also recalled the days just ten or so years earlier when Winston's father, Lord Randolph, himself a noted speaker, had declined mentally to the point that he often was incoherent. Now, a decade later, his son suddenly was struck dumb and unable to go on with a speech. Would it be like father, like son?

Fortunately, it was only a momentary lapse . . . but, another old saying, to be forewarned is to be forearmed. From then on, Winston always made certain that he had a full set of notes to fall back on should he ever lose his place again.

"Uncle" Edward

While Winston Churchill served Great Britain's monarchy from one queen to the next, with four kings in between, his connection with Queen Victoria was fleeting at best. Aside from serving her, somewhat distantly, as a soldier, he did attend her fiftieth anniversary jubilee in London at the age of twelve after writing his mother three letters in which he begged for permission to leave school for the great event. Her reign began in 1837 and ended with her death in 1901, just before Winston took his seat in Parliament.

Her death made him a subject of her son, Edward VII, well known to Winston and his parents for many years as the hearty, womanizing, overly indulgent Prince of Wales. But the familiar "Bertie" taking over the throne, as a fifty-nine-year-old grandfather, surprised everyone as a highly successful monarch noted for goodwill travels and, by contrast with his mother, a decidedly modern outlook.

Despite their wide separation in age, the king and Winston enjoyed an occasionally acerbic but usually cordial relationship—very much like that of a fond uncle and his sometimes outrageous nephew. Indeed, for all his royal relatives spread throughout the courts of Europe, Edward was known far and wide as the "Uncle of Europe." The most troublesome of these relations, of course, would be one of Edward's nephews, Kaiser Wilhelm of Germany. Himself fluent in French and German and the son of the German-born Prince Consort Albert, Edward spoke with a heavy German accent. Thanks to Victoria's marriage to Albert, their son Edward was of the House of Saxe-Coburg-Gotha . . . during World War I, Edward's royal heir and successor as king of England, George V, deemed it wise to change the Germanic family name to the more-acceptable Windsor.

Edward was not yet king when Winston first came to public attention as a writer, both with his newspaper correspondence from the northwest frontier and, at age twenty-three, with his follow-up book, *The Story of the Malakand Field Force*, which was sometimes critical of both military and civilian policy makers. (The fact is, Winston considered the expedition a mistake from the start.) For Winston, the praise heaped upon his book was a new thrill. "I had never been praised before," he wrote in *My Early Life*. "The only comments which had ever been made upon my work at school had been 'Indifferent,' 'Untidy,' 'Slovenly,'

'Bad,' 'Very Bad,' etc. Now here was the great world with its leading literary newspapers and vigilant erudite critics, writing whole columns of praise!"

Winston was especially thrilled to hear words of praise from the Prince of Wales, who said he found the book of the "greatest possible interest" and considered the "descriptions and language generally excellent." He added, "You have great facility in writing, which is a great advantage." The future king, however, also had a prophetic warning: "I only hope you will be prudent in your remarks & shun all acrid criticisms which would be resented by the authorities." Little did Edward know at the time that he himself would be one of those resentful "authorities."

Far from bridling at such a warning (or, as time went on, abiding by it), Winston welcomed the prince's comments as a "great honor." And obviously he viewed the prince as an old family friend, despite the unpleasantness many years before that sent Jennie and Lord Randolph off to Ireland for three years in a kind of exile from the future king's social circle. (See page 377.) Just months after hearing from the prince about *Malakand*, Winston sent him a newsy personal letter explaining how he had been taken prisoner by the Boers even though he ostensibly was a noncombatant journalist. The letter, written on Winston's twenty-fifth birthday, November 30, 1899, wended its way to the prince from the State Schools prison in the Boer capital of Pretoria. Two weeks later, Winston mounted his famous escape from that prison.

By September 1902, as fate would have it, as a Member of Parliament, the fast-rising political star Winston Churchill visited the king at Balmoral Castle in Scotland. "I have been vy kindly treated here by the King, who has gone out of his way to be nice to me," Winston wrote to his mother (employing his usual abbreviations). "It has been most pleasant & easy-going & today the stalking [of deer] was excellent, tho I missed my stags." Winston went on to urge his mother, soon to see the king herself at a social outing, to "gush to him about my having written to you saying how much etc etc I had enjoyed myself here."

Still, the same Edward who once was openly displeased with Lord Randolph Churchill also could call Winston to heel for his political activities or his more intemperate oratorical outbursts. They had dinner together one time in 1905, months after Winston outraged so many in his party and the social circle he shared with the king by ostentatiously leaving the Conservatives in the House of Commons for the Liberals in 1904. Having agreed to meet with Winston for the first time in three years, Edward hoped to "bring home to me the errors of my ways," Winston later reported to his mother. At the same dinner, "He spoke most severely & even vehemently to me about my attacks on [Conservative Prime Minister

Arthur] Balfour," Winston told the Earl of Rosebery. "I accepted it all with meekness. In the end he became most gracious & we talked one hour."

Just a year later, though, the king was angered by the language Winston used in a House debate over a motion to censure the former British high commissioner in South Africa for approving the flogging of Chinese laborers. Rather than censure the official by name, Winston offered a compromise amendment that condemned the flogging of Chinese workers in general, but he used strong language in criticizing the practice, noted Martin Gilbert in *Churchill: A Life*. "'Simply scandalous' was the comment of the king, who protested at Churchill's 'violent and objectionable language,'" Gilbert observed.

Later in 1906, however, the king and Winston obviously were on better than mere speaking terms. Taking a long holiday, Winston sent the king strictly personal but otherwise uninteresting word from Switzerland that he and his host, Sir Ernest Cassel, "propose long walks over the glacier & mountains."

Traveling next to Silesia to attend German army maneuvers as a guest of Wilhelm II (Edward's "hated nephew" noted Winston's son Randolph), Winston received word from on high to be careful in his remarks to the Kaiser. Edward himself, it seems, had asked Prime Minister Henry Campbell-Bannerman to relay the warning "against being too communicative and frank with his nephew."

Just a year later, while vacationing in the French resort of Biarritz, Winston frequently found himself in the king's company plus that of "a great many people I have known a long time—all Tories!" One result for former Tory Winston was "a good deal of chaff & prodding, especially from high quarters." Still, he did receive a letter from Edward acknowledging their recent conversations "on various interesting subjects" and then adding royal sentiments well worth preserving as a family keepsake: "It is quite true that we have known your parents for many years (even before their marriage), & you & your brother since your childhood. Knowing the great abilities which you possess—I am watching your political career with great interest. My one wish is that the great qualities you possess may be turned to good account & that your services to the State may be appreciated."

It was at this point in his young life, incidentally, that Winston uttered one of his best-known self-assessments. Seated next to future prime minister Asquith's daughter Violet at a dinner, Winston, then colonial undersecretary, bemoaned the fact that he was "already" thirty-two years old, then added more brightly, "Younger than anyone else who counts, though." The remark that stuck, however, was this: "We are all worms, but I do believe I am a glow-worm."

It wasn't long after this, in the spring of 1908, that the king and Asquith himself discussed the possibility of a cabinet post for Winston under Asquith as prime minister. Edward was "quite warm in his praise of Winston," said Asquith later, but the king nonetheless was opposed to raising Winston's post as an undersecretary to cabinet level. The king felt Winston simply must wait until a "real Cabinet Office fell vacant."

Indeed, by the time Winston married Clementine Hozier in September 1908, Asquith was prime minister and Winston, at the age of thirty-three, was president of the Board of Trade, a cabinet post. And Edward of course gave Winston a handsome wedding gift—a gold-headed malacca walking stick, "which Churchill was to use the rest of his life," noted Gilbert in his biography. (But perhaps not . . . see pages 89–91.)

There would be other highs and lows in Winston's relationship with Edward VII—royal congratulations for his handling of a threatened coal strike, but royal outrage over Winston's warning of perpetuated class divisions if the budget proposals of 1909 were rejected by the House of Lords. Speaking at Leicester, Winston had said: "If we carry on in the same old happy-go-lucky way, the richer classes ever growing in wealth and in number, the very poor remaining plunged or plunging ever deeper into helpless, hopeless misery, then I think there is nothing before us but the savage strife between class and class, and an increasing disorganization, with the increasing waste of human strength and human virtue."

This time the king was so annoyed that he had his private secretary (himself a lord) write an unprecedented letter of protest to the London *Times*. Undismayed, Winston soon was writing to his new bride, "He and the King must really have gone mad," and "This looks to me like a rather remarkable Royal intervention and shows the bitterness which is felt in those circles. I shall take no notice of it. It will defeat itself."

Actually, as Liberals and Tories fought over efforts to curb the power of the Tory-dominated House of Lords, the king again objected when Winston, by now a leading speaker in the House, publicly suggested the dispute had become an issue of "Crown and Commons acting together against the encroachment of the Lords." Edward this time let it be known through another private secretary that he was not happy with the royal reference and the "various interpretations from various quarters" it received. In fact, came royal word via a note to the Lord Chamberlain, "it has been most distasteful for the King to find speeches, letters to the press, and leading articles discussing the point and attributing various opinions to his Majesty."

In sum, Edward hoped Asquith's cabinet ministers would refrain from mentioning him in their speeches or discussions "as far as possible." Winston at the time was in the Asquith cabinet . . . as home secretary.

The same dispute over the veto power of the Lords was still raging just weeks later when Edward, on May 6, 1910, suddenly died after a series of heart attacks. He thus never would know that it was Winston Churchill who wrote the official letter of condolence to Edward's son George, the new king, on behalf of the House of Commons. It had been just nine years since Winston first had taken a seat in Parliament . . . the very first Parliament that Edward himself had addressed as king. And now Winston was addressing both the "heartfelt sympathy of this House" and "our loyal congratulations" to the next king of England, George V.

Suffragette Troubles

On January 4, 1906, after checking into the Midland Hotel, two out-of-town visitors walked through the slums of Manchester, the great manufacturing center boasting well over half a million in population. Young parliamentarian Winston Churchill, one of the two, remarked to the other, his newly hired private secretary Eddie Marsh, "Fancy living in one of these streets—never seeing anything beautiful—never eating anything savory—*never saying anything clever!*"

So began one of Churchill's trickiest campaigns in search of election to Parliament from a base that was not his home. That was the custom—rather than serve their own home base, MPs often sought out a "foreign" constituency they could represent instead. Thus, Winston first was elected from the cotton-manufacturing town of Oldham; later in life he would represent Manchester, Dundee (Scotland), Epping (just outside of London proper), and Woodford (a new entity carved out of Epping's territory).

In 1906, just two years after leaving the Conservative ranks in the House of Commons for the Liberals, he chose to seek reelection in Manchester, seemingly an odd and challenging choice since eight of its nine seats were held by Conservatives or "Unionists." An aristocrat by personal background but now a Liberal by political label, he hoped to break into the northwest constituency (one of the city's six such divisions) of this Conservative bastion.

As explained by his son Randolph, "Churchill realized his future did not lie with Oldham, and he had for some time been on the look-out for a constituency which he could fight in the Liberal interest." As a result, "unofficial feelers were put out by the Liberals in the North-West division of Manchester."

Actually, Winston seemed perfect for Manchester and Manchester for him because it "was the citadel of doctrinaire Free Trade and Churchill had proved his credentials by intimating that he was about to break with the Tories on this very issue [as indeed he had] and by his capacity for expounding the Free Trade argument in the liveliest and most-up-to date fashion." Indeed, a major landmark of the city, standing in that same northwest section, was Manchester's *Free Trade* Hall.

Ever since its formation in 1884, ten years after Winston's birth, a powerful Tory had represented the northwest Manchester district in Parliament, but now he was stepping aside and a newcomer from London, forty-year-old solicitor William Joynson-Hicks, was running on behalf of the Conservatives. In virtually no time, however, it was the flamboyant Winston who was seen as "the most exciting candidate in the city," noted William Manchester in his unfinished biography *The Last Lion*. Typical of Winston's dramatic style, when a heckler presented him with a pamphlet "quoting his past scorn for his present party [the Liberals]," Winston tore it into pieces and declared: "I said a lot of stupid things when I worked with the Conservative Party, and I left it because I did not want to go on saying stupid things."

Meanwhile, the focus of public interest in Manchester's general election was "the personality of Mr. Winston Churchill," agreed the *Daily Mail*, adding, "You can hardly see the rest of the political landscape for this dominant figure." Biographer Manchester added: "Men discussed his alliterative rhetoric, the mammoth posters bearing his name in letters five feet high, the reviews of his . . . [latest] book, and the startling youthfulness of his mother, who was stumping for him every day."

Adding to the political undercurrents here were Churchill's run-ins with suffragette hecklers, an irony since he ultimately would vote in Parliament *for* the women's vote. As reported by his son Randolph years later, "Manchester was the home of the suffragette movement, and indeed of the Pankhursts, the remarkable mother [Emmeline] and daughters [Sylvia and Christabel] who founded and sustained the cause." Thus, at one meeting covered in detail by the *Manchester Guardian*, Winston suddenly stopped when answering questions to say, "You have got it the wrong way round."

He was looking at a woman holding the same black and white flag often seen at his meetings and saying "Votes for Women." The woman in the audience was holding the flag upside-down.

"It is believed that when she began to speak, the audience showed the liveliest indignation, and utterly refused to hear her," reported the *Guardian*. "The Chairman, in a loud voice, said: 'If that lady interrupts again she is to be carried out.'"

Also appealing for order, Winston started addressing audience questions again, but immediately was interrupted as the woman cried out, "Will you give us a vote?"

At this, reported the *Guardian*, "there was a great uproar."

Winston then invited the woman to join him on the platform. As she complied, "The audience hissed her vigorously," said the *Guardian*, "and the complacent smile with which she regarded them in return appeared to cause still more irritation."

She settled in an empty chair, and Winston again pleaded for order, saying, "Will everybody be quiet. Let us hear what she has to say."

The *Guardian* reported the rest of the spirited exchange of January 9, 1906 (reprinted in Randolph's biography of his father, *Winston S. Churchill: Young Statesman, 1901–1914*):

> The woman then stood up and said: "Men and women—" Cries of "We want to hear Churchill" (Cheers)—"I should like to ask Mr. Churchill as a member of the Liberal government whether he will or will not give a vote to the women of this country?"—(loud cries of "Never.") It was noticeable that the women of all classes of society, who were among the audience in considerable numbers, joined heartily in the cries of "No," "Never," which followed upon the question. A woman's voice said, "You are disgracing us," and still another said, "Leave it to the men." Mr. Churchill said: "This lady has asked me a question. She has a perfect right to ask it, but I don't know why she didn't send up a notice of it on paper like everyone else has done." (Cheers.) The woman said she had done that before. (A voice: "And you have had your answer.") Mr. Churchill: "We should be fair and chivalrous to ladies. They come here asking us to treat them like men." (Laughter) "That is what I particularly want to avoid. We must observe courtesy and chivalry to the weaker sex dependent upon us." (Hear hear.)

Actually, Winston added, the only time he had voted on the issue in the House of Commons so far, was "in favor of woman's suffrage, but"—beginning to show apparent irritation himself—"having regard of the perpetual disturbance at public meetings at this election, I utterly decline to pledge myself."

Another time, obviously irritated at the tactics of the more militant suffragettes, Winston remarked, "I am not going to be henpecked on a question of such grave importance."

As events turned out, he won a handsome victory in Manchester in 1906 but lost the seat in a by-election—required by his appointment as president of the

Board of Trade—just two years later. At that point, he shifted quickly (just two weeks later) to Dundee, the Scottish seaport and ship-building center on the Firth of Tay famous for its marmalade, won a seat there, and held it for twelve years.

In the interim, suffragettes constantly plagued him. Once, when a woman followed him about repeatedly ringing a loud dinner bell, he impulsively shouted, "Get away, woman." When she demurely replied, "It's no use your being cross," but kept on ringing the bell, he more calmly said, "I won't attempt to compete with a young and pretty lady in a high state of excitement."

Another time, though, in a potentially ugly incident, he and his wife, Clementine, were traveling to Bristol for a speech-making occasion when a young suffragette attacked Winston with a dog whip at the Bristol railroad station. To fend her off, he held her by the wrists, but she steadily pushed him back toward the tracks—the train behind just then beginning to pull out. Clementine came to his rescue, climbing over a jumble of suitcases to grab Winston's coattails and pull him to safety. As his assailant then was led away by the police, she shouted, "You brute, why don't you treat British women properly?"

Additional note: "Henpecked," did he say that day at Manchester? He did, but did he—as some people apparently once thought—coin the term? Not so, according to Randolph Churchill. "This word," said Randolph, "dates back at least to 1680. [Jonathan] Swift used it in referring to the relationship between the great Duke of Marlborough [Churchill's own illustrious ancestor] and his Duchess Sarah. The phrase also occurs in Byron's *Don Juan*. Churchill had long been familiar with his writing:

> But—oh! Ye lords and ladies intellectual
> Have they not henpecked you all? (book I, canto xxii)

Meeting Clementine

Could this twain ever meet? Asked to dinner at Lady St. Helier's as a last-minute fill-in, twenty-two-year-old Clementine Hozier, tired from teaching French lessons, told her mother, "I really can't. I don't want to go, I've got nothing to wear and have no clean gloves." In another part of London, at No. 12 Bolton Street to be exact, fast-rising political star Winston Churchill, then thirty-three, was lolling in his bath rather than rushing off to dinner.

Private secretary Eddie Marsh interrupted. "What on earth are you doing, Winston?" he asked. "You should be at dinner by now." The politician merely replied, "I'm not going. It will be a great bore."

But Winston did go, arriving late, as the chicken was being served . . . and Clementine went also, to fill an unexpectedly empty seat at the dinner party given in March 1908 by her great-aunt Mary (Mrs. John Stanley through an earlier marriage and now Lady St. Helier).

The dinner, explained Winston and Clementine's son Randolph, was in honor of Lady Lugard, "wife of Sir Frederick Lugard, the great West African colonial administrator, and a considerable authority on colonial matters in her own right." As Flora Shaw, she, in fact, had been the colonial editor at the London *Times*, Randolph also noted.

Interestingly, Winston at the time was undersecretary for the colonies in the Liberal Asquith government, but that didn't mean his views and the honoree's coincided . . . not in the least, it appears. In a biography by Margery Perham, Lady Lugard referred to that "wild Winston" and called him "an ignorant boy, so obviously ignorant in regard to colonial affairs and at the same time so full of personal activity that the damage he may do appears to be colossal."

At the dinner, Winston was seated, fatefully, next to Clementine and "appears to have ostentatiously ignored Lady Lugard." Instead, he "devoted all his attention to his beautiful young neighbor, much to the latter's embarrassment." The fact is that Winston and Clementine had first met at a dance four years prior, with nothing coming of it. "Churchill saw Clementine, then barely nineteen years old," wrote their son Randolph, "and asked his mother who she was and if he could be introduced to her. Lady Randolph said she did not know the girl but would find out; and when she came back she said: 'how very interesting: she is the daughter of a very old friend of mine, Blanche Hozier, whom I haven't seen for years.'"

Clementine was born in the drawing room of 75 Grosvenor Street in London on April 1, 1885. Officially, she was the daughter of Sir Henry Hozier and his wife, Lady Blanche. Three years later, the Hoziers separated after the birth of Clementine's twin siblings Bill and Nellie. Apparently a bitter estrangement ("Sir Henry did not even list his marriage in *Who's Who*"), the separation meant Lady Blanche had to raise her children on her own, in "reduced" financial circumstances. Sir Henry, a colonel in the 3rd Dragoon Guards, had come from a "brilliant military career" and "cut a gay and flamboyant figure in the City of London." He died in 1907 . . . and he may *not* have been Clementine's father.

Clementine, "beautiful but penniless," had lived at times in Dieppe, France, and attended the Sorbonne. A tournament-class tennis player, she taught French to eke out a small living. All this, and more, Winston learned in due time . . . but not on the occasion of their first meeting.

After Lady Randolph introduced Winston to Clementine, the young lady quite naturally responded, "How do you do?" She told their son Randolph that his father just stood there and stared. "He never uttered one word and was very *gauche*—he never asked me for a dance, he never asked me to have supper with him. I had of course heard a great deal about him—nothing but ill. I had been told he was stuck-up, objectionable, etcetera. And on this occasion he just stood and stared."

Understandably, she gestured for help from one of her admirers. Here, Randolph's recounting of his parents' meeting departs from his usually dispassionate recital of his father's life story to August 1914: "All his life Churchill was always apt to be *gauche* when he met women for the first time. He had no small talk. He greatly preferred talking about himself. He could scarcely do this with strangers: hence the embarrassment he often caused."

But now, in March 1908, at the dinner neither one wished to attend, they had met again. And what does he try as a conversational gambit? He asks if she has read *his* two-volume biography of *his* father, Lord Randolph!

Well, no, she admitted, despite the urging of her mother, "she had so far not opened it."

"If I send you the book tomorrow, will you read it?" he apparently asked.

"Clementine assented, but he did not send the book. 'That made a bad impression on me,' she recalled."

Perhaps it all would have ended there, but strings were being pulled . . . the two would meet again, this time more agreeably, on a Sunday the next month, at Salisbury Hall, Winston's mother's rented home near St. Albans. Both Lady Blanche and her daughter Clementine came avisiting, even though they were due to leave the next day for a six-week tour of the Continent.

Apparently the prospective couple's elders had sensed something was afoot because, "Lady St. Helier had told Lady Blanche that she was mad to let Clementine disappear just when she thought Churchill was interested in her."

Significantly, too, Clementine wrote a thank-you note to Lady Randolph from Paris that took note of Winston's "dominating charm and brilliancy." And Winston wrote to Clementine just four days after the Salisbury Hall visit to say "how much I liked our long talk on Sunday and what a comfort & pleasure it was to me to meet a girl with so much intellectual quality & such strong reserves of noble sentiment." This obviously wasn't just polite acknowledgment of a passing encounter, since he added, "I hope we shall meet again and come to know each other better and like each other more: and I see no reason why this should not be so." Please write, he urged, and "above all" let him know when she would be returning home.

Not so incidentally, in the short time since the dinner at Lady St. Helier's, Winston had been appointed president of the Board of Trade—for such a young politician, a plum post that carried cabinet status in the Asquith government. Not only that, but this particular cabinet, Randolph Churchill noted, "has long been held up as the most glittering of modern times—perhaps of all times."

Was newcomer Winston to be intimidated by such brilliant company? Apparently not. Randolph observed: "Churchill, at the early age of thirty-three, did not feel at all ill at ease in this company. Indeed he, together with [David] Lloyd George, was the most scintillating in the Government, and they were soon to become known as the 'heavenly twins of Social Reform.'"

Churchill of course would be a busy man, perhaps more so than ever, but he wasn't about to neglect the personal side of his life, where there was a certain void. He was in a serious mood for marriage. He had been in love before. He had been unofficially engaged to Pamela Plowden, whom he met in India, and he also had proposed to Muriel Wilson and to Ethel Barrymore (yes, the actress).

But first, as a new cabinet member, under the rules of the day (since changed), he had to run for reelection to Parliament. However, he lost his seat from northwest Manchester, and so he turned to Dundee, where a fellow Liberal had been elevated to the peerage and thus had left his parliamentary seat open. Mounting a vigorous campaign in a four-way race for the open seat, Winston won with 44 percent of the vote. He would serve a working-class constituency, and in the course of the campaign he attacked the House of Lords as "filled with old doddering peers, cute financial magnates, clever wirepullers, big brewers with bulbous noses." Even more hotly, he proclaimed, "All the enemies of progress are there—weaklings, sleek, smug comfortable self-important individuals."

After that, it was back, ever so briefly, to personal business. That would mean, first, attending the civil and religious marriage services on August 4–5, the latter one at Oxford, for his brother Jack and Lady Gwendeline Bertie, otherwise known to the family as "Goonie." Then, on the night of August 6, 1908, a fire broke out in the home where Churchill and others were staying as guests. Typically, it was Winston, donning a fireman's hat, who was seen on the roof plying a hose from a "tiny fire engine" brought over from a nearby village.

Events now were moving at a rapid pace. Invited to visit Winston, his mother, and the Marlboroughs at Winston's birthplace, the magnificent Blenheim Palace, Clementine arrived on August 10. Recalling she only had one clean cotton frock available, she later said, "Everyone except me had a maid and I remember having to stand for fear of getting it crumpled."

The first morning there, she came down for breakfast at a decent hour and . . . no Winston! "Churchill, as was his wont," reported Randolph, "stayed in bed late, which somewhat mortified Clementine."

Coming to the rescue was Winston's cousin "Sunny," the sitting Duke of Marlborough, who "sent a message to Churchill to bestir himself and in the meantime took Clementine for a drive round the park." Not a good start to the visit, one might speculate, but before the day was out, Winston had proposed, they were engaged, and it was official.

How did the engagement come about? Randolph recounted: "In the late afternoon Churchill took Clementine for a walk. It came on to rain, and they took shelter in the ornamental temple which stands some 200 yards to the west of the palace and which overlooks the lake. There Churchill proposed to Clementine and was accepted."

Their engagement would be a secret, they agreed, until she could tell her mother, but on their way back to the massive Marlborough structure, they came across Winston's friend F. E. Smith on the lawn. "Churchill danced across the grass and, in full view of the servants, flung his arms around his neck and blurted out the news." So much for secrecy.

Mary's Story

Winston's daughter Mary Soames has also told the story of her father's sometimes bumbling courtship of her mother, beginning with their first meeting at a ball at the home of Lord and Lady Crewe in the summer of 1904. This was right after Winston "abandoned his father's party, crossing the floor of the House to sit on the Liberal benches."

He had done so "in defense of Free Trade" and in opposition to the Conservative Party's "drift towards Tariff Reform." As a result, in his own party "he was regarded as a renegade and a turn-coat." While he had his friends and supporters, he was already, at the age of thirty, "a controversial figure and, especially among his own class and contemporaries, was judged by many to be bumptious, an opportunist and generally insufferable."

Since politics "were more vehement in those days, and permeated social life to a marked degree," and Lord Crewe happened to be a Liberal Party member, his was one of the few prominent homes of England still open to Winston socially. Thus, he came to the ball . . . as did Clementine.

Winston arrived with his mother and there, standing alone in a doorway, was the fair Miss Hozier. Upon his asking who she was, his mother discovered not only that she was the daughter of an old friend but that her brother-in-law, Winston's uncle, Sir Jack Leslie, was Clementine's godfather. "These links made it easy and natural for Lady Randolph to introduce her son to Clementine," noted Mary.

As Randolph also recounted, Winston "stood rooted to the spot, staring at the vision which had so powerfully beguiled him," Mary added. Embarrassed and even "mortified," Clementine "imagined that Lady Randolph had noticed that she was, for the moment, without a partner and, taking pity on her plight, had out of kindness introduced her son."

From what Clementine had heard about him, she was "not at all favorably disposed towards him." Moments after signaling for help, she was dancing with a "beau" who came to her rescue, and he was asking what she was doing with "that frightful fellow Winston Churchill."

Quite true, Clementine and Winston would not cross paths again for nearly four years . . . but they were a busy four years for each. Winston, never a ladies' man, was no habitué of the ballroom or "fashionable country-house parties," Mary noted. "Politics were always to fill and dominate his thoughts—and now his star was on the ascendancy." With the Liberals coming into power in the general election of 1906, "Winston at once began to play a prominent part in affairs, for although he was only a junior Minister, his chief, Lord Elgin, the Colonial Secretary, sat in the House of Lords. Winston, as Under-Secretary, was therefore the chief government spokesman on Colonial Affairs in the House of Commons."

Clementine, on the other hand, went through—and broke off—two engagements, one of them a secret engagement and the other a brief and sudden betrothal to a man almost twice her age, on top of which came her father's death while he was traveling in Panama.

Then came that fateful night in March 1908 when Clementine "arrived home rather bent and weary after giving French lessons to find a message from Lady St. Helier asking her to dine that very evening, as one of her guests had fallen out, and she was in danger of being an unlucky thirteen." Randolph's and Mary's accounts agree that Clementine was reluctant, she was tired, she had no gown ready, had no clean gloves . . . but her mother insisted.

Private secretary Eddie Marsh, in the meantime, prodded an equally reluctant Winston, who had decided the evening "would be a great bore." Marsh reminded him that a decade earlier, Lady St. Helier had used her influence to help with the backdoor arrangements that allowed Winston to join Kitchener in the Sudan. "So, with none too good a grace, Winston hurriedly dressed and set out, already late, for the dinner party." Before he could get there, the guests were seated and eating, Clementine with a gap to her right . . . Winston's seat. "Halfway through dinner," he finally arrived, "full of explanations and excuses," and took his place. If their first meeting "had not been a signal success," of course, "things went very differently this time."

Instead of discussing colonial affairs with Lady Lugard to his right, otherwise known as the colonial columnist Flora Shaw, "he turned almost at once to the ravishing young woman on his left, and monopolized her for the rest of the dinner."

Then, as the gentlemen rejoined the ladies later, he made a beeline for Clementine, "in whose company he remained for the rest of the evening." In fact, "His attentions were so noticeable that Clementine had to endure a little gentle teasing from the other ladies, when they all went to get their cloaks."

The fact is, each had found a soul mate. "The romantic in Winston Churchill's nature sought in women beauty, distinction and nobility of character: Clementine Hozier possessed all three. On their first brief encounter he had recognized the first two qualities; now, after an evening spent in her company, he realized that here was a girl of lively intelligence and great character. Clementine, for her part, was enthralled by the brilliance, warmth and charm of his personality, which filled his whole being and made his attraction so irresistible, despite his forgetful, unpunctual and even at times un-gallant ways." In fact, after promising her a copy of his biography of his father, he forgot to send it.

As it turned out, his forgetfulness was no great matter . . . and the plot thickened anyway. Quite smitten, Winston asked his mother to invite Clementine and her mother for an overnight visit at Salisbury Hall the second weekend of April. "To her lasting credit, Lady Randolph from the first welcomed Winston's attachment to Clementine. It would clearly have been advantageous for him to have married a girl with some money, and Lady Randolph was a worldly woman. But she instantly recognized in Clementine those sterling qualities which were to make her the perfect wife for her brilliant son."

During that same weekend, newly appointed Prime Minister Asquith announced his top government choices. They included Winston as president of the Board of Trade—his first cabinet level appointment. In her book *Clementine Churchill*, Mary could only suggest the excitement this added to the April visit for Winston, his mother Jennie, and Clementine.

Next, though, came that interruption for the latter's long-planned Continental tour . . . interruption also for Winston's two election campaigns—wherein he lost at Manchester but gained a new constituency at Dundee, Scotland. And the interruption for Jack's wedding, followed by the house fire, wherein Winston "had taken a leading part in salvaging pictures and other valuables . . . and had escaped possible death or serious injury when, just as he left one part of the house carrying two marble busts, the roof, which had been blazing furiously, collapsed."

Clementine immediately wrote him that her heart stood still with terror on hearing the news that the house had burned down . . . but now she was wrestling with another issue: what to wear for their next get-together! Unexpectedly, Winston had arranged for his cousin Sunny, the Duke of Marlborough, to invite her for a two-day visit to Blenheim before going on another previously planned visit to Salisbury Hall. "Lots of things to talk about," Winston had promised about the Blenheim stay, and, besides, his mother would be present "to look after you."

For Clementine, the last point had to be somewhat reassuring, since the duke for the moment was single—he and his first wife, American-born Consuelo Vanderbilt, had separated after eleven years in a marriage that produced two sons (and expended considerable Vanderbilt monies for the upkeep of the vast Marlborough manse).

Then, too, since Clementine had been attending the sailing races and balls at Cowes, the invitation caught her "down to her last laundered and starched dress and, having no personal maid, she would have to make this one last the unexpected visit."

Lots of things to talk about, did he say? Come be with him at Blenheim? Things were moving awfully fast . . . he had been born there, he loved the place, it was his alternate home, and now he insisted she visit. What to think or to expect?

Riding the train from Cowes to Oxford (before riding the eight miles to Blenheim by car), Clementine wrote her mother a quick note: "I feel like in a dream & can do nothing more intelligent than count the telegraph posts as they flash by or the pattern on the railway cushions."

Upon arriving and settling in at the truly imposing palace, she found it indeed was a small house party (by Blenheim standards!): the duke, Winston, his mother, a private secretary furnished to Winston by the Board of Trade, and MP F. E. Smith and his wife.

As events edged toward their climax, Winston that first night, Monday, August 10, asked Clementine to walk with him in the rose garden the next morning after breakfast . . . but then, as son Randolph reported, he wasn't there at the appointed hour. "Appearing punctually at breakfast was never at any time in his life one of Winston's more pronounced qualities," recounted Mary. "Even on this day of days he was late!"

Clementine, in a word or two, "was much discomfited." She considered returning to London, but then, thankfully, Sunny Marlborough came to the rescue. Noting her obvious irritation, "He dispatched a sharp, cousinly note to Winston and, deploying his utmost charm, suggested to Clementine that he should take her for a drive in his buggy. He whirled her round the estate for about half an hour, and upon their return there was the dilatory Winston anxiously scanning the horizon."

And so, on to the climatic moment of the episode. With all apparently forgiven, Clementine and Winston walked late that afternoon and, while walking, were caught by "a torrential rainstorm." They took shelter in the replica of a Greek temple by the estate's great lake. "When in due course, and the rain shower being over, they emerged from the temple—they were betrothed."

Wedding Story

The marriage of Winston and Clementine on September 12, 1908, just a month after their engagement, took place on a Saturday at St. Margaret's Westminster, the parish church of the House of Commons, with an estimated sixteen hundred guests looking on. Thousands crowded the streets outside and the church "was packed to the doors," said daughter Mary (Lady Soames) in her biography of her mother. "For a day a truce was called between Radical and Tory, and indeed one of the first guests to arrive was the Tory member for N. W. Manchester, Mr. [William] Joynson-Hicks, who had so narrowly defeated Winston earlier in that same year."

More comfortably for Winston, his new political ally of recent years, Chancellor of the Exchequer David Lloyd George, signed the official register, "and Winston immediately set to talking politics with him."

While the crowds outside included many suffragettes, they did not demon-strate, as had been feared. Instead, the predominate cries as bride and groom drove off to the reception at their onetime dinner hostess Lady St. Helier's home on Portland Place were "Good Old Winnie!" and "God bless Winnie!"

Clementine, escorted up the aisle by younger brother Bill, a sublieutenant in the Royal Navy, was "a glorious sight" in a gown of shimmering white satin, topped with a veil of tulle and a coronet of orange blossoms. The bridesmaids wore biscuit-colored satin "with large romantic black hats wreathed in roses and camellias." They carried bouquets of pink roses. For the leave-taking from the re-ception, Clementine wore an ensemble of gray cloth, topped by a large black hat of satin, "adorned with one long sweeping ostrich feather."

The jostling onlookers in the street included a number of "Pearly Kings and Queens," dressed in clothes "resplendent with pearl buttons sewn in intricate pat-terns." Mary explained: "As President of the Board of Trade, Winston had helped to protect the costermongers' rights to trade in the streets; so, on this his wedding day, many of them gathered in their splendid traditional finery to wish him well." When they spotted Clementine's feathered hat, "The Pearly Queens, whose own large hats are always decorated with waving ostrich plumes, were delighted. 'Ooh, wot a luv'ly fevver!' they cried, as Winston and Clementine got into their carriage."

For the happy couple, step one in their honeymoon was a trip by train from London to Woodstock, and from there to adjoining Blenheim Palace, where they had become engaged. Step two, after a couple of days at Blenheim, would be a honeymoon trip to Italy's Lake Lugano and Venice, followed by a visit with Win-ston's old friends Baron (Tuty) de Forest and his wife in Austria.

Returning from abroad a month later, they took up residence at Winston's bachelor quarters at No. 12 Bolton Street before house hunting in earnest for something more permanent and suitable for a young married couple. Walking into her bedroom, though, Clementine had a shock—in their absence, it had been completely redecorated, courtesy of Winston's mother.

To Clementine's "simple and rather austere taste, the sateen and muslin covers trimmed with bows, which decked the chairs, dressing-table and bed, appeared vul-gar and tawdry." She would do "her best, however, to conceal her lack of apprecia-tion of her mother-in-law's well-meant efforts." Winston himself, in fact, had asked his mother to prepare the house for their return. And what about that famous and flamboyant mother-in-law? How would these two strong-willed women, each one so central to Winston's life story, get along during the years they would be sharing that story? According to Mary, daughter and granddaughter, respectively:

Clementine was never to have a really close relationship with Lady Randolph. This once supremely beautiful woman was still, in her fifties, remarkably handsome; but, accustomed all of her life to attention and adulation, Lady Randolph had now to accept a long, cool look from her new daughter-in-law. Although as time went on Clementine came to salute her courage and her unfailing zest for life, now in these early years of her marriage she passed (in her heart) a fairly harsh judgment on her celebrated mother-in-law. She thought her vain and frivolous and, in her marriage to a man [George Cornwallis-West] so much younger than herself, somewhat ridiculous.

Wisely, though, Clementine appreciated "how dearly" Winston loved his mother "and she kept (for the most part) her opinions and reservations about Lady Randolph to herself." Thus, "mutual good manners, surface affection and a shared loyalty to Winston maintained a civilized relationship between these two very different women."

Additional note: Another shock of sorts for the frugal Clementine were Winston's superexpensive, pink undies of silk. According to Prime Minister Asquith's daughter Violet, Clementine "confided to her that 'Winston was most extravagant in his underclothes'" and that "these were made of very finely woven silk (pale pink) and came from the Army and Navy Stores and cost the eyes out of the head.'"

According to daughter Mary, when Clementine raised the issue, Winston "protested that he had a most delicate skin (which was true) which necessitated such luxurious lingerie." In fact, Mary recalled "that he always wore very fine silk underclothes."

King's Cane Lost

As a long-lingering aftermath of Clementine and Winston's wedding, there was the tale of the king's cane that Winston treasured for years. A handsome malacca stick and a wedding gift from Edward VII, it boasted a gold knob at the top engraved "W.S.C. Turf Club."

Winston loved the cane and took it with him whenever he traveled, recalled newspaperman Jack Fishman in *My Darling Clementine*. Thus Winston was greatly upset one day between the world wars when he noticed the cane he was carrying, "identical in every respect except for the inscription," was *not* his.

"He realized at once what had happened. He had picked up the wrong stick when leaving some function or other. But when? And where? It could have been at any of a hundred places on any of as many days."

As often was the case, Clementine immediately and efficiently rallied to Winston's need by quickly organizing a search. "She went methodically through Winston's engagement book, making inquiries at every house, club, and business office that he had visited." When that effort failed to produce results, "Winston, who hated even to lose worn-out clothes, was in deepest misery."

Then came Clementine's stroke of genius. She inserted an advertisement in the personal classifieds of the London *Times*: "LOST, probably on Friday, March 28, a gold-headed malacca cane, marked 'W. S, C., Turf Club.' Mr. Churchill has taken by mistake an almost identical cane, but since this has neither the name nor the address upon it he is unable to return it—2 Sussex Square, W.2."

The result was a telephone call that came in just before noon of the day on which the ad ran. It was a message from the Marlborough Club (ironically). "It reported that the stick was 'safe and well' and in good hands, but—in Germany!"

Germany? How could that be? Simple enough. Winston had been entertained at a luncheon at the club and, leaving hurriedly for another appointment, "he had picked up the stick which so markedly resembled his own, while its owner, coming . . . later, had taken the other and left immediately for Germany."

And so, the appropriate swap was arranged, and in short time Winston had his precious cane back again. "Now, thanks to his wife's detective work, Winston was happy again." But that wasn't quite the end of the story behind Winston's malacca cane.

The day came, some time later, when Winston and Clementine visited the Limbless Ex-Servicemen's Center for wounded war veterans at Wellhampton. "Winston, carrying his beloved cane, stopped to talk to an ex-soldier from Norfolk, who had lost a leg in the First World War and was having an artificial limb fitted."

Asked Winston, with apparent interest and sympathy: "You have a special limb and can walk without a stick?"

Quite true, said the veteran, "but I should like that stick of yours."

Perhaps taken aback, surely not by any plan, Winston turned first to Clementine, then to the old soldier. "Here are my hand, my heart—and my stick," he said. "Look after it. It has been all over the world with me."

Young Marrieds

As Winston and Clementine embarked on young married life, they shared a political focus on "Radical" social reform. On a more personal level, Clementine would be learning all about his late-night working schedule, and both, it turned out, would be working on his speech-making skills.

If politics was Winston's consuming interest in life, Clementine was "thrilled" with politics, wrote their daughter Mary. And now, as Winston's wife, she "flung herself with passion into Radical politics."

While Winston is best remembered today for his great speeches, his World War II leadership, his old anti-Bolshevik animus, his postwar "Iron Curtain" speech in Fulton, Missouri, and possibly his Conservative Party ties, the fact is that he *was* a leader at the time of his marriage in radical political initiatives helping to make Britain what many call a welfare state. And Clementine was all for it. Or, as Mary summarized, the "noble, puritan element in her nature responded naturally to the great reforming measures in which Winston, working closely with [David] Lloyd George, was deeply involved."

More specifically, in 1908, "Old Age pensions had been introduced . . . and Winston, who had taken up the cause of social reform with ardor and determination, was now pushing forward the schemes for Trade Boards, which would attack the exploitation of sweated labor, and of Labor Exchanges to combat the scourge of unemployment."

Proud as Clementine might be over her new connection with Winston's causes, she did pay a price. "Bitterness in politics had spread into social life, and there were certain Tory houses where Clementine was no longer welcome," daughter Mary wrote. "Some die-hard Tory acquaintances would even cross the road rather than meet her in the street now that she was Mrs. Winston Churchill." On the other hand, she, with Winston, had a coterie of brilliant new friends, associates, and acquaintances. Their circle ranged from "government colleagues, eminent Civil Servants, Radical politicians and writers and journalists drawn from the galaxy of talent surrounding the Government in these years before the Great War [World War I]. And Winston maintained his links across the 'barricades' with such Tories as F. E. Smith, Lord Hugh Cecil [best man at their wedding] and [former Prime Minister] A. J. Balfour, whose friendship never faltered."

Meanwhile, Clementine was adapting to domestic life with a superenergetic husband "who enjoyed staying up half the night working or talking," noted Jack Fishman in *My Darling Clementine*. Fishman added: "Careless in personal matters, brooding, sleeping by day, working throughout the night, uplifted by success, desolate in failure, Winston was, to put it mildly, a handful for any girl, but she handled him gently, tactfully. She nourished him with calmness, constancy, and content. She could humor him magically, make him laugh when he wanted to cry."

She soon learned that her husband, so well known today as a great orator, had to struggle to make speeches. "An impediment of speech, which would have deterred lesser men even from attempting to enter public life, made his words unintelligible in moments of stress," Fishman asserted. Thus, Winston "would frequently return home to his wife physically weak from the simple strain and effort of public speaking." He added, "He was exhausted by a tongue that refused to give the standard of eloquence he desired to the torrent of thoughts flooding from his brilliant mind."

According to Fishman, this "vocal handicap with its intrusive sibilance was daunting to himself and an embarrassment to his audience." Hard to believe today, the early Winston Churchill "was often reduced to an agonizing stammer, and at times there was a fierce, silent struggle to voice the first syllable of a word."

Never mind, though. Winston now had a close and sympathetic ally—his wife. "When he rehearsed his speeches with Clementine, she noticed his vocal difficulties were most apparent during his opening sentences. The painful effort of mastering his utterance would make his normally pale cheeks flush angrily." As soon as he established a rapport with his audience, however, "his speech became almost clear and the fiery patches in his cheeks disappeared."

It took a sympathetic and loving Clementine to recognize that "the accent of brutality in his speech was the mark, not of a truculent nature, but of a highly strung temperament fighting its own sensibilities for the mastery of its own mind." Thus, she realized Winston was "fighting himself more often than his enemies."

Determined to help, Clementine became both his coach and his most ardent fan. As she listened and made suggestions in the privacy of their home, and always with understanding, "the emotion and eloquence that were locked within his heart began to flow," wrote Fishman. "She would share his mood as, with tears running down his cheeks, he would declaim from a newly written speech some passage dwelling on an incident of pathos or disaster. She would laugh appreciatively at his touches of wit or nod in endorsement of his carefully prepared debating point."

Or she might be sitting in the House gallery. "Often he would look to Clementine . . . for silent, smiling encouragement, as he fought to make his points with clarity. He took heart from her, in his determination to overcome his dreadful handicap, as she helplessly watched one or two sadistically cruel young Members mercilessly mocking his affliction on the very floor of the House."

But Winston of course had his own definite ideas. For one, "short words are best, and old words the best of all." Insisting on well-turned and balanced sentences, he despised "officialese" such as "lower-income group" for the poor, or "accommodation units" for homes.

At the same time, he paid attention to Clementine's well-meant critiques as he rehearsed. "If she told him, 'I would not say that, Winston,' he would remove the offending phrase or passage, recognizing the wisdom of her caution.'" And she did "tell him frankly that many of his early speeches were too impetuous, overelaborate, and frequently harsh and strident."

Fishman observed: "Gradually, he curbed and softened faults and interjected the understanding tolerance, which was to make his outstanding speeches models of good temper as well as of elocution. He was no longer diffident about showing his emotions, about revealing that sympathy with suffering and misunderstanding that was part of his natural makeup. With her influence, his genius lightened and mellowed."

Another sign of their rapport was the short list of affectionate pet names they adopted for each other from the earliest days of their marriage. "Clementine was always the 'Cat' or 'Kat,'" wrote daughter Mary, "and her letters were invariably adorned with cats in various moods and poses. But although resembling more the drawings on a child's slate, they are full of character and meaning."

Winston, for his part, began as the "pug" then became the "amber Pug," but with more change yet to come. Mary noted: "And pugdogs rampant, joyful, fatigued or frivolous always accompanied his signature. In one letter Clementine wrote, 'I must have lessons in Kat-drawing as your pugs are so much better than my Kats.' Gradually the Pug motif was replaced by the Pig symbol, and many are the pigs, expressive of every varying mood, which adorn Winston's letters to her throughout their correspondence; but Clementine's cipher always remained a cat.

In due course their children, unborn or born, acquired 'pet' names, some of which stuck to them in the family for all time."

Accordingly, when Clementine announced she was expecting their first child, the future Diana almost immediately, long before she was born, became "Puppy Kitten."

Howled Down at Dundee

The year 1909 set the stage for yet another election for Winston—and the first of fifteen campaigns in which his bride Clementine would be taking part, sometimes as a very active campaigner herself. That summer Winston had warned Clementine "she would need all her strength and energy later in the year, and he was proved right," wrote daughter Mary in her biography of her mother.

The election itself wouldn't come until early 1910, but political feelings were running high, especially among the more militant suffragettes. At Bolton, a young woman was arrested for throwing a heavy piece of iron wrapped in a political message at Winston's car. This was the same year that a whip-wielding suffragette nearly pushed Winston into the path of a train at Bristol, but he wasn't always the target.

"Such incidents were the constant lot of all prominent members of the government, and were difficult to guard against because of the fanaticism of the women involved, who courted arrest, and were indifferent to personal pain or injury," wrote daughter Mary.

While Winston, no barn burner on the issue, "never publicly opposed the principle of giving women the right to vote," Clementine, for her part, strongly supported an organization called the Suffragists, "which sought by legal and constitutional means methods to press for the right for women to vote, but which was opposed to the militant, law-breaking activities of the Suffra*gettes.*"

Those activities were a bane to England's politicians for the decade leading up to World War I. Until then, Mary noted, "prominent politicians were subject not only to disturbances and interruptions at public meetings, but also to personal physical attacks of quite astonishing violence at the hands of the militant Suffragettes."

Meanwhile, Prime Minister Asquith's Liberal Party colleagues in the House of Commons had passed the controversial "People's Budget," which then was blocked by the Conservative-dominated House of Lords, "thus shattering the centuries-old tradition that control over the raising and spending of revenue was the exclusive prerogative of the Lower House." This action late in November precipitated a crisis in governance leading to the general election of early 1910—the first of two elections to be held that year, as events turned out.

In the first one, Winston came through handsomely at Dundee, but his Liberal Party lost 104 seats in Parliament, which meant Asquith must rely upon the lower chamber's minority Irish Nationalists and Labor members to push through any controversial programs. After this vote, too, Asquith appointed Winston as home secretary—"At thirty five he was the youngest holder of that office since Sir Robert Peel."

While Winston now faced a raft of unfamiliar issues in his new post, the parliamentary crisis continued throughout 1910. First, the hotly debated People's Budget finally passed through the House of Lords, but the Liberals then introduced their Parliament Bill, aimed at breaking the power of the Lords to veto House legislation. In the meantime, Edward VII, once a good friend to Winston's mother and father, had died. The national mourning that followed his death brought "only a brief respite to the parliamentary struggle." All the tumult led by year's end to a second general election, this one intended by Asquith to test the issue of reforming the House of Lords. Winston maintained his seat from Dundee, but on the national level there was no real change in the balance of power among the contending parties.

In the meantime, it cannot be said that Winston found his dour Scottish town to be an absolute joy as a constituency. For one thing, noted Douglas J. Hall in the Winter 1999 issue of the Churchill Centre's *Finest Hour*, it was situated more than 440 long miles from Parliament's home base in London—"in those days, only practically accessible by a rather joyless overnight sleeper train." Even worse, "Dundee was hardly a joyful place in which to arrive on a morning, dark . . . and grimy, with much unemployment, poverty and drunkenness."

At first this workingman's town had welcomed its aristocratic new MP with surprisingly open arms—perhaps, Hall wrote, feeling "honored to be represented by a Cabinet minister" and willing at the same time to overlook his "long absences." Theirs would be a happy marriage lasting throughout World War I and then some. By 1922, however, various strains had set in. Hall cited "Churchill's own controversial escapades compounded with much local bitterness and disillusionment." Then, as Winston prepared to campaign in defense of his seat that year, he was struck by appendicitis. He would be hospitalized . . . and Clementine campaigned in his stead.

Here, just weeks after giving birth to their fifth and last child, Mary, Clementine spoke at one turbulent meeting after another. "Although she was frequently shouted down, she was undaunted by the general uproar," wrote daughter Mary. Taken along with her mother, the newborn Mary was called Clementine's "unbaptized infant" by the local press." And when Clementine attended a meeting wearing a string of pearls, women at the meeting spat at her. Said an admiring friend (a bit chillingly, to be sure), "Clemmie's bearing was magnificent—like an aristocrat going to the guillotine in a tumbrel."

Clementine wrote to Winston that their campaign organization in Dundee was "in chaos." She warned that the upcoming Drill Hall Meeting, which he might arrive in time to address, "is pretty sure to be broken up." She added, "The misery here is appalling, [and] some of the people look absolutely starving." She also reported that the "idea" against Winston locally "seems to be that you are a War Monger." To offset that impression, she was "exhibiting" him as "a Cherub Peace Maker with little fluffy wings round your chubby face." Further, his "line" should not be "so much Smash the Socialists, as to try with your great abilities to help in finding a solution of the Capital & Labor problem."

Winston finally arrived in Dundee late in the campaign. Still weak from his operation, he often had to deliver his speeches while sitting instead of standing, and the meetings he attended at this stage of the campaign "were particularly violent and noisy," noted daughter Mary. He indeed was "howled down" at the Drill Hall affair, headlined the *Dundee Advertiser* after he was forced to cut short his appearance there. The paper described the scene as "pandemonium" and reported that "Police Draw Batons." The newspaper went on to report that a section of the audience gave such trouble from the beginning, "the candidate never really got his address started." When Winston tried to "placate the opposition" by taking questions, the questioners were interrupted.

To no one's surprise, Winston was not fated to prevail. He lost his Dundee seat, and nationally the Liberal Party took a drubbing as well. As he famously said in the aftermath, he was left "without an office, without a seat, without a party, and without an appendix." With both the Conservatives and the socialistic Labor Party now on the ascendancy, Winston next, in 1923, tried running for Parliament from West Leicester as a "Liberal Free Trader." When that effort failed, he tried again in 1924, this time as an "Independent anti-Socialist" from the Abby division of Westminster, again to no avail. This time, though, "many prominent Conservatives supported him," daughter Mary reported, and "the campaign aroused much excitement." In fact, he lost by only forty-three votes.

Then, Conservative Party leader Stanley Baldwin "publicly abandoned his party's pledge to introduce Protective Tariffs," and that "removed the last great obstacle to Churchill's reconciliation with the Conservative Party." Far more happily, Churchill ran again in the fall of 1924 in the general election after the fall of the Labor government then in power. His constituency choice this time was Epping (West Essex), and he won reelection to Parliament with ease. Mary noted: "He was to represent this constituency—later re-named the Wansted and Woodford Division for Essex—for forty years." Even better, the Conservatives returned to power, Baldwin became prime minister, and Winston was appointed to the high office of chancellor of the exchequer, a post he would hold for the next five years.

Additional note: In all, noted Douglas J. Hall in his article for *Finest Hour*, Churchill boasted a parliamentary career spanning a total of sixty-four years. He represented five constituencies (Oldham, Manchester, Dundee, Epping, and Woodford), served under thirteen prime ministers, sought election to Parliament twenty-one times, won sixteen times, and lost only five times. For that matter, starting with his military service under Queen Victoria, he also served six monarchs: Victoria, Edward VII, George V, Edward VIII (who abdicated in order to marry Wallis Simpson), George VI, and Elizabeth II.

Big Boy Now

As a cabinet minister, Winston now was a big boy politically, and as such he attracted—and engaged in—big-boy controversies. For one, there was his commitment to radical social reform, to remembering "the left-out millions." For another, there would be the long-stewing business of women's suffrage, and for still more issues there would be the famous People's Budget and Parliament Act, plus a town in Wales called Tonypandy and a street in London called Sidney.

Even before going to the Board of Trade (but after joining the Liberals in the House of Commons), he said his new party hoped to "promote the cause of temperance, [to] nationalize and extend our system of education, develop proper methods of technical instruction, to mitigate the sorrows of old age, in opening the land more freely to the millions, in adjusting more fairly the burden of taxation upon earned and unearned increment."

The years 1907 and 1908 had been depression years in England, with unemployment growing fast. But the Asquith government taking power in 1908, with Winston Churchill included as president of the Board of Trade, attacked the country's social problems with vigor, noted Randolph Churchill. "Asquith's own accession, and the zeal, dynamism and determination of Churchill and Lloyd George gave the impetus necessary to overcome any obstacles in the way of this new departure," he wrote. Randolph also cited a key speech by his father, given before the Birmingham Liberal Club on January 13, 1909, in which he said: "The social field lies open, there is no great country where the organization of industrial conditions more urgently demands attention. Where the reformer casts his eye he is confronted with a mass of largely preventable and even curable suffering . . . whilst our vanguard enjoys all the delights of all the ages, our rearguard struggles out into conditions which are crueler than barbarism."

While backing the entire sweep of social reform measures the Liberals supported, Winston also favored temperance legislation—ironic for a man know to enjoy his own measure or two—and in foreign policy he confidently—and ironically—"discounted any conflict as possible between Great Britain and Germany." Calling this last stance "wrong-headed," son Randolph dutifully quoted his father as saying that England's island position "freed us from the curses of Continental militarism." This, just six years before England was plunged into war with the same Germany, thanks to Continental militarism!

Meanwhile, taking his seat at the Board of Trade, Winston had no qualms about speaking in favor of a coal miners' relief bill that would limit the number of hours a miner must work underground to just eight a day. Soon, too, he was espousing unemployment insurance, paid in part by the state and by employers, along with other measures strengthening the rights of workers, such as labor exchanges, a minimum wage, even allowance for the famous English tea break. Publishing two books containing his recent speeches (*Liberalism and the Social Problem* and *The People's Rights*), he at one point advanced the now-well-known phrase "War on Poverty."

Mounting one of his sharpest attacks on the House of Lords the same day suffragette Theresa Garnett attacked him with a dog whip at the Bristol railroad station, he said the "proud" Conservative peers considered themselves "the only persons fit to serve the Crown." Martin Gilbert in *Churchill: A Life* noted Winston's comment that the peers regarded the government "as merely an adjunct to their wealth and titles." As expected, though, the Lords rejected the so-called People's Budget originated by the Asquith government and sent forward by the House. "Four days later," Gilbert observed, "Asquith prorogued Parliament and . . . [a] General Election campaign began. Its war cry for all Liberals, including the grandson of a Duke of Marlborough [Winston Churchill] was 'The Peers versus the People.'" And who should lead the Liberal "onslaught against the House of Lords" in the campaign that followed but Winston.

In the meantime, he had successfully arbitrated a major coal strike, he and Clementine had moved into new quarters at 33 Eccleston Square in London, their first child had been born, and Germany had begun a disquieting naval buildup.

In the election interrupting the power struggle with the Lords, the Liberals retained a bare majority of 275 seats in the House, to the Conservatives' 273, the Irish Nationalists' 84, and Labor's 42.

Winston, though, moved up the cabinet ladder with his appointment on February 15, 1910, as home secretary, a post placing him in charge of police, prisons, and prisoners. And now his reform focus would be the prisons and their inmates—he ordered innovations such as separating criminals from political prisoners like the militant suffragettes. He instituted prison libraries and some forms of recreation and entertainment for the prisoners and reduced the number of young offenders held in prison. "He would have a fine Army to command, the Police Force," Asquith's daughter Violet said later, "but he was mainly preoccupied with the fate of their quarry, the criminals. His own experience of captivity [by the Boers] had made him the Prisoner's Friend."

His parliamentary duties hadn't slackened, however, and Winston now became "the main Government speaker" in the campaign to curb the powers of the Lords, Gilbert noted. In April, rather than continue a constitutional crisis, the Lords passed the government budget, but that wasn't the end of the matter . . . still looming was the Parliament Bill, which would take away their veto power. "Not wanting to risk further interference by the Lords in financial measures, Asquith decided to go forward with the Parliament Bill, even if it meant asking the King to create up to five hundred new Liberal peers to ensure the Bill's passage," Gilbert wrote. "But on May 6, as controversy raged over the possibility of the creation of so many new peers, Edward VII died."

The transition to the inexperienced George V resulted in a temporary truce between the two sides, and that summer Winston took Clementine on a two-month cruise of the Mediterranean and Aegean seas aboard his friend Baron de Forest's yacht *Honor*. And who else but Winston would have risked life and limb on the same holiday to ride a train across Turkey . . . ride 260 miles up front, that is, in a seat attached to the cowcatcher. "No better way," he said, "of seeing a country in a flash."

Back home in England, though, more of the big-boy controversies lurked and awaited his return. The first of these to demand his attention was Tonypandy, a small Welsh village subjected to violence during a coal strike in the Rhondda Valley. Winston's response was to send police reinforcements, but to hold off on sending troops.

When the rioting appeared to be spiraling out of control, he permitted a cavalry unit to move close by in warning, but he still insisted the police should deal with the disorders . . . which the police did until the violence abated. As a result, though, Winston was damned, on the one hand, for appearing too lenient, and on the other, for calling in the military on striking coal miners, even though the last was not quite true. In the meantime, he had brought a government arbitrator into the picture to mediate the labor dispute. "The owners are very unreasonable as well as the men," he informed the king. In the end, wrote biographer Gilbert: "For Liberals, Tonypandy represented the success of moderation. For Labor it became part of a myth of Churchill's aggressiveness."

Meanwhile, a scuffle broke out on Downing Street, home of the prime minister, during a cabinet meeting pitting militant suffragettes and their male supporters against police and cabinet ministers. "Asquith had to be hustled into a taxi and another Minister was badly hurt," Gilbert wrote. The onlooking Churchill called out as the police struggled with one of the militants: "Take that woman away; she is obviously one of the ringleaders."

Unfortunately, Gilbert recounted, Winston was overheard by suffragette sympathizer Hugh Franklin before he himself was hauled away by the police. Four days later, Franklin repeatedly heckled Churchill at a speaking engagement at Bradford, then followed him onto the evening train back to London. As Winston made his way to the dining car, Franklin attacked him with a whip, shouting, "Take that, you dirty cur." The result for Franklin was six weeks' incarceration for assault. Ironically, despite such incidents, Winston at heart remained in favor of giving women the vote, and in 1917 he so voted in the House.

A second general election in twelve months was held late in 1910, resulting in no great change in political control, and now, in early 1911, the controversial Parliament Bill resurfaced. First, though, came the "Sidney Street Affair" in the East

End of London—like Tonypandy, it became a Churchill myth often exploited by his political enemies.

After a botched burglary, three suspects retreated to a house on Sidney Street after they shot and killed three policemen trying to arrest them. They were trapped in the house but continued to fire at the police, killing yet another police officer. Hearing about the situation, Home Secretary Churchill retroactively approved the dispatch of twenty military riflemen to the scene and hurried there himself. "It was a striking scene in a London Street," he later told Prime Minister Asquith by letter, "firing from every window, bullets clipping the brickwork, police and Scots Guards armed with loaded weapons, artillery brought up, etc." Soon the house caught fire, and after the blaze burned itself out, the police found two bodies inside. The third suspect, a Russian anarchist named Peter the Painter, was never found.

In the immediate aftermath, noted Gilbert, Winston was accused "of having taken charge of the siege, and of having given orders which ought to have been given by the police." Not so, argued the biographer . . . the closest the onlooking Churchill came to giving any orders was when a fire brigade officer approached him and said the firemen understood they were to stand by without attempting to fight the fire.

"Quite right," Churchill apparently said. "I accept full responsibility."

Added Gilbert's account: "From what he saw at that moment, Churchill later told the Coroner, 'it would have meant loss of life and limb to any fire brigade officer who had gone within effective range of the building.'" Despite this seemingly reasonable view, Gilbert noted, "Churchill's presence at the Siege of Sidney Street was rapidly to become part of the Conservative mockery of his actions."

In Winston's remaining months at the home secretary post, meanwhile, he dealt with significant dock and rail strikes, formed the nonpartisan political dinner group The Other Club, wondered at times how to deal with bouts of his "black dog" depression, and become much more concerned by the growing German aggressiveness on the Continent. The great constitutional crisis over the Parliament Bill came to a head in July 1911 . . . and quietly fizzled when the Lords, with no peer-packing by the king, agreed they could not veto money bills adopted by the House.

Not long after that, Winston ordered secret inspection of mail directed to anyone suspected of taking instruction from Germany, reported Gilbert. The letters, Winston explained, showed England to be "the subject of a minute and scientific study by the German naval and military authorities." That would be a matter of even greater interest to him after he was named first lord of the admiralty on October 24, 1911, at the age of thirty-six.

King George V

Edward VII may have had a short reign of just nine years, but his passing in 1910 was marked by a blowout of a funeral in London that brought together an amazing assemblage of European "royals," one of the greatest ever seen at any one time and place before or since. "This was the occasion of the celebrated Parade of Kings, when over 50 royal horsemen—a swaggering cavalcade of emperors, kings, crown princes, archdukes, grand dukes and princes—followed the trundling coffin through the streets of London," noted Theo Aronson for the BBC's history home page on the Web.

Despite such grand display of monarchial glory, Edward's son and successor, George V, would be notably quiet and sincere—a startling contrast to the turbulence of the world around him during his years as king. Running from 1910 to his death in 1936, his reign encompassed World War I, the Bolshevik revolution in Russia, the Irish Home Rule controversy, the vote given to women, America's Prohibition era and the stock market crash, followed by the Great Depression and Adolf Hitler's rise to power in Germany.

The second son of Edward VII and born in 1865, almost a decade before Winston Churchill, George probably would have made the Royal Navy his permanent career. The death of his older brother in 1892 forced him to stand by as royal heir-presumptive to royal heir-presumptive Edward, his father. Meanwhile, George married his brother's fiancée, Princess Mary of Teck.

He then succeeded to the royal helm at the time of the still-unresolved constitutional crisis stemming from the Liberal government's attempts to curb the power of the House of Lords. "After the Liberal government obtained the king's promise to create sufficient peers to overcome Conservative opposition in the Lords (and won a second election in 1910), the Parliament Bill was passed by the Lords in 1911 without a mass creation of peers," noted the BBC history Web site (www.bbc.co.uk/historic_figures/george_v_king.shtml).

George V reigned as king during a still-remarkably young Winston Churchill's steady ascent of high government posts, followed by the latter's fall from favor and first years in a political "wilderness." The relationship between the king and this ambitious politician began on a smooth note, with the king showing kindnesses both to Winston and to Clementine . . . but, as with Edward, there soon would be

a few bumps as well. The more noteworthy kindnesses began at George's coronation on June 22, 1911, in the form of special seating arrangements for Clementine,
who recently had become a mother for the second time with the birth of Randolph. Not only did George provide access to his own box at Westminster Abbey,
but, wrote Clementine's daughter Mary, "a royal brougham called for her at her
house and drove her to Westminster Abbey, so that she arrived at the latest possible
moment." This meant the nursing mother could watch the ceremony "until the actual crowning of the King before slipping discreetly away, to be driven home to the
hungering Randolph."

The next day, Clementine was able to join Winston, then still serving as home
secretary in the Asquith cabinet, in accompanying King George and Queen Mary
in the first of their "Coronation State Drives" through London. After Clementine
left London to spend a month at the seaside in Seaford, Winston was treated to
"another of the Coronation 'royal progresses'" with the royal couple. "The King,
Winston told Clementine, had been most friendly, and the Queen had asked solic-
itously after her and had 'urged the importance of a full rest before beginning gai-
eties.'" Winston added—as a measure of how well known he already was in
1911—he was cheered "all the whole route" but in places also "booed vigorously."

Ironically foreshadowing Winston's role in two world wars yet to come, the
coronation festivities in London were accompanied by news that Germany had
sent a gunboat to Agadir "as a challenge to French claims to Morocco," daughter
Mary recalled in her biography of her mother. Although the crisis only briefly
"galvanized Europe" and then passed, "to those who could read the omens aright,
this incident meant only one thing—that Germany was bent on trouble, and that
her expanding economic vitality and growing physical power made her a grave
threat to the peace of Europe."

Meanwhile, the new king soon criticized Winston's tendency to be outspoken. As home secretary, Winston followed the tradition of writing a routine
letter—a daily report of sorts—to the king on the debates in Parliament. He
raised the king's hackles one day, though, by commenting, "it must not be forgotten that there are idlers and wastrels at both ends of the social scale."

That observation, the king charged, was "very socialistic." The rebuke took
the form of a letter from the king's secretary, Lord Francis Knolly, to the prime
minister's private secretary. As a result, Winston apologized, saying he only wished
to make his parliamentary reports "interesting and reliable," but also acknowledging, "it is always possible that some sentiment or opinion may occur which has
not received the severe and deliberate scrutiny and reconsideration which should
attach to a State Paper." Further, Winston said, he had never been given guidance

on how to frame his letters to the king. For that matter, he only was following the pattern established with the late Edward VII.

The fact is, according to his son Randolph's biographical coverage of those years, for all his brashness, Winston "was much taken aback, mortified, indeed affronted at this rebuke." Apparently, the king and his staff were surprised to learn this, because Lord Knolly soon wrote a follow-up letter directly to Winston saying that the king "regrets that your feelings should have been hurt by anything which the Prime Minister may have said to you in consequence of HM having taken exception to two passages in your House of Commons letter." But Knolly added there was no concealing the fact "that the King would have preferred it, had you seen your way to suppress this remark [about 'idlers and wastrels']." Bitingly, Knolly added his own observation that the late King Edward "did not always appear pleased with certain occasional passages" in Winston's letters to him. As for having never been given guidance on what the king might expect: "I hope you will forgive my saying that you never asked for any, or else it would have of course have been most cheerfully given."

George V, on the other hand, was most grateful when Winston successfully prosecuted the author of a published statement claiming that the king had been secretly married in Malta while serving in the Royal Navy. That would have made his current marriage to Queen Mary a "sham," as the author had claimed.

Generally, in fact, the king and his home secretary exchanged cordial views. In late summer of 1911, after a period of widespread labor unrest, strikes, and a clash at Llanelli in South Wales between rioters and police, backed up by soldiers, the king sent Churchill a laudatory telegram acknowledging that Winston's "prompt measures" had "prevented loss of life in different parts of the country."

Brouhaha at Blenheim

Naturally, Winston's political alignment with David Lloyd George and the various social reforms they achieved in the years prior to World War I didn't always sit well with the blue-blood social and family circles that had been Winston's heritage and background. As a case in point: wife Clementine's highly visible break with

Winston's cousin Sunny, the sitting Duke of Marlborough, at Blenheim Palace in October 1913.

Already behind was the bitter, months-long battle over Lloyd George's 1909 budget known as the People's Budget for its social insurance terms, which would be financed in part by new property and income taxes. Its rejection by the House of Lords was the impetus for the 1911 Parliament Act that resulted in the upper chamber losing its veto power.

Winston's daughter Mary wrote in *Clementine Churchill*, "It is hardly surprising that the controversies surrounding the People's Budget and the Parliament Bill should have caused tension between the ducal and radical branches of the family." Not only had Lloyd George "pilloried the dukes" in a famous 1909 speech, but "Winston too had had fiery things to say about peers and primogeniture which did not pass unnoticed and must have been extremely irritating to Sunny Marlborough, despite his tolerant and hospitable ways." By 1913, Winston's partnership with Lloyd George in such affairs still was difficult for some family members to swallow . . . and now came "an incident between Clementine and Sunny Marlborough which resulted in a distinct chill between the cousins for nearly two years."

Normally repressed feelings burst forth the day after Lloyd George had made another landmark speech, this time at Swindon on October 22, presenting "the Government's proposals for Land Reform, which, as can be imagined, held no joy for the land-owning classes who, in addition, were roundly castigated and held up to ridicule in the more inflammatory passages of the . . . oration." Clementine was visiting Blenheim at the time with her sister Nellie and sister-in-law Goonie, Jack's wife, among others. On this particular morning, sisters Clemmie and Nellie were reading newspaper reports of the speech in the great library of the palace "not only with interest, but with loud expressions of admiration and approval." This, Mary commented, "cannot have failed to have caused displeasure to the Duke, already ruffled by his own perusal of the morning's papers."

Clementine wrote a note to Winston saying the speech by Lloyd George was "I think . . . the greatest speech I have ever read."

The real trouble arose at lunchtime, but not before the duke had lit a fuse or two at mealtimes by "teasingly referring to Mr. Asquith's drinking habits, which were the subject of comment at the time." Asquith still was the prime minister, Lloyd George his chancellor of the exchequer, and Winston the first lord of the admiralty. The teasing had offended Clementine's sense of loyalty to Winston's chief, daughter Mary noted, "and she begged Sunny to refrain from these unseemly jokes (particularly while the servants were in the room); whereupon he repeated them in a clearer tone."

Thus, the atmosphere already was tense when, during lunch, Clementine was handed a telegram from none other than Lloyd George himself. It was about "some arrangements in which Winston and she were involved." Clementine rose from the table, saying she must reply at once, "and proceeded to write a reply at one of the writing tables which were in the Green Room where the family lunched when they were few in numbers."

For the duke, that apparently was a last straw. "Please, Clemmie," he said—with some sharpness, it can be imagined—"would you mind not writing to that horrible little man on Blenheim writing paper."

For Clementine, that was a last straw. She immediately marched upstairs to her bedroom, rang for the maid, and told her to pack her things—she was leaving Blenheim, the place where Winston had been born and where he had proposed to her. Minutes later Jack's wife Goonie appeared. "You're not really going?" she wanted to know. And when Clementine said yes, Goonie "loyally said she would go too," but Winston's wife dissuaded her.

"When the packing was done," added Mary, "Clementine descended to the front hall, where she was met by Sunny Marlborough, who begged her not to leave, and apologized for upsetting her. But Clementine, once aroused, was not easily calmed, and despite this proffered twig of olive, left the house and took a train from Woodstock to London."

Winston, busy elsewhere with his duties as civilian chief of the Royal Navy, of course had missed the upsetting episode, and when he heard of it, he "thought the whole affair a storm in a teacup." When he, in fact, only "half-heartedly" took her part, that "caused her deep mortification, for she felt she had nobly defended his colleagues against Tory malice." Left "very much" upset at the time, Clementine finally, years later, "said she thought she had been wrong not to have accepted Sunny Marlborough's apology."

Additional note: In the meantime, possibly the distressing Blenheim incident "or perhaps some other passing cause of friction," prompted this exchange between Clementine and Winston in letters written less than two weeks later.

First, Clementine to Winston on November 2, 1913: "My sweet and Dear Pig, when I am a withered old woman how miserable I shall be if I have disturbed your life & troubled your spirit by my temper. Do not cease to love me. I could not do without it. If no one loves me, instead of being a Cat with teeth & Claws, but you will admit soft fur, I shall become like the prickly porcupine outside, & inside so raw & unhappy."

His remarkable reply: "I loved much to read the words of your dear letter. You know so much about me, & with your intuition have measured the good & bad in my nature. Alas I have no good opinion of myself. At times, I think I cd conquer everything—& then again I know I am only a weak vain fool. But your love for me is the greatest glory & recognition that has or will ever befall me: the attachment wh I feel towards you is not capable of being altered by the sort of things that happen in this world. I only wish I were more worthy of you, & more able to meet the inner needs of your soul."

To which a happier Clementine answered: "Thank you my darling for your dear letter. I feel so good now, as if I could never be naughty again!"

Up in the Air

"As an instructor," Group Capt. Ivon Courtney once told Winston's son Randolph, "one was *over*-careful with WSC. We were all scared stiff of having a smashed First Lord on our hands." So scared that even after Winston had accumulated twenty-five hours in the air, no one among all his Royal Navy instructors dared let him solo. "If anything happened to WSC the career of the man who had allowed him a solo flight would be finished," commented future Air Commo. Eugene Gerrard.

Winston also took lessons from Royal Marine Capt. Gilbert Wildman-Lushington . . . only Lushington crashed and was killed one day in December 1913. But still, despite entreaties of family and friends, Winston kept on flying . . . for a while.

He at this point was first lord, or civilian head of the admiralty and Royal Navy, but his interest in aviation had begun much earlier, when it still was in its infancy on both sides of the Atlantic. As early as 1909, "when he was still president of the Board of Trade," his son Randolph noted, "he had been appointed a member of the Committee of Imperial Defense, and intervened in one of its earliest discussions on aviation." At a subcommittee meeting on February 23, he had proposed getting in touch with Orville Wright, one of the two American brothers who had flown a powered airplane (at Kitty Hawk, North Carolina) for the first time in history just six years before.

Then, as newly appointed head of the admiralty, wrote Randolph, "One of . . . [his] most enterprising and successful roles was as founder of the Royal Naval Air Service." To do this, however, he had to fight for funding and overcome the resistance of the army (War Office) and its Royal Flying Corps. As Winston himself wrote in his history of World War I (*The World Crisis*), the War Office had its own funding problems. "Seeing this and finding myself able to procure funds by various shifts and devices, I began in 1912 and 1913 to form under the Royal Naval Air Service flights of airplanes as well as of seaplanes for the aerial protection of our naval harbors, oil tanks and vulnerable points, and also for a general strengthening of our exiguous and inadequate aviation."

While many generals and admirals failed to appreciate the full potential of the airplane as a weapon of war, Winston did. Randolph recounted that when one of his instructor crew shot "some wild duck for him from a plane [that is, in midair] and the officers were treating it as a great lark, he surprised them by making a short speech on aerial war in the future, including the arming of planes with weapons—until then [1913] they had been regarded as suited only for reconnaissance."

All well and good, but the troubling aspect of Winston's early fascination with airplanes, so far as friends and family were concerned, was the fact that he was taking to the air at every opportunity. They were upset when Winston's instructor Lushington was killed on December 2, 1913, and upset all over again when pioneer aviator Gustav Hamel disappeared while flying across the English Channel in May 1914 to give an aerial demonstration in England . . . at Winston's invitation.

Quickly reacting to the Lushington accident, Winston's friend F. E. Smith sent him a note just four days later, asking, "Why do you do such a foolish thing as fly repeatedly?" The same note warned that Winston's insistence on flying was "unfair" to family, career, and friends. His cousin Sunny Marlborough also protested . . . and then there was Clementine's growing concern.

For Clementine, pregnant in 1914, this time with daughter Sarah, "There had been for many months a constant fear which gnawed away at her," wrote daughter Mary. "Winston had taken up flying." With aircraft in only a "rudimentary state of development," noted Mary, "these early machines took their toll of the daring men who experimented with them." Thus Winston's many flights in 1912 and 1913 were a cause of "deep anxiety" for Clementine. And it didn't help when he tried to share the thrill by writing as he did on October 23, 1913: "Darling: We have had a vy jolly day in the air. . . . It has been as good as one of those old days in the S. African war, & I have lived entirely in the moment, with no care for all those tiresome party politics & searching newspapers, and awkward by-elections."

Instead of sharing in the excitement, Clementine, "much alarmed," sent him "an imploring telegram," followed by a letter, saying, "please be kind & don't fly any more just now." But he did . . . again and again.

Mary recounted: "Winston was aware of the immense urgency for Great Britain to develop this new science, with all its far-reaching implication for both war and peace. And not only did flying grip him, but also he came to know and admire many of the men who were developing and testing these new machines, and he loved to share some of the risks taken by them; and he always found in physical danger a release from mental care. That winter, Winston, no longer content to be merely a passenger, started receiving instruction in the art of flying."

That naturally just made Clementine all the more fearful for him. He tried to mollify her a bit in a lighthearted letter on November 29, 1913: "I have been naughty today about flying. Down here with twenty machines in the air at once and thousands of flights made without mishap, it is not possible to look upon it as a vy serious risk. Do not be vexed with me."

Just days later, noted Mary, Wildman-Lushington was killed . . . the same instructor "with whom Winston had spent such a happy day on 29th November."

As Winston kept on with his lessons and his many sojourns in the air over the next few months, the same tug-of-war—reassurances in response to pleadings—kept on between husband and wife. In the meantime, there were a couple of minor mishaps. Engine failure in a seaplane one day forced Winston's pilot to make a sudden descent uncomfortably close to a jetty. Another time, while landing under instruction, "he bent an undercarriage," Ivon Courtney informed Randolph years later. Rather than discourage Winston, the "shock" made him more eager, "so up we went again."

Finally, a distraught Clementine's "dream" letter prevailed upon Winston to reconsider. With their children Diana and Randolph (five and three in age), she was staying with her mother, Lady Blanche, in Dieppe, where Clementine had spent part of her childhood years. After a quick one-day visit by Winston—dropped off and then picked up again by the admiralty yacht *Enchantress*—she wrote a letter, saying, "I cannot help knowing that you are going to fly as you go to Sheerness & it fills me with anxiety." But then, the next day, came the dream letter. Clementine related that she had dreamed about having her baby, but the doctors and nurses wouldn't let her see it. She ran all over the house looking for the baby. "At last I found it in a darkened room. It looked all right & I feverishly undressed it & counted its fingers and toes. It seemed quite normal & I ran out of the room with it in my arms. And then in the Daylight I saw it was a gaping idiot. And then the worst thing of all happened—I wanted the Doctor to kill it—but he was shocked & took it away & I was mad too. And then I woke up & went to sleep again and dreamt it a second time. I feel very nervous and unhappy & the little thing [the unborn baby] has been fluttering all the morning."

On top of all that, she had "a fright" receiving a telegram from Winston the night before, "after we were in bed," because every time she now saw a telegram, "I think it is to announce that you have been killed flying." She then found ("to my horror") the next morning that instead of being from harmless Dover, his first intended stop, the telegram came from the flying base known as Sheerness. "So," she wrote at the end of the dream letter, "you are probably at it again at this very moment."

Possibly he was, but his reaction to her entreaties and fears this time "was instantaneous," daughter Mary recounted. He stopped flying "at once." And he wrote to her:

> This is a wrench, because I was on the verge of taking my pilot's certificate. It only needed a couple of calm mornings; & I am confident of my ability to achieve it vy respectably. I shd greatly have liked to reach this point wh wd have made a suitable moment for breaking off. But I must admit that the numerous fatalities of this year wd justify you in complaining if I continued to share the risks—as I am proud to do—of these good fellows. So I give it up decidedly for many months & perhaps for ever. This is a gift—so stupidly am I made—wh costs me more than anything wh cd be bought with money. So I am vy glad to lay it at your feet, because I know it will rejoice & relieve your heart.

End of story? Not quite, because in 1919, after World War I had come and gone, Winston again took up flying lessons. This time, it was only a brief flirtation, thanks to an incident in which he barely escaped with his life. It happened in July, just a month or so after he had been forced to make an emergency landing at Buc aerodrome outside Paris. Now, on July 18, Winston was taking off from Croydon airfield in a dual-control plane with war ace Col. Jack Scott as his instructor. Seventy to eighty feet above the ground, the plane lost speed and then dropped, out of control. It hit the ground hard. Scott was severely injured but recovered, and Winston, saved by his seat belt, "was badly shaken, his forehead scratched, and his legs covered with bruises." Even so, "two hours after this misadventure he presided at a dinner in honor of [U.S. Gen. John J.] Pershing, and made a speech."

Happily for Clementine, their family, and friends, "despite his debonair demeanor," the accident shook Winston to the core, and he gave up "any further attempts to qualify as a pilot," Mary wrote.

Additional note: On that day, November 29, 1913, that Winston had such a "naughty" outing with his instructor Lushington, the young captain from the Royal Marines himself had found their time together memorable. Writing his fiancée, Airlie Hynes, the next morning, he said, "Yesterday turned out to be quite a strenuous day." He and Winston began their instruction session about 12:15 p.m., "& he got so bitten with it, I could hardly get him out of the machine, in fact except for about 3/4 hour for lunch we were in the machine till about 3.30." Lushington added: "He showed great promise, & is coming down again for further instruction & practice."

That night, the eve of Winston's thirty-ninth birthday on November 30, Lushington was a dinner guest aboard the *Enchantress* "and sat on the right of WC." Earlier in the day, "We sent a machine . . . for oysters for lunch, but they didn't arrive till too late, so I took them on board as a birthday present from the [officers'] mess for WC." In sum, "I've never had such a day in my life."

Meanwhile, Winston wrote Lushington a quick note on some technical questions about handling the controls, and on December 2, prior to his crash, Lushington replied. With the young man then killed, Winston sent the captain's fiancée a letter of condolence: "To be killed instantly without pain or fear in the necessary service of the country when one is quite happy and life is full of success & hope, cannot be reckoned the worst of fortune. But to some who are left behind the loss is terrible."

She responded to say her fiancée had been "so pleased at having given you your first instruction and his last letters were all about it and he was so happy." His was a "splendid end," and she was "only proud to think that I always encouraged him to fly."

As events turned out for these proud and patriotic people, Randolph Churchill reported, Airlie Hynes married a British army major in 1918, and two of their sons were killed in World War II. Meanwhile, Lushington's younger brother Godfrey, also a Royal Marine, fought as a Naval Air Service pilot in World War I, then served on Lord Mountbatten's staff during World War II, and wound up taking over his wartime chief's post as chief of combined operations in 1947.

Taking Over the Fleet

When Winston Churchill became first lord of the admiralty, or civilian chief of the Royal Navy, just before World War I, the admirals and sailors of England's great fleet didn't quite know what hit them. "He was an enthusiast," noted Keith Robbins in his *Churchill*. "He wanted to know everything about his new responsibilities and to know it immediately. He prodded and probed every aspect of the navy with a cheerful indifference to *amour-propre*."

In his triple biography *The Mountbattens*, Alden Hatch observed: "In their sober afterthoughts most naval officers admitted that much of Churchill's 'meddling' was good for the Navy, but they found it damned annoying at the time. His self-confidence and original thinking negated their cherished theories, short circuited their sacred channels, and upset their dignity."

In *Churchill and War*, Geoffrey Best noted: "Curt speech, short tempers and professional pride, even arrogance were part of their mystique. . . . The Admiralty was not going to be sorted out by soft soap and sweet reason. Churchill was put there to be tough and to be, so far as was necessary, unpleasant."

As home secretary immediately before becoming head of the Royal Navy, Winston had already had a taste of naval affairs that could stand a change or two. In the summer of 1911, when tensions with Germany were building, he discovered the navy's reserves of cordite at three magazines in London were unguarded. As it turned out, the Home Office was responsible for their security, noted Hatch in his Mountbatten book. "He tried to get the Admiralty to send Marines. They refused. He then asked Army Secretary Lord [R. B.] Haldane [secretary of state for war] for a company of troops to supplement his own police reserves. They were promptly sent." Score one for the army . . . but even so, it was the navy he soon came to know and bring along to his way of thinking.

The night of the day he was offered the admiralty post by Prime Minister Asquith—in Scotland—Churchill saw the stately silhouettes of two British battleships through his bedroom window as they cruised slowly down the nearby Firth of Forth. "From that moment Churchill in his powerful imagination became part of and dedicated to the British Navy," wrote Hatch. "And remained so all his life."

Until now, ironically, all his military interests and experience had been with the army. "He had begun adult life as a soldier and always prided himself on being one," wrote Best in *Churchill and War*. "By the time he was in his thirties he had come across many generals—indeed he had made sure that many generals came across him." Until recent times he more or less had taken it for granted that the Royal Navy was there, for all his lifetime it always had been there and no doubt always would be there, as the most powerful navy in the world—"apparently guaranteeing protection of the home island against invasion and its imperial properties against predators."

Even with his Sandhurst and 4th Hussars-21st Lancers background, all strictly army, he had from his early politician years (as a Conservative Party member from Oldham) "made no attempt to conceal his low opinion of the War Office," wrote Best. Churchill once complained in the House of Commons that "it is necessary to stand over the War Office with a stick to get anything done." And now, with his new portfolio announced on October 24, 1911, he would be taking his stick to the sometimes-moribund Royal Navy.

Moving into his admiralty office on October 25, 1911, Churchill soon made sure the cordite magazines received a naval guard. He also issued orders, wrote Hatch, "that naval officers, instead of just a sleepy guard, must remain on duty at the Admiralty all night and holidays so that never a moment should be lost in giving an alarm, and that one of the Sea Lords [the highest-ranking admirals] must always be on duty in or near the Admiralty to receive it. He then set about reorganizing the whole place."

Among his key changes, he brought in Prince (and Adm.) Louis of Battenberg from the home fleet as his second sea lord, in charge of personnel . . . but only temporarily, since Churchill in a year's time would be moving Battenberg up a rung to first sea lord.

At a time of growing anti-German feelings in England, this was a shock to some onlookers both in and out of the navy because of Battenberg's well-known heritage of German royalty . . . a burden he felt so keenly after the war with Germany had begun in 1914, he changed his name to Mountbatten. Back in 1911, however, rather than war, Battenberg's consuming focus had to be his civilian chief, Winston Churchill, the "energetic fireball . . . [who] had set out to make himself the world's greatest expert on naval affairs."

For some notion of the scope of Churchill's activities, one need only look at his words: "The Admiralty yacht, *Enchantress* [crewed by 196 officers and sailors], was now to become largely my office, almost my home, my work, my sole occupation and amusement. In all I spent eight months afloat in the three years before the war. I visited every dockyard in the British Isles and in the Mediterranean, and every important ship. . . . I got to know what everything looked like and where everything was, and how one thing fitted into another."

Mountbatten biographer Hatch wrote: "Wherever he went Churchill invited officers of all ranks aboard *Enchantress* and shot searching questions at them. He learned a great deal, but he upset many officers of flag rank, who thought lieutenants should be seen and not heard. There had never been a First Lord like this, they said, quite truly."

Indeed, typical of the newcomer's minute interests, noted biographer Sir Martin Gilbert in *Churchill: A Life*, within two weeks of his appointment Winston sent Asquith a note: "I have come across one disconcerting fact: there is a shortage of 120 21-inch torpedoes, meaning that thirty of our best destroyers would have to go to sea without reserves of any kind other than the two they carry." The note was written on Churchill's first day aboard the *Enchantress*.

Meanwhile, the British had been quite alarmed in the summer of 1911 by the sharp German response to a French expedition to Fez in Morocco. Perceiving this as a possible prelude to annexation of Morocco, Germany reacted by sending a gunboat to the nearby port of Agadir on the west coast of North Africa, supposedly to protect German nationals in the unsettled region. *Supposedly* . . . but perhaps really to establish a naval base on the west coast that could interrupt Britain's mercantile lanes to South Africa and South America? This was a real fear in government and other well-informed circles. Indeed, as Best summed up the tense situation, "For many weeks, war felt close."

The additional fact is that the European Continent at the time had become an armed camp, with Germany not only possessing a large army but also engaged in building a seagoing navy for the first time in history. And . . . to what purpose, the British of course had to wonder. Whatever Germany might be up to, Churchill was determined the Royal Navy would be ready for any contingency. Meanwhile, on his first cruise aboard the *Enchantress*, ironically, he set sail from Cowes, the spot where his mother and father had first met.

After inspecting naval facilities at Portsmouth, Winston set forth a few days later to join the escort for George V as he set out for India as the first British monarch to visit the subcontinent. After that, Winston launched a new battleship, the *Centurion*. And so on . . . typically, he hardly paused up to the day World War I erupted three years after the Agadir crisis. By then the Royal Navy was prepared for any possible action, not only because of the precautionary dispersal he and Battenberg ordered on the eve of war, but also because Winston as first lord had approved the installation of 15-inch guns on battleships and switched from coal to oil as fuel for His Majesty's ships at sea.

Countdown to War

On July 24, 1914, the first lord of the British admiralty wrote dire words to his wife: "Europe is trembling on the verge of a general war. The Austrian ultimatum to Serbia being the most insolent document of its kind ever devised."

That was Friday. Saturday, no general war yet. For a few hours that weekend, Winston managed to join the family—then consisting of Clementine, Diana, and Randolph—at the seaside, at their Pear Tree Cottage at Cromer on the Norfolk coast.

That Sunday morning, he recalled, "We damned little rivulets which trickled down to the sea as the tide went out. It was a very beautiful day. The North Sea sparkled to a far horizon."

He kept in touch with the office by borrowing a neighbor's telephone.

At midday, he hustled back to London, where his chief admiral, Prince Louis of Battenberg, issued orders halting any dispersal of Britain's first and second fleets in the wake of a recent test mobilization and review by the king at Spithead. It was the obvious order to send.

Background note: all three of the Royal Navy's battle fleets had taken part in the test mobilization rather than stage the usual grand maneuvers . . . canceled this year as an economy measure. Thus, on the same July 24 that Europe was "trembling on the verge of a general war," the first and second fleets were still gathered at Portland, whereas ships of the reservist-manned third fleet already had dispersed to their homeports. The first and second fleets would have done the same as of Monday, July 27 . . . but not now.

On Sunday, July 26, splitting time between family and the tensions preoccupying all of Europe, Winston and Battenberg made the decision to keep the two fleets in place for the moment.

Monday, still no war . . . Clementine and Winston kept in touch by telephone. She borrowed the neighbor's phone because the Pear Tree Cottage didn't have one.

The news, as the hours ticked by, only grew worse and worse. It all sounded so grim. In one of her many notes to Winston that week, she wrote, "It would be a wicked war."

By Tuesday, July 28, wrote Geoffrey Best in *Churchill: A Study in Greatness,* "it seemed desirable to move the First Fleet to its war stations at Scapa Flow, the

Firth of Cromarty and (for the battle-cruisers) Rosyth, and to do it stealthily lest [German Grand Adm. Alfred von] Tirpitz launch the preemptive torpedo attack which had become one of the Admiralty's nightmares."

The fleet's movement through the night of July 29, added Best, prompted Winston's own wonderful description in his *The World Crisis* of "scores of gigantic castles of steel wending their way across the misty, shining sea, like giants bowed in anxious thought."

And to this, Winston had added, "We may picture them again as darkness fell, eighteen miles of warships running at high speed and in absolute darkness through the narrow Straits, bearing with them into the broad waters of the North the safeguard of considerable affairs."

That same Wednesday night, July 29, Winston wrote Clementine from the admiralty, "Everything tends towards catastrophe & collapse." But at St. James Park lake, the two black swans she knew so well had had a baby swan, a cygnet— "grey, fluffy, precious and unique," he reported.

Two days later, July 31, he could report somewhat contradictorily: "There is still hope, although the clouds are blacker and blacker."

This coming weekend he wouldn't be back at the Pear Tree Cottage. Instead, on Sunday August 2, the cabinet sat and agonized for hours. At 1:00 a.m. that same day, he wrote to her: "It is all up. Germany has quenched the last hopes of peace by declaring war on Russia."

The next day, August 3, Germany declared war on France. German troops rolled toward Belgium after issuing an ultimatum demanding the right to cross through . . . on their way, obviously, to France. By afternoon, they were actually in Belgium. Great Britain, bound by treaty to Belgium and by sentiment to France, issued its own ultimatum demanding a halt to these activities.

The next night, at eleven o'clock in England, the deadline for Britain's cease-and-desist ultimatum came and went, with no halt in Germany's aggression. Not even an acknowledgment. And so, First Lord Winston's order, telegraphed to all of the Royal Navy's ships at sea, to British naval bases around the world: "Commence hostilities against Germany."

Winston and Clementine, all of Great Britain, its peoples and dominions, were now at war. The Great War. World War I.

Additional note: With the British Grand Fleet held in fighting readiness at its Scapa Flow anchorage above Scotland, the German Grand Fleet would be blocked from the Atlantic until the battle of Jutland two years later (a loss for the Germans).

War Under Way

Winston Churchill, first lord of the admiralty, was excited, even eager to get on with it. Certainly so. But . . . happy? Was that really what David Lloyd George, his old partner in radical reform legislation and now chancellor of the exchequer, meant? Not fifteen minutes after the war officially started, Winston burst into Prime Minister Asquith's residence at No. 10 Downing Street: "He was radiant, his face bright, his manner keen, one word after another pouring out on how he was going to send telegrams to the Mediterranean, the North Sea and God knows where," Lloyd George told a friend later. Could he have been merely excited? Or did Lloyd George have it right when he added, "You could see he was a really happy man"?

The fact is that Winston justifiably could take pride in his role as his country committed itself to war. "Churchill was proud to have made sure that, when war with Germany began, Britain's first line of defense [the Royal Navy] was in good order," wrote Geoffrey Best in *Churchill.* "He was also able to make sure that it was ready for action more promptly than might have been expected."

The truly surprising fact for many of us today is to learn that within days of the war's start, Winston Churchill, the British cabinet minister in charge of the navy, was in Belgium doing his best to line up enough ground forces to stem or at least to hinder the onrushing German army . . . described by American war correspondent Richard Harding Davis in a dispatch from Brussels as "not men marching, but a force of nature like a tidal wave, an avalanche or a river flooding its banks."

Operating on many fronts, the ubiquitous, energetic Winston in the last days of peace not only had sealed off the Dover Strait from German invasion, he essentially had safeguarded the English Channel for the crossing of the British Expeditionary Force. On August 8, Martin Gilbert reported, the first ships had sailed; within two weeks, 120,000 men had been carried across the Channel "without the loss of a single ship or life." Among other activities in the days immediately after hostilities commenced, the first lord of the admiralty ordered a naval blockade of Germany's North Sea ports, took on the responsibility for the aerial defense of Britain, established an all-volunteer Royal Naval Division, sent submarines and troop transports to help the Russians in their sector of the war against the Central Powers, became the first cabinet member to cross over the Channel to embattled France, sent three squadrons of his Royal Naval Air Service to Dunkirk (each one commanded by his former flying instructors), and last but far from least, almost invented the tank, the great tactical innovation of the ground war.

Most spectacularly, however, in early October he motored up to the key Belgian port city of Antwerp in a singled-handed effort to stiffen its resistance . . . and then offered to resign his naval post in order to stay on in Antwerp in charge of a hastily thrown-together command of defenders, if given a sufficiently high rank. The British thinking was that Antwerp must hold out for a few extra days, or, noted biographer Martin Gilbert, "the Germans would win the race to the sea, and that Dunkirk and even Calais might be overrun, endangering Britain itself."

Once on the scene in person, Winston offered the Belgians a brigade of Royal Marines already at Dunkirk and two brigades of the new, hardly trained division of Royal Naval volunteers ("Churchill's Pets"). There was talk also of the French throwing in a force, as well as a British division of forty thousand men already on their way.

The idea, Prime Minister Asquith wrote to his young love, Venetia Stanley (a cousin of Clementine's), the morning of October 3 was that the "intrepid" Winston, not quite yet forty years old, "will go straightway & beard the King & Ministers, & try to infuse into their backbone the necessary quantity of starch." Later, noted Gilbert, "it was to become fashionable, even for Asquith, to mock Churchill's mission to Antwerp. On the morning of October 3, however, much seemed to depend upon it."

Two days later, after turning down Winston's offer to resign as the admiralty's first lord in order to stay in Antwerp, Asquith told Venetia, "Winston succeeded in bucking up the Belges, who gave up their panicky idea of retreating to Ostend, and are now holding Antwerp for as long as they can, trusting upon our coming to their final deliverance." When Asquith informed the cabinet of Winston's offer to stay on (in command and with a high military rank), however, "I regret to say it was received with a Homeric laugh." For one thing, he noted, the former lieutenant would have been "in command of two distinguished Major Generals, not to mention Brigadiers, Colonels, etc., while the Navy was only contributing its little brigades."

Urged by Asquith to return home, Winston nonetheless lingered. As he explained in a telegram to War Secretary Kitchener on the afternoon of October 5: "In view of the situation and developing German attack, it is my duty to remain here and continue my direction of affairs unless relieved by some person of consequence. If we can hold out for next three days, prospects will not be unfavorable. But Belgians require to be braced to their task, and my presence is necessary."

That night, as the German bombardments continued, an Italian reporter saw Winston near a Belgian fort "tranquilly smoking a large cigar and looking at the progress of the battle under a rain of shrapnel, which I can only call fearful." His naval brigades finally arrived the next morning, but the men were too tired to take the offensive right away. That afternoon, Gen. Sir Henry Rawlinson arrived ahead of his forty-thousand-man division, still disembarking at Ostend. But too late . . . with the German heavy howitzers drawing close enough to bombard the city center, the Belgians decided to abandon the city. "That evening," Gilbert noted in *Churchill: A Life*, "Churchill made a final visit to the front-line positions. Then, leaving Rawlinson in charge, he returned overnight through Ostend and Dover to London."

That very morning, October 7, Clementine delivered their third child, daughter Sarah. After a quick visit to mother and child, Winston reported to his fellow cabinet members on his three and a half days in Antwerp. And now Asquith told Venetia, "Winston is in great form & I think has thoroughly enjoyed his adventure. . . . He was quite ready to take over in Belgium, and did so in fact for a couple of days—the army, the navy & the civil government."

Additional note: After Winston left Antwerp, the city's situation became dire, and the forty thousand men of Rawlinson's division were kept back. The evening of October 8, with Antwerp in flames from the German shelling, he agreed the Royal Marines and the Royal Naval Division holding out in the city—totaling eight thousand—should leave. "Poor Winston is very depressed," Asquith informed Venetia Stanley, "as he feels that his mission has been in vain."

But not so, not totally . . . despite all the criticism and mockery Winston would undergo in the months and even years ahead for his bold, and, yes, impulsive reaction to Antwerp's peril in the opening days of World War I, the fact is, noted Gilbert, "the extra six days' resistance of Antwerp since Churchill had persuaded the Belgians not to evacuate the city enabled the British Army to return safely to the Channel Coast, and to reform in Flanders." The delay in the fall of Antwerp, as Asquith said at the time, "may . . . have even been of vital value."

Spies in the Woodwork

While Winston and his colleagues in London now worried over the movement of fleets and armies, the town fathers of Cromer and environs worried over the premature flight of tourists from their coastal area and its beaches. To stem the tide, Churchill's daughter Mary recounted, they even ran an appeal on the screen in a local movie theater saying: Why Leave? After all, Winston Churchill's wife and children are staying here, aren't they? If it's safe for them, it's safe for you.

Winston wrote to Clementine (none too reassuringly): "It makes me a little anxious that you should be on the coast. It is a 100 to one against a raid—but still there is the chance, and Cromer has a good landing place near." He mentioned that she should have the car he had left with her in good repair, "so that you can whisk away at the first sign of trouble." Meanwhile, Clementine and sister Nellie believed their mother shouldn't be staying in Dieppe, so Nellie "was therefore dispatched to bring her home," Mary wrote. "Clementine invited her to join them at Pear Tree Cottage, where she arrived around the middle of August."

Just about then, the whole area was rife with spy mania—"an epidemic of highly colored (and generally not well substantiated) stories of spies and their alleged activities, which swept through the country." Soon, Clementine was reporting to Winston that a local woman saw two men walking along the cliff by the shore, and they released four carrier pigeons from beneath their coats. Also incriminating, they spoke to each other in a foreign tongue. She told two officers about it; they "pursued the men & caught them."

End of story, so far as Clementine had heard. . . . but she went on to tell Winston: "Mother is much alarmed at the 'carrier pigeon story' & insists that the message carried by the pigeons was that 'the wife of the First Lord is at Overstrand [Cromer and area] and that the Germans are to send an airplane to kidnap me & that then I am to be ransomed by the handing over of several of our handsomer ships.'"

If all this happened, she went on to say in seemingly facetious vein, "I beg of you not to sacrifice the smallest or cheapest submarine or even the oldest ship. . . . I could not face the subsequent unpopularity whereas I should be quite a heroine & you a Spartan if I died bravely & un-ransomed."

The fact is that Clementine, then pregnant and close to term with Sarah, was "in a highly agitated, almost hysterical state of mind, engendered by what she considered to be Nellie's inconsiderate and wrong-headed behavior." Instead of coming to the seashore with their mother and taking care of her while Clementine enjoyed some time with Winston in London, it seems, Nellie sent Lady Blanche on down alone ("in a feeble and exhausted state") with a letter explaining that Nellie was off to Cliveden (the Astors' house) to help turn it into a convalescent home.

Clementine was then even more put out with her sister when a second letter arrived explaining that Nellie was now off with a "nursing unit" to Belgium, which was about to be overrun by the advancing German army. Little did Clementine know that her precious Winston also would be in endangered Belgium in the days just ahead. And of course no one had the slightest idea that by New Year's Eve of that same year, 95,654 British soldiers would have died on what became known as the western front.

George V Revisited

Not long after Winston moved up the cabinet ladder as the civilian head of the Royal Navy, he and George V had been at mild loggerheads again. This time it was over naming new battleships—the king balked at naming one of them for Oliver Cromwell, leader of the Parliamentary forces that won the English Civil War of the 1640s and beheaded Charles I.

As Randolph Churchill explained in *The Young Statesman*, the king took a great interest in anything having to do with the Royal Navy. "It was not for nothing that he had seen fifteen years' service, and was known as the Sailor King," Randolph explained. Thus, when Winston submitted the name of the still-controversial Cromwell two years in a row, the king emphatically said no (and prevailed) both times. In 1914, meanwhile, with World War I just under way and Winston serving as civilian head of the admiralty, the king again remonstrated against Winston's choice of language, this time at a political rally in Liverpool where he had threatened to have the German fleet "dug out like rats in a hole."

That remark, said the king, somewhat stuffily, "was hardly dignified for a Cabinet Minister." Unfortunately, the Germans just a day later sank three British cruisers, with more than fourteen hundred men killed . . . by further misfortune, the cruisers were on station despite Winston's instruction of four days earlier that they should not be stationed there. His instruction was unknown to the public, "and subsequently kept secret by the Government," wrote biographer Martin Gilbert in *Churchill: A Life*. "As a result he was blamed for the loss of the ships and their men."

Meanwhile, it was almost simultaneously with Winston's hurry-up trip to Antwerp that Clementine's sister Nellie also went to Belgium with a volunteer medical unit . . . and, along with her companions, was captured. Temporarily locked up in the waiting room of a railroad station, the defiant sister-in-law of Winston Churchill memorialized their king back in England with this jingle scrawled on the wall:

> Our good King George is both
> Greater and Wiser,
> Than all other Monarchs,
> Including "der Kaiser."

As events turned out, both Churchill and Nellie returned home safely, and Clementine in the meantime had given birth to Sarah. Upon returning from Antwerp, Winston was "received at Buckingham palace by the King," and Foreign Secretary Edward Grey sent Clementine a friendly note saying he felt "a glow" sitting in a committee meeting with her Winston—"next to a Hero."

Others, though, derided Churchill's Antwerp mission—or "escapade," Mary reported—as typical of his impulsive nature and in that sense it hurt his reputation on the eve of the Dardanelles disaster of the following year. Even before the full scope of the Dardanelles-Gallipoli fiasco dawned, with Winston becoming the prime scapegoat (the concept largely was his, but the faulty execution of the plan was not), he was out of the cabinet loop. And it may surprise some to know that George V was undismayed to see Winston go. At least that's the inference to be gained from a note to Queen Mary, in which he said (according to biographer Gilbert's *The Challenge of War*): "Personally I am glad the Prime Minister is going to have a National Government. Only by that means can we get rid of Churchill from the Admiralty. He is intriguing also with French against K. He is the real danger." (By prime minister, the king of course meant H. H. Asquith, and by National Government, he meant the coalition government Asquith briefly formed before he fell away to David Lloyd George's government. The reference to French is to British army Gen. Sir John French, then commander of the British forces in France. And by K he meant Winston's cabinet colleague Lord Kitchener.)

Not all was lost for Winston, meanwhile. He certainly would suffer long-festering wounds over the entire affair, and not only because of the king's very minor role in the outcome. Later, under Lloyd George as prime minister, Winston would be brought back into the government to finish the war as minister of munitions. The king, meanwhile, went about the kingly duties that might be expected in wartime—"public respect for the king increased during World War One, when he made many visits to the front line, hospitals, factories and dockyards," noted the BBC's history Web site.

Before his reign came to an end in 1936, the Irish Free State had been established, India was inching toward independence, and "the Statute of Westminster of 1931 meant dominion parliaments [such as Canada's] could now pass laws without reference to United Kingdom laws." Meanwhile, in 1924, he had accepted Britain's first Labor government. Then, with the faltering economy stirring a political crisis in 1931, "the king promoted the idea of a coalition national government of Labor, Conservatives and Liberals, which eventually was formed."

Winston went though good times and bad during the same period, first reappearing for four and a half years in the mid- to late 1920s as chancellor of the exchequer in a Conservative government headed by Stanley Baldwin, then losing that lofty cabinet seat (and tenancy of No. 11 Downing Street) with the Conservative government's general election defeat of May 30, 1929, to enter his "Wilderness" years out of government . . . out of public favor as well, except for his books.

In the meantime, though, he had enjoyed another "shooting" visit to Balmoral Castle, this time of course with George V as host. Apparently, Winston no longer was a "real danger."

While enjoying four days of grouse and stag shooting on this occasion, noted Gilbert in *Churchill*, Churchill met the king's granddaughter, two-and-a-half-year-old Elizabeth. "The last is a character," he wrote to Clementine in 1928. "She has an air of authority & reflectiveness astonishing in an infant." That same tyke, of course, would grow up to become, in 1952, Winston's second queen, by which time the aging Churchill was serving his second stint as prime minister (1951–55).

Meanwhile, after celebrating his silver jubilee in 1935, George V died less than a year later—to be succeeded, however briefly, by Edward VIII, also well known to Winston Churchill, who was twenty years his senior.

Gleam in Their Eyes

Yes, England was at war with Germany, but even so, in Scotland, close to Loch Ewe, where the British grand fleet was anchored, the owner of a large private home was startled one night to find Britain's first lord of the admiralty, two admirals, and at least two other naval officers at his doorstep.

It was all about that searchlight on his roof, they announced—and not in entirely friendly tones. Brushing aside his explanations, they insisted upon seeing the light for themselves. Moments later, with Adm. Horace L. A. Hood standing guard at the bottom, Winston led his small raiding party up a narrow, winding staircase with their host, a former Conservative MP, in tow as a "potential hostage," reported Martin Gilbert in *Winston S. Churchill: The Challenge of War, 1914–1916.*

The visitors were armed with pistols from the armory of the battleship *Iron Duke.* After all, it was wartime, and there had been reports of an airplane buzzing the area. And now . . . now, here was a private home with a searchlight on its roof. The incident stemmed from First Lord Winston S. Churchill's planned visit to the fleet on September 3, 1914, just two weeks into the war with Germany and its allies. Taking a train to Inverness, he and his party of two admirals and two commodores then "motored westward towards the Loch, where the Grand Fleet was at anchor."

On the way, at a small town named Achnasheen, they noticed the searchlight on someone's roof. "The sailors were mystified." One of the party was the Royal Navy's director of intelligence, Adm. Henry Francis Oliver, and he "knew of no Admiralty searchlight in the area, and there seemed no explanation for this one." Motoring on for the moment, Winston and his companions fell into sometimes wild speculation. "Each wondered whether it might not be a spy's searchlight, used to signal to a Zeppelin information about fleet movements, and able to direct a Zeppelin to naval anchorages," wrote Gilbert. "On reaching Loch Ewe they mentioned their fears to [Adm. John] Jellicoe [commander in chief of the first fleet], who added to the alarm by saying that an airplane had been seen in the neighborhood since the war began, but had never been traced."

That was quite enough for Winston, his "sense of adventure" now thoroughly aroused. Nothing would do but to go to the suspect house in Achnasheen and determine what was going on there. "But if it belonged to a German spy, there was danger in a senior Minister [Churchill] arriving unexpectedly." Ergo, he and his companions would be armed with pistols and ammunition from the *Iron Duke*'s armory, courtesy of Jellicoe. "Returning across the highlands, they stopped outside the house, put the pistols in their pockets and marched up the drive, prepared for violence." Neither Hollywood nor J. Arthur Rank could have played out the ensuing melodrama any better. First, a butler answered the door. He "calmly" told them it was the home of a former conservative MP, Sir Arthur Bignold. Churchill and company then "demanded" to see the master of the house. Sir Arthur, who was entertaining guests, broke off and hurried to the door.

There he met their questions head on. "To their amazement, he admitted without demur that he did have a searchlight on the roof."

But why? What on earth for? They demanded to know. Admiral Oliver, revealing he was director of naval intelligence, asserted he had every right to know.

None of them was quite prepared for their host's answer this time. He was using the searchlight "to catch the gleam [in] the eyes of the deer lying on the hillside, so that he would know where to stalk them the next morning."

That explanation seemed to Churchill "so improbable," he was "convinced that he had indeed stumbled upon a nest of spies." Now, nothing would do but to climb the narrow winding staircase to see the offending light, with "their pistols ready for any emergency." As history knows, "nothing untoward happened." The somewhat muted outcome of the affair was a partial dismantling of the light and departure of the high-level party, with "various essential parts of its mechanism" in tow . . . and an obviously indignant Bignold left behind to fume and wonder on his own.

Churchill, for his part, still had his doubts, and on his return to London he ordered a full report "on the circumstances in which this searchlight came to be placed in position, together with all other facts about Sir Arthur Bignold, his guests, friends and servants." He wanted to know if there were any aircraft landing fields in Bignold's neighborhood—and he had a real point in wondering why there had been no "police report" on the sightings of a searchlight placed on the roof of a house "in close proximity to an anchorage of the fleet."

As events turned out, noted biographer Gilbert, there really had been little to worry about. "The party Bignold was entertaining consisted of quite innocent and respectable people. No Germans could be found in the neighborhood. No confirmation could be obtained of airplanes crashing or flying near the estate. Nor indeed, so the experts reported, was the searchlight itself capable of being used at that particular moment. The adventure had been harmless." Still, if the house had been full of German spies, "instead of a patriotic Scotsman, it might have had a less simple ending."

Family Row Patched Up

The first days of World War I brought an end to two separate estrangements in Winston Churchill's life, one professional and the other highly personal. Horatio

Herbert Kitchener, the famous general of England's nineteenth-century African wars, figured in both settlements. One of them involved his relationship with Churchill, which went back to the days when Winston, a minor officer in Kitchener's command at Omdurman in the Sudan, had the temerity in his writings to criticize Kitchener's conduct of the Sudan campaign. But that was in the previous century (albeit as late as 1898), and now, in 1914, in the days just before Continental Europe became embroiled in war, their circumstances—and the world's—had changed drastically. Still, Kitchener, now field marshal and Lord Kitchener, British agent and consul-general in Egypt, could be expected to be a bit testy over those earlier days, and Winston, now a civilian and the first lord of the admiralty . . . would he be still highly critical?

Not so, recounted biographer Martin Gilbert. "Both at Army maneuvers in 1910 and at the Malta Conference of 1912, Church had been impressed by Kitchener," wrote Gilbert in *Winston S. Churchill: The Challenge of War, 1914–1916.* "The old hostilities . . . were already assuaged by 1914." Then, too, after two meetings in late July 1914, as the specter of war loomed ever more obviously, "Churchill had formed an even more favorable impression."

He, in fact, "felt that if war came, Kitchener's presence in the Government would be a necessary strength." Prime Minister Herbert Henry Asquith could not be expected in the press of war to hold both his leadership post and his office of secretary of state for war at the same time. In that case, who better to take over the war reins than Kitchener? And so it would be . . . intercepted on his way back to Egypt on August 4, the day hostilities between England and Germany commenced, Kitchener was offered the post of secretary of state for war, which he readily accepted.

Two days later, Winston saw the new defense chief in decisive action. At issue in a meeting between Winston and Kitchener and staffs was the need to transport a British Expeditionary Force of more than 120,000 men across the English Channel to France. "He asked what would happen if the Germans made a dash into the Channel with their fast ships to attack our transports," Winston recalled. "I replied that we should know of their movement . . . in time to suspend the transportation till we could deal with them."

But what about submarines, Kitchener then wanted to know. That was a serious risk, Winston conceded, but it must be accepted. Of course, he added, the danger would be greater in daytime hours than at night.

Everyone present then was "astonished" at Kitchener's immediate reaction. "Without further discussion," Gilbert noted, "Kitchener turned to the Chief of the Imperial General Staff, General [Charles W. H.] Douglas, and gave him a direct order to suspend all day crossings at once." While decisive, it turned out, this really would not do. For one thing, night crossings would take nearly twice as long to complete. For another, such a schedule would throw off railroad connections, embarkation times, and other logistical arrangements, with even more delays resulting.

So advised, "Kitchener immediately canceled his veto on daytime crossings," Gilbert reported. Churchill privately considered the episode "a revelation of the War Minister's personal authority, of his readiness to accept unlimited responsibility, and to take the gravest decision by word of mouth as if he were a commander issuing orders on the field of battle, and also of the inevitable but very serious limitations of his knowledge of the business in hand at the moment of taking up his new duties."

That night, Kitchener was present, among other luminaries of the day, for a dinner meeting of The Other Club, the dining club founded by Winston and his friend F. E. Smith. The next day, Winston's former field commander in the Sudan wrote to say: "My dear Churchill, . . . Please do not address me as Lord as I am only yours, Kitchener." Clearly, any past differences between them were patched up, at least for the moment. So patched up, in fact, that a few weeks later Winston was willing to ask his former chief a personal favor aimed at smoothing over a troublesome family squabble. It was that unhappy episode of two years earlier when Winston's cousin Sunny (officially, Charles Richard John Spencer-Churchill), the ninth Duke of Marlborough, objected to Clementine's writing a note to David Lloyd George on Blenheim Palace stationery. He later tried to apologize, but "Clementine Churchill had not been mollified, and the Churchills had subsequently refused to spend their usual Christmas at Blenheim," wrote Gilbert.

In September 1914, with World War I freshly under way, Cousin Sunny, "intent on settling the family quarrel," paid a visit on Winston at his admiralty offices with his two sons and asked for appointment to "some position in which he could help the war effort." His politics were wrong for a political appointment under the Liberal Prime Minister Asquith, and he was too old to serve as a soldier at the front. And it was Kitchener who now came to the rescue for the Churchills, by agreeing, "at once," to give the duke a War Office post as a "special messenger."

As a result, War Minister and Army Chief Kitchener received a thank-you note from his former subaltern and public critic Winston Churchill, saying (in his usual shorthand): "I am touched by the promptness with wh you have looked after Marlborough. It is a gt pleasure to work with you, & the two departments [Army and Navy] pull well together. As you say—they are only one department really."

If their old differences were now patched up, the two wartime leaders later would have their differences again, especially over the disastrous Dardanelles-Gallipoli campaign. Just when Churchill was drumming up support and laying plans to show Kitchener's neglectful role overseeing the campaign from London, however, came shocking word of the war minister's death at sea on June 5, 1916. His warship, HMS *Hampshire*, bound for Russia on a secret mission, had struck a mine. It promptly "sank in a few minutes beneath the icy waters of the North Sea," noted Gilbert—an especially horrifying end for a man who all his life hated cold water.

Fall from Grace

For Winston Churchill, the first months of World War I were a frenzy of activity, a time of tremendous responsibility, a catalog of various triumphs (disregarding his gaffe of volunteering to give up the admiralty to stay and defend Antwerp). He more than competently led one of the nation's two fighting services, as biographer Martin Gilbert pointed out.

Thus the Royal Navy "depended upon him for its orders and morale." His Naval Air Service had launched bombing attacks on Germany itself. His all-volunteer Royal Naval Division had fought at the siege of Antwerp. And he had taken charge of the nation's air defenses. Moreover, as a member of the War Council from its start in November 1914, added Gilbert, "he was at the centre of British war policy." Virtually alone, he had stiffened little Belgium's back and slowed the German advance on Antwerp. As anyone would agree, too, he and Lord Herbert Kitchener, when appointed secretary for war, were the two war experts of the Asquith cabinet.

"His authority was wide, extending over every aspect of naval planning and action," added Gilbert, Churchill's consummate biographer. "These responsibilities exhilarated him. He was only thirty-nine at the outbreak of war; his youth, energy and zeal made possible continuous exertions, plans and stratagems, not all limited to naval affairs."

Indeed, wrote Prime Minister Asquith's wife, Margot, in her diary after a weekend of visiting friends with the Churchills, Winston had enthused aloud over the war, saying, "Why I would not be out of this glorious, delicious war for anything the world could give me (eyes glowing but with a slight anxiety lest the word 'delicious' should jar on me)." He then apparently added a disclaimer, "I say, don't repeat the word 'delicious'—you know what I mean."

At the same time, Winston, like everyone else, was appalled by the endless slaughter of men in the static trench lines of the western front . . . thus, among other schemes, Winston made the mistake, however wisely or well intended, of suggesting a breakthrough to the east—to establish a supply line to struggling Russia, on the one hand, but primarily as a flanking movement opening a new front to the east in any case. How? By seizing the Turkish Dardanelles and attacking Constantinople. That strategy, if successful, would allow supplies to reach Russia unfettered, by way of the Black Sea, while also shifting the war's focus away from the western front, where little was being accomplished by either side.

Actually, noted biographer Gilbert, Winston Churchill was not the first to suggest the attack at the Dardanelles. And further, he "initially . . . preferred, and pressed continually for, an assault upon the north German coast." Nor did he always regard a purely naval attack as "the ideal operation." Instead, "he argued repeatedly at the War Council that troops must assist the navy, and protested when they were not made available."

Gilbert also reported in *Churchill: A Life* that Kitchener argued in February 1915 that no troops would be needed against the supposedly weak Turkish defenders. As the weeks passed, he repeatedly balked at releasing the eighteen thousand men of the 29th Division for a landing at the Dardanelles, in addition to an Australian and New Zealander force being readied for a possible such assault. Even Prime Minister Asquith had to wonder at this. "One must take a lot of risks in war," he wrote to Venetia Stanley, the love of his life, after one War Council meeting on the subject, "& I am strongly of the opinion that the chance of forcing the Dardanelles, & occupying Constantinople, & cutting Turkey in half, and arousing on our side the whole Balkan Peninsula, presents such a unique opportunity that we ought to hazard a lot elsewhere rather than forgo it."

As events turned out, the operation began on February 19 as an all-navy affair, with Adm. Sir Sackville Carden's flotilla of twelve fairly ancient French and British warships opening a four-week bombardment on the Turkish forts at the entrance to the Dardanelles. Next, with the forts at Cape Helles and Kum Kale well "reduced," by military terminology, Allied minesweepers came forward and, working at night, began the unenviable job of clearing away an estimated eleven belts of mines that guarded the inner passage. Called the Narrows, the passage led to the Sea of Marmara just beyond. But this is when the entire enterprise began to come apart, starting with a collapse at the very top—Admiral Carden's health, or nerves, broke down, and he had to be replaced by Adm. Sir John de Robeck.

In London, meanwhile, Kitchener again turned down an appeal from Winston for troops, on grounds the Turks couldn't be taken seriously.

Now, determined to carry out Carden's plans, de Robeck launched an all-out attack on the narrow neck—and the forts—with ten battleships at 10:45 on the morning of March 18, but with the minesweepers going first. His leading warships actually reached the mouth of the Narrows, but that's all. A single mine destroyed the French battleship *Bouvet* (with six hundred men lost), while field guns on the Turkish shore raked the minesweepers. As events then went from bad to worse, the British themselves lost three battleships, at least two of them to mines still floating in the waterway. It was all too much for de Robeck, who then withdrew.

At his request, the army joined the effort at opening the key waterway by storming the Gallipoli Peninsula running alongside the western side of the Dardanelles strait. In the end, however, the army only produced even more disastrous results. Unaware how skillfully German Gen. Otto Liman von Sanders had built up the Turkish defenses and deployed the sixty-thousand-strong Turkish Fifth Army in the targeted area, the Allies first landed two forces, amounting to fifty-two thousand men, at the southern end of the peninsula.

That was not until April 25. The largest group, divided into five parts, hit the beaches at the extreme tip of the peninsula . . . and were held to the beaches and nearby heights. The second group, the Anzac Corps of Australians and New Zealanders, landed a bit farther up the western coastline, only to be held on their beachhead as well. In the stalemate that ensued, the Allies were unable to press inland, but the Turkish defenders were unable to push the invaders off the beaches.

In August, twenty-five thousand more men were landed still farther up the western coast of the peninsula, but again the invaders were held to their precarious coastal lodgment. Stalemate merely continued. Meanwhile, de Robeck never again attacked the Narrows with his ships.

Nobody could really blame Winston for this repeated drum roll of disaster (though they did!). As Gilbert pointed out in his minutely detailed biography, Winston neither planned nor supervised the army landings of April and August, "but once those landings had been made, he pressed Kitchener to reinforce them, and wanted a military victory even if the cost were high." In the meantime, however, the government at home underwent a reshuffle, and Winston was left out in the cold. Worse, he became the chief scapegoat for the Dardanelles-Gallipoli affair, which didn't end until the Allied troops quietly were withdrawn from the theater in December 1915 and January 1916.

Thus the young politician on top of the government world one moment now, in the next moment, had been dashed to the ground. "His enthusiasm, first for the naval, and then for the military, attacks at the Dardanelles and on the Gallipoli Peninsula, convinced many of his contemporaries that he was a man of blood, lacking sound judgment, and unfit for high office," wrote Gilbert. The unhappy failure of Winston's Dardanelles strategy and the blame game that followed "shattered Churchill's career and deeply affected his character."

The result was a new and different Winston Churchill. "The ebullient politician of August 1914, confident of his powers, exuberant in manner, certain of a distinguished future, optimistic in his assessment of men and events, was gone by the summer of 1916; men saw instead a broken figure, unsure of his career, pessimistic about the outcome of the war, lacking faith in the country's leaders, consumed by brooding and bitterness."

Pushed to the very outer rings when Asquith formed a coalition government, in May 1915, Winston was named chancellor of the Duchy of Lancaster, an archaic post allowing him to appoint the magistrates in the county of Lancaster and not much else, noted biographer Roy Jenkins in his *Churchill.* After six months in that come-down capacity, Winston decided to go to war . . . and literally, he would. A reservist all these years with the Oxfordshire yeomanry based at Woodstock, he donned his army uniform and headed for the trenches of the western front.

Romance in High Places

As if it weren't enough to have a rampant world war on his hands, not enough to have daily encounters with prima donnas Winston Churchill, David Lloyd George, and Herbert Kitchener, Prime Minister Herbert Henry Asquith also, in the midst of his cabinet crisis of May 1915, had to cope with a broken heart. This month he learned that the woman he loved would be leaving him for another man. And no, she wasn't his sharp-witted younger wife, Margot Tennant Asquith.

Instead, she was his daughter Violet's best friend and therefore a woman about thirty years younger than he.

For months he had been writing her daily letters, sometimes three and four times a day—a total of more than 560 at last count. For months he had been telling her what was going on in the cabinet, the very center of the country at war with Germany and the other Central Powers. Telling her quite often what Winston said, what Lloyd George said, what Kitchener said—what his own protégé in the cabinet, Edwin Montagu, said. Telling her the grand strategies and even the small tactical decisions of the war. What troops, how many of them, when and where they were going.

In one such missive, he told her the code name "Sylt" for the proposed seizure of Borkum Island on the north German coast. In addition, he shared with her the latest intelligence on German ship movements gained from decoded signals. Even more frequently, he passed along personal observations and gossipy tidbits about his cabinet members and what went on in their meetings. After an informal lunch on the eve of the Great War, he told his young love, Beatrice Venetia Stanley, of a warning by Lord Kitchener "that if we don't back up France when she is in real danger, we shall never be regarded or exercise real power again."

On the other hand, after a later cabinet meeting: "Lloyd George, all for peace, is more sensible and statesmanlike for keeping the position open. . . . . Winston very bellicose and demanding immediate mobilization."

Or when Winston first went to Antwerp to buck up the Belgians, "The intrepid Winston set off at midnight & ought to have reached Antwerp by about 9 this morning." But he also warned, "Don't say anything of Winston's mission, at any rate at present; it is one of the many unconventional incidents of the war."

Or, in a more reflective, even poetical note in December 1914, "I am writing in the Cabinet room, at the beginning of twilight, and thro' the opposite window across the Parade I see the Admiralty flag flying & the lights 'beginning to twinkle' from the rooms where Winston and his two familiars [Winston's secretaries Eddie Marsh and James Edward Masterton-Smith] are beating out their plans."

The prime minister sometimes wrote Venetia in the midst of cabinet meetings. Significantly, however, just down the table, Edwin Montagu also was writing letters on occasion—writing probably to the very same young woman, because he was the "other man" in the triangle, and for months he had been asking Venetia to marry him.

Who was this woman who so fascinated at least two members of the highest governmental panel in the land? "She was the daughter of a family of intellectual, faintly eccentric, aristocratic liberals, a sympathetic, well-read, charming young woman who until the war thought about little except the smarter pleasures," observed British journalist Godfrey Hodgson in a 1983 book review for the *New York Times*.

Asquith, on the other hand, was "an orphan from a modest background who had made his way in politics by sheer intellectual ability." Until May 1915, he had been "the virtuoso ringmaster of a political three-ring circus," a ringmaster who "tamed and manipulated such strong-willed and unruly colleagues as Winston Churchill, David Lloyd George and Kitchener of Khartoum." He was a prime minister who "dominated the House of Commons and inspired the country." Born outside society, "he enjoyed spending time 'in society,' entertaining and being entertained by the elite that still exercised a pervasive influence in British politics, though the tide of democracy had been rising since all adult British males won the vote 30 years earlier."

Hodgson's useful summary of the Asquith-Veneteia-Montagu triangle appeared in a review of *H. H. Asquith: Letters to Venetia Stanley*, edited by Michael Brock and Eleanor Brock. "Almost certainly there was no physical intimacy between Asquith and Venetia," Hodgson noted. "They met, usually in the family setting, at country house weekends or dinner parties, sometimes alone."

Ironically, Asquith and Venetia first became friends when all three principals had gone on holiday to Sicily with Asquith's daughter Violet. At the time, Montagu was Asquith's political secretary and protégé. "In 1912 Montagu had proposed to Venetia and at first been accepted, then turned down. What Asquith did not know was that while he was becoming more and more emotionally dependent on Venetia, Edwin Montagu had not given up and in the spring of 1915 Venetia confessed to Montagu that she returned his love." He then "persuaded her that she must tell Asquith the truth."

And she did, but she did so on the same day in mid-May, noted Geoffrey Best in *Churchill: A Study in Greatness*, that the London *Times* broke the news "on how Sir John French's army was suffering from a shortage of shells: the first time that Asquith's government's ability to manage the national war effort had been seriously questioned."

This double whammy then was followed the next day by the resignation of Winston's combative and aging first sea lord (or top admiral), Sir John Fisher, all of which, together, conspired to bring about a coalition government with Asquith still at its head, but now including key Conservative Party leaders. And their price for cooperation was the removal of Winston Churchill from his admiralty post. . . . soon, by May 25, done.

Meanwhile, Venetia married Montagu, later to be secretary of state for India, but he died young, at age forty-five. Soon replaced as prime minister by Lloyd George in yet another government shuffle, Asquith apparently was shattered by Venetia's rejection. "Most loved," he had written upon learning of her plan to marry Montagu, "as you know well, this breaks my heart. I couldn't bear to come and see you. I can only pray God to bless you and help me."

Worse yet, Asquith lost his son Raymond in the battles of the Somme. Sadly, too, he had one meeting with Venetia after her marriage—in 1927, after returning to his home at The Wharf, by a mill pond in Sutton Courtenay near Oxford. By then he had been stricken with partial paralysis, leading to an overall physical and mental decline and, finally, to his death the following February.

Support for a Landship

Prescription for victory in the trenches: "It would be quite easy in a short time to fit up a number of steam tractors with small armored shelters, in which men and machine guns could be placed, which would be bullet proof. Used at night, they would not be affected by artillery fire to any extent. The caterpillar system would enable trenches to be crossed quite easily, and the weight of the machine would destroy all wire entanglements. Forty or fifty of these engines, prepared secretly and brought into positions at nightfall, could advance quite certainly into the enemy's trenches, smashing away all the obstructions, and sweeping the trenches with their machine-gun fire, and with grenades thrown out of the top."

The recipient of this memo in January 1915 was Prime Minister Asquith. The author . . . who else but the wide-ranging first lord of the admiralty, Winston Churchill (before his abrupt departure, of course).

Subject: Creation of a new weapon of war.

Initial military development funded by: £70,000 in admiralty monies.

First code-named: "Water carriers for Russia."

Winston's name for the machine: "Landship"

Next known as: "water-tanks."

Finally birthed in World War I and known ever since as tanks.

Actually, Englishman James Cowen was awarded a patent in 1855, two decades before Winston's birth, for an armed armored vehicle based on the steam tractor, but using wheels for its mobility. Next, an armored self-propelled variant built in England in 1900 was used to haul supplies in South Africa during the Boer War, when Winston was very much alive, well . . . and actually on the scene. Next, an armed armored vehicle built by Vickers, Son and Maxim was exhibited in London in 1902. In France, two years later, another variant appeared, complete with a turret. Austria's Austro-Daimler Company also developed a wheeled armored machine.

Still missing among all these prototypes, however, was the one element that Winston would seize upon as the horrendous slaughter of the trenches unfolded on the western front: caterpillar tracks that enabled such a vehicle to overcome obstacles in its path.

Ironically, as early as 1903, such a tracked vehicle had been proposed in France. The same concept was brushed aside in England in 1908, with similar designs then turned down by the Germans and Austro-Hungarians in 1911 and again by the British in 1912. Then came the war, with the belligerents immediately going to armored cars—excellent on roads, not so good on broken ground, at crossing shell holes, or breaking through barbed wire. And now came the British tank, thanks in large part to the memo Winston sent Asquith on January 5, 1915, and a follow-up conference Winston held in his admiralty bedroom (he was confined by a bout of flu) on February 20. The January memo had been inspired, in turn, by a proposal from Maurice Hankey, a former Royal Marine colonel and secretary to the War Council, "for a trench-crossing machine," biographer Martin Gilbert reported. Asquith in turn sent Winston's memo to Lord Kitchener, "who set in motion a certain amount of design work at the War Office."

None too certain much would come of the army's thoughts on the matter, Winston briefly bided his time . . . until focusing in late February upon a proposal advanced by Maj. Thomas Hetherington, who was attached to the admiralty's own Royal Navy Air Division for experimental work. The major's proposal was for "a large cross-country armored car that would not only carry guns, but would surmount obstacles, trenches and barbed wire," Gilbert wrote. Winston immediately asked Capt. Eustace Tennyson D'Eyncourt, head of naval construction, to try designing "such a 'landship.'" Explained Gilbert: "To mystify those who might accidentally see the designs, they were called 'water-carriers for Russia,' but when it was pointed out that this might be abbreviated to 'WCs for Russia' [meaning water closets, or toilets] the name was changed to 'water-tanks,' then to 'tanks.'"

The February 20 conference at Winston's sickbed was held to discuss the best way to go forward with development of the tank, with D'Eyncourt leading the effort as chairman of a newly formed Land Ship Committee. The committee reported back to Winston two days later; he approved its proposals, and "an order for the first tank was placed with a firm of agricultural engineers, who suggested using a tractor as the model for the new machine."

Meanwhile, "having obtained Asquith's approval for his experimental activities," Winston gave the D'Eyncourt's Land Ship Committee £70,000 in admiralty funds to pursue development of the future tank, "with as much speed as possible." On March 9, shown the first designs, Winston responded, "Press on."

Next, just days after Admiral de Robeck's ill-fated attack at the mouth of the Dardanelles in mid-March, D'Eyncourt sought permission to build eighteen different prototypes. Well convinced by now of the tank's likely usefulness in breaking the stalemate of the trenches, Winston naturally approved. "Most urgent," was his response this time. "Special report to me in case of delay."

At this point, as no one yet could know, Winston's days as a prominent member of the Asquith government were numbered. Two months later, his reputation shattered by the continuing failures of the Dardanelles-Gallipoli campaign, he would be relegated to the humiliating post of chancellor of the Duchy of Lancaster, yet remaining a member of the War Council. Before he went, however, the seeds leading to development of the tank as a new weapon of war had been well sewn. Indeed, noted biographer Gilbert, the Royal Commission on War Inventions reported after the war that "it was primarily due to the receptivity, courage and driving force" of Winston Churchill that the concept of the tank as a war-making weapon "was converted into a practical shape."

That conversion of concept to practical application had proceeded by September 1915 to construction of Britain's first tank, called "Little Willie," followed by a second model, "Big Willie," which was able to cross wide trenches. In February 1916 the army ordered one hundred of the latter model, to be called the Mark I. Proceeding on their own, the French ordered four hundred of their first tank the same month—the French Schneider tank featured an armored cab set on a tractor chassis.

The British first tried 49 of their fledgling tanks in battle on September 15, 1916, but they achieved only mixed results. The real baptism of the tank as an effective weapon of war came more than a year later, on November 20, 1917, when the British threw 474 tanks into the battle of Cambrai . . . resulting in a spectacular breakthrough of the German lines. Although still primitive, the tank had proved itself and was here to stay. By war's end a year later, Britain had built 2,636 tanks and the French, 3,870. Germany, so noted during the early stages of World

War II two decades later for its tank-led blitzkrieg tactics, produced a grand total of just 20 tanks during World War I.

Sojourn on "Plug Street"

"The whole household was upside down while the soldier-statesman was buckling on his sword, " wrote Winston's friend Max Aiken (Lord Beaverbrook) after a visit to the combined Winston and Jack Churchill family quarters at London's 41 Cromwell Road. "Downstairs, Mr. 'Eddie' Marsh, his faithful secretary, was in tears. . . . Upstairs, Lady Randolph was in a state of despair at the idea of her brilliant son being relegated to the trenches. Mrs. Churchill [Clementine] seemed to be the only person who remained calm, collected and efficient."

And true, once the cabinet decided to reduce the size of the Dardanelles Committee, with Winston's seat among those eliminated, he had no further voice in decisions affecting the heartrending, costly standoff on the Gallipoli Peninsula. "I could not accept a position of general responsibility for war policy without any effective share in its guidance and control," he wrote in his letter of resignation to Prime Minister Asquith. But he wasn't backing down from his stances of the immediate past. "I have a clear conscience, which enables me to bear my responsibility for past events with composure," he insisted. And so off he would be . . . to the horrors of the stalemated trench warfare on the western front, where his own Oxfordshire Yeomanry was stationed.

Oddly enough, other than an again-tearful Eddie Marsh, the only nonfamily personages attending a farewell luncheon at the Cromwell Road home on November 16, 1915, were Asquith's wife Margot and his daughter Violet. "It may seem surprising," Mary Soames acknowledged in her biography of Clementine. "Violet was a close friend and political confidante, and despite the fact that Winston and Margot never really got on together, there was a long story of liking, shared endeavor and loyalty between the Asquiths and the Churchills."

Meanwhile, as a former cabinet minister, former head of the Royal Navy, still-colorful personality supreme, and only incidentally a reserve army major, Winston was far different from the average officer deploying to France for duty. Upon arrival at Boulogne, in fact, he was greeted by a car sent by Sir John French, commander in chief of the British Expeditionary Force. After checking in with his familiar Queen's Own Oxfordshire Hussars, he met with French at general headquarters (GHQ). He then was offered the choice of assignment as an aide de camp (ADC) or command of a combat brigade, and for a night or two he was quartered, he wrote to Clementine, "in a fine chateau, with hot baths, beds, champagne and all the conveniences." Such luxuries were not to be his for very long, even though Winston always would remain a special case.

To no one's surprise, he chose the brigade command, but asked first to spend some time in the trenches with an active unit to gain a bit of experience. As a result, he temporarily was assigned to the 2nd Battalion of the Grenadier Guards, whose officers at first received him coldly, said Mary, and with considerable "suspicion," wrote biographer Martin Gilbert. Now, on the front lines, he would see what the world of trench warfare was all about.

What it was all about, he wrote very soon to Clementine, was "filth & rubbish everywhere. Graves built into the defenses & scattered about promiscuously, feet & clothing breaking through the soil, water & muck on all sides; & about this scene in the dazzling moonlight troops of bats creep & glide, to the unceasing accompaniment of rifles & machine guns & the venomous whining & whirring of the bullets which pass overhead." But here, out of the political limelight, he had found "happiness & content such as I have not known for many months." Here, he wrote his mother, "Do you know I am quite young again."

Actually, his forty-first birthday was fast approaching—on November 30—and he almost didn't make it. Ordered on November 26 to meet his corps commander at a point behind the lines but some distance away, he set off on foot just as German artillery shells began falling on the front-line trenches. He spent a good hour traipsing across "sopping fields on which stray bullets are always falling, along tracks periodically shelled" before he finally reached the crossroads where he was supposed to meet the corps commander's car. "But," Gilbert reported, "it had been 'driven off' by shells, and a Staff Officer who arrived to tell Churchill this informed him that the General had only wanted a chat 'and that another day would do equally well.'"

Thoroughly annoyed, Winston brooded over the inconvenience all the way back to his dugout, now crossing the same "sopping fields" in the dark, wind, and rain, only to learn that fifteen minutes after he left his dugout that morning, it was squarely struck by a shell that destroyed the structure and killed one of the three men inside. "When I saw the ruin," he wrote to Clementine, "I was not so angry with the General after all."

"It is all chance, and our wayward footsteps are best planted without too much calculation," he also told Clementine. "One must yield oneself simply & naturally to the mood of the game and trust in God, which is another way of saying the same thing."

Meanwhile, during his six days at the front with the grenadiers, less than a week, he reported, "Our total casualties in the battalion were 35 out of 700 in six days [of] doing nothing." On a more personal level, though, Winston won quick acceptance among his fellow soldiers. Whereas the battalion commander at first had greeted him by saying "your coming was not a matter in which we were given any choice," Churchill commented that now was "all smiles & hand waves & pressing invitations to return whenever I liked & stay as long as I liked, etc."

He would be with the battalion another eight days, however, all spent behind the front lines at Melville, beyond German artillery range. Then it was back to GHQ at St. Omer, "where he amused those present by referring to himself as the 'escaped scapegoat,'" reported Gilbert. During this period, Winston was unhappy to hear that Gallipoli was about to be evacuated . . . left to the Turks. But, never still, he sent his friend F. E. Smith (serving the Asquith government as attorney general) a memo for cabinet attention in which he elaborated upon an earlier suggestion for a giant mobile shield of bulletproof metal on caterpillar tracks that would cross trenches and crush barbed-wire obstacles in its advance, with attacking infantrymen crouched safely behind.

Back home on Cromwell Road, his wife and mother quite naturally "feared for Churchill's life at the front." Clementine wrote that if he overexposed himself and was killed as a result, "the world might think you had sought death out of grief for your share in the Dardanelles." Lady Randolph, on the other hand, urged him to be "sensible" and "remember you are destined for greater things than even in the past."

Politics did follow him to his life as a soldier. Some of his friends and supporters thought, as he himself hoped, he could arrange a brigade command . . . others, more realistically, thought that a unit so large (five thousand men) would be a reach for an officer of his limited experience and thus would be further ammunition for his detractors. They urged him to take a battalion instead (one thousand men commanded by a lieutenant colonel).

As events rapidly unfolded, Winston first was told to expect a brigade command, with the rank of brigadier general. But then Sir Douglas Haig replaced General French; worse, for Winston, French also received a letter from Prime Minister Asquith rejecting the idea of a brigade command for Winston and suggesting battalion command instead. Explained Gilbert: "Asquith knew that . . . he was going to be questioned in the Commons by a Conservative MP as to whether Churchill had been promised an infantry brigade, if he ever had ever commanded even a battalion of infantry, and for how many weeks 'he had served at the front as an infantry officer?' Asquith was determined to dodge this particular attack." The result was Winston's command of the 6th Royal Scots Fusiliers as one of thirteen colonels commanding battalions in the 9th Division, most of whom he knew from his days at Sandhurst and in India, the Malakand, the Sudan, or during the Boer War. The battalion itself would be new to him, and it unfortunately was in woeful condition after suffering heavy losses at the battle of Loos. All but one of its remaining officers were nonprofessional volunteers from civilian life.

Once again, Winston's arrival was received coldly, and it probably didn't help that he arrived with "a long bath and a boiler for heating the water." He then promptly launched a campaign against body lice. In short time, however, he apparently won the admiration of his men. "After a very brief period," reported one of the officers, Jock MacDavid, "he had accelerated the morale and officers and men to an almost unbelievable degree."

As always when he took on a new post, Winston threw himself into the job, with no detail considered too minor for his close attention. He was considered scrupulously fair with the men brought before him on discipline charges; he trained his men well; he even organized a sports day, concert, and banquet for them before the battalion was sent back into the front lines.

Not all was to his liking, however. Nor was he always happy to be out of the political lines of fire. No, with Winston, no matter where he might be, there always were worries and thoughts about what was going on politically back home. Thus, in early 1916, when he saw German aircraft spend the morning "in combat in the sky above his billets," Gilbert reported, Winston was quick to blame his political colleagues back home. "There is no excuse for our not having command of the air," Winston wrote to Clementine. "If they had given me control of this service when I left the Admiralty, we should have supremacy today. Asquith wanted this, but in contact with the slightest difficulty & resistance, he as usual shut up."

Political regrets or no, the war continued. January 23, 1916, would be the battalion's last day of training at Moolenacker behind the lines. Winston took his officers to dinner in a nearby village. As the battalion then moved to the village of La Creche for two days, he wrote to his son Randolph, then just four: "Soon we are going to go close up to the Germans, and then we shall shoot back at them and try to kill them. This is because they have done wrong and caused all this war and sorrow."

The pause at La Creche gave him a chance also to write his old parliamentary colleague Lloyd George about the controversial issue of a military draft . . . and fears that the Tory-dominated cabinet might repeat the failures of Gallipoli in an even larger theater of war such as the Balkans. "Lloyd George made no reply," wrote Gilbert. "He knew Churchill's anguish, but could not yet help." Keyword . . . *yet.*

After that, it was on to the serious and this time long-lasting business of war at the Belgian village of Ploegsteert, which the British called "Plug Street." Here the 6th Royal Scots Fusiliers were to hold down a thousand-yard line—alternating between six days in the front trenches and six days in "immediate reserve." And there they would stay for the next three and a half months, with no offensive—British or German—to disturb their routine. Even so, "the German shellfire was continuous, and machine-gun and rifle fire a constant hazard," Gilbert noted.

Very important to Winston, he still had his portable bath and hot-water tank with him. And he was cheered when his old colleagues Lloyd George, F. E. Smith, and Bonar Law all visited him at St. Omer on January 31, a "drop-in" allowing all four to agree that Asquith must go at the first opportunity. After that, the days dragged on, broken sporadically by dangerous artillery fire, near misses, and occasional casualties. After a time, Winston "amazed his young officers by setting up an easel and starting to paint."

Oddly, his worst crisis came during a brief visit home on seven days' leave in early March—he impulsively made plans to speak in Parliament (he still was a member) on the Royal Navy's budget needs and call for the return of controversial Lord John Fisher as first sea lord. Clementine was vehemently opposed, telling Fisher to his face at a lunch on Cromwell Road: "Keep your hands off my husband! You have all but ruined him once." And indeed they had gone through a spectacular dispute at the time of Winston's fall from his admiralty post.

Against Clementine's advice, however, Winston did speak in Parliament, urging a more vigorous naval war policy and the return of the seventy-five-year-old Fisher to his post as chief admiral. "The House was amazed and aghast," Gilbert wrote. "Ridicule of Churchill followed at once." He would be "shattered," said Gilbert, "by the hostile, mocking reaction to his [Fisher] proposal." But now he stubbornly planned to extend his leave and stay on for the pending debate in Parliament on the army budget estimates. He obtained permission from Kitchener and Asquith, even meeting briefly with Asquith, only to be told he really had no political support among those "who count at all."

Thus was set the pattern of the next year, during which Winston stubbornly obtained permission to leave the "Plug Street" trenches and return to the political wars at Westminster, with the conviction that he would be more effective in government than in the trenches. While given no opportunity for months to act in the field, he at least could speak out in Parliament—where one of his themes was a plea for greater use of machines instead of precious manpower to achieve military ends. Learning that the tank, the "landship" he previously had endorsed so fully, was about to be tried at the Somme in mid-September 1916, he pleaded with Asquith to hold back until a large number of the new machines could be sprung on the Germans as an overwhelming surprise. Although Asquith "listened . . . attentively," reported Gilbert, only a few of the new machines appeared at the Somme. "My poor 'land battleships' have been let off prematurely & on a petty scale," Winston wrote to Fisher.

During this fallow period, Winston was doing his best to make sure the governmental panel inquiring into the Dardanelles-Gallipoli debacle would be fully briefed upon his role at the beginning of the affair. "There was reasonable prospect of success," he argued. When the investigating committee finally issued its report in March 1917, it placed "no blame" on Winston, noted Gilbert. "But although the report made clear that Asquith had been as keen to attack Turkey as any of his colleagues, and that it was Kitchener who had failed to give the War Council sufficient details of his military plans, it did not, to Churchill's mind, answer many of the specific charges that had been made against him personally."

In a response submitted to the commission, Winston argued that the report "failed to set the Dardanelles in the context of the wider war," especially in reference to the trench stalemate on the western front, added Gilbert. Or, as Winston himself once again stated his case: "A fifth of the resources, the effort, the loyalty, the resolution, the perseverance vainly employed in the battle of the Somme to gain a few shattered villages and a few square miles of devastated ground, would, in the Gallipoli Peninsula, used in time, have united the Balkans on our side, joined hands with Russia, and cut Turkey out of the war."

Meanwhile, the Asquith government had collapsed in December 1916, with Lloyd George then becoming prime minister. He sent word that he would consider a minor appointment for Winston, but not until the Dardanelles report was published . . . some months later, as it turned out. Meanwhile, Conservative opposition to Winston remained fierce and deep-seated.

When an appointment finally came, in July 1917, it was to succeed Christopher Addison as minister of munitions. "For several days there was a storm of Conservative and newspaper protest," wrote Gilbert. The *Morning Post*, which Winston so famously served as a correspondent during the Boer War, now charged that he imagined himself to be a "Nelson at sea and a Napoleon on land." Nonetheless, the appointment stuck, although, as Gilbert reported, Winston's aunt Cornelia, his father's sister, offered a cautionary note: "Stick to Munitions, and don't try to run the Government."

New Roosevelt Encountered

With Winston resurfacing as Lloyd George's minister of munitions (despite continuing dissent by the coalition government's Tory members to anything having to do with Churchill), the Cromwell Road house the Churchills shared with brother Jack's family (as well as their mother Jennie) suddenly became Winston's "second" war headquarters, since the Admiralty House no longer was available to him.

Situated in London's South Kensington section, the new Winston headquarters bore "only the remotest resemblance to a home," newspaperman Jack Fishman pointed out in *My Darling Clementine.* "Prime Minister Lloyd George and other Cabinet Ministers came and went at all hours; official dispatch boxes piled up in the hall and on stairs, and as soon as one lot of the boxes was cleared another pile appeared. Telephones and secretaries pounding typewriters were everywhere; and the two mothers [Clementine and Jack's wife, Goonie] and the domestic staff had their work cut out for them keeping the children out of the way."

Winston—always uniquely Winston—did the traffic flow no favors when he joined the children in building a bridge with a toy construction set . . . and when that wouldn't do, with several more construction sets, until a huge edifice fifteen feet long and eight feet high had risen, wall to wall, across the dining room. "Finally, yielding to protests about the loss of the dining room, he transferred the bridge to the hall, where visitors, including Cabinet Ministers, had to stoop under the raised center section of the bridge to get through the door."

More seriously, the Munitions Ministry may have an unglamorous sound to it, but it was a vital job that, in Winston's hands, went well . . . and, not so incidentally, led him into a resumed relationship with the land of his mother's birth.

He hadn't set foot in America since 1901, but he nonetheless had kept up a few close ties, especially with Bourke Cockran, who followed Winston's political career from afar, even advising him at one point to disclaim any thoughts of a cabinet post in hopes the high offices he sought would come to him, rather than his appearing to go after them. It didn't work out that way, since Winston, always a young man in a hurry, unblushingly scrambled up the career ladder while gradually accumulating a short list of controversial, even ill-conceived decisions. But in 1917, thanks to Lloyd George, Winston had come to life again in the strictly nuts and bolts but absolutely vital munitions post.

This meant constant contact with high-level British and American industrialists and financiers—among the latter was Bernard Baruch, head of the U.S. War Industries Board and soon to become a lifelong friend. Another new acquaintance was Charles Schwab, head of Bethlehem Steel, who early in the war had agreed to make submarines for England, but ship the parts for assembly in Canada to avoid violation of America's neutrality status.

Later, with America fully involved in the war, Winston met another interesting American—at a banquet in London for the allied ministers of war, noted Martin Gilbert in *Churchill and America*. This was Assistant Navy Secretary Franklin Delano Roosevelt, then thirty-six, who rose toward the end of the evening and told his British hosts, "We are with you to the end."

Oddly, Winston would have no memory of FDR's speech nor of any conversation held with his future ally of World War II. And what FDR recalled of their first meeting is no less startling. Twenty years later, he apparently told Ambassador Joseph Kennedy that Winston acted "like a stinker" to him and was "one of the few men in public life who was rude to me."

Meanwhile, it's only fair to report here that Theodore Roosevelt, FDR's distant cousin, had been so impressed by Winston's mobilization of the British fleet on the eve of the war that he asked a mutual British friend to pass along his congratulations. On another positive note, after filling the post of munitions minister until war's end, Winston could note with justifiable pride that the first million American troops to reach Europe had been "almost entirely" equipped by Britain and France with essentials such as artillery, machine guns, rifles, trench mortars, and munitions of all kinds, biographer Gilbert noted.

Thus the war effort had brought the two countries into close communion on goals while also establishing a historically unprecedented, close working relationship, thanks in great part to Winston's daily efforts. But then, immediately after the war, a shock. The Americans refused to join the nascent League of Nations, much less embark upon any serious military effort against the Bolshevik regime in Russia. Winston, rebuffed by his own cabinet on the latter point, was greatly disappointed on both scores.

He then would be angered outright by U.S. pressure in the years ahead for prompt payment of Britain's war debts to the United States and by U.S. insistence on naval parity with Great Britain, which Churchill saw as threatening both to Britain's tradition as a great maritime nation and to the Royal Navy's age-old domination of the seas. Still, at the bottom of the Anglo-American equation, America had been Britain's ally in the Great War, had spilled her own blood on behalf of England and the Allied powers of Continental Europe, and that meant the most.

Additional note: Even the largely sedentary munitions job added yet another hair-breadth escape to Winston's ever-growing list of close calls. In this instance, he, Clementine, and private secretary Eddie Marsh were returning by automobile from a visit to a munitions factory outside London when another car barreled into theirs broadside, "turning it completely over," Fishman reported in his biography of Clementine. Marsh later said that Clementine wound up sitting on him "in what struck me at the time as a remarkably becoming attitude." They weren't frightened, he added, until "Winston began banging on the glass over our heads. . . . He explained that he wanted us to get out before the car caught fire (which it didn't), so we forgave him."

★ PART 3 ★
Betwixt and Between

Until Now II

From erudite British journalist and longtime PBS television host for *Masterpiece Theatre* Alistair Cooke some years ago came a useful retrospective of Britain during the rise and fall of Winston Churchill's political star prior to and during World War I. Cooke was, after all, an eyewitness, albeit a bit young at the time.

"I was on the verge of eight years of age," Cooke recalled in a speech to the Churchill Society's 1998 international convention at Bretton Woods, New Hampshire, "and I saw in the *Daily Mail* a very strange picture of Major Churchill in uniform. I said to my father, 'Why is he in uniform?' He replied, 'Because of the Dardanelles.' This didn't mean very much to me at the time but it very soon did. I don't need to tell you about the enormous tragedy of Gallipoli, but believe me, if you lived in Britain then—even as an unquestioning boy of eight—it was one of the great disasters. The other was the battle of the Somme in which, in three nights, the British lost 160,000 men and the Germans lost about the same."

As a child, Cooke knew the Dardanelles was Churchill's conception. And when it was all over, concluded with a remarkable evacuation of the remaining troops, he and his family knew the casualty lists "went on for pages." For them, the Dardanelles was "the greatest failure of the war" perhaps because a local regiment had fought at Gallipoli. On their Manchester streets, Cooke said, "suddenly every other young woman was wearing black." Further, "we knew that Churchill, disgraced, had gone to France to fight in the trenches."

Then came a day, June 6, 1916, when meeting his mother after school, Cooke found on her face "an expression I had never seen." She must have been in her late thirties, but just that moment, "she looked suddenly old, gray, startled—yet not wanting to frighten me."

She took his hand and said, "Kitchener has died."

Not quite the end of the world, but "even at that age I felt the sky had fallen in on us. Kitchener had seemed an [Dwight D.] Eisenhower-[Bernard] Montgomery-[Chester] Nimitz, all rolled into one. He wasn't, but we thought he was. We didn't know then that his power was declining, drastically; or that he was more than

149

anyone morally responsible for the failure of the Dardanelles: he would not support the original expedition—would not produce the manpower or the materiel." Kitchener drowned, "and he got the halo," whereas, "Churchill got the blame."

If the Dardanelles was Churchill's conception, "We did not know at the time that it was also, as Clement Attlee would say, 'the only great strategical idea of the First World War.'"

Embittered by the Dardanelles fiasco and about Churchill, Cooke's father did have fonder memories. "He had been a young man during what he always said were Winston's great years—from 1904 to 1910, during the memorable Liberal Parliament, when the two great radicals, Lloyd George and Churchill, embarked on the reform of British society."

How so? "This strange alliance—the poor country boy and the aristocrat—abolished sweatshops and gave the miners an eight-hour day. They set up labor exchanges that led to unemployment insurance."

More generally: "If you were an English Liberal, 1904 through 1910 were very stirring years. Here on the one hand you had the crackling, sarcastic, brilliant Lloyd George; and on the other the witty, devastating Churchill, following each other like a great vaudeville team up and down the country. Churchill at one point even spent a week on the road begging—pleading—for the abolition of the House of Lords: 'This second chamber as it is, one-sided, hereditary, unpurged, unrepresentative, irresponsible, absentee.' It is still there, though shorn of all power."

Then came the Dardanelles, and "all this was forgotten," Cooke said. "In 1917, Lloyd George brought Churchill back into the Government as Minister of Munitions, against much opposition, especially in the press. And from then until 1923, Churchill could not go before a British audience, especially during an election, without thirty or forty people suddenly starting the chant, 'What about the Dardanelles? What about the Dardanelles?' He had a very rough time."

Ups and Downs Ahead

The decade coming after the end of World War I in 1918 meant wild roller-coaster years for Winston (and Clementine!), wherein he reached great heights at times and plunged again to startling depths . . . all the while surviving one political or physical threat after another, even possible assassination attempts. These were years when it was not unusual to find both of them combating hecklers at political meetings—or, on one occasion, to find them showered with glass as an angry mob stoned their train in Egypt.

The hostile audiences at Dundee during the 1922 elections were but one of the travails to dog both Clementine and Winston. In the early 1920s also there would be distressing family deaths—a child, a famous parent, a sibling's suicide, among others. The child was Marigold, their latest daughter, younger sister to Diana and Sarah—"Duckadilly" was the family nickname for her. Often beset by colds and sore throats, she was stricken with yet another sore throat while the children were at the seaside with a young French governess in August 1921. This time, though, the infection possibly was meningitis. Within days, with Winston and Clementine rushing to her side, her condition progressed fatally. She was not quite three years old.

Still to come was the following year's "rough go" at Dundee, and it surely didn't help that in 1920 the socialist Scottish Independent Labor Party had called for Winston's arrest and impeachment on grounds that—as the postwar secretary of state for war in Lloyd George's government—he supposedly had made war on the Soviet Union. And true, he briefly obtained grudging cabinet approval for prolonging the British share of the short-lived Allied intervention against the Bolsheviks in Russia.

In early 1921, meanwhile, he was appointed colonial secretary, and as such he produced a white paper acknowledging Jewish claims to Palestine as a national home but also recognizing Arab rights. Originally a supporter of continued British rule of Ireland, associated even with the hated "Black and Tan" auxiliary police sent over from England to impose firm, sometimes ruthless order, Churchill then played a key role in negotiations that resulted in the Irish Treaty of 1921.

The Dardanelles resurfaced once again in 1922 as a troublesome issue in British political affairs, with Winston typically urging a firm stand against apparent Turkish designs on the postwar Dardanelles neutral zone, which was now protected by a small British force. The public feared a possible war over the issue, and the coalition government in power at the time collapsed as a result. Thus Winston—and more pointedly Clementine—had to defend his parliamentary seat from Dundee just when he was stricken by appendicitis. This, then, was the lost election in which both had to endure insult and catcalls at their campaign stops, including Winston's last-minute appearances in a wheelchair.

Observed the *Observer*: "The circumstances were such that Mr. Churchill, on personal grounds, has, we believe, the generous sympathy of the country. Stricken by illness at the beginning of the struggle, late in the field, not fully recovered even then, yet assailed by Communist rowdyism, he was cruelly handicapped. The burden of the task fell on his devoted wife, but, in the dour circumstances of Dundee, the odds were too great."

More fruitfully, meanwhile, with Winston wearing two hats as both air minister and colonial secretary, the Churchills traveled to the Middle East together in March 1921. He attended conferences on the future of the volatile area, hoping that air power could be substituted for the more expensive army garrisons protecting the region's British mandates—Iraq among them. Clementine accompanied him despite a warning from the head of the Egyptian police that Winston would be "in the greatest danger," according to Jack Fishman's *My Darling Clementine*. Indeed, from the very moment of their arrival in Alexandria, local police had to protect them from "shouting, threatening demonstrators" lining the streets.

When Winston visited a nearby British air base, demonstrators outside the perimeter sent the local police into retreat until reinforcements arrived and fired into the crowd, wounding at least nine rioters. In the same incident, twenty policemen were injured by stones and rocks. "Although Winston had nothing to do with Egyptian affairs," Fishman noted, "as far as the country's nationalists were concerned, he represented Britain, and the danger to both him and Clementine grew with every hour they remained in the country."

When the couple slipped out of town by taking a secret route to the railroad station, "angry mobs" appeared along the rail line anyway. As the train rolled down the track, the demonstrators threw stones. "One large stone shattered the window beside Clementine, and glass spattered all over her. Miraculously she was unhurt. Her reaction was to calmly and meticulously brush the pieces of glass from her clothes. More stones hurtled through the broken window. Throughout the attack, Winston, unperturbed, sat smoking a cigar."

At a crossing, "more stones were flung at the windows," said Fishman. "Some tried to jump [onto] the train and cling to the doors. Window after window was smashed, glass splinters were everywhere." They were aboard King Faud's personal train—painted entirely white, locomotive included, it was easy to spot.

Crowds awaited the train in Cairo. As a result, Winston and Clementine were met outside the city by a party in cars and safely whisked to their hotel. When the train arrived at the railroad station, meanwhile, "mobs broke through police cordons to storm it." Despite all the excitement, the Churchills soon were off to see the pyramids and then the excavations at Sakkara, accompanied by Col. T. E. Lawrence—Lawrence of Arabia. The plan called for a two-and-a-half-hour ride by camelback, which started well enough . . . until Winston fell off, due to an improperly tightened saddle girth. Unhurt, he insisted upon finishing the long ride aboard his camel.

Returning to Cairo, they laid plans to visit the Holy Land, despite warnings from the British high commissioner for Palestine "of a plot to murder them with a bomb or shoot them somewhere along the route from Cairo to Jerusalem." Indeed, when their train stopped to allow them a visit to Gaza, a mob refused to back down before mounted police and, in fact, moved forward, ready to swamp the small party. Just then, Lawrence's voice rang out. "He spoke only a few words, and miraculously, the great crowd parted like the Red Sea, allowing the party to return to the train."

The return trip to London did not, however, guarantee safety and relaxation, so far as Winston's security officials were concerned. And concerned they were, for now the danger included Irish militants who had previously assassinated Gen. Sir Henry Wilson, former chief of the imperial staff, gunning him down in the street. During the following weeks, Fishman observed, "their home was guarded like a fortress, and Clementine was aware that the danger was not only to him, but also to herself and the children, for the stop-at-nothing Sein Feiners might decide to use the kidnapping of one of them as a weapon against Winston."

Thus "she daily watched her home searched from top to bottom for bomb plants. A Rolls-Royce car completely armored with half-inch steel plates and weighing two and a half tons, was placed at their disposal, and two Special Branch men— expert shots—were detailed to shadow the Rolls in a motorcycle and sidecar. . . . The Rolls took Winston to Whitehall by a different route every day, as a precaution against possible ambush."

One morning, in fact, traveling through Hyde Park, Winston spotted two men "standing back, almost in some bushes, by the side of the road." One of them appeared to signal a third man by a tree a hundred or so yards ahead. The detective guarding Winston that day quickly ordered the chauffeur, "No stopping—get your foot down and get going!" In seconds, the car slid harmlessly into the middle of the traffic, screened from the park by other vehicles.

As yet another safety precaution, a steel plate was fitted into the back of Winston's favorite bedroom chair, Fishman reported. Clementine covered it with a piece of tapestry. "Every night, Winston would place a fully loaded .45 Colt on this chair. 'If they come, Clemmie,' he said, 'they will receive a warm welcome, and not obtain a walkover.'"

Thankfully, he never had to use the pistol . . . and in fact he secretly arranged a meeting between the head of Unionist Northern Ireland and Sein Fein leader Michael Collins. So involved was Winston with the many negotiations that Lloyd George "gave him the task of guiding the Irish Treaty through Parliament," noted biographer Martin Gilbert in *Churchill: A Life*. The result was the creation of the largely Catholic Irish Free State with dominion status in the south of Ireland and of Protestant-dominated Northern Ireland, or Ulster, to the north as a part of the United Kingdom. The 1921 treaty did not immediately end age-old discord in Ireland, but the two side-by-side national entities have enjoyed a peaceful calm and dramatic economic growth in recent years.

As event piled upon event that tumultuous year, Winston's sixty-seven-year-old mother broke an ankle. Painful as it was, no one suspected the accident would bring about her death . . . until, upon her return to London, gangrene set in. Thus her leg was amputated above the knee.

With Jennie's much younger third husband, Montagu Porch, away on business in Africa, where he previously had lived, Clementine often sat with her mother-in-law during her recuperation. "Although Clementine and Lady Randolph had never been very close," wrote daughter Mary Soames in her biography of her mother, "understanding and a real affection had grown over the years." And now, "as Clementine witnessed the indomitable courage with which this vital, worldly woman faced the ordeal and pain of amputation, she felt a new admiration for [Jennie]."

For a time, Jennie's prospects for recovery looked good—so good that Winston cabled her husband on June 23 that "she was out of danger," Mary reported. But early in the morning of June 29, just six days later, "Lady Randolph had a sudden, violent hemorrhage." Alerted at his home just around the corner, Winston "came running through the streets." But too late, she was dead, or at least unconscious, never to recover by the time he reached her side.

Winston was devastated but said that his mother's passing was a loss, not a tragedy. "Her life was a full one," he said. "The wine of life was in her veins. Sorrows and storms were conquered by her nature & on the whole it was a life of sunshine."

Barely two months before, Clementine's younger brother Bill had died in a Paris hotel room, a suicide, reasons unknown. Overall, 1921 and 1922 were two very difficult years for both Winston and Clementine.

"Most Exciting Election"

If Winston (and of course Clementine) thought Dundee had been a difficult fight, Leicester would prove hardly any easier . . . and only slightly less rancorous.

And still ahead would be the Abbey division of Westminster, perhaps the most glamorous and most varied constituency of all. With Parliament suddenly dissolved in 1923, and Winston recovered from his appendectomy after a period of relaxation and painting on the French Riviera, he now attempted to regain a seat in Parliament by running as a Liberal Free Trader from Leicester West. This and the recent publication of the first volume of his history of the Great War, *The World Crisis*, gave his enemies opportunity to flay old wounds. In response to accusations of his responsibility for the Dardanelles disaster, he said: "The Dardanelles might have saved millions of lives. Don't imagine that I run away from it. I glory in it."

Also out on the hustings, Clementine took on a critic's comment that Winston couldn't speak for the working classes. Saying her blood "boiled" at that, she shot back, "With the single exception of Mr. Lloyd George, my husband has been responsible for the passing of more legislation for the benefit of the working classes than any other living statesman," Jack Fishman noted in his Clementine biography. She then ticked off Winston's efforts behind labor exchanges, mine safety rules, limited shop hours, and many other labor reforms. Rather than being essentially a military man, she argued, "I know that he is not that at all; in fact, one of his greatest talents is the talent of peace making."

Be that as it may, when Clementine and Winston arrived together at an election stop in Essex, "a brick smashed through the window of their car, narrowly missing injuring them both." In addition, "violent crowds did everything but rush them on the platform." All of this prompted Winston to declare it "the worst crowd I have ever seen in England in twenty-five years of public life."

After losing his Leicester bid by a wide margin, Winston decided to do battle in a by-election for a seat from the Abbey division of Westminster, home to some of London's best-known landmarks, including Buckingham Palace and the Houses of Parliament. Here, for Winston, was familiar and comfortable territory. By contrast, so far as is known, he never had visited the East Midlands city of Leicester prior to running for election there, but this colorful legislative district in London, as he pointed out in a letter to Clementine, encompassed more familiar features, such as Westminster Abbey, Victoria Station, part of Soho, Drury Lane, and Covent Garden.

Having run a distinctly lackluster campaign in Leicester, he turned on the dazzle for this plum seat. "He drove around the West End of London in a coach and four with a trumpeter on the box, a stunt organized by his new acolyte, Brendan Bracken, then aged twenty-three, who was to remain both close and faithful for the rest of his life," wrote Roy Jenkins in his Churchill biography. "The chorus girls of Daly's Theatre were said to have sat up all night addressing envelopes for Churchill's election address, although a kernel of truth may here have become exaggerated into an often repeated myth. Was it all night and was it the whole chorus line?" In any case, "The contest inevitably attracted tremendous attention, equally because of Churchill's fame and personality and because of its location."

For all its glamour, however, the "very cosmopolitan" Abbey Division also had its poor and downtrodden. And even here Clementine and Winston ran into occasional rowdyism. After one campaign meeting, Jack Fishman recorded, the driver of their car made a wrong turn into a cul-de-sac. "A large crowd closed in. A man jumped from the crowd onto the running board of the car, and the fight started." Winston's personal detective and bodyguard "sent several attackers sprawling." Fortunately, "the mob eventually gave way," but then it was discovered that Winston's aide Bracken, himself an MP, had been stabbed in the thigh during the fracas.

Still, the show had to go on, and Clementine, for her part, "organized and led an army of canvassers ranging from peeresses and beautiful society girls to theater chorus girls." On the day before the election, "a great car procession, with Winston and Clementine in the lead vehicle wound its way through every street in the constituency until the small hours of the morning, sounding their horns, whirring rattles and shouting 'Vote for Churchill!'"

When the count was made after the voting, Winston was down by a mere thirty-three votes. His side demanded a recount since the tally was so close. But close it would remain . . . Winston was still out of the running, this time by forty-three votes.

Even so, noted biographer Jenkins, running under the label Independent Anti-Socialist, Winston "had shown his vote-drawing power in a rich constituency, much better suited to him than Dundee or Leicester West." Thus, Winston could be somewhat philosophical about the Abbey campaign, which he, nearly ten years later, called "incomparably the most exciting, stirring, sensational election I have ever fought."

Additional note: It was in a general election held later that same year, 1924, that Winston finally found and won his lifetime constituency of Epping, later Woodford, composed of outer London suburbs and rural areas in West Essex, this time running as a Constitutionalist, a label that made him acceptable to local Conservatives. Thus, for Winston and Clementine, the roller-coaster 1920s rolled on . . . with a surprise move to Downing Street just ahead.

All from His Pen

Driving down to Kent from London one autumn day in 1922 with children Diana, Sarah, and Randolph, Winston proudly showed them a deteriorating, ivy-covered Victorian mansion set on a hillside—part of a gently sloping combe actually—with a magnificent view of the greenish Weald stretching on for miles beyond. Built of brick, the house was dark, romantic . . . but full of dry rot and in need of extensive remodeling. Sarah recalled, "[The house] was wildly overgrown and untidy, and contained all the mystery of houses that had not been lived in for many years."

After what she called "a complete tour" of house and grounds, Winston anxiously asked if they liked it. "Did we like it?" wrote a grown-up Sarah in *A Thread in the Tapestry*, "We were delirious." He told them he was thinking of buying it . . . by the time they returned to London, twenty-five miles away, he told them he already had bought it. And so, the "writing factory"—where he produced hundreds of articles, speeches, and the four-volume biography of his illustrious ancestor, the Duke of Marlborough, where he would spend his so-called Wilderness Years, where he informally would gather intelligence about Germany's rearmament, where he would write his history of World War II, where so much Churchillian legend would be conceived and fostered—came into the family's possession as a base, refuge, sanctuary, oasis for the next forty years. A final, real home for Winston especially.

It was the view across the Weald that captivated him, he said. And the setting certainly was captivating. "Fertile soil overlays the local ragstone, and the trees, mainly chestnut, beech and oak, grow to great size," commented Robin Fedden in a short history and guidebook about the home. "Their shadows at dawn and sunset are thrown across the combe." Woods, waters, and smooth pasturelands all combine here. Plus a spring, historically known as the Chart Well, fed the small lake just below the brooding manse. And so the name of Winston's new country home . . . Chartwell.

The only hitch was that Clementine never quite loved it as much as Winston. She did . . . initially, after a first viewing, reported daughter Mary. She did send Winston a note saying, "I can think of nothing but that heavenly tree-crowned hill—it is like a view from an airplane being up there." She added, "I do hope we shall get it—If we do I feel we shall live there a great deal & be very very happy." But then, Mary added, "a closer and more thoughtful inspection of the house and property quickly moderated her first impression. The house frankly appalled her."

It really did have major faults. Among others, the house had been built near the edge of the property and only eighty yards from a public road. Worse, a public right of way "ran right through the garden, slicing it inconveniently in two, and diminishing its privacy."

A high bank, steep, wooded, and replete with wild mauve and purple rhodo-dendrons—colors that Clementine "particularly disliked"—rose on the other side of the road. It thus dominated the house, screening it from the afternoon sun. And yet nothing could be done about it . . . the high bank wasn't their property.

The house had been built on the site of a much older structure—it was "damp, dreary and ugly." Worse, despite the "pleasing prospect to the south, look-ing over the Weald, the house had been built facing west." In short, Clementine quickly realized "that in order to correct (for to cure was impossible) the faults in-herent in the siting and aspect of the house, it would be necessary to all intents and purposes to rebuild it."

Winston, on the other hand, "was blind to the drawbacks and deaf to rea-son." Still, after voicing her objections, Clementine thought he had given up on the house. "But he had done no such thing: he had merely 'gone to ground' for the time being." When it turned out, months later, that he had made an offer on the house without further consulting her, "she was frankly devastated."

It wasn't that he didn't care about her feelings (even if he did make such a major commitment on his own); he, in fact, "longed for her approval over this major step in their life." He was convinced that she in time would see it his way. "Everything, he assured her, would be done to transform the house according to her wishes; difficulties and defects would melt away like the morning dew: his confidence and enthusiasm were boundless and touching."

But he was wrong. "In all the forty years Chartwell was to be their home, Clementine never came to love the place as did Winston. For her, the beauty of the valley, the eventual charm and comfort of the house, and the possibilities of the garden, never outweighed the worries and difficulties of running the house and property."

The bottom line is that Winston bought the old house and eighty acres in November 1922 for £5,000, then spent another £18,000 revamping it and the grounds, with the family finally occupying the house in 1924. Both Mary and Fedden indicate that the initial £5,000 did not come, as many biographers assert, from the first volume of his *World Crisis*. "More relevant is the fact that in 1921

Churchill inherited a considerable sum on the death of a relative, Lord Herbert Vane-Tempest," noted Fedden.

Meanwhile, misgivings or no, Clementine did her best to make it work out. "She worked like a Trojan to make it the home and haven for us all that [Winston] dreamed of," wrote Mary. "But it never acquired for her the nature of a venture shared; rather, it was an extra duty, gallantly undertaken, and doggedly carried through."

In the days, months, years ahead, Chartwell went through many changes. It housed a family of six (two adults and four children); it played host to a constant stream of guests ranging from world statesmen, past, present, and future, to actors such as Charlie Chaplin, and it served as a backdrop for Winston's most ambitious schemes, books, or other multifaceted projects. Here, too, he did much of his painting, raised pigs, built the children a tree house in a lime tree, even learned to build brick walls at the pace of one brick a minute.

Clearly, Chartwell was an expensive indulgence. "For life there to be easy and comfortable," Mary wrote, "eight or nine indoor servants were needed: two in the kitchen; two in the pantry; two housemaids; a personal maid for Clementine (who also did a good deal of family sewing); a nursery-maid; and an 'odd-man' (boots, boilers, dustbins)—these made up the tally of personnel necessary to run this enlarged manor house in the [nineteen] twenties. In addition there was a nanny or governess and always two secretaries, one being available for late-night work whenever necessary."

It was a "wonderfully agreeable and enriching life, enjoyed equally by Winston, his family and his guests," wrote daughter Mary, but it could only be supported by Winston's incredibly hard work, late hours, and "prodigious literary output." Indeed, as he once told a visiting Ethel Barrymore with a sweep of his hand, "All this is out of my pen!"

Additional note: Among the substantial changes that rendered Chartwell more livable for Winston and his entourage, architect Philip Tilden added a four-story wing at right angles to the east end of the house to accommodate Clementine's bedroom, a drawing room, and a dining room with fireplace and arched, floor-to-ceiling windows affording a gorgeous view of the sweeping lawn and lake below. The hoary ivy covering the old Victorian front was scrubbed away, while inside a new study with open-timbered ceiling appeared—now historic as Winston's working place. Not to be forgotten, meanwhile, the outdoor setting was considered so special, noted Fedden, that no less than six doors entered onto the garden.

"Hour of Polo"

Even before any family members moved into Chartwell, Winston's grandly refurbished country abode, his polo ponies took up residence in the manor's stables—and, yes, while still in his early fifties, he still occasionally played polo, the "Emperor of Games," as he called it. His introduction to polo had come at Sandhurst, but the greatest thrills probably were those he experienced in India with the 4th Hussars. He described the cavalry regiment's "first incursion into the Indian polo world" as no less than "dramatic."

The prevailing theory among the British then (the 1890s) in India, where modern polo originated, was that no team from a newly arrived regiment could be expected to win a "first-class" polo tournament. Or as Winston stated the case in his autobiographical *My Early Life*, "A regiment coming from home was never expected to count in the Indian polo world for a couple of years." For one thing, it took at least that long to gather a good string of polo ponies.

To break with this onerous tradition, the polo buffs among the 4th Hussars decided to pool their finances and, upon arrival in India, buy out the entire string of twenty-five polo ponies belonging to the Poona Light Horse, a well-established native regiment "strongly officered by [the] British." This was done "so that these ponies should form the nucleus around which we could gather the means of future victory in the Inter-Regimental Tournament."

A note here: not only were newly arrived regiments expected to bide their time before achieving significant polo victories, but "never in the history of Indian polo had a cavalry regiment from south India won the Inter-Regimental cup." The 4th Hussars were stationed at Bangalore . . . in south India, and they were determined to break this mold. If they should fail, it wouldn't be for lack of practice. As recorded in Winston's *Early Life*, the cavalry regiment's daily Bangalore routine included a late-afternoon session of polo. This would come only after early-morning parade, with drilling and maneuvering for ninety minutes, followed by a bath and then breakfast in the officers' mess. Next, there would be duty at the stables or the orderly room from nine to half past ten. The Englishmen then took shelter from the blazing sun during the midday hours, with a quick sojourn to the mess again for lunch, followed by nap time until five o'clock. "Now the station begins to live again," Winston wrote. "It is the hour of Polo. It is the hour for which we have been living all day long."

A real lover of the game, he played as much as possible. Then, "as the shadows lengthened over the polo ground, we ambled back perspiring and exhausted to hot baths, rest and at 8:30 dinner, to the strains of the regimental band and the clinking of ice in well-filled glasses." After that, a game of Whist or simply sitting and smoking in the moonlight before bed at half past ten or eleven o'clock. "Such was 'the long, long Indian day' as I knew it for three years; and not such a bad day either."

Less than six weeks after the regiment's arrival, its polo team was off to Hyderabad for the Golconda Cup Tournament. The 4th Hussars were unlucky enough in the first round to draw the Golconda team itself—"incomparably the best team in Southern India."

The great event began after a morning review staged by the local garrison, which was quite a spectacle. "At the end came a score of elephants drawing tandem-fashion gigantic cannon. It was then the custom for the elephants to salute as they marched past by raising their trunks and this they all did with exemplary precision." In the afternoon came the polo match.

"Tournaments in Hyderabad were a striking spectacle. The whole ground was packed with enormous masses of Indian spectators of all classes watching the game with keen and instructed attention. The tents and canopied stands were thronged with the British community and the Indian rank and fashion of the Deccan [the region south of the Narbada River]." The newcomer 4th Hussars were expected to be "easy prey" for the powerful Golcondas in the opening round, "and when our lithe, darting, straight-hitting opponents scored 3 goals to nothing in the first few minutes, we almost shared the general opinion." But not quite, it turns out. Instead, the upstart Hussars from Bangalore defeated the Golcondas 9-3. "On succeeding days we made short work of all other opponents, and established the record, never since broken [as of his book's publication in 1930] of winning a first-class tournament within fifty days of landing in India."

There were other tournaments in the months ahead, one of them an interregimental affair at Meerut and witnessed by Sir Robert Baden-Powell, future founder of the Boy Scouts organization but at the time a member of the host Meerut regiment. In his book *Indian Memories*, Baden-Powell recalled the spirited hijinks and speechmaking that occurred the final night of the affair. A memorable highlight was provided by one Winston Churchill:

> When all was over and a sigh of relief was going round, there suddenly sprang to his feet one of the members of the 4th Hussars' team, who said: "Now, gentlemen, you would probably like to hear me address you on the subject of polo!" It was Mr. Winston Churchill. Naturally, there were cries of: "No, we don't! Sit

down!" and so on, but disregarding all their objections, with a genial smile he proceeded to discourse on the subject, and before long all opposition dropped as his honeyed words flowed upon their ears, and in a short time he was hard at it expounding the beauties and the possibilities of this wonderful game. He proceeded to show how it was not merely the finest game in the world but the most noble and soul-inspiring contest in the whole universe, and having made his point he wound up with a peroration which brought us all cheering to our feet.

When the cheering stopped, one of his listeners commented that was enough of Winston for the evening, while others took him in hand and placed him under an overturned sofa, "upon which two of the heaviest were then seated, with orders not to allow him out for the rest of the evening." But Winston was far too resilient to be silenced so easily. Soon afterward, "he appeared emerging from beneath the angle of the arm of the sofa, explaining: 'It is no use sitting upon me, for I'm India-rubber,' and he popped up serenely and took his place once more in the world and the amusement that was going on around him."

As the evening's hijinks continued, the young officers staged polo pony races "over jumps made up of furniture round the billiard room" and conducted "a musical ride on camels in the ante room." But none of the foregoing "made such an impression on my memory as did the first great speech of the future First Lord [of the admiralty]." In addition, Baden-Powell often thought of the sofa incident when, "in politics or elsewhere," Winston gave proof that he was like India rubber and couldn't be kept down.

Such a tenacious attitude also was seen in his game of polo, which Patrick Thompson once described: "He rides in the game like heavy cavalry getting into position for the assault. He trots about, keenly watchful, biding his time. . . . Abruptly he sees his chance, and he gathers his pony and charges in, neither deft nor graceful, but full of tearing physical energy—and skillful with it too. He bears down opposition by the weight of his dash, and strikes the ball. Did I say strike? He slashes the ball."

It was the young Winston's preference for the cavalry rather than infantry that led to his discovery of the joys of polo, explained Barbara J. Langworth in the Churchill Centre's *Finest Hour* publication (vol. 72, 1991). Writing his mother from Sandhurst back in 1894, Winston said, "I hate the infantry—in which physical weaknesses will render me nearly useless on service & the only thing I am showing an aptitude for athletically—riding—will be no good to me."

It wasn't long before polo became such a consuming interest to him that he wrote in 1895: "It is the finest game in the world and I should almost be content to give up any ambition to play it well and often." In the same breath, though, he did more realistically concede "that will no doubt cease to be my view in a short time." In January 1898, while engaged in writing *The Story of the Malakand Field Force,* he wrote from India that a major polo tournament was coming up soon, "but it fills a vy different position in my mind to what it did last year."

Still, he played in the pending tournament—held at Meerut, it so happens. He and his fellow 4th Hussars took along a string of twenty-four ponies. They did well at first, but then lost to "the famous Durham Light Infantry," but only after "a gallant fight." Thus, he and his team "escaped without disgrace."

Ironically, it appears that Winston, from February 1898 onward, was forced to play hurt . . . with what amounted to a physical weakness. Possibly a contradiction to what he wrote in his *Early Life* book thirty years later, he wrote to his brother Jack that he suffered a shoulder dislocation (and sprained ankle) when he fell down some stairs at the home of Sir Pertab Singh, administrator of Jodhpore. "I am going to struggle on to the polo ground this afternoon," Winston wrote, "but I fear I shall not be able to play in the Tournament as my arm is weak and stiff and may come out again at any moment."

But in his book he indicated that he suffered the shoulder dislocation when he grasped an iron handhold while standing in an unsteady boat as it was docking at Bombay on the day of his arrival in India. After that, he wrote, he had to have his arm strapped to his side when he played polo.

Is this a contradiction? According to Barbara Langworth's article, "His letters at the time made no mention of [the Bombay] incident," and, "It was his habit to mention injuries." Whatever the case, in the February 1898 tournament at Jodhpore, "even with his arm immobilized," Winston and his team played so well, they advanced to the final round, in which they defeated the 4th Dragoon Guards, "making them Inter-Regimental Champions!"

Few of his team, he later reflected, "were destined to see old age," while he himself would become a "sedentary politician increasingly crippled by my wretched shoulder." Even so, he continued to play polo for another two decades or more after leaving India for his adventures in the Sudan and the Boer War. "Into his forties," Barbara Langworth noted, "polo still was very much a hobby with Churchill." Long after he and Clementine were married, his wife once commented, "Politics are absolutely engrossing to you . . . and now you have painting for leisure and polo for excitement and danger."

As late as 1925, Langworth noted, "Churchill's [House of] Commons team defeated the House of Lords." And it may have been a year later when, in an economizing measure, he suggested to Clementine that they rent out Chartwell while the family stayed in London and sell all the livestock *except* his two polo ponies. "The polo ponies were still sacred!" commented Langworth.

His last game, though, finally came . . . a long-planned match at Malta in early 1927 at the invitation of Admiral of the Fleet Sir Roger Keyes, while Winston was on a holiday cruise in the Mediterranean. They originally met in 1904, when Keyes and friends played on hired ponies at Wembley, as did members of Parliament, Winston among them. Now, twenty-three years later, after his last game ever, Winston wrote to Clementine from the Admiralty House at Malta: "I got through the polo without shame or distinction & enjoyed it very much."

Downing Street Abode

Could he be teasing? She, Winston, and the children all moving to that famous Downing Street address? "I had the greatest difficulty in convincing my wife that I was not merely teasing her," Winston said. And true, at only forty-nine—almost fifty—he had been named to his highest governmental position yet . . . to the second-highest governmental position in the land. And they would be living on Downing Street! But no, *not* at No. 10 Downing, the prime minister's official residence, but next door, at No. 11, the residence of the chancellor of the exchequer.

"'Number Eleven' was then a charming house for a family, with the discreetly shared use of the 'Number Ten' garden," explained Mary Soames. "Clementine loved the house, and always remembered with pleasure the five years they lived there."

With Chartwell remaining the "ideal solution for week-ends and holidays," the family's London home from late 1924 until the spring of 1929 was No. 11 Downing Street. In other words, this was the time when the three oldest children "were passing through their teens" and while Diana as the oldest "made her debut and 'did' the London season," added Mary.

Meanwhile, on the political front, Winston's tenure as chancellor would be best remembered for Britain's return to the gold standard under his stewardship, which was followed by economic woes and the disastrous general strike of 1926. "Churchill was not a financial innovator," notes the online *Columbia Encyclopedia*: "He basically followed conventional advice. Nevertheless, Churchill's decision to return the country to the prewar gold standard increased unemployment and was a cause of the general strike of 1926. He advocated aggressive action to end the strike, and thus earned the lasting distrust of the labor movement."

But once again, as in the case of the Dardanelles fiasco, perhaps the fault was not entirely his. Biographer Martin Gilbert recounted that Winston was "uneasy" with the treasury's decision "to go back to Gold." This, he said in January 1925, "favored the special interests of finance at the expense of the interests of production." Rather than buck the anti-gold advice of John Maynard Keynes, as many histories assert, Winston gave a dinner for the economist and "his own officials," noted Gilbert, "to bring to bear the best arguments possible against a return to gold."

The key factor in the end was the fact that Stanley Baldwin, "with his authority both as Prime Minister and a former Chancellor of the Exchequer, urged Churchill not to rock a boat which was already virtually launched, and to which the Bank of England was committed." And so Winston "gave way." Unfortunately, it was a decision he had to defend for years to come.

The general strike of 1926, noted Mary in her biography of Clementine, "brought Britain very near the precipitous edge of civil strife . . . [while] for nine days in May there was a nation-wide stoppage in transport, printing, heavy industry, gas and electricity." This stoppage included newspapers, and who should step into this vacuum but the writer-journalist-historian Winston as organizer and editor of the Conservative government's own hastily issued newspaper, called the *British Gazette*. "It was the only newspaper to be published during the period of the strike," added Mary's account, "and its circulation reached 2½ million."

Since it was the chancellor's duty to present an annual budget, traditionally carried into the House of Commons in a red briefcase called the Red Box, Winston also was known in his years as chancellor for long but erudite and sometimes spellbinding speeches in the Commons in support of the potentially dry financial statement. In his first such speech, noted Gilbert, Winston spoke for two hours and forty minutes—"showing, Baldwin told the King, 'that he is not only possessed of consummate ability as a Parliamentarian, but also all the versatility of an actor.'" As for Gilbert's assessment: "Lucidity, rhetoric, levity and humor, each had its part in his speech, the centerpiece of which was . . . insurance and pension schemes."

Ironically, one of Winston's first jobs as head of the treasury was "devising and financing a substantial extension of national insurance, the social reform he had been instrumental in creating fifteen years earlier, at the height of his Liberal activities." As further irony, he now would be working "closely" with the newly named minister of health, Neville Chamberlain, whom Winston would succeed as prime minister in 1940 to lead the nation through World War II.

Meanwhile, Chancellor Churchill continued in the late 1920s to be a star attraction in his House appearances. Presenting his fourth budget in May 1928, once again before packed public galleries and this time in a speech of three and a half hours, he "fascinated and amused the House," wrote Gilbert. All the more remarkable, he suddenly "was seen to sway," reported *Time* magazine on May 7, "and then to hurry from the House." Winston had the flu and thus missed the debate that followed his speech, which Baldwin called "almost the most remarkable of his career."

The chancellorship had come Winston's way as a surprise, thanks to Prime Minister Baldwin. First, as Winston made his way back through various political shadings to the Conservative Party, Baldwin had helped him to select Epping as a constituency. Then, with both Winston and the Conservative Party overall winning in 1926, Baldwin summoned Winston. Until then, Winston didn't believe he would be offered a post in Baldwin's government. Only "impeccable" Conservatives would be selected, he told a friend. Clementine, though, was hoping that perhaps he might be offered the ministry of health and urged him to take it.

As recounted by Gilbert, Baldwin asked, "Will you help us?" And Winston of course said yes, "if you really want me."

Would he take the chancellorship?

Would he! "'Will the bloody duck swim?' Churchill had wanted to reply. But, he later wrote, 'as it was a formal and important conversation I replied, "This fulfils my ambition. I still have my father's robe as Chancellor. I shall be proud to serve you in this splendid office."'"

Thus Winston not only would fill a major governmental seat his own father once held but five years later he would survive the parliamentary shellacking the Conservatives took in 1929 that sent Baldwin's Tory government packing . . . and left Winston entering a lonely decade with no governmental post other than his seat in a decidedly unfriendly House of Commons.

Anthill Disturbed

Years rolled by before Winston Churchill visited the United States for a third time. It had been such a long absence, World War I had come and gone, his good friend Bourke Cockran had died, his mother Jennie had died . . . indeed, America in the time since his last visit had seen its government pass from the assassinated William McKinley to Theodore Roosevelt and reside now in the care of Herbert Hoover, who was ill-fated in another way.

This time, traveling with son Randolph, brother Jack, and Jack's son Johnny for much of the time, Winston took a long and meandering path to Canada, the western United States, then the East Coast. This was not a lecture tour, but primarily a socializing and sightseeing trip, although Winston had lined up eager outlets for twenty-two articles on his travels in North America. And for one of his few talks, given before the Bond Club of New York, there would be the startling, onetime fee of roughly $12,500 provided by a British industrialist interested—as was Winston—in strengthening ties between Britain and America.

Before reaching New York, though, Churchill would be spending time with William Randolph Hearst at Hearst's castlelike San Simeon estate and in Hollywood—with Hearst's mistress, movie star Marion Davies, on hand. He also would be hobnobbing with comedian Charlie Chaplin and William McAdoo, the former U.S. treasury secretary who married President Woodrow Wilson's daughter Nell (who was twenty-six years his junior) in the White House and later ran for the Democratic nomination for president himself (but lost).

Quite fascinating to Winston were the towering, massive California redwoods . . . and a new roadside phenomena soon to be seen everywhere across the country. "Every dozen miles or so, rest camps—'motels' as they are called—have been built for the motorist population," he wrote. "Here simple and cheap accommodation is provided in clusters of detached cabins, and the carefree wanderers on wheels gather round great fires, singing or listening to the ubiquitous wireless music [radio]." After visits to Yosemite and Chicago, the Churchill party was on to New York, Washington, and Richmond, Virginia, with, to be sure, an occasional talk along the way. Winston often traveled by private railroad car, thanks to friends such as financier Bernard Baruch or steel magnate Charles Schwab. For Winston, the added highlights were a visit to Virginia's Civil War battlefields, where hundreds of thousands had died, and the Stock Market crash of 1929, which took place while he was in New York City, the epicenter of the financial earthquake.

As a keen student of military history, he loved the tours of the battlefields around Richmond, the former Confederate capital on the James River, and Fredericksburg on the Rappahannock. He was amazed, he noted in the *Daily Telegraph* (cited by Martin Gilbert in *Churchill and America*), "by the many traces of the fighting which still remained, more than seventy years after the Civil War."

Outside of Richmond, for instance: "The farm-houses and the churches still show the scars of shot and shell. The woods are full of trenches and rifle pits; the larger trees are full of bullets." He also noticed a "tattered" rebel flag still flown before the "War Museum" in Richmond and said, "If you could read men's hearts, you would find that they, too, bear the marks."

To really understand what happened in the Civil War, books and maps alone were insufficient for him. "You must see the ground; you must cover the distances in person; you must measure the rivers and see what the swamps were really like." After spending a day tramping the battlefields of the Fredericksburg area just a decade after World War I, Churchill was struck by the fact that quite possibly, on one local tract of land, "more soldiers have perished in an equal space than anywhere excepting [the WWI battlefields] Ypres and Verdun."

When he arrived in New York City, Churchill hoped to meet the latest Roosevelt to serve as governor of New York. But FDR sent word he would not be in the city during the two days Winston would be there—October 28–29. Regardless, with his usual flair for the dramatic, Winston now managed to be in the Big Apple on Black Thursday, October 29, the day of the Stock Market Crash of 1929.

Winston had dinner that night with Bernard Baruch. "He had gathered around his table forty or more of the leading bankers and financiers of New York," the visitor wryly noted later, "and I remember that when one of them proposed my health he addressed the company as 'Friends and former millionaires.'"

Although Winston himself lost money in the crash, his compensation for the articles he was writing helped to offset his losses. Quite unforgettable, however, was a grim event that supposedly occurred the day before Churchill was to sail for England. As he told the story later, "Under my very window a gentleman cast himself down fifteen stories and was dashed to pieces, causing a wild commotion and the arrival of the fire brigade." But that may not really have been the case. According to the Churchill Centre's Autumn 2007 issue of *Finest Hour*, a man jumped or fell from a high floor of the Plaza Hotel, where Churchill was staying, but this happened on October 24, not October 29 or 30, as Winston's statement seems to imply.

In striking contrast, regardless of the time or place of the apparent suicide, Churchill saw surprising "calm and orderliness" on the floor of the New York Stock Exchange after the crash of October 29 instead of the pandemonium he expected to see. "So there they were, walking to and fro like a slow motion picture of a disturbed ant heap, offering each other enormous blocks of securities at a third of their old prices and half their present value, and for many minutes together finding no one strong enough to pick up the sure fortunes they were compelled to offer." Even though he lost money in the crash, Churchill saw that his American hosts could take the long view, rather than dwell on the short-term pain.

Looking out a high window and seeing the teeming streets below, the towering New York structures, seeing all the great shipping activity on the nearby Hudson and East rivers, along with the industrial smokes and steam clouds pouring out of the nearby New Jersey shore, no one, he thought, "could doubt that this financial disaster, huge as it is, cruel as it is to thousands, is only a passing episode in the march of a valiant and serviceable people who by fierce experiment are hewing new paths for man and showing all nations much that they should attempt and much that they should avoid."

Thus, as Gilbert also noted, when Churchill sailed home this time, he had seen America "at its most magnificent and its most tormented."

Mustard for the Ham, Please

If Winston always seemed to stir up legend, myth, or simply a good story wherever he alighted in the world, his lengthy 1929 visit with Governor and Mrs. Harry F. Byrd of Virginia was no exception . . . and in fact was a mere warm up to his famous White House visit of Christmas 1941, right after Pearl Harbor. As is well known from the latter visit, he could be imperious, he could be demanding, and in both cases he was. If one hostess was glad to see him go, so was the other. If he allegedly sallied forth "in his underwear" in Richmond, he once greeted FDR in the altogether at the White House not that many years later.

In Richmond, at a formal dinner one night, he balked when served a proud local delicacy—Virginia ham. His granddaughter Celia Sandys recalled the incident and how she heard about it in a talk she gave in Richmond on November 3, 2007.

While researching her book *Chasing Churchill: The Travels of Winston Churchill*, she recalled, "I thought it would be impossible to meet anyone who had witnessed my grandfather's visit to America nearly eighty years before." But then she was "thrilled" to meet former U.S. Senator Harry Byrd Jr., "who does,

I believe, have the oldest living memory of my grandfather right here in Richmond."

This "delightful man," she added, "remembers with astonishing clarity how he met Winston Churchill. Senator Byrd [the younger] was fourteen when his father, Governor Harry Byrd, told him a very distinguished British politician was coming to stay at the governor's mansion. The young Harry saw the guest at close quarters and heard what his parents thought about him."

One of the younger Byrd's recollections, it seems, included the time Winston surprised his hosts at a "State dinner" one night by asking for mustard to go on the Virginia ham. "Mrs. Byrd sent to the kitchen for it, only to be told that there was none in the house. She apologized and said if he really wanted mustard she could send to the store." Instead of dismissing such an idea as being far too much trouble, he astonished his hostess by saying that would be fine, he would like the mustard. "And the whole party had to toy with their food while they waited for this apparent necessity."

As to another apparent necessity that often came up during the visit, "Prohibition was bypassed by serving Churchill brandy in his bedroom."

One morning after a formal dinner the night before, goes yet another story from Churchill's visit, Winston came downstairs from the private family quarters on the second floor in his bathrobe and, spotting a prominent attorney from Winchester who had been a guest at dinner the night before, flipped him a coin and said, "Here, Boy, fetch me the morning paper will you?" Of course he had not recognized his fellow dinner guest, but . . . 'tis also said, the paper indeed was fetched for him.

The allusion to a bathrobe echoes the notation by granddaughter Celia Sandys in her Richmond speech that Mrs. Byrd had "considerable reservations" about the guest from England. "Apart from the mustard saga," she said, "Churchill wanted not only to decide at what time meals should be served, but also to choose the menus. To add to her consternation he would walk around (one assumes upstairs) dressed only in his underwear."

According to another of Sandys's stories, an American woman attending a meal with Churchill corrected him when he asked if the chicken being served was from the leg or breast. In this country, she said, we say white meat or dark. Allegedly, Churchill followed up the next day by sending her a corsage with a note saying, "Pin this to your white meat." (See also page 347.)

Meanwhile, related Sandys, the Churchill visit with the Byrds dragged on for ten days, and as they waved good-bye to their guest, the first lady told the governor, "Don't you ever ask that dreadful man here again."

No Writer's Block Here

Which came first? The writer in Winston Churchill? Or the statesman and politician? Truly, the one fed the other and the other the one. The fact is, he began writing—mostly personal letters, to be sure—as a boy, a lad just sent off to school, not yet quite eight and constantly writing home to Mama and Papa. The further fact is, the early death of Lord Randolph in 1895 not only left Winston fatherless but also close to penniless at the age of twenty. Just ahead for the young Churchill was his short, impetuous, and often heroic military career as a cavalry officer just out of the Royal Military College at Sandhurst. He always had been fascinated by warfare and things military, but even then he knew this was not to be his permanent track. He did have hopes that a short burst of exciting military service would be a base for his start in politics, but it was as a soldier and correspondent going to the empire's frontiers that Winston first embarked on an amazing professional writing career that, in the end, won him the Nobel Prize in Literature (for all his writings in the aggregate, rather than for any one literary or historical work).

Never a slacker, and always needing money, he produced forty-two books amounting to sixty volumes before he finally put down his pen, to say nothing of his five thousand speeches and "pot boiler" articles for newspapers, magazines, and various journals. And all coming to a total of thirty million words (estimated by those in the know).

Politics, it seemed would have to wait . . . but only until 1900, when he first followed his father's footsteps by winning election to Parliament. Thus the writing came before the politics. And once started, he was on a fast track and rarely if ever flagged. "He never had writer's block," Richard M. Langworth, editor of the Churchill Centre's quarterly journal *Finest Hour*, once observed in a speech at the Boston Athenaeum. "When he went to work, usually late at night, he shut himself up in his study, banned loud noises, hired teams of stenographers, and arranged his papers at a stand-up desk. And there, padding up and down in his slippers, he reeled off prose in the small hours."

So accustomed was Churchill to his fast pace, he once told an audience, a bit facetiously to be sure, "I'm going to give a long speech tonight; I haven't time to prepare a short one."

The serious fact is that even as a statesman and politician in later years, he always wrote his own speeches, noted grandson Winston S. Churchill in *Finest Hour*, which was named for Winston's "Finest Hour" speech after the fall of France in 1940. For his inspiring speeches of World War II, certainly Winston's own finest hour, he "would regularly devote an hour of preparation to each minute of delivery," wrote the grandson, author of *The Great Republic*, a collection of his grandfather's writings about America. "Thus it was not unusual for him to spend 30–40 hours preparing a single speech." Echoing Langworth's depiction of Churchill the writer, his grandson also noted that after World War I, at the start of the future prime minister's so-called Wilderness Years, he turned his country home of Chartwell in Kent County "into a literary factory where the lights would burn to a late hour every evening."

Added his grandson: "He would employ a team of up to half a dozen 'gentleman-researchers,' for the most part Oxford graduates, who would work for him part-time, preparing material and doing research work. In addition he had a raft of half a dozen secretaries, at least two of whom would remain on duty until he retired for the night."

The younger Winston cited the recollections of Grace Hamblin, who began work as one of Churchill's secretaries in 1930. "She recalls that even when my grandfather had dinner guests, which was most evenings, the guests would be encouraged to leave or go to bed by about 11 p.m. when the two secretaries on the 'late shift' would be summoned. Work would continue until two or three in the morning. Indeed it was by burning the midnight oil that he achieved such a phenomenal output, doing his best work in the quiet hours of the night when there were no interruptions, such as visitors or the telephone to distract him."

As a boy of five or six, Churchill's grandson was exposed to the trappings of Churchill the Writer, especially when spending school holidays at Chartwell.

At about 9 each morning, I would make my way through my grandfather's study on the first floor, with its high vaulted ceiling and old oak beams, his works of reference on the shelves and galley-proofs of his latest book set out on his upright desk where he would stand to make his corrections, and through to his small bedroom beyond. There, through the thick haze of cigar smoke I would find the venerable Grandpapa. He would be propped up in bed, wearing a quilted silk bed-jacket. Before him was a bed-table [tray], cut out to accommodate the shape of his ample belly! To his right, on a narrow book-shelf would stand a weak whiskey and soda, from which he would take the occasional sip. While puffing one of his Havana cigars, usually a Romeo y Julieta, he would be dictating a speech or a letter to one of the secretaries.

Never to be forgotten, however, is the fact that the writer also became the politician and statesman, that when he wrote history, as he did, it often was history that he had experienced and indeed had made himself. Didn't he once say (as Langworth noted in his Boston speech), "It will be found much better by all Parties to leave the past to history—especially as I propose to write that history myself." And about his World War II memoirs, he proclaimed, "This is not history, this is my case."

The fact is, noted Langworth: "Writing and statesmanship went hand in hand, for Churchill lived politics and writing furthered his political aims. The soaring oratory he made famous in World War II occurred because Britain was led by a professional writer."

Impact of Buckshot

The next time Winston Churchill visited the land of his mother's birth, just two years after his last U.S. sojourn, he brought along Clementine, their daughter Diana—and a bodyguard, thanks to perceived threats posed by Sikh terrorists based in San Francisco. But the real menace—to life and vitally needed income, as events turned out—was Mario Contasino's taxi on Fifth Avenue in New York City on the night of December 13, 1931.

The visit was to be a serious lecture tour, with expectations of thousands of dollars for forty lectures, plus articles for the *Daily Mail* that also would pay a handsome fee. The bodyguard accompanied the Churchills for fear of some threatening action by Sikhs who wanted an independent nation established in India.

After arriving in New York by ship on December 11, 1931, Winston and family hardly had checked into their rooms at the Waldorf-Astoria Hotel before he was off to Worcester, Massachusetts, to deliver a talk that very night on the need for close Anglo-American ties. As another way of expressing the thought, he also called for unity and cooperation among the world's English-speaking peoples.

Two nights later, after having dinner at the Waldorf, Winston received a call inviting him to drop by Bernard Baruch's house on Fifth Avenue that evening to meet a few mutual friends. Going without his address book, Winston set off alone in a taxi but found he couldn't recognize Baruch's home as the driver drove up and down Fifth Avenue.

Exasperated to the core, frustrated also by an innovation called traffic lights—not yet seen in London—he finally, after nearly an hour of searching, jumped from his cab on the Central Park side of Fifth Avenue and started across the famous New York thoroughfare toward what he thought was Baruch's house on the opposite side. That's when he and Mario Contasino's taxi met—collided, that is, with the taxi coming out the winner despite Winston's growing bulk of two hundred plus pounds.

"A man's been killed," one onlooker shouted. Winston himself thought (for the umpteenth time in his life, it would seem), "Perhaps it is the end."

The taxi had been traveling at a hardy thirty to thirty-five miles per hour. Even so, Winston's injuries were not life-threatening, although painful and tough on the overall system of a fifty-seven-year-old man. Either way, he spent eight days in the hospital and then another two weeks in bed at the Waldorf. While invalided, though, he made up for a portion of his canceled lectures by dictating a story on his accident for the *Daily Mail* back in London . . . for a handsome fee. He, Clementine, and Diana then took time for more rest and recuperation in the Bahamas for three weeks.

It had been quite a scare, to be sure. Suffering severe shock and a concussion, he sustained ugly, painful bruises on his right arm, chest, and leg, plus lacerations of his forehead and nose that had to be stitched. How had it happened? Habit, he said . . . habit played him a deadly trick.

I got out of the cab somewhere about the middle of the road and told the driver to wait. Then I instinctively turned my eyes to the left. At about 200 yards away were the yellow headlights of a swiftly approaching car. I thought I had just time to cross the road before it arrived and I started to do so in the prepossession— wholly unwarranted—that my only dangers were from the left. The yellow-lighted car drew near, and I increased my pace toward the pavement, perhaps twenty feet away. Suddenly upon my right, I was aware of something utterly unexpected. I turned my head sharply. Right upon me, scarcely its own length away, was what seemed a long dark car rushing forward at full speed. I thought quickly, I am going to be run down and probably killed. Then came the blow. I felt it on my forehead and across the thighs. But besides the blow there was an impact, a shock, a concussion indescribably violent, I do not understand why I was not broken like an eggshell or squashed like a gooseberry. I certainly must be very tough or very lucky or both. I did not lose consciousness for an instant.

He was taken to the nearby Lenox Hill Hospital, where both Clementine and Baruch were on hand when he opened his eyes. How close was he to the right address, he immediately asked Baruch. "Not within ten blocks," was the reply.

Before going to the Bahamas in early January, Winston asked his friend Professor Frederick Lindemann, also his scientific and economic adviser, for an estimate of the impact he had suffered. Part of the answer received by telegram: "Collision equivalent to falling thirty feet onto pavement equal six thousand foot pounds energy equivalent stopping ten pound brick dropped six hundred feet or two charges buck shot point blank range."

Additional note: Returning to New York on January 25, Winston resumed his hectic lecture tour. Taxi driver Contasino attended Winston's first lecture, given in Brooklyn before a crowd of two thousand on January 28. In it, Winston warned that the English-speaking peoples faced a new tyranny and opponent in the form of the Soviet Union.

After that, rushing from one city to another, Winston went nonstop, recalled Phyllis Moir, a secretary working with him at the time. "It [the tour] means revising speeches in taxicabs and dressing out of suitcases," she recalled. "It means always being the social lion for the lion hunters, however tired and out of sorts one may feel. It means eating caterers' meals. It means living by a train schedule."

Through it all, Winston accepted the hardships and steamed ahead, with no slackening of his pace. Furthermore, he never gave the same speech twice. "After each engagement he would think of a number of improvements and would get to work the next morning on the text of his address," Moir noted. "He polished and re-polished his speeches endlessly so that they seemed to grow considerably in scope and depth."

He returned often to the themes of English-speaking peoples and the menace posed by the Soviet Union. He predicted a major war would be coming soon, but urged his American listeners to be of good cheer despite the economic doldrums afflicting their country . . . and indeed the world.

He fought on, you might say, despite episodes of sore throat, laryngitis, threats against his life, and his car being stoned in Detroit. In one speech, he cited a quote from his friend Bourke Cockran, who had died in 1923. He also visited Rochester, New York, where his American grandfather Leonard Jerome once lived. Asked somewhat facetiously if he ever would become an American citizen in order to serve as president of the United States, he said (also somewhat facetiously): "There are various little difficulties in the way. However, I have been treated so splendidly in the United States that I shall be disposed, if you can amend the Constitution, seriously to consider the matter."

Meanwhile, traveling and lecturing, he had a second audience with President Herbert Hoover in Washington, he again visited Richmond and its Civil War battlefields, escorted this time by Robert E. Lee's famous biographer, Douglas Southall Freeman, and he crammed in a tour of Gettysburg, where he proved so knowledgeable about the three-day battle of 1863 that he found himself correcting the professional tour guides from time to time. While in Washington he was presented to the House of Representatives . . . a prelude of sorts to his future address to a joint session of Congress in 1941, just ten years later.

While he was staying at the British Embassy, he and British ambassador Sir Robert Lindsay made quite a picture together, as described by traveling secretary Phyllis Moir. "These two made the oddest contrast," she recalled. "The immensely dignified diplomat standing extremely ill at ease at the foot of the old fashioned four poster and the Peter Pan of British politics sitting up in bed, a cigar in his mouth, his tufts of red hair as yet uncombed, scanning the morning newspapers."

All this time—and in his two previous visits—Winston received extensive press coverage. As early as 1908, for that matter, the *New York Times* devoted two columns to his marriage to Clementine. Without a doubt, to Americans of all stripes, he was one of the best known of all Englishmen.

And he kept pounding on the theme of what miracles America and England working together could achieve. Speaking in Atlanta, Georgia (and introduced there by the governor of Georgia), he said: "Whatever the pathway of the future may bring, we can face it more safely, more comfortably, and more happily if we travel it together, like good companions." Certainly the two countries had their "quarrels" in the past, but even then "great leaders on both sides were agreed on principle," he said. For the future, then, "Let our common tongue, our common basic law, our joint heritage of literature and ideals, the red tie of kinship, become the sponge of obliteration of all the unpleasantness of the past."

Not long after uttering those words, in mid-March 1932, he was on his way back to England. There, he would be in a political wilderness while in America that other Roosevelt, Franklin Delano, would be elected president in 1932, defeating Herbert Hoover. In Germany, the Nazis would win a majority in the Reichstag, as prelude to Adolf Hitler's ascension to chancellor in 1933. From the very start, Winston liked the New Deal and FDR's vigorous approach to solving the problems of the Depression. From now on also, however, Winston would be alarmed by the direction Germany was taking.

As he feared, a war, the worst ever, was looming.

Meet Hitler?

If World War II adversaries Adolf Hitler and Winston Churchill might possibly have been only a few miles apart while stationed in the trenches of the western front during World War I, they came even closer to "meeting" just one other time in their respective lives. That potentially history-making occasion came in 1932 at a hotel in Munich, Hitler's "hometown" in the years (and very last months) before he became chancellor of Germany in 1933.

During World War I, Hitler was a front-lines runner repeatedly sent racing, under fire, across the barren landscape of the trenches with messages. He received the Iron Cross for his bravery, and he was badly wounded and almost blinded by gas during the war. After slowly recovering from his injuries and severe depression, the Austrian-born would-be artist was sent by the postwar German authorities to infiltrate a suspect political group in Munich by posing as an enthusiast. That group was the fledgling Nazi party, and instead of betraying its secrets and goals, he became an enthusiast for real, its leader, and then Nazi Germany's leader, or Führer.

Winston Churchill also was notable for his bravery in combat, though never wounded, and he, too, suffered from depression. He was an amateur artist of some note who, after many trials and tribulations, eventually worked his way into the leadership of his country during World War II . . . which, so far as Britain was concerned, was waged chiefly against Hitler's Nazi Germany.

Married and a family man, Winston also was a great many other things that Hitler's twisted mind never could aspire to, among them Nobel Prize–winning author and historian. It was in that role that Winston traveled to Belgium, Holland, and Germany, including Munich and Bavaria, in the late summer of 1932, while out of ministerial office, to carry out research for his four-volume biography of the Duke of Marlborough. It was his intention, wrote biographer Martin Gilbert, "to see the scenes of Marlborough's military victories."

Catching up with Winston at various points of his tour were his good friend and scientific adviser Frederick Lindemann (an Oxford professor and later Lord Cherwell) and military historian Lt. Col. Ridley Pakenham-Walsh, plus family members Clementine, Sarah, and Randolph, the latter by now himself a young journalist. With Winston on his way in September to visit the scene of Marlborough's famous victory at the battle of Blenheim (which eliminated Bavaria as a factor in the 1701–14 War of the Spanish Succession), his entourage stopped for three days at the Regina Hotel in Munich. Here, early Hitler spokesman Ernst "Putzi" Hanfstaengl, a tall and gangly German American acquaintance of Randolph, joined them and tried to arrange a meeting between Winston and Hitler.

As later related by Winston, Putzi first entertained them by playing a piano in the hotel restaurant. He played and sang "many tunes and songs in such remarkable style that we all enjoyed ourselves immensely," Winston commented, adding that Putzi "seemed to know all the English tunes that I liked."

Hanfstaengl then suggested a meeting between Winston and Hitler. "He said I ought to meet him, and that nothing would be easier to arrange. Herr Hitler came every day to the hotel about 5 o'clock, and would be very glad indeed to see me." At that early date, Winston noted, he had "no national prejudice against Hitler. . . . I knew little of his doctrine or record and nothing of his character. I admire men who stand up for their country in defeat, even though I was on the other side. He had a perfect right to be a patriotic German if he chose." But Winston said he couldn't understand why Hitler was so anti-Jewish. Hanfstaengl later recalled, Winston "taxed me about Hitler's anti-Semitic views."

By Martin Gilbert's account, "Hitler made no appearance that night." The next day, Putzi "again tried to persuade him to meet Churchill, but in vain." Argued Hitler, "What part does Churchill play? He is in opposition [in Parliament] and no one pays any attention to him." To which Hansftaengl replied, "People say the same about you."

Just a few months later, Hitler was chancellor of Germany. Winston, in the meantime, had visited the Blenheim battlefield as planned but then fell dangerously ill with paratyphoid fever. "Too ill to be brought back to England, he spent two weeks in a sanatorium in Salzburg," wrote Gilbert. "But after a few days he began dictating from his sick bed twelve articles for the *News of the World*, which had commissioned him to retell 'The World's Great Stories.'"

Home again by September 25, Winston resumed work on his life of Marlborough, considered by many to be a classic and his best historical effort. He was helped in those days by historian and aide Maurice Ashley, who spent hours poring through documents at Marlborough's Blenheim Palace. Also fully engaged in the project was Winston's faithful secretary Violet Pearman—"Mrs. P" to intimates of the Churchill household.

Two days after returning from the Continent, however, as he and Ashley were walking the grounds at Chartwell, Winston collapsed. He recovered in due time (after a spell in a London nursing home). Typically, he had pushed too hard, too soon.

Additional note: Back in Germany, Putzi Hanfstaengl's fortunes tended to rise and fall at the whim of his boss, Hitler. By the time CBS radio correspondent William L. Shirer, author of *Berlin Diary*, arrived in Nazi Germany in 1934, Putzi was settled in as the official government spokesman dealing with the foreign press. In his book, Shirer first blamed Putzi for expelling an unfriendly American writer (rapier-witted Dorothy Thompson), then described him as "an immense, high-strung, incoherent clown who does not often fail to remind us that he is part American [on his mother's side] and graduated from Harvard." Even so, Shirer said, British and American correspondents "rather like him despite his clownish stupidity." It wasn't long before Putzi fell out of Hitler's favor and fled the country. Later, during the war, he was held in England as an enemy alien and then sent to help the Americans develop a psychological profile of Hitler.

Long Time Apart

Clementine always loved traveling and sightseeing, her daughter Mary noted. But she and Winston often went off in different directions . . . in short, apart. Still, this proposed trip of five long months on her own, without Winston, to the home of the Komodo dragon on the far side of the globe, would be an unprecedented experience for them both. Especially since, briefly, another man would enter the picture. Just fifty years of age, Clementine "was still exceptionally beautiful, and slender and graceful," wrote Mary. He, the other man, was younger, "suave, good-looking, charming and cultivated—it is hardly surprising to relate that Clementine fell romantically in love with him."

And much of the time, Winston's letters from home were full of news about the monster digger he had engaged to turn the peninsula in their bottom lake at Chartwell into an island . . . only the digger, prosaically enough, became stuck in the mud and was a center of attention for weeks instead of the few days originally planned. Interesting perhaps, but hardly the stuff of romance.

The potentially disastrous travel adventure began with the Churchills' friend Walter Guinness (Lord Moyne, a former financial secretary to the treasury) and his oceangoing yacht, the *Rosaura*. After both Winston and Clementine enjoyed a cruise aboard the yacht during the summer of 1934, Guinness invited them to join in a cruise to the Dutch East Indies (Indonesia), where he proposed to capture one or more large monitor lizards known as Komodo dragons for the London Zoo. "Winston saw how much Clementine longed to go," wrote daughter Mary, "but he himself did not really enjoy sea travel for long periods of time." In addition, he was still "engrossed" in the successive volumes still under way of his biography of his illustrious ancestor, the Duke of Marlborough. "He was loath to let her go so far, for so long without him. But perhaps he recognized that again and again in their life together her plans or preferences had been subordinated to his needs and wishes, and here was a chance for her which would not be likely to occur again."

Thus, she would go—on a months-long journey destined to become "one of the great events of Clementine's life." To be sure, she kept up with Winston and the family frequently, and he with her—he both by personal letter and by twelve issues of "long, minutely detailed 'Chartwell Bulletins'" providing the latest news of the household as well as a recitation of parliamentary activities.

Naturally, the longer and farther away Clementine sailed, the slower the mail was in reaching either of them. It already had been a wrench the day—December 17, 1934—Clementine bid farewell to Winston and family at Victoria Station in London for the start of her immense journey, first by train across Europe to Messina to join the yacht. Daughter Mary noted that Clementine had no idea just then that her "odyssey through tropical seas and coral-fringed islands" was "a sunshine interlude before the darkening, anxious ending of the decade ushered in a period when, yet again, the utmost effort and commitment would be demanded of her [that is, World War II]."

As the yacht steamed eastward, meanwhile, with Clementine happily settled aboard since leaving Sicily, the only noncrew were herself, Lord Moyne's cousin Lee Guinness, his wife, and the suave Terence Philip, "a very personable and agreeable man in his forties" who worked in an art gallery back in London. The rest of the party would be joining them in Rangoon. "But," added Mary, "from Messina to Rangoon, a distance of some 6,000 miles and twenty days' steaming, the Guinnesses, Terence Philip and Clementine were *a quartre*, and they all combined most agreeably."

Still, letters between Winston and Clementine flowed back and forth, thanks to the yacht's ports of call. On New Year's Day, she wrote that she was thinking of him, loved him . . . and wished they both were "young again." It took three weeks for a reply to reach her, but it, too, was a heartwarming love letter.

At Chartwell, Winston was continuing his personal wall building, laying the bricks himself of course, but the big news was the arrival of the mechanical digger for work on a ditch north of his swimming pool (which he created himself). Most important, though, the monster machine would carve an island out of the peninsula in their bottom lake. The two jobs should take no more than a week and cost only £25, Winston assured her. A month later, however, the digger was still engaged in creating the island. Almost two months later, it was bogged down after getting itself "into a hole." By March 2, Winston doubted he would "get out of it under £150." The monster digger had "wallowed himself into an awful pit [and] it became necessary to bring [in] four hydraulic jacks." Finally, the monster was out of its hole and practically finished, "though there is still a fortnight's tidying up for five men."

At Singapore, at the tip of Malaya, where the British maintained a major naval base (destined to be attacked and captured by the Japanese just a few years later), Clementine not only looked over the docks but dropped in to the principal bookshop to see how Winston's books were doing. "They said that the compressed *World Crisis* [his book about World War I] had gone very well," she reported. "The second volume of *Marlborough* was doing better than the first."

But now, bookstores, city streets, big guns . . . all such trappings of civilization soon dropped behind as the yacht plugged on, to make short stops in such primitive climes as Borneo and coastal New Guinea.

From the largely unknown estuary of the Eilanden River, she wrote, "This is the 'genuine article!' uncharted seas, unexplored territory, stark naked savages." After the party paid a more civilized visit to Australia, the disconcerting day came when Clementine found herself separated from her companions on an uninhabited island populated by large, dog-sized tuatara lizards. Soaked by a sudden downpour, exhausted, and lost, she was eyeballed for long minutes by one of the lizards . . . which, after a time, moved off. Her companions then found her, and all was well again.

The voyage continued . . . until they reached their goal, the island of Komodo, home of Lord Moyne's intended prey, the really large "dragon" lizards. As a result of a week's stay on the island, he returned with two Komodos for the London Zoo, with both surviving until 1946.

As Winston later learned, Lord Moyne and party didn't reach Komodo Island until March 18, 1935. "For all this time," Mary dutifully noted, "and on all these thrilling expeditions to strange peoples and enchanted islands, Clementine's constant companion was Terence Philip." Romantic settings, a romantic interlude . . . what did it all mean in the long run? Nothing lasting, apparently. Their relationship, said Mary, "was like a fragile tropical flower which cannot survive in greyer, colder climes." Once Clementine returned home, her "real life, and the one and only great love in it, claimed her back entirely." Terence visited Chartwell a few times, then "came no more." He died in New York City, where he worked at another art gallery.

Meanwhile, just before turning for home, Clementine and party would spend two days in Bali, which she quite naturally described as "enchanted." It was a place, she wrote (with no commas), where the inhabitants work two hours a day, and the rest of the time "play musical instruments dance make offerings in the Temples to the gods attend cock fights & make love!" After Bali and Java's capital of Batavia, as Winston joyfully noted, her "nose" was turned homeward. Saying, "Now on yr return journey you will be meeting yr mails, instead of them lagging behind," he decorated his letter with a pig labeled "On guard & waiting." In her reply, she signed off, "Your loving Homing Clemmie."

All this time Winston not only had been fighting the battle of the digger in the lake but also, in Parliament, against the government's India bill. But overarching all of his concerns by now, noted daughter Mary, "was the growing might of Nazi Germany." As he wrote to Clementine about the time the yacht reached Komodo Island, "the political sensation of course is the statement by Hitler that his air force is already as strong as ours," which, Winston said, "vindicates all the assertions that I have made."

And still Britain did little to prepare for war. Still Winston was sounding warnings again and again as Clementine returned on April 30 to England and reality . . . just in time, not yet for war, but for the Silver Jubilee of George V and Queen Mary.

Oils to the Rescue

From her childhood days, Winston's daughter Mary once wrote, "I took it for granted that painting was a grafted-in part of my father's life—at Chartwell painting had to fight it out with bricklaying—but both occupations had their share of the hours carved from full-time politics (in or out of office) and writing (mostly at night), the profession by which he kept us all." Anytime a holiday trip loomed, Lady Soames added in her foreword for the book *Winston Churchill: His Life and His Paintings* by David Coombs with Minnie Churchill, the "impedimenta" of painting piled up in the front hall at Chartwell, ready to go with the master of the house, "and on his return home, it was a treasured treat for the stay-at-homes to have displayed the holiday pictures for them." Not only a family treat, many of Winston's paintings were, in fact, quite impressive from a professional view.

But it was the meaning of painting to Mary's father on a more personal level that really mattered . . . just how much, she did not realize until she was in her sixties. In the writing of her *Winston Churchill: His Life as a Painter*, she at last came "to realize what painting had really meant to my father."

For Winston, painting was an accidental discovery made "fortuitously and suddenly, at a moment of disaster in his political career after the Dardanelles catastrophe (when as my mother would much later tell his biographer Sir Martin Gilbert, 'I thought he would die of grief')." Painting was to be a happy discovery that "opened up to him a complete new world of color, light and shade, or proportion and perspective," she wrote. Not only that, "but even more, this compelling occupation, I came to understand, nourished deep wells."

It all began, Winston once explained in a two-part article for *Strand* magazine, soon after he had lost his admiralty post in 1915, in the aftermath of the Dardanelles fiasco. Since he briefly would remain in the cabinet and in Prime Minister Asquith's war council, he wrote, "In this position I knew everything and could do nothing." He added:

> The change from the intense executive activities of each day's work at the Admiralty to the narrowly measured duties of counselor left me gasping. Like a sea beast fished up from the depths, or a diver too suddenly hoisted, my veins threatened to burst from the fall in pressure. I had great anxiety and no means of relieving it; I had vehement convictions and small power to give effect to them. I had to watch the unhappy casting-away of great opportunities, and the feeble execution of plans which I had launched and in which I heartily believed. . . . And then it was that the Muse of Painting came to my rescue . . . and said, "Are these toys any good to you? They amuse some people."

A bit more succinctly stated, Winston and Clementine had rented the Hoe farm in Surrey for the summer of 1915. They and their three children (this was before Mary appeared on the scene) spent weekends there, often with brother Jack's wife Gwendeline ("Goonie") and their two children (John George and Peregrine) while Jack served as a major in the British army. "One June day at Hoe Farm," related David Coombs with Minnie Churchill, "Gwendeline sat in the garden sketching in watercolors. Winston, passing by deep in thought, noticed this and after watching for a few minutes borrowed her brush. Taking her son John George's painting box, Gwendeline encouraged Winston to paint a picture." And with that, Winston the painter was off and running.

Almost.

"He soon decided he wanted to experiment further by using oils and Clementine rushed into [the nearby village of] Godalming to buy whatever materials she could, without realizing the need for turpentine—hence Churchill found it virtually impossible initially to paint with the oils."

Back in London, however, and now advised by Sir John Lavery and his wife Hazel, both of them friends, neighbors, and themselves artists, Winston made the appropriate purchases: an easel, palette, brushes and paints, canvasses . . . and turpentine! "He began to paint in oils. His first subjects were exterior and interior views of Hoe Farm."

As Winston recalled the key moment for readers of *Strand*, he was "gingerly" applying a bean-sized dab of blue onto his virginal, snow-white canvas, when:

at that moment the loud approaching sound of a motor-car was heard in the drive. From this chariot there stepped swiftly and lightly none other than the gifted wife of Sir John Lavery. "Painting! But what are you hesitating about? Let me have a brush—the big one." Splash and the white, frantic flourish on the palette—clean no longer—and then several large, fierce strokes and slashes of blue on an absolutely cowering canvas. Anyone could see that it could not hit back. No evil fate avenged the jaunty violence. The canvas grinned in helplessness before me. The spell was broken. The sickly inhibitions rolled away. I seized the nearest brush and fell upon my victim with berserk fury.

I have never felt any awe of a canvas since.

As Winston's life and career continued to evolve, he then painted scenes from "Plug Street," where he was stationed on the western front as an infantry officer for nearly six months. He moved on to portraits, the Laverys among his subjects, along with Group Capt. Jack Scott, "who in 1919, when acting as co-pilot, saved Churchill's life when the plane he was flying crashed at Croydon Aerodrome." Upon his return from the front, determined to reenter the political fray, Winston bought Lullenden Manor in East Sussex as a safe haven for Clementine and the children from the Zeppelin raids on London. It, too, became a subject of his early paintings, by this time considered the perfect antidote for his spells of the "Black Dog," or depression.

Soon, too, Winston painted the Pyramids while attending the 1921 conferences in Cairo on the future of the Middle East. He by now was painting landscapes, seascapes, mountainscapes, even cityscapes, all seen on his travels. Of course he painted scenes, both interior and exterior, from his birthplace, Blenheim Palace, and from his beloved home of forty years, Chartwell. He continued painting all his life, up to five hundred canvasses it has been estimated, until he simply was too infirm to continue. Prior to that, his painting halted only during World War II—except for one painting, which he gave to wartime ally Franklin Delano Roosevelt.

Notable for their composition and color, Winston's paintings often went well beyond the typical amateur's work. His good friend John Lavery wrote: "We have often stood up to the same motif, and in spite of my trained eye and knowledge of possible difficulties, he, with characteristic fearlessness and freedom from convention, has time and time again shown me how I should do things. Had he chosen painting instead of statesmanship, I believe he would have been a great master with the brush."

In 1921, the year he and Clementine toured the Middle East, Winston visited an exhibition in Paris of paintings by Charles Morin. Shown at the prestigious Galerie Druet, six Morin works were sold . . . and Morin in reality was Winston Churchill!

In the *Strand* magazine piece, though, he said he was merely "a weekend and holiday amateur who during the last few years has found a new pleasure and who wishes to tell others of his luck."

Afloat, But Barely

If Chartwell was maintained in fairly lavish style by Winston's pen, so, in the 1930s, was his and the family's entire lifestyle dependent upon the output of his pen as well. After all, with no ministerial office to engage him, or pay him, he had the time and he needed the money.

Once again demonstrating his remarkable resiliency by bouncing back from the injuries suffered when struck by the taxi in New York, he soon was back at work at Chartwell on his biography of Marlborough, actually a labor of love as well as of need. "He also conceived the idea of writing a history of the English-speaking peoples, uniting that of his father's nation with that of his mother's country, and soon arranged a highly profitable contract, a quarter (five thousand pounds) payable in advance," noted British military historian John Keegan in a succinct biography titled *Winston Churchill.* Money always cheered him up, Keegan noted. "The book would not see the light of day for nearly twenty years. In the interval it helped to sustain his perennially extravagant way of life."

Explained Keegan: "Large houses (he was now living in and expensively improving Chartwell . . .), cruises, foreign holidays, opulent motor cars (though he had been given a Daimler by friends after his accident), dinners, grand hotels, squads of secretaries and servants, the best schools for his children, silk underwear and Havana cigars for himself, champagne for his guests [and himself]—all the ingredients of ducal life—seem to have been necessary to Churchill's well being."

Politically in the wilderness, left out of government when Ramsay MacDonald formed his "National Government" in 1931, Keegan commented, Winston nonetheless continued to live "very well, if on tenterhooks about finding the means to carry off appearances." Keegan added: "Articles were written for press baron friends, delivered by the chauffeur with orders to wait for the check. Creditors were stared down. Somehow he swam rather than sank."

Political Mistake

Even his best friends (and his wife) realized that Winston Churchill had misstepped badly when he publicly threw his support behind Edward VIII in the latter's abdication crisis of 1936, a domestic storm over the king's infatuation with American divorcee "Wally" Simpson. As daughter Mary Soames wrote in her biography of Clementine, this issue was one upon which her mother "found herself at variance with Winston."

The storm over the new king's romance with a twice-married commoner from abroad took an uninformed British public by surprise in late 1936, months after he succeeded his late father, George V . . . and quite a while after the rest of the world had become aware of Edward's interest in Mrs. Simpson. "The British press, by common agreement, had not made any mention of this romantic situation," wrote daughter Mary, "but it had been the subject of discussion and grave speculation in Court and government circles after Mrs. Simpson's divorce from her second husband, Ernest Simpson, in October 1936."

Once the news broke in Britain, however, "chiefly" the young and romantic-minded "saw no reason why the King should not marry the woman he loved." Others, "a larger but less vocal section of the public," felt he "should sacrifice his personal happiness to his royal duty." On a more official level, it fell to Prime Minister Stanley Baldwin to inform the king "that Mrs. Simpson would not be acceptable as Queen." As the crisis played out for Edward, it boiled down to a choice between the throne or Mrs. Simpson. He chose her, and on December 11, 1936, less than a year after his father's death made him king (but prior to his coronation), Edward abdicated.

All of which placed Winston on a hot seat of his own, since he was a longtime friend of the king who tried to defuse the constitutional crisis by urging the various parties to take more time in considering the options. "He felt this momentous decision was being resolved with wanton haste, and that given more time and consultation a happier issue might be devised," Mary explained.

At the same time, there was no mistaking where Winston stood, since he openly "espoused the king's cause with loyalty and vigor." Not only were they friends, but Winston believed strongly in the monarchy. Or, as his daughter stated: "Always a monarchist, every instinct of personal loyalty and chivalry was aroused by the dilemma of his Sovereign, for whom he had always had a true regard."

By taking the romantic view, Winston hoped for some arrangement allowing Edward to marry yet remain king . . . and thereby spare the nation "the convulsion of the crisis which would be caused by his abdication." Quite mistakenly, Winston also "was certain the King commanded wide sympathy among the people of this country, who would rally to support him."

As events turned out, that certainly did not include Clementine, who "disagreed profoundly with Winston, both in his view of the problem and in his estimation of what public feeling really was." In her view, Edward owed his heart to duty, not to his personal happiness. Moreover, the prime minister had read the public pulse quite correctly "and in no circumstances would Mrs. Simpson be acceptable to the British either as Queen Consort or even as merely the wife of the

King." For that matter, Winston's championship of the king's cause would be fresh grist for his critics. "In all of this she was proved right," Mary pointed out.

Just how right was seen on December 7 of that year when Winston was shouted down in the House of Commons just as he rose to warn "no irrevocable step should be taken." It was an embarrassing rebuff—"the most humiliating event of his parliamentary career" in the eyes of Churchill biographer Geoffrey Best.

The further fact is that Edward, while a friend of Winston's, personally was no paragon evoking public sympathy. But that apparently didn't dissuade Churchill. "The attributes which many wrote down as defects of character—lack of seriousness of mind, liking for flashy company, irreligion, sexual adventurism—did not particularly bother Churchill, who knew how often monarchs had been like that and how little it need matter constitutionally," wrote Best in *Churchill: A Study in Greatness*. "Besides, Churchill was not himself a religious man and, although not personally interested in divorce or amorous adventures, he was far too familiar with them in his own extended family and social circle to think that account should be taken of them in public life."

What the entire episode came down to for Winston was a mistake . . . a major political mistake. Or as summed up by Best: "His brief campaign did Edward no good and did Churchill himself some harm, which fortunately for his country proved to be short-lived. He had excitedly underrated Edward's resolve to marry Mrs. Simpson and to make her Queen—over optimistic though Churchill was about other things, he never thought that possible—and he had overrated the degree of popular support that might be aroused on Edward's behalf." Short-lived harm or not, both for Winston and his country, the abdication crisis couldn't have come at a worse time—just when he was warming to his theme that a nasty, fast-rearming Nazi Germany loomed on the horizon.

More immediately, once Edward abdicated on December 11, 1936, Clementine and Winston were agreed upon one aspect of the disheartening affair, reported daughter Mary, and that was their shared anger against those, "many of them in high places," who had turned against the king "in his hour of anguished decision." Mary's mother "was particularly scornful of those in the social world who had been only too willing to entertain King Edward and Mrs. Simpson during the months that led up to the final crisis, but who turned cool when the day of reckoning came."

Touchingly enough, Winston reacted with tears when they attended the coronation of Edward's brother as George VI at Westminster Abbey in May 1937 and saw George's wife Elizabeth crowned consort, "after making vows of the utmost solemnity, and receiving tokens of grace for her special task." Turning to Clementine, Winston said: "You were right; I see now the 'other one' [Wallis Simpson] wouldn't have done."

Additional note: According to Mary Soames, the period after the abdication crisis "was probably the lowest point in Winston's political fortunes since the dark days immediately following the Dardanelles disaster." Not only were his warnings of "national peril ahead" unheeded, there was a feeling also that he really had supported the king out of antipathy toward Prime Minister Baldwin. "To those who knew him well this was malicious nonsense: Churchill had reacted to the King's plight spontaneously and naturally, as one would expect of someone possessing his instincts of loyalty and chivalry. Nonetheless, this unjust appraisal blunted, in a most critical moment, his power to act and to persuade."

Clementine of course grieved for him, even if he had gone against her advice in supporting Edward's position during the abdication crisis. Asked at this low period in their lives if she thought he would ever become prime minister, she said, "No, unless some great disaster were to sweep the country, and no one could wish for that."

Winston himself wasn't optimistic about his future prospects. In a letter discussing the possibility they might have to sell the beloved Chartwell country home, a depressing thought in itself, Winston told Clementine, "no good offer should be refused, having regard to the fact that our children are almost all flown, and my life is probably in its closing decade."

Commented daughter Mary, "These words read strangely indeed: Churchill had nearly three more decades to live, and his life's supreme task and achievement lay ahead."

Voice in the Wilderness

When historian Geoffrey Best was growing up in a middle-class London suburb, he had only to look up and down the street to be reminded of the ravages of war.

And, no, he wouldn't be looking at damage to buildings . . . but at people, at the veterans and survivors of the Great War. For the young Geoffrey and his family—indeed, for all of England—there was no escaping the grim human residue of the recent war that had been so terrible it had been called the war to end all wars.

"Upright Mr. Davis next door had lost an eye in it," Best wrote in *Churchill: A Study in Greatness.* "Giant Mr. Piercy from twenty houses along our road, whose daughter was one of my occasional playmates, had lost a leg in it and thumped up to Osterley station each morning on large wooden crutches. Our dear friend Mr. Draisey had served alongside my Uncle Harold on the Somme and had come out of it in one piece; poor Harold lost an eye, was shell-shocked, and never wholly recovered. Cousin Henry from Australia died of wounds at Gallipoli and lay buried at Malta. . . . My father went early in the war to an officer's training school but contracted pneumonia and pleurisy, which left him with a cardiac weakness for the rest of his life." Furthermore, a "treasure" for the youthful Best was a piece from the metal skeleton of a German Zeppelin his father had seen shot down over north London during World War I.

Such were the memories and the artifacts of the British people in the 1930s as an out-of-favor, out-of-power political figure from the recent past tried his best to rally them for the possibility of yet another Great War. He was, of course, Winston Churchill, and for the most part his pleas and his warnings, even his threats, fell on deaf ears. But were they really deaf?

At first perhaps. For a good long while after his government service during and immediately after World War I—that is to say, during his out-of-power "wilderness years"—Winston was more or less tolerated as a somewhat celebrated, somewhat eccentric parliamentary figure. "He was not as popular a figure in the House [of Commons] as he once used to be, and he felt it. His absences were noted, and his presumption when he was there was resented," wrote Best. Still, "Liberals and Conservatives acknowledged his supremacy as a speaker and crowded to hear him when he was in action; they admired the form, but often reserved judgment on the substance."

He had run into a buzz saw for his stand against dominion status for India, and he soon would be shouted down in the House when he voiced support for Edward VIII during the 1936 abdication crisis. But both before and after 1936, Winston's focus was on the growing danger posed by Adolf Hitler's Nazi Germany. Best ably stated: "Churchill's attitudes regarding India and the abdication were of some importance in the history of the British Empire, but the great matter with which he was dramatically connected through the 1930s, the rearmament and nazification of Germany, was of importance in the history of civilization."

Thus, among many other firsts to his credit, Winston would go down in history as "the first British statesman of any note to identify, and to call public attention to, the dangerous twist given to German national aspirations (which he well understood) by their confluence from 1933 with Nazi ideology and Hitler's leadership."

Ironically enough, the great orator and wordsmith who emerged in twentieth-century England was at first eclipsed in the public view by another crowd-pleasing spellbinder—Hitler. "The British public in the 1930s," wrote Best, "was curiously suggestible, and Hitler was a politician of genius and a platform orator of unusual skill whose words became listened to (literally listened to, by whole families sitting round the loudspeaker of the wireless, though few in Britain could understand him) with unparalleled attention." British and French politicians and their constituencies, Best added, "were, to put it crudely, keener on hearing what Hitler said about peace than what Churchill said about war."

Understanding their fears of war, Hitler cleverly used "yo-yo" tactics against those tempted to heed the warnings of Winston Churchill and his small coterie of supporters. For every bold step forward by Hitler, such as the remilitarization of the Rhineland in 1936, there was the promise of no further demands. Or a threat. "Everyone knew how each successive advance was advertised as 'positively my last territorial demand,' and how every delay in meeting his demands provoked the warning that 'my patience is nearly exhausted.'"

Thus, the out-of-power Winston faced both a "crafty" opponent abroad and a domestic shrinking back from the slightest consideration of another "German" war so soon after the last, a nightmarish disaster even in victory. In contrast to the obvious menace embodied in the fast-strengthening Third Reich, Best wrote, "the idea of any sort of armed confrontation with Hitler, which was the logical conclusion of Churchill's arguments, was extraordinarily unpopular, nearly as unthinkable as a thought can be, and it is not difficult to understand why." Indeed, as the wounds borne by his own family and neighbors attested: "The prospect was a fearful one, whether you looked forward or back. If forward, there was the widely held (and until the end of the 1930s, officially endorsed) belief that London was accessible to German bombers, that it was indefensible against them and that, besides causing vast destruction, they would rain poison gas. If you looked backwards, the experience of the Great War was, to adult men and women, only fifteen years behind them."

Not that long before . . . and just as Best said, right there in his own neighborhood, a middle-class suburb of London, were the "upright Mr. Davis" minus an eye, and just twenty doors away, "Giant Mr. Piercy" stumping about minus a leg.

Additional note: True, as Best wrote, among other factors influencing the British public's apparent deaf ear there was a hopeful faith in the League of Nations, a view held by people who "believed that two League talismans called Collective Security and Economic Sanctions would turn fighting into a last resort so remote as scarcely to require serious consideration." Further, some felt, as Hitler took his steps re-asserting German power, that Germany had been overly punished by the terms of the Versailles Treaty ending the Great War. Then, too, some, even in England, a handful to be sure, were outright fascists or Nazi sympathizers themselves.

"Only Hours Away by Air"

Here, for the Royal Air Force, was a quandary indeed. A German Air Mission led by Nazi Germany's air minister, Gen. Eduard Milch, was coming for a visit. What to let them see? How poorly prepared the British were for war with a fast-arming Germany? Or unveil the latest innovations to show him how advanced, and therefore threatening, were some RAF developments? Either way, Winston Churchill, lone but perennial gadfly extraordinaire, was on the case once again. As always with his drumbeat of warnings in the 1930s, this one, in the fall of 1937, was serious business.

One issue: Should the visiting Germans be allowed to see the newly developed power-driven gun turret? Writing to his old World War I admiralty colleague Maurice Hankey, Winston said, "We have invited the German Mission over—why I cannot tell." And he added: "Highly competent men are coming. A desperate effort is now being made to present a sham-show. A power-driven turret is to be shown, as if it was the kind of thing we are doing in the regular way. Ought it to be shown at all?" And further, from the secret documents he was sending along, Winston said, "You will see that a special telegram has to be sent to fetch one of the only men acquainted with this turret to give a demonstration."

As explained by biographer Martin Gilbert, Winston had received his latest inside information from RAF Group Capt. Lachlan MacLean, whom he described to Hankey (without naming MacLean) as "a high Staff Officer of the

RAF." By the same official notes, Winston told Hankey, "You will also see the statement, made by the Air Officer-in-Chief Bomber Command . . . [Air Chief Marshall Edgar] Ludlow-Hewitt, how he is forced to address himself to the task of making a show; and what exertions are necessary to put little more than a hundred bombers in the air—the great majority of which (as the Germans will readily see) can barely reach the coast of Germany with a bomb load."

Understandably, with Nazi Germany's Luftwaffe growing in strength and capability almost daily, Winston was concerned by Ludlow-Hewitt's confidential lament "that we should have to comb the country in order to produce sufficient aircraft to get up any sort of show." The fact was that by 1937 it was late in the day for England to try to stay ahead of or to stay even with . . . or was it too late to catch up with the Luftwaffe?

The fact was also that Winston had been sounding grim warnings since the decade began. Nor was it always Hitler he inveighed against, although Hitler very soon became the focal point. No, in the beginning and always, it was Germany . . . always it was a militant, rearming Germany vengeful in its thinking.

And no, Winston also argued early in the game, simple equality or parity in arms was not what Germany wanted. Not at all. "All these bands of sturdy Teutonic youths marching through the streets and roads of Germany, with the light of desire in their eyes to suffer for the Fatherland, are not looking for status," he told fellow parliamentarians in late 1932, before Hitler became chancellor in early 1933. "They are looking for weapons, and, when they have the weapons, believe me they will then ask for the return of lost territories [stemming from the Versailles Treaty]."

For Winston, the danger first took the form of a nationalistic, militarist, and expansionist Germany, noted historian Geoffrey Best in *Churchill and War*. "For those with eyes to see and ears to hear, that essential Germany had been there since Versailles, under the hopefully liberal cover of the Weimar Republic," Best wrote. But Weimar was doomed from that moment in 1930 that the young Nationalist Socialist Party—the Nazis—suddenly became the second-largest party in the German parliament, or Reichstag. "Their Fuhrer, so far known only to specialists in German politics, began to be a figure of international interest. Churchill does not seem to have paid any attention to him until 1932 and, like many others viewing the German situation from afar, was at first neither surprised nor particularly alarmed by him."

But then, even though out of the government (except for his seat in Parliament), Winston had many other interests to juggle. For one, his ongoing but losing fight against the movement to give India somewhat limited self-government with dominion status. For another, he was financially stressed, thanks to his losses in the great stock market crash that he had personally witnessed while visiting the United States in late 1929. So stressed was he, Best reported, Chartwell had to be partially shut down. "Most of it was placed under wraps; only Churchill's study was kept open so that he could carry on writing without interruption. When not occupying the garden cottage there, the Churchills stayed in hotels or places rented by the month."

Then, in addition to his outpouring of magazine and newspaper articles, he had several major writing balls in the air, all of book length—he was finishing up the popular *My Early Life*, he was well into his biography of the Duke of Marlborough, and he was negotiating the future publication of *History of the English-Speaking Peoples*. By now, his *World Crisis*, about World War I, was in the bookstores. All of the last three were multivolume book projects. Despite all this activity, along with sundry other distractions—building sturdy brick walls or the cottage at Chartwell, plying his hobby of painting or overcoming an occasional serious illness such as paratyphoid fever—he soon acquired the great new mission of his life. Geoffrey Best stated it well when he wrote: "Raising public consciousness regarding the German danger became Churchill's preoccupation and main mission in life in the course of the year 1933." And not only in 1933. By 1935: "The German danger had come to command the greater part of his attention. In speech after speech, article after article and (not that they were yet numerous) broadcast after broadcast, he called attention to Germany's rearmament and its implications for the peace of Europe, perhaps the peace of the world."

As for Britain itself, Winston said in a 1934 broadcast: "Only a few hours away by air there dwells a nation of nearly seventy million of the most educated, industrious, scientific, disciplined people in the world, who are being taught from childhood to think of war and conquest as a glorious exercise, and death in battle as the noblest fate for man . . . a nation . . . in the grip of a group of ruthless men preaching a gospel of intolerance and racial pride, unrestrained by law, by parliament or by public opinion."

Meanwhile, say what he would, Winston was left out of the national government formed in 1931; he still had no ministerial post when Stanley Baldwin came back as prime minister in 1935 . . . but now he at least was given a seat on a secret committee on air defense research. That gave him official access to vital intelligence on top of the secrets he was being fed by a small coterie of select contacts in the military and the government, among them the RAF officer who told him about the coming visit of the German air minister.

Others in the group included Desmond Morton, a military intelligence expert, and foreign office specialist Ralph Wigram, made famous by the BBC-HBO film *The Gathering Storm*. According to the story line in that docudrama, Wigram and his wife become very close to the Churchills, but they were pressured to stop their Chartwell visits, and then Wigram mysteriously died, apparently a suicide. "The emphasis placed on Wigram's role . . . is being questioned by some historians," reported the *London Observer* in 2002. Said biographer Roy Jenkins (according to Vanessa Thorpe's *Observer* article): "The film is rather good, but Wigram's role is ludicrously exaggerated." Not so, responded the film's screenwriter Hugh Whitemore, "The more I talked to people, the more I realized how significant he was."

According to Whitemore, Wigram's story was little known even though Winston's history of World War II called him a "great unsung hero." A couple of biographers "mention him," but only in passing. "There is also a letter from Wigram's wife begging Churchill to attend his funeral, which he did. . . . His death certificate says he died of a pulmonary hemorrhage, but if I had to guess I would say it was suicide. His own parents did not attend his funeral."

In contrast, Winston gave a small luncheon at Chartwell for the mourners, noted biographer Martin Gilbert. In addition, he wrote the widow, Ava Wigram, citing her husband's "courage, integrity of purpose, high comprehending vision," and saying his death (at forty) was "a blow to England and to all the best that England means."

It often was from such sources that Winston gathered his secret information, data that allowed him to puncture official government claims. Thus, if defense coordinator Sir Thomas Inskip told the House of Commons in a debate on January 27, 1937, right after Wigram's death, that 120 of a promised 124 British air squadrons would be ready by a certain date, "though not all brought up to their complement," Winston could argue, no, only 100 would be ready, and of those, 22 would not be combat ready. "This left only seventy-eight squadrons instead of the promised 124, a shortage of forty-six," noted Gilbert. Not everybody approved of Winston's methods, not even some who might otherwise have joined in his unpopular cause—his old admiralty friend Hankey, for instance.

In the process of sending Hankey MacLean's confidential information about the German air minister, Winston marked his letter "Secret and personal," reported Gilbert. In it, Winston said: "As one small installment of the alarming accounts I have received of the state of the RAF, I send you the enclosed. It is for your own personal information, and I trust to our friendship and your honor that its origin is not probed." But Hankey responded with a stiff eight-page rebuke accusing Winston of receiving "backstairs" information that his informants should advance through channels in their own departments of government.

Obviously stung, according to Gilbert's account, Winston replied stiffly himself: "My Dear Maurice, I certainly did not expect to receive from you a lengthy lecture when I went out of my way to give you, in strict confidence, information in the public interest. I thank you for sending me the papers back, and you may be sure I shall not trouble you again in such matters."

Additional note: Winston first heard from Ralph Wigram, head of the Central Department at the Foreign Office, in April 1935. Wigram, alarmed by Nazi Germany's aggressive posture, volunteered information that Germany was close to placing its aircraft-manufacturing plants on an emergency wartime footing, Martin Gilbert reported. A week later, Wigram sent Winston "the Government's own most recent, and secret, figures, which showed that the minimum German first line air strength had reached 800 aircraft, as against Britain's 453." Said Winston later: "He was a charming and fearless man. . . . He saw as clearly as I did, but with more certain information, the awful peril which was closing in upon us." Maj. Desmond Morton, meanwhile, first brought into government intelligence work in 1919 by Winston, now was a neighbor to Chartwell and head of the Imperial Defense Committee's industrial intelligence unit. He monitored the import and uses of raw materials from around the world for the production of weaponry by the European powers. "Fortified" in early 1933 by Morton's information, Gilbert also reported, Winston "contrasted Hitler's quest for rearmament with [Prime Minister Ramsay] MacDonald's continuing pursuit of disarmament." Germany or a German ally equal militarily to France, Poland, or even the smaller European states would mean "renewal of a general European war." In the same House of Commons speech, Winston also decried "this [Nazi Germany's] persecution of Jews."

Motive for Appeasement

What were the leaders of Britain's government thinking during the 1930s while, just a short airplane flight away, Nazi Germany was busily rearming? Not only did they fear a repeated war, like World War I, it seems, but economics as well. *Money.*

After all, the leading nations of the free-enterprise world had just been through a global depression that began with the American stock market crash of 1929. The aftereffects of the "world crash and the subsequent British slump," noted John Keegan, "set the tone for British politics in what, for Churchill, would be his Wilderness Years."

More specifically, "Neville Chamberlain, chancellor of the exchequer for most of the period, took it as his responsibility to protect by every means the slow process of industrial recovery." That would mean, so far as Chamberlain was concerned, the lightest possible tax burden on the people and the least government spending possible. Worthy aims, of course, but under his stewardship, Keegan noted, the British armed services "were starved of funds." Thus, "[Chamberlain] denied the Royal Navy new capital ships and the Royal Air Force modern aircraft." Further, "the army was left in an almost archaic state, with equipment suitable only for conducting colonial operations."

To compound Chamberlain's tight-fisted spending policy, the managers of the air services put their few eggs, so to speak, into bombers, on the mistaken theory, added Keegan, that "Britain's best defense against air attack lay in the acquisition of offensive means, a policy so belatedly reversed that it was only by the narrowest of margins that Fighter Command acquired the Spitfires and Hurricanes which would win the Battle of Britain in 1940."

In Germany, meanwhile, Hitler was turning the losers of World War I into "the world's leading military power." Stripped by the 1919 Versailles Treaty of any air force, of capital ships and submarines, of heavy artillery and tanks, and left with only a "token" army, Germany under Hitler was a nation transformed by the late 1930s. Keegan, in his short biography of Winston Churchill, outlined the transforming steps Hitler took, one by one, after his elevation to chancellor of Germany in January 1933.

In 1934, "he ordered the German army to begin building a tank fleet."

In 1935, "he decreed the creation of an air force, the Luftwaffe, the elements of which were already in existence."

In 1935, he reintroduced the draft, taking young men into military service. "At a stroke, a German army artificially restricted to inferior status vis-à-vis its neighbors began to expand, first to match and then to exceed their strengths." In 1934, the Germans under arms were outnumbered by their counterparts in Czechoslovakia, France, Great Britain, Poland, and, of course, the Soviet Union. "Within the next three years, however, the balance of military power in Europe would be transformed. By September 1938 the German army, which in 1933 possessed only seven infantry and three cavalry divisions, stood at a strength of forty-six infantry divisions and five panzer (tank) divisions, with a numerical strength of six hundred thousand. By comparison the British army had only six infantry divisions and one national tank division; many of its two hundred thousand soldiers were dispersed abroad in colonial garrisons. The Luftwaffe, with three thousand combat aircraft, already outnumbered both the Royal Air Force and the [French] Armee de l'Air. The French army, though large, was hidebound and poorly equipped."

In 1936, meanwhile, Hitler even talked the British into accepting a change in the Versailles Treaty allowing Germany "to build and deploy submarines."

In fairness, the British cabinet "did during 1934 take steps to reverse some of the damage done by more than a decade of underspending on defense. It accepted a report that placed the needs of the air force at the head of a list of requirements and, to the dismay of the proponents of bombing in the Air Ministry, gave priority to the procurement of new fighters and other air defense measures. It was still preoccupied, however, with the need to nurture industrial revival and refused to make large increases in the defense budget."

All this time, all these years, Winston stood virtually alone, publicly, in speaking out on Britain's lack of preparedness. He had his secret sources within the governmental bureaucracy, he always filled the House chamber when he spoke, "and his speeches were privately admired, but his message was too uncomfortable and too much at variance with official policy to command parliamentary support," wrote Keegan. "Moreover, an aura of unreliability still clung to him. Conventional Conservatives too easily regarded Churchill as 'unsound'"—a reputation only enhanced, unfortunately, by his support of Edward VIII in the 1936 abdication crisis.

On the Continent, meanwhile, Hitler, taking advantage of the short-term benefits from a state-directed economy, remilitarized the Rhineland unchallenged. He then annexed Austria in early 1938, the *Anschluss*. During the Spanish Civil War of the late 1930s, he was able to test much of his new weaponry in support of Francisco Franco's victorious rebels. Late in1938, he assumed control of the Czech Sudetenland, and Winston spoke up once again: "Silent, mournful, abandoned, broken, Czechoslovakia recedes into the darkness." Early in 1939, Nazi Germany's troops took over the rest of the country, and Hitler slept that night in Prague.

Poland obviously would be next . . . and was, on September 1, 1939, as World War II began in earnest.

★ PART 4 ★
Battle for Survival

1940

The year 1940 broke quiet, cold, and somewhat frightening in England. Thus far, no bombs . . . but one never knew. One thing *was* known—the Control of Noises (Defense) Order was in full, silent effect. That meant no sirens allowed, no factory whistles, no noises, *period*. "Church bells, however, might be rung," reported British journalist Laurence Thompson in his book *1940*. "Their turn for silence came in June."

It had been different back in September, when Hitler had launched his blitzkrieg against hapless Poland, when the British government had issued its war ultimatum to Nazi Germany, then had found itself at war when the ultimatum was ignored. That was when "some had fainted upon hearing Prime Minister Neville Chamberlain's sad, flat voice on the radio proclaim war; others had awakened that night, in terror, from the nightmare of a sky black with bombing planes wingtip to wingtip."

The radio announcement by Chamberlain, always a tall, gangly, faintly ridiculous-looking figure in his bowler hat, came on a "bright, breezy morning," Winston's daughter Mary wrote later. It was Sunday, September 3, 1939.

Said a middle-aged schoolteacher from a small country town: "At 11:15 I went up, and we sat round listening to Chamberlain speaking. I held my chin high and kept back the tears at the thought of all the slaughter ahead. When 'God Save the King' was played, we stood."

No sooner had Chamberlain relinquished the microphone than the sound of air-raid sirens startled London. But it was a false alarm. No air raid. After that, except for Poland, a few scattered shots here and there, and the serious (but seemingly distant) war at sea—nothing. No war . . . no slaughter. Not yet.

Still, that winter did present a war of sorts, a war waged by Mother Nature. "From the end of December until mid-February, with only a single break, Britain experienced its coldest winter for forty-five years," Thompson observed. An eight-mile stretch of the river Thames? Frozen over, solid ice. And snow! Snow up to cottage rooflines. Trains slowed, up to a full day late. Snowplows "engulfed in thirty-foot drifts."

Thankfully, the same bad weather affected Continental Europe as well; it delayed Hitler's planned leap beyond Poland; he had to "postpone his long-expected offensive against the French and British armies." Even so, to some British and American observers, the French already looked shaky. "The American Under-Secretary of State, Sumner Wells, touring Europe in the spring of 1940, reported to his government that French officers complained about the lack of discipline among their men. Fears were expressed that, if Hitler delayed his attack on the Western front for long enough, the French rank-and-file would spontaneously disband themselves and go home."

In England, meanwhile, the nonwar was wearing thin in a thousand ways. Nearly everyone hated the blackout—nighttime traffic fatalities increased. So did highway robberies. Also difficult were the massive population shifts rippling through British society, a social upheaval in magnitude. "By the beginning of 1940, half the families in the country had one or more members on the move," noted Thompson. *Half!* "Wives and children had been evacuated from the towns . . . young men were called up for the services, workers moved from the depressed areas . . . to busy armament centers like Coventry and Oxford. Another two million young men, warned that they would shortly be called up, found it difficult to take their civilian jobs seriously."

Meanwhile, many of those going into service, or moved about for other reasons, suddenly found their income cut as well. Then, too, among the million and a quarter mothers and children evacuated from cities and towns—and among their hosts—there were problems. A number of the refugees came from city slums—"and people who had been intellectually aware for some time of such abstractions as 'problem families,' 'depressed areas,' 'the underprivileged,' found themselves confronted by the reality in their own living rooms. Some of the children were verminous, and quickly distributed the vermin among others."

Even Churchill's beloved country retreat of Chartwell was assigned its share of evacuees—two mothers with seven children from the East End of London. But, said Mary, they joined thousands of others who soon "drifted back" to their city homes despite the dangers of bombing.

George VI, meanwhile, set off a mild tumult with his Christmas Day speech. Despite a stammer that made public speaking an onerous chore for him, he thought it his duty on this first yuletide of the new war to speak to his people. He picked up a few words from a newspaper clipping someone had sent Buckingham

Palace. They came originally from a postcard found on a deceased doctor's desk and used by his daughters on their greeting cards. A recipient then sent one of the cards to the London *Times*, and from there a clipping wound up on the king's desk. Thinking they would be a good morale boost, he used the quotation as his closing: "I said to the man who stood at the Gate of the Year, 'Give me a light that I may tread safely into the unknown.' And he replied, 'Go out into the darkness, and put your hand into the Hand of God. That shall be to you better than light, and safer than a known way.'"

The king's use of the unattributed quote, wrote Thompson, "led to a frantic search" in newspaper offices for the source, "and cables came from New York seeking enlightenment for the American public." All sorts of suggestions for the authorship were reviewed and discarded. It wasn't from G. K. Chesterton nor from Bunyan nor the gospels. "It was not until midnight that the BBC was able to announce the name of the author, sixty-four-year-old Miss Minnie Louise Haskins."

Who? It turned out she was a retired lecturer at the London School of Economics then living in Sussex . . . she had missed the king's midafternoon speech, but thought when she heard a BBC summary that night that the words were somehow familiar. Indeed, she had written them for a slim volume of poetry privately printed back in 1908 and sold to help fund mission work in India. Within days, she was famous, noted Thompson. "Her volume of verse, republished, passed through eight editions and remained in print until 1948, by which time forty-three thousand copies had been sold."

During all the hubbub, Winston and his family passed a quiet Christmas in London, "gathering around them quite a number of the family, and two old and valued friends and 'Chartwell regulars,' Brendan Bracken and 'The Prof' [Frederick Lindemann]," reported daughter Mary.

For Winston, in contrast to Britain as a whole, the last few months of 1939 had been a time of frantic initiatives, of repeated reaction to enemy hostilities . . . as befitted a first lord of the admiralty at a time of renewed war with Germany. For such, at the invitation of Prime Minister Neville Chamberlain, Winston once again had been since September 3, the day that marked the beginning of World War II for Britain. "Winston reported to the Admiralty at six o'clock that evening," wrote Mary. "It was a moment fraught with emotions and memories of which Winston wrote: 'So it was that I came again into the room I had quitted in pain and sorrow almost exactly a quarter of a century before.'"

Now, the word went out to the fleet: "Winston is back!" Back indeed, and busy with a war at sea. That first night, a German U-boat sank the liner *Athenia*, "with heavy loss of life," and in October a U-boat penetrated the Royal Navy's sacrosanct Scapa Flow anchorage and sank the old battleship *Royal Oak* in its home base. In November, magnetic mines sank sixty thousand tons of British shipping, reported Mary, but soon there was better news: the Germans had scuttled their pocket battleship *Admiral Graf Spee* in the river Plate off Montevideo, Uruguay, on the east coast of South America after a battle with three British cruisers (one was New Zealand's *Achilles*). "It was a glorious victory, and brought a gleam of light into a dark December," commented Mary.

Additional note: For Winston, the first weeks and months of 1940 were no less active. First, in February, came the *Altmark* incident, like the *Graf Spee*, a coup for Winston's Royal Navy. A supply ship for the *Graf Spee*, the *Altmark* ran for cover toward neutral Norwegian waters but was spotted by aircraft. On the theory it carried prisoners taken from British merchant ships previously sunk by the *Graf Spee*, the British destroyer *Cossack* drove the *Altmark* aground in a Norwegian fjord. A boarding party then freed about three hundred captured merchantmen, mostly British, being held on the German ship.

Next, however, came a fiasco in Norway for the British. Even while plans (largely Winston's!) to mine Norwegian waters and possibly set British troops ashore in neutral Norway were being advanced in London, the Germans suddenly struck on April 9—six battle groups against six major Norwegian ports along a thousand-mile coastline. The operation, also against Denmark, involved paratroops and even soldiers hidden in the holds of merchant ships "peaceably" at dock, with all supported by a completely air-dominant Luftwaffe. While the shocked Norwegians courageously fought against the first large-scale combined operation by land, sea, and air forces in history, the British mounted a pair of hastily assembled counterthrusts in mid-April, one of them in the Trondheim vicinity of central Norway and the other at Narvik to the north. The Trondheim forces had to be evacuated just two weeks later, while the Narvik defenders held out against the German invaders for nearly eight weeks.

The results at sea were painful for both sides, but it was the Germans who suffered the greater loss (three cruisers, ten destroyers, eleven transports, and eight submarines) compared to the Allies' (one aircraft carrier, two cruisers, nine destroyers, and six submarines). Even so, by subjugating Norway, Nazi Germany in the long run secured a northern flank and the "Leads" supply line along the Norwegian coast for crucial iron ore mined in Sweden. In London, meanwhile, recriminations flew fast and furious.

PM at Last

Oliver Cromwell had said the very same words to the Long Parliament of the 1600s, nearly three hundred years earlier: "You have sat too long for any good you have been doing. Depart, I say, and let us have done with you. In the name of God, go!" Only *these* words, spoken before the House of Commons to Prime Minister Neville Chamberlain by his old friend, political colleague, and fellow Conservative Leopold Amery on May 7, 1940, were the beginning of the end of Chamberlain's premiership. And as events turned out three days later, they were the beginning of the beginning of Churchill's ascent, at long, long last, to prime minister.

On May 8, the second day of debate on the Norway fiasco, Winston did not shrink from defending his and the Chamberlain government's role. "I take full responsibility for everything that has been done at the Admiralty, and I take my full share of the burden," he declared. But both Lloyd George and Harold Macmillan warned him against taking too much of the blame, recalled Martin Gilbert in *Churchill: A Life*. "Why not?" Winston asked, and Macmillan answered, "Because we must have a new Prime Minister, and it must be you."

Certainly, the tide was running . . . in for Winston, out for Chamberlain. That night as Chamberlain left the House chamber, it was to cries of "Go! Go! Go!" Gilbert described Chamberlain as "devastated," and he went to Buckingham Palace for a visit with George VI—"not to resign but to tell him he would try to form an all-Party Government, bringing in Labor and the Liberals." The next day, May 9, Chamberlain told Sir Kingsley Wood, "one of his closest confidants," he would resign if the Labor Party refused to serve under him.

That very afternoon, he asked Labor Party leaders Clement Attlee and Arthur Greenwood if they would be willing to serve in a re-formed coalition government under himself or under another Conservative Party figure. Labor's response was no to Chamberlain, and thus the die was cast. His foreign secretary, Lord Halifax, briefly appeared a possibility for prime minister, but his prospects rose and fell quickly, in part because members of the House of Lords normally could not become prime minister. Entire books have been written on how the tides within the House membership flowed and ebbed these last days of Chamberlain's tenure, but in the end it was obvious to all that Churchill would be the man for the job, that he would become Great Britain's next wartime leader.

"On the night of 9–10th May," summarized daughter Mary, "German forces invaded Holland and Belgium. These events clinched the political situation at home. At six o'clock on the evening of the 10th May Chamberlain went to Buckingham Palace to tender his resignation; half an hour later the King sent for Churchill and asked him to form a Government, and a few hours later Churchill returned to the Palace to submit the first list of names of members of the new Government for the King's approval."

More Details Told

The night before Winston became prime minister of England, according to biographer Martin Gilbert, he was asked by son Randolph, himself now a soldier, what was the latest news. And Winston replied, "I think I shall be Prime Minister tomorrow." He already had heard that Chamberlain was dependent on the unlikely support of Labor, and if that didn't work out, he would defer to someone else: "Thus, by the afternoon, I became aware that I might well be called upon to take the lead. The prospect neither excited nor alarmed me. I thought it would be by far the best plan. I was content to let events unfold."

The next morning, May 10, though, the British leadership was thrown into confusion by the long-awaited German onslaught against the rest of Western Europe. Upon learning early on May 10 of the German invasion of Holland and Belgium, with France obviously to come next, Chamberlain decided this was no time to change prime ministers after all. He should stay on.

His war and air ministers, meanwhile, had breakfasted with admiralty chief Churchill. "We had had little or no sleep," wrote Air Minister Sir Samuel Hoare, "and the news could not have been worse. Yet there he was, smoking his large cigar and eating fried eggs and bacon, as if he had just returned from an early morning ride."

Randolph called to ask the news again. "Well," said Winston, "the German hordes are pouring into the Low Countries." But what about that prime minister business? "Oh, I don't know about that," answered Winston. "Nothing matters now except beating the enemy."

It was in a meeting later in the morning at No. 10 Downing Street that Chamberlain learned Labor wouldn't stick by him, no matter what. At eleven o'clock, Winston was called to another meeting at No. 10 . . . this time with only himself and his chief rival, Lord Halifax, facing Chamberlain across a table. "He told us that he was satisfied that it was beyond his power to form a National Government," Winston reported in *The Gathering Storm.* "The question, therefore, was whom he should advise the King to send for after his own resignation had been accepted. His demeanor was cool, unruffled, and seemingly quite detached from the personal aspect of the affair. He looked at us both across the table."

For Winston, the moment of truth at last had arrived. "I have had many important interviews in my public life, and this was certainly the most important," he noted. "Usually I talk a great deal, but on this occasion I was silent." A "very long pause" followed.

At last, Lord Halifax spoke . . . to say that as a peer, and not a member of the House of Commons, he would find it difficult to discharge the duties of a prime minister. "He spoke for some minutes in this sense, and by the time he had finished, it was clear that the duty would fall upon me—had in fact fallen upon me."

For the moment, however, Winston still was head of the admiralty, where his attention urgently was needed. He rushed back to find, first, the Dutch government ministers at his offices. "Haggard and worn, with horror in their eyes, they had just flown over from Amsterdam. Their country had been attacked without the slightest pretext or warning. The avalanche of fire and steel had rolled across the frontiers." And so Winston had much to deal with as this historic day rolled on.

The Moment Comes

As May 10, 1940, sped on, the dogs of war fully unleashed just beyond the English Channel, someone told Winston that Chamberlain had gone from Downing Street to see the king. "Presently," Winston recalled, "a message arrived summoning me to the Palace at six o'clock."

It was only a two-minute trip from his admiralty offices to Buckingham Palace. No crowd waited at the palace gates. "Although I suppose the evening newspapers must have been full of the terrific news from the Continent, nothing had been mentioned about the Cabinet crisis. The public had not had time to take in what was happening either abroad or at home."

At the palace, no time was wasted as Winston was taken before George VI. "His Majesty received me most graciously and bade me sit down," Churchill recounted. "He looked at me searchingly and quizzically for some moments, and then said: 'I suppose you don't know why I have sent for you?' Adopting his mood, I replied: 'Sir, I simply couldn't imagine why.' He laughed and said: 'I want to ask you to form a Government.' I said I would certainly do so." Winston told the king he would send for Liberal and Labor Party leaders and try to form a national, or coalition, government. "I proposed to form a War Cabinet of five or six Ministers, and that I hoped to let him have at least five names before midnight."

Returning to his admiralty offices, Winston sent for Clement Attlee, who arrived between 7:00 and 8:00 p.m., accompanied by fellow Labor leader Arthur Greenwood. Asked if Labor would join Winston's proposed cabinet, Attlee said yes. Winston suggested Labor could probably have a third of the five or six cabinet seats.

Meanwhile, what to do with, or about, the outgoing prime minister? "I invited Mr. Chamberlain to lead the House of Commons as Lord President of the Council," Winston recounted, "and he replied by telephone that he accepted and had arranged to broadcast at nine that night, stating that he had resigned, and urging everyone to support and aid his successor. This he did in magnanimous terms." Lord Halifax, later to be ambassador to Washington, remained foreign secretary for now. At about ten o'clock, Winston sent the king "a list of five names, as I had promised."

Still to go was the appointment of his military service chiefs, but he already planned on naming (future prime minister) Anthony Eden as head of the war (or army) office, Liberal Party leader Sir Archibald Sinclair (once Winston's second in command on the western front) civilian chief at the air ministry, and A. V. Alexander at the helm of the admiralty. Winston himself would become defense minister as well as prime minister. "Thus, then, on the night of the tenth of May, at the outset of this mighty battle," he recalled in his account of the war, "I acquired the chief power in the State, which, henceforth I wielded in ever-growing measure for five years and three months of world war, at the end of which time, all our enemies having surrendered unconditionally or being about to do so, I was immediately dismissed by the British electorate from all further conduct of their affairs."

It of course was one thing to anticipate winning the great prize, as he so calmly had just two days before, but what about now . . . now that the title and all its awesome responsibility at last were his? Most people would have felt somewhat overwhelmed, surely. But not Churchill. During the last few "crowded" days, he insisted, "my pulse had not quickened at any moment." He simply took events as they came. Going to bed at 3:00 a.m. on May 11, he added, "I was conscious of a profound sense of relief."

That and more, actually:

> At last I had the authority to give directions over the whole scene. I felt as if I were walking with Destiny, and that all my past life had been but a preparation for this hour and for this trial. Eleven years in the political wilderness had freed me from ordinary party antagonisms. My warnings over the last six years had been so numerous, so detailed, and were now so terribly vindicated, that no one could gainsay me. I could not be reproached either for making the war or with want of preparation for it. I thought I knew a good deal about it all, and I was sure I should not fail. Therefore, although impatient for the morning, I slept soundly and had no need for cheering dreams. Facts are better than dreams.

Until Now III

Winston Churchill had planned further lecture tours in the United States in the 1930s, but growing tensions in Europe over Nazi Germany's aggression kept him at home despite his pressing financial needs. In the meantime, Churchill met President Roosevelt's son James at a dinner in England and continued to champion Anglo-American unity against the aggressive postures of both Nazi Germany and, now, Japan in the Far East.

At that 1933 dinner, incidentally, asked what he most wanted to do, Winston said it would be to become prime minister and communicate every day with James's father. "There is nothing that we could not do if we were together," he said.

The rest of that story is well known. Once Winston Churchill became prime minister on May 10, 1940, and the full fury of the new war in Europe, World War II, broke upon France and Britain, the Roosevelt administration was poised to provide significant moral and material support, but slowly and within the bounds of U.S. neutrality laws in respect to war supplies. Another restraint was the nation's longstanding isolationist mood, but this gradually softened as the picture emerged of a brave Britain . . . nay, of Winston Churchill as the very symbol of brave Britain, both battered but unbowed in the face of terrible odds.

Even so, another year and a half elapsed before Churchill's hope for unity and salvation took concrete form—with the Japanese attack on Pearl Harbor on December 7, 1941, which propelled a suddenly antagonized United States into World War II. During the period beforehand, the United States provided Britain with various war supplies through the Lend-Lease Act, approved by Congress in 1941. Also welcome to the desperate "island race" were fifty old U.S. destroyers made available in exchange for leases of British bases in the Western Hemisphere.

Meanwhile, Churchill and his military chiefs had their eye on Japan's activities even while undergoing the German bombing of London and other civilian centers. Thus Churchill knew from intelligence in late March 1941 that the Japanese foreign minister had been visiting Berlin, where the Nazi regime urged a Japanese attack on British possessions in the Far East. Also aware that the Japanese envoy would be visiting Moscow on his way home to Japan, Churchill sent him a list of questions pointing out the folly of taking on a war with an England helpfully supplied by the United States and backed by America's great naval strength.

"From the answers to these questions," said Churchill, "may spring avoidance by Japan of a serious catastrophe, and a marked improvement in the relations between Japan and the two great sea powers of the West." Meanwhile, orders already had gone out to the RAF's Bomber Command to be sure and give Berlin an extra heavy pasting on the night the Japanese diplomat was expected to be there.

In August 1941, with the Soviet Union now under German attack also, Churchill traveled to Placentia Bay, Newfoundland, for a key meeting with Franklin D. Roosevelt that produced the Atlantic Charter, military staff meetings, and a series of U.S. commitments to provide additional aid to both the USSR and Britain. For instance, barely short of becoming an official belligerent in the war, the United States agreed to provide an escort of five destroyers and a cruiser for every convoy bound for England or Russia across the U-boat-infested North Atlantic.

Coming less than six months later, the Pearl Harbor attack of course made the United States a full-fledged partner in the war against the Axis powers. And once the smoke cleared from the Japanese attack, it appeared Japan had greatly reduced any threat it faced from the U.S. Pacific Fleet, for which Pearl served as homeport. After all, 7 of 8 battleships in port that fateful morning were sunk or damaged, as were 80-odd other naval vessels. In addition, 187 aircraft at adjoining army and marine airfields were destroyed. Shamefully, too, more than 2,400 U.S. military personnel were killed.

To Japan's later sorrow, it turned out that the American carriers were safely at sea and not all the battleships and other vessels were totally knocked out of commission. More important in the long run, the Japanese fatally underestimated the nation's anger and resiliency, expressed both in the form of its fighting soldiery and its breathtaking industrial power. As an indication of the unified American response, Congress agreed the very next day, December 8, 1941, to a declaration of war against Japan with only a single nay vote cast.

In England, meanwhile, Churchill had learned of Pearl Harbor shortly after 9:00 p.m. London time with, it so happened, U.S. Ambassador John G. Winant and special U.S. envoy Averell Harriman as his dinner guests at Chequers, the PM's official country retreat. Hearing vague references on the radio news that evening to a Japanese attack on U.S. shipping at Hawaii and British ships in the Dutch East Indies, Churchill quickly called Roosevelt.

"Mr. President," he said, "what's all this about Japan?"

"It's quite true," said FDR. "They have attacked us at Pearl Harbor. We are all in the same boat now."

Three days later, Churchill learned the shocking news that Japan had sunk Britain's mighty warships *Repulse* and *Prince of Wales* off Malaya. For now, on paper at least, it appeared the Japanese enjoyed unchallenged naval supremacy in the Pacific. More important in the long run, Italy and Germany declared war on the United States as of December 11, which—much to Churchill's relief and gratification—made America Britain's ally in Europe as well as in the Pacific. That development, he said, "makes amends for all, and with time and patience will give certain victory."

It also meant he would be visiting Washington, the White House, and FDR, forthwith.

Victory at All Cost

It was just three days after he became prime minister that Winston gave the first of his great wartime speeches to the House of Commons . . . in effect to all of

Britain and the world. It was in this oration that he said, "I have nothing to offer but blood, toil, tears and sweat." It was here and now that he warned "many, many long months of struggle and suffering" lay ahead, that he said to expect "an ordeal of the most grievous kind." It was in this speech that he fervently spelled out his and his newly formed government's approach to war: "You ask what is our policy. I will say, it is to wage war with all our might, with all the strength that God can give us, to wage war against a monstrous tyranny never surpassed in the dark, lamentable catalog of human crime."

And the aim? "You ask what is our aim? I can answer in one word: Victory. Victory at all costs. Victory in spite of all terror. Victory however long and hard the road may be. For without victory there is no survival."

As PM

As prime minister, Winston still was the same old (at age sixty-five) Winston that he had been for years: unflagging, fingers in every pie, absolutely determined, unstinting, and yet surprisingly considerate at times with his subordinates, still napping by day in order to work by night . . . working, working into the wee, dark hours of just about every morning.

And his presence was felt everywhere. As France was invaded and not so gradually collapsing before the weight of the German onslaught, he flew across the Channel five times in May to buck up the French leadership. "Usually escorted by guardian Spitfires," wrote daughter Mary, "on one occasion he had to leave France and return without his escort; during this flight his aircraft had to dive down to about 100 feet above sea level to avoid attracting the attention of two German planes which were strafing fishing boats."

Another time, reported biographer Martin Gilbert, flying to Paris with Clement Attlee and two generals also aboard, Winston's plane had to avoid German fighters north of the city. As a result, they flew "first to Weymouth to pick up an escort of nine Hurricanes, then across the Channel to Jersey, then crossing the French coast west of St. Malo, then due east to Villacoublay near Versailles, where, for a while, the plane was virtually lost at the wrong end of the vast airdrome."

Another no-change for Winston was his unusual sleeping regime, just right at least for him. As he had for years, he insisted on taking an hour's rest in the afternoon or early evening. Observed Mary: "He undressed and went right to bed, and awoke a giant refreshed. He was then able to work after dinner long into the night. This system undoubtedly contributed to Winston's ability to survive the strains and support the burdens of five long years of war. It enabled him as he wrote himself, 'to press a day and a half's work into one.'"

The same regime might not have been so perfect for others, such as Britain's military chiefs, who had to work all day, with no nap, and then often deal with Winston's nighttime demands as well. Most accepted the added strain "with understanding and loyalty," Mary said, but for many it wasn't easy.

Meanwhile, with the fall of World War I ally France in mid-June, both Winston and Clementine felt "intense grief and dismay over the downfall of that great country," Mary wrote. France for years had been a place they loved for travel and holidays of all kinds. Clementine of course had lived there, at Dieppe, as did her mother in her final years. But now the France of old was gone. Now, only Gen. Charles de Gaulle remained out of German hands and able to lead the Free French from Britain for the time being. He would not always be easy to get along with—Clementine once felt compelled to dress him down at the luncheon table—but at least he was strong and resolute, like Winston.

With France gone, Britain basically stood alone against the barbarians. And now, when would the ax fall? "It is difficult to recapture the atmosphere of those times," wrote Mary. "There were indeed to be many more days of anxiety, and many hard tidings to bear in the course of the next five years; but never again, I think, did one feel one could scarcely breathe. We got through the days almost automatically, living from news bulletin to news bulletin, and dreading what each would bring."

Still, there were certain domestic arrangements afoot once Winston became prime minister. For one, the family again would be on the move, this time from the admiralty apartment to No. 10 Downing Street, the traditional home for the prime minister. "A charming house where the Prime Minister can both live and work," Mary noted. "On the ground floor are the Cabinet Room and the Prime Minister's Private Office; on the first floor is a series of beautiful and dignified rooms leading one into the other, including a large state dining room, and a delightful white-paneled passage room, where we always lunched or dined when we were not more than eight people. Upstairs the bedroom floor with its egg-shell blue passages, cheerful red carpets and pleasantly sized rooms with sash windows, gave the impression of a country house."

Speaking of country homes, Chartwell was all but shuttered for the war years. If and when the Germans began bombing—and surely they would—it was on their target route "and easily identifiable from the air."

Taking Chartwell's place as a weekend retreat—almost always a working weekend retreat—would be Chequers, the prime minister's official country residence. A commodious Elizabethan home in Buckinghamshire near Aylesbury, it was "fully staffed and run by a charming and efficient Scottish curator, Miss Grace Lamont," Mary noted. "Winston and Clementine spent their first weekend at Chequers on 1st June, while the evacuation from Dunkirk was reaching its climax."

From then on, like No. 10 Downing Street, Chequers played a major role in the direction of Britain's war effort. Often descending here on weekends were "a skeleton Private Office, two or three telephone operators, the detectives, chauffeurs and dispatch riders, as well as the family and up to eight guests," reported Mary. "Quite soon the pattern for the weekends took shape: there was nearly always a nucleus of the family, and occasionally a close friend or two, and superimposed on these intimates would be succeeding waves of service chiefs, Cabinet colleagues, or specialists in various subjects, who were bidden to 'dine and sleep.'"

For "many an overworked general, Civil Servant or government colleague," these working weekends could mean "a grueling twenty-four hours." But never mind, they were invaluable sojourns that "often resulted in far-reaching and vital decisions, or closer understanding, between Churchill and those in whose minds and hands lay the waging of the war." In time, Chequers was staffed by women volunteers from the Auxiliary Territorial Service and the Women's Auxiliary Air Force.

☆   ☆   ☆

Additional note: Not even a sometimes superhuman-seeming Winston Churchill could take on the burden he did in May and June 1940 without some deterioration. Simply, "he drove himself, and he drove others with a flail," Mary noted. As a result he sometimes "must . . . have become extremely overbearing and tyrannical." Winston became so domineering that Clementine was moved by a "devoted friend's" warning to send him a cautionary note citing his "rough sarcastic & overbearing manner" and saying she had noticed he wasn't as "kind" as he used to be. Mary noted, "The letter surely bore fruit, for although Winston could be formidable and, indeed, overbearing, many people who served him at all levels during those hard years have put on record not only their respect and admiration for him as a chief, but also their love for a warm and endearing human being."

The Beaches, the Streets, the Hills...

The battle of Flanders raged for twenty-six days, and the Allies (British, French, Belgians) lost a million men as prisoners. The French alone lost thirty divisions. The Belgians lost their entire army and their country (with the French about to lose theirs). Survivors of the British Expeditionary Force (BEF) clustered around the coastal town of Dunkirk, just above the narrowest part of the English Channel. Now, beginning on May 29, 1940, came the evacuation of Dunkirk.

Thus began a historic saga, with 861 vessels of all shapes and sizes, ranging from Royal Navy warships to private yachts and sailboats, removing 338,000 Allied troops from the embattled town's beaches, jetties, and piers and carrying them to at least temporary safety in Britain. Much of their equipage and 30,000 of their fellows were left behind on the bloody beaches, killed or taken prisoner. Of the vessels employed in the great rescue, to England's possible salvation in the event of a German invasion, 243 were sunk, including 6 destroyers. In addition, a holding force at Calais was sacrificed for the sake of the men at Dunkirk.

In all, the story of Dunkirk was a heroic story that led to the second of Winston's greatest and most memorable addresses to the House of Commons in his first days and weeks as wartime prime minister. On June 4, 1940, just after the last soldier was plucked from Dunkirk, he rose so memorably to say: "We shall not flag or fail. We shall go on to the end. We shall fight in France, we shall fight on the seas and oceans, we shall fight with growing confidence and growing strength in the air. We shall defend our island, whatever the cost may be. We shall fight on the beaches, we shall fight on the landing-grounds, we shall fight in the fields and in the streets, we shall fight in the hills. We shall never surrender!"

Additional note: At the height of the evacuation, Winston made it clear that French as well as British soldiers must be taken off the embattled beaches of Dunkirk.

Given up, though, were the gallant Scotsmen of the 51st Highland Division, who, in a rear-guard action at St. Valery-en-Caux, "were still fighting in France ten days after the evacuation at . . . Dunkirk had been completed," noted Bill Innes, editor of the book *St. Valery: The Impossible Odds*.

Ready to Die

It's not often that a committee meets and the chairman declares, to every member's approval, that all of those assembled might die, might end up "choking in his own blood upon the ground." Yet on the eve of the Dunkirk evacuation, during secret discussions within the British cabinet of possible peace negotiations with Hitler, that is what happened.

In the first place, recalled biographer Martin Gilbert, the five-member War Cabinet on May 28 briefly debated Lord Halifax's "suggestion that Britain should take up an offer from [Hitler's Italian ally Benito] Mussolini to negotiate a general peace" if "decent terms" were offered.

Winston, "dismayed and angered," retorted that chances were a thousand to one against any decent terms presenting themselves. "Nations which went down fighting rose again, but those who surrendered tamely were finished," he declared.

Supported in this stance by Labor members Clement Attlee and Arthur Greenwood, Winston addressed all twenty-five members of the full cabinet to repeat his "belief that Britain would rather go down fighting than negotiate peace," Gilbert recorded. Peace with the Germans, Winston predicted, would mean turning over the British fleet, "her naval bases and much else." Their country would become a slave state under the rule of a puppet government.

Warming to his task, Winston declared Britain still had "immense reserves and advantages." He went on to say: "I am convinced that every man of you would rise up and tear me down from my place if I were for one moment to contemplate parley or surrender. If this long island story of ours is to end at last, let it end only when each one of us lies choking in his own blood upon the ground." It was a dramatic moment, one of the most dramatic of Winston's entire life. Not only were there cries of approval, but "quite a number," he later wrote, "seemed to jump up from the table and come running to my chair, shouting and patting me on the back."

In sum: "I am sure that every Minister was ready to be killed quite soon, and have all his family and possessions destroyed, rather than give in."

Said Hugh Dalton, the newly named minister of economic warfare and one of those in attendance: "He was quite magnificent. The man, and the only man we have for this task."

Their Finest Hour

Just a day after Winston rose in the House in the wake of Dunkirk to pledge England would never surrender but would fight in the streets, on the beaches, and in the hills, German armies unleashed their full fury on France. After losing a third of its strength in the battle of Flanders, France now could muster only 65 divisions to defend against 140 German divisions crushing all opposition before them across a hundred-mile front, with the help of the Luftwaffe's fighters and terrifying dive-bombers.

By June 11, the government had declared Paris an open city and retreated to Tours. By June 17, newly installed Premier Henri Petain, the hero of World War I, was suing for peace, and on June 22 France formally surrendered. The armies of implacably hostile Nazi Germany now stood unchallenged at the water's edge directly across from England, a distance in places of less than thirty miles.

And so, on June 18, the day after Petain's capitulation, Churchill again rose in the House of Commons to voice perhaps his greatest speech of all. With the battle for France now over, he said:

> I expect that the battle of Britain is about to begin. Upon this battle depends the survival of Christian civilization. Upon it depends our own British life, and the long continuity of our institutions and our Empire. The whole fury and might of the enemy must very soon be turned on us. Hitler knows that he will have to break us in this island or lose the war. If we can stand up to him, all Europe may be free and the life of the world may move forward into broad, sunlit uplands. But if we fail, then the whole world, including the United States, including all that we have known and cared for, will sink into the abyss of a new Dark Age, made more sinister, and perhaps more protracted, by the lights of perverted science. Let us therefore brace ourselves to our duties, and so bear ourselves that if the British Empire and its Commonwealth last for a thousand years, men will still say, "This was their Finest Hour."

Additional note: Of the thousands of French soldiers evacuated to Britain in May and June, most returned to France and submitted to the Vichy government.

Attack on the French

Soon after becoming prime minister, Churchill felt compelled to turn British guns against a faithful ally . . . and for his troubles won a demonstration of approval by the House of Commons that left him in tears. In the midst of the Battle of the Atlantic, with bombing and an invasion of England expected at any moment, the day, the hour came when London ordered the shelling of several French warships at the Mers el-Kebir naval base and adjoining Oran in North Africa. In just minutes on July 3, 1940, a battleship was blown up and two other capital ships were seriously damaged while nearly thirteen hundred French sailors were killed.

To attack Britain's ally against Germany in two back-to-back wars was certainly a painful task for the British, but the Vichy French leadership that agreed to an armistice with Nazi Germany no longer could be viewed as an ally . . . and the French warships it controlled could not be allowed to fall into German hands. Sir James Somerville, the admiral whose fleet was ordered to carry out the distasteful attack, commented, "We all feel thoroughly dirty and ashamed that the first time we should have been in action was an affair like this."

No one was happy with the outcome. Certainly not Charles de Gaulle, leader of the Free French, who, while despising the Vichy French, also felt "pain and anger" over the British action—in fact, it was his complaint about the shelling that prompted Clementine's sharp rebuke to his face at the luncheon table at No. 10 Downing Street. Meanwhile, he complained elsewhere that the British press announced the shelling "as if it were a victory."

It definitely had not been a victory, not when so many French sailors cheered at the orders to relight the fires aboard their dormant ships in the belief, reported journalist Laurence Thompson in *1940*, that "they were sailing in support of the British." No great victory, either, when some of the French warships were "anchored in such a position that they could not use their guns."

As Thompson noted, the French Atlantic Squadron harbored at Mers-el-Kebir and Oran comprised about one-fifth of the French navy, itself the fourth largest in the world at the time. The squadron consisted of two battle cruisers, two battleships, a seaplane carrier, four submarines, and thirteen destroyers.

Winston wrote in his history of the war that the two battle cruisers "in German hands on our trade routes would have been most disagreeable." He noted that the decision by the War Cabinet to act against the French ships "was a hateful decision, the most unnatural and painful in which I have ever been concerned." Still, "the life of the State and the salvation of our cause were at stake."

As a result, during the night of July 2–3, French vessels moored at the British ports of Plymouth and Portsmouth were seized, with only token resistance offered by crewmen aboard a French submarine. Although "overwhelming force" and surprise were key elements in the double takeover, Winston commented, 'the whole transaction showed how easily the Germans could have taken possession of any French warships lying in ports which they controlled."

The subsequent shelling by Somerville's squadron on the evening of July 3 followed a British warning and ultimatum to the French admiral that included the options of fighting with the Allies, turning over the ships without their crews, or scuttling the vessels on the spot. Refusing to bow under threat of force, French Adm. Marcel Gensoul refused all choices—instead, he gave the order to relight the boilers and clear for action *against* the British.

When Gensoul's six-hour grace period ran out, Somerville reluctantly opened fire. The barrage lasted just thirteen minutes, with only one of the capital ships able to slip away to safety in Toulon.

In America, as well as Britain, the outcome was greeted as a relief and as convincing evidence that Churchill's Britain would fight the Nazi-led Axis powers to the bitter end . . . no surrender. Before now, fearing for the future of both the French and British fleets, the Americans calculated they might have to shift part of their Pacific fleet to the Atlantic in their own defense. Now, that might not be necessary. Now, too, if the British were so ruthlessly determined to fight it out to the end, a few American supply strings would loosen up. White House insider Robert Sherwood commented that the Oran shelling "served forcibly to underscore Churchill's defiant assurance that 'we will fight them in the streets' and 'never surrender.' It exerted a particular effect on Roosevelt."

That, of course, suited Winston, for he not only wanted to keep the French ships out of German hands, he also wished to demonstrate Britain's determination to fight on, despite the terrible odds arrayed against the island nation. In addition, noted Thompson, "Churchill seized the opening offered by the impact of Oran to revive the question of the loan to Britain of fifty old American destroyers, which he had raised as long ago as May 15, in his first telegram to the President as Prime Minister."

The destroyer request had been put aside because of American anxieties about the future of the British fleet, but now the Marquis of Lothian, the British Ambassador to Washington, was able to report progress on the issue. "Informed

American opinion was at last beginning to realize that if America remained neutral and Britain went down, the British fleet might be lost altogether," Thompson noted. If the destroyers were to be given over, however, there must be assurances "that, if the United States entered the war, the British fleet would cross the Atlantic in the event of Britain being overrun."

As Thompson (and many other historians of the war) noted, negotiations over the simple-sounding destroyers deal dragged on for several weeks . . . and acquired an historic symbolism in the process. As Thompson stated, "The loan or gift of destroyers to Britain would mark a major step forward in American commitment to eventual war with Germany; the sale or lease of British territory to the United States [in exchange] would be a tacit admission that Britain was no longer capable by herself of defending her imperial interests. The transaction did indeed mark the first step in the eventual transfer of world power from Britain to the United States."

The final deal announced on September 5 gave Britain the destroyers and the United States leases on British bases in Newfoundland and Bermuda, along with several in the Caribbean. Meanwhile, assurance had been given that warships of the British fleet would retire to American or Dominion ports if Britain "went down," although FDR publicly said the fleet proviso only "happens to come along at the same time."

Meanwhile, the day after the shelling of the French fleet at Oran, Winston had gone before the House of Commons to report on the terrible deed. "I spoke for an hour or more that afternoon, and gave a detailed account of all those somber events as they were known to me," he recalled. Although he didn't say so, it was the unanimity in the reaction of the House that moved him to tears.

Until now, Winston had remained a controversial, even hated figure in some circles. As noted by John Lukas in his *Five Days in London: May 1940*, "Some of his enemies often referred to him as a 'half-breed' (his mother having been American and a woman with more than one past) or a 'mongrel' [while] the words 'crooks,' 'gangsters,' and 'wild men' appear in many of the diaries and letters of the period, referring to Churchill's new government."

The reserve demonstrated toward Churchill among the Conservative ranks of the House had been palpable, but that changed with his "long and emotional report" of July 4, noted Thompson. "There were tears in his eyes as he spoke of the British ships firing upon their former allies. When he sat down there was silence. The Labor benches began to cheer. The Conservative benches remained silent." But then they, too, "as if at a signal . . . rose and burst into enthusiastic cheering." (Actually, there may have been a signal from the chief Conservative whip, David Margesson, but no matter, the effect was the same.)

Winston recounted that the House was "very silent" during his recital of events, "but at the end there occurred a scene unique in my own experience." Unique but of course very moving. "Everybody seemed to stand up all around, cheering, for what seemed a long time. Up till this moment the Conservative Party had treated me with some reserve, and it was from the Labor benches that I received the warmest welcome when I entered the House or rose on serious occasions. But now all joined in solemn stentorian accord."

And so it was that Winston was in tears again as he sat down.

Additional note: The "violent action" eliminating the French navy as an important factor "in a single stroke" made a profound impression "in every country," Winston wrote in *Finest Hour*. Said he: "Here was this Britain which so many had counted down and out, which strangers had supposed to be quivering on the brink of surrender to the mighty power arrayed against her, striking ruthlessly at her dearest friends of yesterday and securing for a while to herself the undisputed command of the sea. It was made plain that the British War Cabinet feared nothing and would stop at nothing. This was true."

Tribute to "the Few"

The battle was far from over when Winston Churchill returned from visits to Fighter Command airfields in southern England and went before the House to pay his unforgettable tribute to the intrepid airmen defending their island nation. Who can forget the incredible story of "the Few"?

How few? The Battle of Britain, the air battle of 1940, began with 2,670 German aircraft—Junkers, Dornier, and Heinkel bombers; Stuka dive-bombers; and Messerschmitt fighters—ranged against only 600 Royal Air Force (RAF) Hawker Hurricane and Supermarine Spitfire fighters. Naturally, it was the bombers, all 1,015 of them, that were the real threat to the homeland and its defenders. Naturally, based in the newly captured airfields of France and Belgium, they didn't have far to go.

After weeks of wondering, indeed even fearing, when the war would come home to them, the British citizenry had its answer on July 10. On that day the now legendary Battle of Britain began with heavy German raids on ports in southern England, presumed to be a likely invasion site. From then on, almost daily, bombers escorted by swarms of fighters struck at shipping and harbor facilities in port cities stretching from Bristol to Plymouth. The low point came on August 15, the day both southern and northern England took a beating from an estimated 940 German aircraft—with 76 German planes shot down to the RAF's loss of 34 fighters and 21 bombers destroyed on the ground.

By this time, thanks to Fighter Command's relentlessly fierce defense of the homeland, a new phase in Luftwaffe strategy had developed: the RAF itself became the target. Thus, the Luftwaffe went after airfields, radar facilities, and aircraft factories supporting Fighter Command in this all-out two-week effort to negate the RAF's threat to German bombers. During this critical phase, the British lost 466 Hurricanes and Spitfires, along with 103 pilots killed and another 128 badly wounded—a fourth of the pilot pool in Fighter Command. These were terrible losses, difficult to overcome, but it is estimated the Germans lost twice as many aircraft and even more pilots and aircrews.

But on September 7 the Luftwaffe changed strategy again and began targeting the civilian population of England. London became the target of the German blitz, no holds barred. The new phase began with a daytime raid on London by 300 German planes. On September 15, 400 German bombers attacked the capital city, with 56 lost to RAF fighters and antiaircraft fire. Another change in tactics quickly followed. Now, the Germans would bomb only at night, with an average of 200 planes striking London with high explosives and incendiaries night after night—57 nights in a row during the peak period. On one of those nights, October 15, an estimated 480 German aircraft struck the capital city with 386 tons of high explosives and 70,000 incendiaries.

"The repetitive, heavy raids killed more than 43,000 British and wounded five times that number, caused tremendous property damage, and curtailed war and food production," noted David Eggenberger's *Encyclopedia of Battles*. "But the change to night attack made it clear that British fighter pilots . . . had broken the back of the Luftwaffe bomber offensive and unequivocally ended Nazi invasion plans. Although the air battle raged on for another two months . . . the issue had been settled in September."

By November 3, Germany had lost 1,733 aircraft (although the British claimed to have downed 2,698 planes). By comparison, the RAF lost 915 fighters.

The air war continued, but the major targets were now the big industrial centers. This was when Coventry, on the night of November 14, suffered its infamous pasting by 500 bombers dropping 600 tons of high explosives and leaving even the city's cathedral shattered. Birmingham was another high-value target and absorbed heavy raids into the fall and winter months. Meanwhile, London and the port cities continued to be intermittent bomber destinations as well.

The bombing campaign went on until May 1941. "During this time British air defenses destroyed an average of 15 to 20 planes a month," reported Eggenberger. "In the first ten days of May [1941] alone, 70 Luftwaffe planes were shot down by ever improving defensive weapons—more antiaircraft guns (almost 500 in London alone), better radar, and the addition of rocket batteries." Indeed, the prewar British invention of radar, allowing Fighter Command to "see" where and when the attackers were coming from a minimum of sixty miles out was crucial to England's survival. So was its solution to Nazi Germany's own radio-based weapon—a radio beam that led pilots to their targets. But the British, discovering the beam's presence, devised a way to "bend" it, thus often leading the German bombers to empty fields instead of blacked-out cities.

The Luftwaffe's bombing campaign ended with a proverbial bang on May 10, the anniversary of Winston's elevation to prime minister, when German bombers in their last major raid launched their most destructive raid of all on London. "Bombers started more than 2,000 fires and killed or injured over 3,000 people, at a cost of 16 planes (the most planes destroyed in a night attack throughout the blitz)," Eggenberger noted.

After a pause of five weeks, the Luftwaffe next became fully engaged in Hitler's surprise invasion of his wartime ally of nearly two years: the Soviet Union. Long before this, however, long before the salvation of Britain could be known, Churchill on August 20, 1940, had gone before the House to proclaim, "The gratitude of every home in our island, in our Empire, and indeed throughout the world, except in the abodes of the guilty, goes out to the British airmen who, undaunted by odds, unwearied in their constant challenge and mortal danger, are turning the tide of the world war by their prowess and by their devotion."

Indeed, none could ever forget "the few" after he went on to say, long before the outcome of the Battle of Britain was resolved: "Never in the field of human conflict was so much owed by so many to so few."

☆   ☆   ☆

Additional note: While the myth persists that Winston knew from intelligence reports that Coventry was about to be bombed, and he allowed the bombing to take place unimpeded rather than compromise the highly secret Ultra code decrypts, historians say that isn't the case. To the contrary, it seems that Winston was traveling in the countryside when he was misinformed that London was about to be attacked. He immediately returned to London and only learned later that Coventry was the night's main target.

Days of Blitz

With the start of the London blitz, Winston was in the streets. No holding him back. "Winston, who disliked exercise, walked miles among the rubble and still-smoking skeletons of buildings," wrote newspaperman Jack Fishman in *My Darling Clementine*. "As darkness began to creep up on the day, dock authorities became anxious for Winston to leave for home."

On that first time out, too, "he was in one of his most obstinate moods and insisted that he wanted to see everything," wrote Lord Ismay, his chief of staff at the Defense Ministry and constant wartime companion. "Consequently we were still with him at the brightly lit target when the Luftwaffe arrived on the scene and the fireworks started. It was difficult to get a large car out of the area, owing to many of the streets being completely blocked by fallen houses. As we were trying to turn in a very narrow space, a shower of incendiary bombs fell just in front of us. Churchill, feigning innocence, asked what they were. I replied that they were incendiaries and that we were evidently in the middle of the bulls-eye!"

Naturally, they were worried about the wandering PM back home.

"It was very late by the time we got back to No. 10 Downing Street," Ismay commented, "and Cabinet Ministers, secretaries, policemen, and orderlies were waiting in the long passage in great anxiety. Churchill strode through them without a word, leaving me to be rebuked by all and sundry for having allowed the Prime Minister to take such risks." Ismay said he may have used "the language of the barracks" in telling anybody who thought they could control Winston "on jaunts of this kind" that they were welcome to give it a try on the next occasion. Unfortunately, there were many such next occasions as the bombings of London continued.

Again and again, Winston was in the streets with the suffering Londoners.

But Clementine figured out a way to keep him from seeking the most dangerous pathways in the besieged city—namely, she insisted on going with him.

Thus, "Day after day Winston and Clementine walked together over rubble that was once homes, talking to the homeless, listening to their needs," wrote Fishman. "He became the idol of the people, and the people were lucky in their idol—they could trust him with a tyrant's power because they knew he would not use it like a tyrant."

One day, cheered as they toured bombed-out streets in the East End, Winston turned to her and said, "They greet me like a conquering hero. God knows why. They are a great people."

On that first tour, after the initial bombing of London and its docks, he indeed had been greeted that way. The moment he stepped out of his car, "hundreds who had been battered mercilessly, mobbed him, shouting 'Good old Winnie! We thought you'd come and see us.'"

He couldn't hold back the tears as he surveyed the destruction wrought by the bombs and noticed the tiny paper Union Jacks planted defiantly on the great piles of debris. "You see, he really cares; he's crying," said a woman from a few feet away.

His walking tours, his frequent rounds by Jeep, his V-sign hand gestures and defiantly tilted cigar, his obvious caring, all undoubtedly helped the British people to keep a stiff upper lip during their time of trial. But it took Clementine to realize, Fishman added, that Winston "undertook these journeys not only to instill encouragement into the people by his appearance among them, but also because their continued spirit in turn strengthened him."

Personal Glimpse

One day early in the war, thirteen-year-old Edith Harmer was walking in a small village with a young mother, her three-year-old daughter, and a baby in a carriage. Suddenly, German airplanes swooped down out of nowhere. They machine-gunned the village streets for a few seconds . . . and just as suddenly they were gone.

Edith and her friends escaped harm. As she later explained on the BBC's "WW2 Peoples' War" Web site (an archive of wartime memories from the public), this was not an isolated incident in the village of Woodchurch. "This did happen from time to time, and, as always, we dived for cover into the nearest ditch."

The only harm done this time was some damage around the village and a blackthorn wound to the three-year-old's bottom. That was on a September afternoon in 1940 or 1941, and later that day the teenaged Edith was sent back to the village to buy some potatoes. She found the grocer sweeping up glass from his shop window—shattered during the strafing attack.

As the real excitement of the day, however, along came a "big black car." It stopped across the road from the grocer's, and out stepped the king and queen of England and the prime minister, Winston Churchill! No escort, no security detail—"just them and their driver."

Edith, of course, could hardly believe it. Especially as the queen approached and spoke to her while Churchill and the king made a beeline for a nearby group of soldiers. "She asked if it had been a bad raid and if anyone was hurt.

"I managed to stutter out, 'No, no one.'

"'I'm so glad,' she replied and returned to the car."

Within moments the car drove off, the royal couple seated in the back and Churchill up front with the driver. Meanwhile, Edith was so "dumbfounded" by the whole affair, she only then remembered that she had forgotten to curtsey to the queen.

No. 10 Under the Bombs

On October 14, 1940, as the Churchills dined in the garden rooms at No. 10 Downing Street, the prime minister's official residence, bombs began dropping—"the usual night raid," he termed it later. But this time not quite.

"The steel shutters had been closed," he wrote *Their Finest Hour*. "Several loud explosions occurred around us at no great distance, and presently a bomb fell, perhaps a hundred yards away, on the Horse Guards Parade, making a great deal of noise." Since No. 10 Downing Street consisted of two houses joined together, one facing Downing Street and the other the Horse Gardens Parade, this last bomb was pretty close.

While dinner continued and "the butler and parlor maid" carried on their service "with complete detachment," Churchill recalled that the kitchen was "lofty and spacious, and looks out through a large plate-glass window about 25 feet high." He quite suddenly "became acutely aware" that the kitchen and its expansive window were to the rear of the Downing Street part of the house and the last bomb had been pretty close to that area. By "provincial impulse" he went into the kitchen. There, he told the butler to put the dinner on a hot plate in the dining room and ordered the cook and other servants out of the kitchen area and into a shelter.

He hardly had taken his seat at the table again when, with a "really loud crash" close by, "a violent shock showed that the house had been struck." Indeed, as he was told moments later, "the kitchen, the pantry and the offices of the [nearby] Treasury were shattered." Worse yet, three civil servants on Home Guard duty were killed in the blast, which came from a bomb landing on nearby Treasury Green. It did extensive damage to the empty kitchen and state rooms at No. 10 Downing Street as well.

Before this, newly appointed Prime Minister Churchill and his wife, Clementine, had resided in the second-floor flat at No. 10. Following his long-established practice, Winston "often dictated speeches, memos and letters to his secretary while lying propped in bed in the morning or later in the evening, cigar in hand," recalls the online history of No. 10 Downing Street. But close calls such as the October 14 bomb, which came as the Battle of Britain raged in the skies overhead, dictated fresh steps to enhance security at the residence.

"Keeping Downing Street, the Prime Minister and the War Cabinet safe became a top priority," notes the historical sketch of the famous residence. "Steel reinforcement was added to the Garden Rooms and heavy metal shutters were fixed over windows as protection from bombing raids. The Garden Rooms provided a small dining room, bedroom and a meeting area which were used by Churchill throughout the war. In reality, though, the steel reinforcement would not have protected him against a direct hit."

Good reason, naturally, for the fact that a year earlier, at the outset of the war, the British cabinet had moved its meeting place from No. 10's traditional Cabinet Room into underground rooms built in the basement of the innocuous-looking Office of Works opposite the Foreign Office . . . into the complex open to public visitation today and known as the Cabinet War Rooms. Although the neighboring complex included office and sleeping quarters for Churchill, his wife, and various aides, plus his beloved map room, the Churchills actually lived most of the time in the "Number 10 Annex" established right above the war rooms.

But Churchill still preferred the prime minister's real home at No. 10 "for working and eating," the official history notes. "A reinforced shelter was constructed under the house for up to six people, for use by those working in the house," the same online source adds. "Even George VI sought shelter there when he dined with Churchill in the Garden Rooms." And "although bombs caused further damage to Number 10, there were no direct hits to the house, allowing Churchill to continue to work and dine there right up until the end of the war."

After that, though, the old home required both cosmetic and structural repairs that took nearly two decades to complete. First, as Labor Minister Clement Attlee and wife succeeded the Churchills in 1945, the attic was converted into a flat for their living quarters. But downstairs, alarming discoveries were made as the repair work advanced. The wartime bomb damage had only made preexisting structural problems worse, problems such as "sloping walls, twisting door frames and an enormous annual repair bill." Still, basic solutions were put off until a committee established by Prime Minister Harold Macmillan reported in the 1960s "that drastic action was required before the building fell or burnt down." Among the recommendations: tear down No. 10 Downing Street and its adjoining Nos. 12 and 11 (the traditional home of the chancellor of the exchequer) and start over.

Of course, that would never do. "The idea was rejected and instead it was decided that Number 12 should be rebuilt; Number 10 and 11 should be strengthened and their historic features preserved."

Only then, as workers began the £500,000 restoration project, was it discovered that the foundations were so rotted "that concrete underpinning was required on a massive scale." As the work proceeded, No. 10 was gutted completely. "Walls, floors and even the columns in the Cabinet Room and the Pillar Room proved to be rotten and had to be replaced." With brand-new features added here and there to Nos. 10 and 11, the project wound up taking an extra year to complete (in 1963) at a cost double the original estimate. Even then, with dry rot turning up on the premises, still further work had to be undertaken. By then two-time resident Winston Churchill long since had gone his inimitable way, followed by Anthony Eden, Macmillan, Margaret Thatcher ("living above the shop," she called it), Tony Blair, and Gordon Brown, among others.

In 1991 an IRA mortar round provided a brief scare during the tenure of John Major. Fired from a van, it exploded harmlessly in the garden at No. 10. Harmlessly . . . true, but uncomfortably close to the PM himself while he was leading a cabinet meeting just yards away from the crater the mortar round created.

☆ ☆ ☆

Additional note: All kinds of history, both momentous and menial, has unfolded behind the front door of No. 10 Downing since Sir Robert Walpole first conceived of the building's role as the home and office for the leading minister of England nearly three hundred years ago. For here, not only Winston Churchill in the 1940s, but his onetime mentor David Lloyd George led the nation through the twentieth century's two devastating world wars. Here, too, William Gladstone strived to convert prostitutes into honest women, and Walpole "openly entertained his mistress Maria Skerett" while still married to, but estranged from, his wife.

The No. 10 tradition began in the 1730s when George II presented both the Downing Street house and the Horse Guards residence directly behind it to Walpole, who held the high office of first lord of the treasury and thus "effectively served as the first prime minister." It was Walpole, taking up residence here in 1735, who conjoined the two houses but refused to accept the Downing Street property as an outright gift. Instead, "he asked the King to make it available to him, and future First Lords of the Treasury, in their official capacity." Thus, "to this day prime ministers occupy Number 10 in the role of First Lord of the Treasury. The brass letter box on the black front door is still engraved with this title."

Was there, however, a Mr. Downing of any kind ever involved with London's most famous address? There was, actually. He was an early housing developer. But Sir George Downing—born in Dublin, Ireland, and raised in America and educated at Harvard University—also was "an enterprising rogue," per the property's online history—"a spy, traitor and shady property developer—who saw building houses on prime London land as a means to get rich quick."

At one time he served as Oliver Cromwell's intelligence chief, and after Cromwell, Downing managed during the Restoration period to ingratiate himself to Charles II, serve as ambassador to Holland, and after various intrigues and adventures, compile his fortune. Gaining title to property near Hampden House and Westminster, home of Parliament, he tore down existing structures and in their place created "a cul-de-sac of 15 or 20 terraced houses."

These were not grand structures by any means. "Designed for quick turnover, Downing's houses were cheaply built, with poor foundations for the boggy ground. Instead of neat brick facades, they had mortar lines drawn to look like even-spaced bricks." One of them was the No. 10 Downing Street so widely known today . . . only back then, in the 1680s, it was a much more humble No. 5.

Typing for Winston

Born in Suffolk, England, raised in the Canadian Rockies, and a comely young woman by age twenty-three, newly hired prime minister's secretary Elizabeth Layton one day in 1941 faced her first bout of dictation from the boss, Winston Churchill. The others in the secretarial pool at No. 10 Downing Street had briefed her as best they could. "When you don't hear, you may ask him what he said if you're brave and prepared for a squash," they told her. "Or you may put [down] what you thought he said if you don't mind having your head snicked off. Or you may leave a space and hope from the sense you'll later realize what it was you missed, in which case you can creep back quietly on the typewriter and put it in—and hope he doesn't roar at you for fidgeting."

As events turned out, Layton's first session with the temperamental prime minister was a bit of a disaster. "She didn't notice until it was too late that the silent typewriter had been left set at single spacing instead of the prime ministerially decreed double," reported the London *Times* years later. "On discovering her offense, Churchill 'went off like a rocket,' as she described it in her memoirs [*Mr Churchill's Secretary*], and she was sent away to be replaced by a colleague."

But not for long.

Although for weeks she "seemed unable to do anything right," she finally, in the wee hours of a morning at Chequers, the official country residence, "produced a piece of shorthand writing that . . . passed muster." With that, "she had turned a corner and won his confidence."

As a result, Elizabeth Layton would be a key player in Churchill's close-support team for the duration, a punishing tour of duty indeed. As summarized by the *Times* in her obituary of November 1, 2007: "In war-torn London, during the week she worked three consecutive days from 2 p.m. to anything between 2 a.m. and 4:30 a.m., with duties at Chequers every other weekend, both day and night, plus regular dictation in the car en route between the two venues. Many a night was spent typing before snatching three hours' sleep at 6 a.m. and starting another busy day's work at 10 a.m."

Nor was "the Boss" or "Master," as she called him, an easy taskmaster. "For the sake of speed, Churchill expected his secretaries to take his dictation straight on to a silent typewriter and to hand him a perfect typescript almost as soon as he finished. This wasn't easy when his cigar, speech impediment and habit of walking about conspired to make him inaudible."

As for working conditions in the official car . . . well, she described that experience: "It is a bit apt to put you off your outlines when the car goes swinging round a corner and your spare pencil falls on the floor and his papers (which you are holding) begin to slide off your knee, and his matches (which you are holding) rattle down beside you, and his spare cigar (which you are holding) makes a dive down behind you, and his box (which you are holding in position with your foot) slams shut and rushes across the floor of the car."

Despite all, Churchill soon had won over Layton's total loyalty and devotion. He was "the spearhead of our stand against Nazism," she said later. Moreover, difficult taskmaster or not, she wrote to her parents during the war that he was "sweet" and even more. Said she in one such letter after he spoke at Leeds in May 1942: "He is just as warm-hearted, and one might even say lovable, as he could possibly be."

Another time, on the way back from the Yalta Conference in early 1945, the PM's entourage made a stop in Cairo, then prepared to take off again for the thirteen-hour, nonstop flight to England. While awaiting takeoff in the specially converted American Skymaster that Churchill used at this point in the war, he repeatedly burst into song. "He was in a grand mood, rather sleepy and very funny and I must admit rather lovable," Elizabeth wrote to her parents (as noted by Martin Gilbert in *Churchill: A Life*).

"If he alternately barked at her, ignored her and teased her," added the *Times* obituary, "she bore it for the sake of his occasional sunny smile and word of thanks. This, combined with his fatherly worries about her eating properly and keeping warm in wartime winters, inspired her to the most furious feelings of devotion and loyalty. 'Let me say at once that neither I nor anyone else considered this treatment unfair,' she wrote. 'The Prime Minister carried a heavy load.'"

Born in England in 1917, Elizabeth Layton had moved to Canada with her family at the age of seven to finish growing up on the western slopes of the Canadian Rockies. She returned to England in 1936 at age nineteen "to train as a shorthand typist," then worked for an employment agency. The beginning of the war in September 1939 caught her visiting Canada, where she remained until December 1940 before crossing the Atlantic to the beleaguered land of her birth. In the spring of 1941, she was working in London for the prisoners of war section of the Red Cross. "And it was then that she heard of a vacancy at Downing Street for a third personal secretary to the Prime Minister. She applied at once, and was taken on, starting work on May 5, 1941."

It not only was taxing work but dangerous as well. Five days after she began at Downing Street, England came under its heaviest air raid of the year, with more than fourteen hundred civilians killed, Gilbert noted, "most of them in London." Another "victim" was the historic chamber of the House of Commons . . . unoccupied at the moment, fortunately.

In any case, Elizabeth was at center of the war effort, privy to all kinds of secrets, crucial decisions . . . and a determined prime minister's sometimes wandering and intimate thoughts. In the last week of July 1941, the hundredth week of the war for England, German bomber attacks had slackened, Gilbert noted, but still, five hundred British civilians were killed in air raids that month. In the midst of his late-hours' dictation to Elizabeth on the night of July 28, Churchill made the comment, "We must go on and on, like the gun-horses, till we drop."

Then, too, starting late on the night of May 7, 1945, and winding up at 3:45 a.m. the next morning, quickly dubbed "V-E Day," the same young secretary would be taking Churchill's final nighttime dictation of the war in Europe. "Well," he said as she entered his study that final night of the European hostilities, "The war's over. You've played your part."

Both a perk and an added strain during the many months before victory could be officially proclaimed were her travels with the wartime Churchill entourage—to Washington, to Moscow, to Cairo, to Yalta, even to dangerously besieged Athens, Greece, at Christmastime 1944. She especially loved traveling to America, noted the *Times* obituary, "where steaks overlapping both sides of the plate were an eye-widening sight for anyone used to British rationing."

Nonetheless, the workload was as demanding as ever when Churchill traveled. As Layton finished up one night at the White House at 4:30 in the morning, an American officer said, "Gee, are you crazy? All the American girls went home 12 hours ago."

Churchill's 1944 trip to Moscow proved to be memorable for what appeared a Russian misapprehension of her status as a member of the Churchill entourage. At a refueling stop on the way home, it seems, the chairman of the Crimean Soviet gave a dinner for the travelers from England. "After vodka toasts were drunk to King George VI, Marshal Stalin and their respective air forces," said the *Times*, "a twinkling-eyed Churchill proposed the health of 'Miss Layton, the only lady present.'"

So enthusiastically was this toast greeted that Churchill's private secretary John Colville thought perhaps the Russians had decided the comely Layton must be Churchill's mistress, noted the *Times* account. "One Russian general, fearing perhaps that her hosts had not been attentive enough, grabbed some flowers from a bowl on the table and dumped them, dripping, in Layton's lap, in lieu of a bouquet. The image set Churchill chuckling on at least one occasion in the remainder of their time together."

Meanwhile, the month of May 1945 would always be memorable to the young woman . . . not only because of V-E Day. For this was when she met a South African army lieutenant in London who had just been released from confinement in a German prisoner-of-war camp. They married and moved to South Africa. He died in 2000 and she in 2007 at age ninety, survived by a son and two daughters. Until the end, the *Times* reported, she proved Churchill's enduring champion whenever broadcasters or biographers "attempted to show him warts and all." After all, she wrote, "When one thinks of what Mr. Churchill did, what he actually achieved, he alone, for his country and for the world, then I think he deserves our loyalty."

Twisting in Bed

Thanks to breaking the German navy's variant of the Enigma code, the British by mid-1941 could intercept orders directing U-boats to their destinations and warn North Atlantic convoys accordingly. This also meant it could be a bit safer for Winston to travel across the Atlantic to Placentia Bay, Newfoundland, by ship for his first trip outside of Britain since the fall of France, albeit by fast ship . . . a spanking new battleship at that.

The genesis of the history-making trip, in which Prime Minister Churchill met and conferred with President Roosevelt for the first time, came late in July when FDR's aide and confidante Harry Hopkins visited the garden at No. 10 Downing Street and said, as Winston remembered, "the President would like very much to have a meeting with me in some lonely bay or other."

As Winston recalled in *The Grand Alliance*, the third volume of his World War II history, "I had the keenest desire to meet Mr. Roosevelt, with whom I had now corresponded with increasing intimacy for nearly two years." (As mentioned earlier, Winston had no memory of their brief encounter during World War I.) And so it was decided, just like that. "Placentia Bay, Newfoundland, was chosen, the date of August 9 was fixed, and our latest battleship, the *Prince of Wales*, was placed under orders accordingly."

Moreover, it was to be an important and fruitful meeting. "A conference between us," wrote Winston, "would proclaim the ever closer association of Britain and the United States, would cause our enemies concern, make Japan ponder, and cheer our friends. There also was much business to be settled about American intervention in the Atlantic, aid to Russia [by now invaded by Germany], our own supplies, and above all the increasing menace of Japan."

It was not quite dark on the evening of August 4 when *Prince of Wales* and her destroyer escort set out from Scapa Flow for the Atlantic crossing, which was still dangerous despite Britain's intelligence on some (albeit not necessarily all) U-boat movements. But a problem soon arose. The "spacious quarters" first given to Winston were right above the great ship's propellers. In heavy weather, the vibration rendered these accommodations "almost uninhabitable." As a result, Winston moved "to the Admiral's sea-cabin on the bridge for working and sleeping."

Here, Winston was perfectly happy for the rest of the voyage, but on the second day out, "the seas were so heavy that we had to choose between slowing down and dropping our destroyer escort." The decision was to go on alone—at high speed. "There were several U-boats reported, which we made zigzags and wide diversions to avoid."

Radio silence was a must . . . the great ship could receive messages but could not send out any. "Thus there was a lull in my daily routine and a strange sense of leisure which I had not known since the war began." As a result, Winston indulged in reading for pleasure. He loved C. S. Forester's *Captain Hornblower, R.N.*, but caused a minor squall back home when he later sent Forester a congratulatory telegram. Some of his military officials thought *Hornblower* was a code reference to a pending operation they hadn't been told about.

Another indulgence was movies. "In the evenings we had an excellent cinema, where the latest and best films were presented to our party and to those officers who were off duty." A favorite for Winston was *Lady Hamilton*, which he viewed for the fifth time. After the showing, he addressed those watching: "Gentlemen, I thought this film would interest you, showing great events similar to those in which you have been taking part." Like the *Hornblower* book, the film was about the Royal Navy during the Napoleonic Wars.

Meanwhile, FDR was making his way to Placentia . . . secretly, by U.S. cruiser after the White House put out word that he was vacationing aboard the presidential yacht. His aide Hopkins, in the interim, despite his own frail health, had flown to Moscow since visiting Winston in the Downing Street garden. He returned to England in time to join the PM's party departing from Scapa Flow.

With both leaders safely delivered by their respective navies, they conferred on August 9 aboard the U.S. heavy cruiser *Augusta*. "[FDR] stood supported by the arm of his son Elliott while the national anthems were played, and then gave me the warmest of welcomes," Winston recounted. The next day, a Sunday, the two leaders and their respective staffs interrupted their meetings to attend a worship service aboard *Prince of Wales*. Winston personally selected the hymns: "For Those in Peril on the Sea," "Onward Christian Soldiers," and "O God, Our Help in Ages Past." The service, attended by hundreds of sailors from both navies, "was felt by us all to be a deeply moving expression of the unity of faith of our two peoples, and none who took part in it will forget the spectacle presented that sunlit morning on the crowded quarterdeck," Winston recorded. He then cited "the symbolism of the Union Jack and the Stars and Stripes draped side by side on the pulpit; the American and British chaplains sharing in the reading of the prayers; the highest naval, military, and air officers of Britain and the United States grouped in one body behind the President and me; the close-packed ranks of British and American sailors, completely intermingled, sharing the same books and joining fervently together in the prayers and hymns familiar to both. It was a great hour to live. Nearly half of those who sang were soon to die."

Here, he apparently referred to the shocking news less than six months later, right after Pearl Harbor, that the mighty 35,000-ton *Prince of Wales* and the 33,300-ton battle cruiser *Repulse* had been sunk by Japanese aircraft off Malaya, with a thousand sailors and Adm. Sir Tom Phillips killed. "I saw the *Prince of Wales* lie over on her side like a tired war horse and slide beneath the waters," reported CBS Radio's Cecil Brown, who had survived the attack.

Back in London, by grim irony, Winston and his top aides—"mostly Admiralty," he recalled—were in a meeting barely three hours beforehand to debate the future use of the *Repulse* and *Prince of Wales* in view of the disaster at Pearl Harbor. It was ten o'clock the night of December 9 in London when the group of about a dozen gathered to discuss the ramifications of the American losses and Japan's Pacific offensive. "We had lost the command of every ocean except the Atlantic," Winston noted. "Australia and New Zealand and all the vital islands in their sphere were open to attack."

On a more positive note, so the British officials believed, *Repulse* and *Prince of Wales* had arrived at Singapore and presumably would be available for operations against the Japanese. "They had been sent to these waters to exercise that kind of vague menace which capital ships of the highest quality whose whereabouts is unknown can impose upon all hostile naval calculations," Winston wrote in *The Grand Alliance.* "How should we use them now? Obviously they must go to sea and vanish among the innumerable islands. There was general agreement on that."

Winston's own preference at the moment was to have the two British warships join the tattered American fleet. "It would be a proud gesture at this moment, and would knit the English-speaking world together," he opined. The British already had agreed to the Americans shifting their capital ships based in the Atlantic. "Thus in a few months there might be a fleet in being on the west coast of America capable of fighting a decisive sea battle if need be." The mere existence "of such a fleet and of such a fact would be the best possible shield to our brothers in Australasia."

Such were the possibilities under discussion when the meeting in London broke up because the hour was late. Winston and his advisers planned to sleep on the issue and "settle the next morning what to do with the *Prince of Wales* and the *Repulse.*" And then, "Within a couple of hours they were at the bottom of the sea."

Winston was still in bed the next morning but already opening his "boxes" of paperwork, when his bedside telephone rang. "It was the First Sea Lord. His voice sounded odd. He gave a sort of cough and gulp, and at first I could not hear quite clearly." He reported the grave news of the calamity at sea. "So I put the telephone down. I was thankful to be alone. In all the war I never received a more direct shock. . . . As I turned over and twisted in bed the full horror of the news sank in upon me. There were no British or American capital ships in the Indian Ocean or the Pacific except the American survivors of Pearl Harbor, who were hastening back to California. Over all this expanse of water Japan was supreme, and we everywhere weak and naked,"

Winston went before the House of Commons that morning at eleven o'-clock, "as soon as they met," to tell the House members in person what had happened. Meanwhile, plans were advancing for Winston's departure on December 14 for his first wartime visit to the United States. He again traveled by Royal Navy ship, this time aboard the brand-new battleship *Duke of York.*

Additional note: Meanwhile, in the meeting at Placentia Bay, the United States pledged ever-increasing aid to Britain and the Soviet Union, Martin Gilbert noted in his Churchill biography. In addition to their pledged escort of five destroyers and a capital ship for every supply convoy to Britain, the Americans would ferry bombers to Britain and West Africa with the pilots staying on to provide training. In their jointly issued Atlantic Charter, the two leaders pledged their respective countries had no interest in territorial gain and would respect the right of peoples everywhere to determine their own form of government. They also had asked Japan to withdraw from French Indochina (Vietnam) and halt its aggressive moves in the Southwest Pacific.

An elated Winston returned home to tell his cabinet, "I have established warm and deep personal relations with our great friend [FDR]." Added Gilbert: "That friend had gone so far as to tell Churchill that all American convoy escort vessels had been ordered to attack any German submarine which showed itself, even if it was '200 or 300 miles away from the convoy.'" In fact, Winston told his colleagues, Roosevelt had "made it clear that he would look for an 'incident' which would justify him in opening hostilities."

Across the Atlantic, however, Roosevelt "had hastened to assure the American people that the United States was no nearer to war than before the meeting," Now not so elated, Winston telegraphed Harry Hopkins: "I ought to tell you there has been a wave of depression through Cabinet and other informed circles here about President's many assurances about no commitments and no closer to war, etc." To guests at Chequers, Winston complained, "Though we cannot now be defeated, the war might drag on for another four or five years, and civilization and culture would be wiped out." To his son Randolph, then serving in Egypt, he wrote, "One is deeply perplexed to know how the deadlock is to be broken and the United States brought boldly and honorably into the war."

Prelude to Pearl

FDR to the U.S. High Commissioner of the Philippines, November 26, 1941: "Preparations are becoming apparent . . . for an early aggressive movement of some character, although as yet there are no clear indications as to its strength or whether it will be directed against the Burma Road, Thailand, Malay Peninsula, Netherlands East Indies, or the Philippines. Advance against Thailand seems the most probable. I consider it possible that this next Japanese aggression might cause an outbreak of hostilities between the United States and Japan."

Churchill to FDR, November 30, 1941: "It seems to me that one important method remains unused in averting war between Japan and our two countries, namely, a plain declaration, secret or public as may be thought best, that any further act of aggression by Japan will lead immediately to the gravest consequences. I realize your constitutional difficulties, but it would be tragic if Japan drifted into war by encroachment without having before her fairly and squarely the dire character of a further aggressive step."

Tokyo to the Japanese ambassador to Berlin, November 30, 1941: "Say very secretly to them that there is extreme danger that war may suddenly break out between the Anglo-Saxon nations and Japan through some clash of arms, and add that the time of the breaking out of this war may come quicker than anyone dreams."

Winston Churchill in *The Grand Alliance*, the third volume of his history of the war: "My deepest fear was that the Japanese would attack us or the Dutch, and that constitutional difficulties would prevent the United States from declaring war."

That was the rub: *constitutional difficulties*. That being the case, did he go on to suggest it would have been defensible for the Americans to allow Japan a first strike in order to enter the war and forestall disaster later? Churchill went on to say:

We know that all the great Americans round the President and in his confidence felt, as acutely as I did, the awful danger that Japan would attack British or Dutch possessions in the Far East, and would carefully avoid the United States, and that in consequence Congress would not sanction an American declaration of war. The American leaders understood that this might mean vast Japanese conquests, which, if combined with a German victory over Russia and therefore an invasion of Great Britain, would leave America alone to face an overwhelming combination of triumphant aggressors. Not only the great moral causes which were at stake would be cast away, but the very life of the United States, and their people, as yet but half-awakened to their perils, might be broken. The President and his trusted friends had long realized the grave risks of United States neutrality in the war against Hitler and all that he stood for, and had writhed under the restraints of a Congress whose House of Representatives had a few months before passed by only a single vote the necessary renewal of compulsory military service, without which their Army would have been almost disbanded in the midst of the world convulsion. Roosevelt [and his chief strategists] had but one mind. Future generations of Americans and free men in every land will thank God for their vision.

A Japanese attack upon the United States was a vast simplification of their problems and their duty. How can we wonder that they regarded the actual form of the attack, or even its scale, as incomparably less important than the fact that the whole American nation would be united for its own safety in a righteous cause as never before?

Whatever the factors leading up to the Japanese attack on Pearl Harbor, Winston commented that America's strength "was sufficient to enable them to sustain this hard ordeal required by the spirit of the American Constitution." Moreover, "to them, as to me, it seemed that for Japan to attack and make war upon the United States would be an act of suicide." But then . . . "Governments and peoples do not always take rational decisions."

Tonic for Winston

"Mr. Churchill has been panting to meet the President ever since he heard of Pearl Harbor, so today we are bound for Washington," wrote Dr. Charles Wilson (Lord Moran), Winston's doctor for the duration and then some. That was Moran's notation from the December morning that his precious patient, the prime minister of England, "pulled himself out of a launch and was piped aboard the *Duke of York*" for the transatlantic trip to visit Roosevelt at the White House over Christmas 1941.

And what a change it had been!

"The Winston I knew in London frightened me. I used to watch him as he went to his room with swift paces, the head thrust forward, scowling at the ground, the somber countenance clouded, the features set and resolute, the jowl clamped down as if he had something between his teeth and did not mean to let go." As Moran could see, and worry about, Winston then was "carrying the weight of the world, and [I] wondered how long he could go on like that and what could be done about it."

But now, "in a night it seems," all had changed. "A younger man has taken his place."

On the Atlantic crossing aboard the British battleship, Winston kept busy all day in his cabin, "dictating for the President a memorandum on the conduct of the war," added Moran in his memoir *Churchill at War, 1940–45.* Even so, "The tired, dull look has gone from his eye; his face lights up as you enter the cabin."

Just a month earlier, before the Japanese propelled a reluctant America into the war with the attack on Pearl Harbor, "if you had broken in on his work, he would have bitten off your head. And at night [now] he is gay and voluble, sometimes even playful."

The reason for the change was obvious.

"The P.M., I suppose, must have known that if America stayed out there could only be one ending to this business. And now suddenly the war is as good as won and England is safe; to be Prime Minister of England in a great war, to be able to direct the Cabinet, the Army, the Navy, the Air Force, the House of Commons, England herself, is beyond even his dreams. He loves every minute of it."

White House Visit

Not even Eleanor Roosevelt, the president's wife, was aware of the unusual houseguest coming for Christmas that year . . . until just before the distinguished visitor's arrival on December 22. Once they knew, though, not only White House intimates, but the American public at large were agog.

British prime minister Winston Churchill's sudden appearance at the White House so soon after the Japanese attack on Pearl Harbor and the declarations of war by the Axis powers of Europe electrified the country. For here, in the somewhat stooped form of sixty-seven-year-old Winston, in his cigar-chomping, bulldog face, was the personification of England's unbowed stand against Hitler.

Naturally, with the nation so suddenly at war, it would be a somber Christmas that year for Americans. Indeed, the first survivors of Pearl Harbor arrived at San Francisco on Christmas morning. In the Far East, even as Churchill and FDR discussed strategy in Washington, Hong Kong fell to the rampaging Japanese on Christmas Day. During this crisis time, too, the White House was being fitted with bulletproof glass, the nearby Potomac River was checked for enemy submarines, and wooden antiaircraft guns reportedly joined the real weaponry placed around the White House.

Amid all the grave events of the moment, Winston's sudden, unexpected appearance was quite a distraction both for the White House and the American public. Braving winter storms and U-boats in the North Atlantic, he came by ship, then flew into National (now Reagan) Airport with no public announcement. Roosevelt personally met Churchill and escorted him back to the Executive Mansion in a black Treasury Department limousine confiscated years before from Chicago mob boss Al Capone.

Almost immediately, the papers were full of Churchill stories, although Great Britain's feisty PM wasn't actually seen in public that frequently. He did, on Christmas Eve, join FDR in speaking at the lighting of the National Christmas Tree—a ceremony held for the first time on the south lawn of the White House rather than at the ceremony's previous location on the nearby Ellipse. With security a fresh concern, the grounds were closed to the public until thirty or forty minutes before the president pushed the button to light up the tree shortly after 5:00 p.m. To enter the grounds, spectators had to leave all packages with soldiers stationed outside the perimeter fence and then pass through an "electric searcher" of circa-1940s technology. With patriotism a reawakened passion, the National Christmas Tree was decorated in red, white, and blue.

If Churchill's presence was both a morale boost and a grim reminder of the nation's sudden plunge into war, it also was quite a burden to White House intimates, from the president and first lady on down to butlers, cooks, and other staff. For FDR, Churchill's late hours were exhausting. For Eleanor Roosevelt, his suspected colonialism was an anathema. For the staff, his demands were . . . well, demands. For America's military strategists, his proposals could be appalling.

Imagine, wrote columnist George Will at Christmas 2005, having an uninvited houseguest over Christmas whom the wife dislikes and who tells your butler, with only faintly apologetic preamble: "One, I don't like talking outside my quarters; two, I hate whistling in the corridors; and three, I must have a tumbler of sherry in my room before breakfast, a couple of glasses of scotch and soda before lunch and French champagne and 90-year-old brandy before I go to sleep at night."

Furthermore, Will noted, "This Guest from Hell declares that for breakfast he requires hot 'eggs, bacon or ham and toast' and 'two kinds of cold meats with English mustard and two kinds of fruit, plus a tumbler of sherry.'"

Winston stayed in North America for three weeks, and among other agreements between the two leaders and their respective staffs, the key was the decision to focus a joint war effort first on Germany and then Japan, much to Winston's relief. Not so happily, he suffered chest pains one evening at the White House while trying to open a stuck window in his bedroom. His doctor, Lord Moran, traveling with him, kept this information to himself for fear Churchill would be sidelined for bed rest at a crucial point in the war. He simply told Churchill not to worry and not to overly exert himself either . . . and hoped for the best.

It was on this trip, on December 26, the day after Christmas, that Winston addressed a joint session of Congress with the well-known statement: "I cannot help reflecting that if my father had been American and my mother British, instead of the other way round, I might have got here on my own. In that case, this would not have been the first time you would have heard my voice."

From Washington, Churchill moved on by train to Ottawa, Canada, for more war strategy talks and an address to the Canadian Parliament. After that, a quick stop back in Washington, then on to five days' rest and recuperation in Florida. He wrapped up this first of five wartime visits to the United States with yet another stop in Washington, this time discussing plans for the 1942 Allied landings in North Africa, among other topics.

As if he needed any reminder of the war's dangers, legend has it that Churchill's flight home, begun January 14, 1942, in a flying boat by way of Bermuda, almost came to tragic end when the aircraft strayed a bit too close to German antiaircraft batteries at Brest in occupied France, then aroused British fighters by approaching England from the French coast. Six RAF fighters sent aloft with orders to shoot down what appeared to be a "hostile bomber" were called off in the nick of time. Minutes later, Winston was home again, his island nation still in mortal peril but given new confidence with the United States, his mother's homeland, and its vast resources now locked in battle side by side with his beloved Britain.

Inside View

But first . . . it was almost midnight, and Lord Moran, Winston's doctor, thought the PM was getting ready for bed at the Mayflower Hotel the day the Churchill party arrived in Washington for Winston's first wartime visit to the White House. "I had gone to my room when a page brought a message from the P.M. to say he wanted to see me at the White House," Moran wrote in his postwar memoirs.

At the White House he was taken "up some stairs" to the PM's bedroom, but no one was there. "It smelled of cigar smoke and I tried to open the window. The crumpled bed-clothes were thrown back, and the floor was strewn with newspapers, English and American, just as the P.M. had thrown them away when he had glanced at the headlines; it would have been the first thing he would have done when they took him to his room, for he always wants to know what the papers are saying about him."

The newspapers came in handy, since Moran now had to wait ninety minutes for Winston to reappear from a tête-à-tête with FDR. "He looked at me blankly; he had forgotten that he had sent for me." As it turned out, Winston was so wound up, he wanted a sleeping pill. "He must have a good night." And so, "When I left him, I said he could take two reds [barbiturates] for I could see he was bottling up his excitement."

Moran noted that the crowd attending the lighting of the Christmas tree on the White House grounds on Christmas Eve numbered thirty thousand. The emotional occasion was marked by hymn singing, a sermon, and speeches by both FDR and Winston. In his remarks, Winston said: "Let the children have their night of fun and laughter. Let the gifts of Father Christmas delight their play. Let us grown-ups share to the full in their unstinted pleasures before we turn again to the stern task and the formidable years that lie before us, resolved that, by our sacrifice and daring, these same children shall not be robbed of their inheritance or denied their right to live in a free and decent world. And so, in God's mercy, a happy Christmas to you all."

But afterward, Winston told Moran he had felt heart palpitations during the ceremony. His pulse was 105. Fast.

"It has all been very moving," he said. Actually, Moran wrote, "He lisped with excitement." Winston added, "This is a new war, with Russia victorious, Japan in and America in up to the neck."

Christmas with the Roosevelts

Christmas Day 1941 with Franklin and Eleanor Roosevelt would be a pleasant day, begun with church and ending up with a large family dinner party at the

White House . . . but Winston's mind very much was on the speech he would be making the next day before a joint session of the U.S. Congress.

"He is full of the address he is to make tomorrow," Moran wrote. Winston planned to use a quotation from Psalm 112: "He shall not be afraid of evil tidings: his heart is fixed, trusting in the Lord."

That evening, Winston led the way "to a small room, where the President was making cocktails for his English visitors, the three Chiefs of Staff, [John] Martin [Winston's principal private secretary], and myself." There, Winston tested his biblical quotation on FDR, "who liked it."

At eight o'clock they went down to the family dinner party. "Everybody stood in a circle and Mrs. Roosevelt went round and shook hands. We then went into dinner. The President said there would be no speeches, but he just wanted to remind us that the King and Queen had dined there two and a half years ago, and this had been the beginning of the coming together of the two English-speaking races, which would go on after the war."

Dinner over, the group watched a movie on the history of the war thus far. Winston, though, had been uncharacteristically "silent and preoccupied." Moran thought that perhaps he was "turning over in his mind" the next day's speech to Congress.

In any case, speaking to Moran, he said it had been a tremendous occasion. "He could remember nothing quite like it in his time. The two democracies were to be joined together and he had been chosen to give out the banns."

But he also wondered aloud what the mood of the U.S. Senate would be the next day. "He knew, of course, that some of the senators were not at all friendly to the British. Would they perhaps show it?"

That morning he had decided "that what he was going to say to them was all wrong." And now he had to go and finish his speech before he went to bed. "He yawned wearily. He would be glad when it was all over. It must be getting late. He got up and asked the President to excuse him. 'I must prepare for tomorrow,' he said. It would take him, he thought, until about two o'clock. Smiling vaguely at the company, he withdrew."

After his leave-taking, the group sang Christmas carols until the polio-crippled Roosevelt was wheeled to his bed, but only "after he had waved 'Good night' to us."

Moran's impression of the departing American chief was of "a schoolboy, jolly and carefree." Thus, "it was difficult to believe that this was the man who was taking his nation into a vast conflict in which, until Pearl Harbor a few days ago, she had no thought of being engaged."

History-Making Speech

The day after Christmas, Winston worked on his speech up to the moment he should leave the White House for the brief trip up Pennsylvania Avenue to the U.S. Capitol. "Then we set off from the back entrance of the White House, dashing through the streets with the siren wailing and two G-men on each of the running boards, their pockets bulging with revolvers, ready to jump off in a second if anything happened," wrote Lord Moran. In the streets were a few people waving and cheering, but "without fervor," Moran thought.

At the Capitol, they waited in a small room. "There he sat arranging his thoughts as he gazed at the floor," the doctor recounted. "Once he got up and paced rapidly up and down the room, mumbling to himself; then he stopped, and, looking down at me, he said, with his eyes popping: 'Do you realize we are making history?'"

Moments later, Winston stood before the joint session of the Congress; moments later, he was saying to the senators and representatives: "I cannot help reflecting that if my father had been American and my mother British instead of the other way round, I might have got here on my own." Moran, now a listener himself, could not help but feel Winston "at once got on terms with his audience." In fact, "When the laughter was dying down, it would break out again, and this, coming right at the beginning, convinced him that he had got a grip on things. There was great cheering when he mentioned China and a loud shout when, speaking of the Japanese, he said with passion: 'What sort of people do they think we are?' At this Congress rose as one man and stood cheering as if they would never stop."

There was less acclaim when he chided: "If we had kept together after the last war, if we had taken common measures for our safety, this renewal of the curse need never have fallen upon us." And this was followed by silence, Moran wrote, when Winston added, "Five or six years ago it would have been easy, without shedding a drop of blood, for the United States and Great Britain to have insisted on fulfillment of the disarmament clauses of the treaties which Germany signed after the Great War."

Even so, chiding or not, "taken as a whole, it was Winston at his best." And chiding or not, at the end there was "a great scene." At the end, "The Senators and Congressmen stood cheering and waving their papers till he went out."

In that small antechamber afterward, Winston was "sweating freely, but he said it was a great weight off his chest." And later, at the White House, obviously still taking the measure of his speech, he confided he had been doubtful about the speech overnight—"had not liked it." Then, when he awoke, he "thought" it was all right. Before he got up, "he was sure it would be just right." And now, in the aftermath, he was quite willing to say: "I hit the target all the time."

Doctor's Dilemma

The late morning of December 27, the day after Winston's speech to the U.S. Congress, posed an excruciating dilemma for Lord Moran. "I'm glad you've come," said Winston when Moran responded to an urgent summons from the White House. Indeed, "he was in bed and looked worried."

The night before it was hot in his room, Winston explained. He got up to open the window and get some air. "It was very stiff and I had to use considerable force."

And that's when it happened.

"I noticed all at once that I was short of breath. I had a dull pain over my heart. It went down my left arm. It didn't last very long, but it has never happened before. What is it? Is my heart all right?"

For Moran that last was the crucial question. Was his heart all right? What would it mean to the world if it were not? To the Allied cause? To England!

"There was not much to be found when I examined his heart," Moran wrote in his memoirs. "Indeed the time I spent listening to his chest was given to some quick thinking." Quick thinking, because Winston, never easily mollified, must be told something. He surely would ask "pointed questions," and regardless of Moran's medical findings, he had to have answers.

It didn't take long for Moran to reach a conclusion: "I had no doubt that whether [testing with an] electro-cardiograph showed evidence of a coronary thrombosis or not, his symptoms were those of coronary insufficiency." So there could be a problem. And the "textbook treatment" at the time for such was "at least six weeks in bed."

Clearly that wouldn't do. Nor would the mere diagnosis of heart trouble—in any form. The news immediately would get out, wrote Moran, "that the P.M. was an invalid with a crippled heart and a doubtful future. And this at a moment when America has just come into the war, and there is no one but Winston to take her by the hand."

What to do?

"I felt that the effect of announcing that the P.M. had had a heart attack could only be disastrous. I knew, too, the consequences to one of his imaginative temperament of the feeling that his heart was affected. His work would suffer."

But to say and do . . . *nothing?*

"On the other hand, if I did nothing and he had another and severer attack—perhaps a fatal seizure—the world would undoubtedly say that I had killed him through not insisting on rest."

Such were Moran's thoughts as he listened to Winston's heart. "I took my stethoscope out of my ears. Then I replaced it and listened again."

"Right or wrong," Moran decided on the spot, he would say nothing about it to his patient for his own sake and the world's—"whatever the consequences."

"Well," asked Winston, as expected. "Is my heart all right?"

"There is nothing serious," Moran told him. "You have been overdoing things."

Winston of course was quick to say he couldn't take time to rest. "I can't. I won't. Nobody else can do this job. I must."

But remembering the symptoms from the night before, he asked, "What actually happened when I opened the window?" Then Winston answered for himself, "My idea is that I strained one of my chest muscles. I used great force. I don't believe it was my heart at all."

Churchill then paused for the doctor to respond. Moran said, "Your circulation was a bit sluggish. It is nothing serious. You needn't rest in the sense of lying up, but you mustn't do more than you can help in the way of exertion for a little while."

Fortunately, there was a knock on the door—it was President Roosevelt's aide Harry Hopkins—and Moran didn't have to explain further. He stuck to his decision against telling anyone, but vowed, once they returned to London, to take Winston to a specialist "who will hold his tongue."

Additional note: According to medical researcher and doctor John Mather, president of the Washington (D.C.) Society for Churchill, subsequent medical tests and examinations in London showed no evidence that Winston had suffered a coronary thrombosis or heart damage of any kind.

Who Is This, Anyway?

While he was enjoying a bit of rest in Palm Beach between White House visits in December 1941 and January 1942, Winston thought it only polite to call Wendell Willkie and arrange a time they could get together before he had to return home. After all, the former Republican presidential contender had paid a good-will visit to Britain a year earlier, and they had established "cordial relations" as a result.

It seemed a simple thing to pick up the telephone on the evening of January 5 and place the call. As Winston related the story, it wasn't quite so simple after all.

"After some delay, I was told, 'Your call is through.'"

"I said in effect, 'I am so glad to speak to you. I hope we may meet. I am traveling back by train tomorrow night. Can you not join the train at some point and travel with me for a few hours? Where will you be on Saturday next?'"

The reply was not what Winston expected. "A voice came back," he related. And in answer to his question about Saturday, the voice answered: "Why, just where I am now, at my desk."

Puzzled, Winston said, "I do not understand."

Said the voice: "Whom do you think you are speaking to?"

"To Mr. Wendell Willkie, am I not? "

But it wasn't. "No," said the voice, "you are speaking to the President."

Confused and not sure he heard correctly, Winston said, "Who?"

"You are speaking to me. Franklin Roosevelt."

And it was FDR, Winston's host at the White House in the immediate aftermath of Pearl Harbor. The very man Wendell Willkie had done his best to unseat just months before, in the presidential campaign of 1940.

Potentially embarrassing . . . Winston pressed on anyway. What else could he do but say, "I did not mean to trouble you at this moment. I was trying to speak to Wendell Wilkie but your telephone exchange seems to have made a mistake."

"I hope you are getting on all right down there and enjoying yourself," Roosevelt responded.

"Some pleasant conservation followed about personal movements and plans," Winston recounted in *The Grand Alliance*, the second volume of his history of the war. But there came a point when Winston returned to the telephone gaffe. "I presume you do not mind my having wished to speak to Wendell Willkie?"

"To this Roosevelt said, 'No.' And this was the end of our talk."

But not quite the end of the story, since the incident still worried Winston as he traveled back to Washington for more high-level strategy sessions. He thought he had better check with Roosevelt's aide Harry Hopkins to see "whether any offense had been given." But Hopkins assured him that "no harm had been done."

It's worth noting, of course, that Willkie traveled to England, the Mideast, and the Far East after the 1940 election as FDR's personal representative. At the time of Winston's visit to America, however, "there was tension between him and the President," Winston wrote. In fact, "Roosevelt had not seemed at all keen about my meeting prominent members of the Opposition, and I consequently so far had not done so." But Willkie, because of their meeting in England the year before, was a special case and an exception: "I felt I ought not to leave American shores without seeing him. This was also our ambassador's advice."

Additional note: Another time during the war, Winston picked up the telephone and called a section of the War Office dealing with the Middle East, recalled Max Hastings in the *Oxford Book of Military Anecdotes*. Thinking he had the headman on the line, Winston fired off his questions.

"How do you think the operations are going in Syria?"

"Oh," was the answer, "I think everything is going all right."

And how about that turning movement being executed by the French?

That seemed to be perfectly all right also.

Finally, Winston asked to whom he was speaking.

"Corporal Jones, Duty Clerk." Oops. End of call.

Dictation from the Bath

Patrick Kinna signed on as an assistant to Churchill in time to travel with him to Newfoundland in 1940 aboard the battleship *Prince of Wales* for the meeting with Roosevelt that produced the Atlantic Charter, the early basis for the United Nations.

"Not long after the trip I asked to go to No. 10 [Downing Street] and was offered the position of permanent assistant," said Kinna on the BBC's "WW2 People's War" Web site. "He was particularly impressed because I was a high speed typist!"

Kinna lived and worked in the Cabinet War Rooms, the underground bunker complex opposite St. James Park, from early 1940 to 1945. "I had my own private bedroom in the 'bunker,'" he added. "It was very ordinary and I didn't have many personal effects. We were very well protected and could not hear the usual sounds of war; the air raid sirens, planes flying over or the bombs dropping."

Even so, Kinna and his co-workers were "immersed in the war . . . in the thick of it!" They developed "a very good atmosphere," and all were "keen to give their best." This effort meant an exacting routine of up early and to bed late every day.

"Churchill was very pleasant to me," said Kinna. "You could tell instantly by his expression whether he was in a good mood or not." As Winston's only male assistant, Kinna traveled abroad with him, "because it was more appropriate." How so? Well, Kinna recalled, on a visit to the White House, he was roused one morning to take dictation while his chief wallowed in a bathtub.

"He would submerge himself under the water every now and then and come up and carry on with the dictation," said Kinna. "He was very absorbed in his work that morning and would not keep still for the valet to help dress him; he kept walking around the room speaking aloud."

It was then that a knock was heard on the door, and who should be calling but President Roosevelt himself. Swinging the door open, Winston "simply said that he had 'nothing to hide from Mr. President!'"

Additional note: There are slight variations to this story and to the famous quote, but it seems that Kinna actually was there to see and to hear all that transpired.

Please Don't Look Up

Bob Yuill, a British soldier who once served a light antiaircraft gun near Dover Castle "overlooking Dover town in Kent," later said the harbor and town were surrounded by barrage balloons that could be raised or lowered to different heights as a barrier against low-level attacks by enemy aircraft. He was on duty one day when an "intense" dogfight broke out overhead between Spitfires and Messerschmitts: "The empty cannon fire cartridge cases from the planes overhead are raining down. They are quite large and made of brass, and if they hit an unprotected head they can quite easily kill. We are warned never to look up if planes are immediately overhead."

One time, however, "a figure emerges from a building just below my position. And looks skywards."

"Oh, the fool," thinks Yuill. Then, to his horror, he realizes it is Winston Churchill, well known for his frequent visits to coastal defense positions. "I hastily run forward and throwing a salute (should I salute a Prime Minister?), I respectfully suggest he should take cover from the falling cartridge cases."

Fortunately, Winston complied, with a hurried thanks. No harm done.

At other times, Yuill had seen the PM "standing on the battlements in Dover Castle intently watching the shells from the huge cross-Channel German guns near Calais landing in the harbor and Dover town."

Yuill was present also for a visit to his pioneer platoon at Bexhill on Sea by Winston and other dignitaries just before the Normandy invasion of June 6, 1944. The visitors with him were South African prime minister Jan Smuts and Canadian prime minister Mackenzie King. "What a security risk," thought Yuill, "to congregate three Prime Ministers in one small building."

Meanwhile, telling the assembled soldiers, "Good luck, lads," onetime Boer leader Smuts added, "I know you are dying to get at the horrid Hun. It won't be long now."

Years later, however, Sergeant Yuill still thought the reference to dying was "most inappropriate." Said he: "The majority of the soldiers present on that day were either killed or taken prisoner within six months."

Mole Machine Abandoned

He loved technical innovations like the tank and radar (the latter developed just in time for the Battle of Britain), but another device that intrigued Winston for a time during both world wars was *Nellie*, a dragonlike, earth-gobbling machine that was never built for the first of those wars and came along too late in the second.

Even so, for a time there was a 77½ foot, 140-ton machine that chewed through the earth like a giant slug and left a deep trench in its wake. After pushing development of the tank in the Great War with considerable foresight, Churchill conceived of a fleet of mechanical "moles" like *Nellie* that would burrow trenches up to fixed defenses during the night. At that point, the infantry following the mechanical monster's track would spring to the attack against a startled enemy. In the trench warfare of the First World War, a fleet of the molelike machines would have been very useful. But the mechanicals were not yet developed to accomplish the mission. When the Second World War came along, with the long so-called Phony War that followed Germany's invasion of Poland in September 1939, Churchill resurrected the mole concept, in case of another trench stalemate on the Continent. Such mechanical moles would be useful in approaching static German entrenchments.

But the German blitzkrieg unleashed against France and the Low Countries in May 1940 forever dashed the concept of static defenses withstanding the new mechanized weapons of mass destruction. Nonetheless, shortly after assuming the post of prime minister, Churchill insisted that England should have her *Nellie*.

Apparently for the first time, the full story of the Churchillian project, a well-kept secret during the war, appeared in a 1988 book published by the Society for Lincolnshire (England) History and Archaeology under the title *"Nellie": The History of Churchill's Lincoln-Built Trenching Machine*, by John T. Turner. A press release from the historical group explained that Churchill's initial hope was to avoid "the trench warfare and horrific casualties of the First World War."

Even though the highly mobile tank warfare that Nazi Germany introduced in Poland and then employed to perfection in the conquest of France rendered Churchill's mole-machine unnecessary, a handful were built. The result, said Turner, was "a masterpiece of heavy engineering, the biggest machine of its kind ever built, and it worked." As might be imagined, creation of such a huge, self-propelled trench-digging machine at a time of national emergency and carefully husbanded resources was a mind-boggling feat—"a tale of a challenge accepted, wrestled with, and overcome against terrific odds." Flinging away the loose dirt as it traveled, the fantastic machine "was to travel at .5 mph through no-man's land at night, cutting a trench six feet wide and six feet deep for infantry to follow and penetrate enemy lines."

Fairly successful in field trials, the original *Nellie* carried a three-man crew. The pilot was seated in a conning tower with a slit window for visibility; a driver was seated below him, facing the rear and driving totally blind; and an engineer was trapped in a mechanical cubicle filled with oil fumes and the deafening noise of two 600-horsepower engines. The machine, visited by Churchill during its field trials, consisted of a plow-and-cutting section in front and the "propel" section in the back. Like a very slow-moving submarine, it could dig into the earth, nose first, find its proper level, and then proceed on the chosen course (more or less). Steering, though, was a major problem, and tree roots tended to stop *Nellie* in her self-made tracks. In the end, *Nellie* never was sent to the Continent, and she died a dinosaur's unlamented death. Only six of the giant machines were completed. "On Churchill's instructions," wrote Turner, "they were to be kept serviced and ready in case a need for them arose." It never did, and "all but one were reduced to scrap shortly after the end of the war." The one remaining machine, apparently the original model, was consigned to the scrap heap in the early 1950s. And so vanished the last of Churchill's once farsighted mole-machines—and with it, in Turner's opinion, "much that might have been learnt has been lost forever."

Worst Blow, Greatest Raid

Winston Churchill's "worst blow" in the opening weeks and months of the war, its pain kept a closely held secret, "was President Roosevelt's initial refusal to provide weapons, especially destroyers, that were urgently needed," wrote Martin Gilbert in the London *Times* on the eve of the fiftieth anniversary of V-E Day. Once the United States finally released fifty aging destroyers in return for leasing rights to British bases in the Western Hemisphere, it took just a single World War I destroyer built by Maine's Bath Iron Works to sideline Germany's mighty pocket battleship *Tirpitz* for most of World War II.

Previously named for Civil War–era Confederate Commo. Franklin Buchanan, the USS *Buchanan* became HMS *Campbeltown* upon transfer to the British on September 9, 1940. For the next few months, the *Campbeltown* was assigned to fairly routine wartime duty. First serving with the 7th Escort Group, Western Approaches Command, out of Liverpool, she briefly was loaned to the Royal Netherlands Navy then recalled to Atlantic convoy duty. Several times attacked by U-boats and German aircraft, she escaped damage until taken off her escort duties in early 1942 for a very special role in Operation Chariot, "the Greatest Raid of All."

The plan, aimed at keeping the dangerous *Tirpitz* out of the sea lanes, was to wreck the only drydock on the Atlantic seaboard large enough to accommodate the German battleship if it ever required significant repairs. The theory, proven by later events, was that with no way to repair the ship, the Germans wouldn't risk the *Tirpitz* on any seagoing ventures.

As the British realized, the one way to keep the *Tirpitz* bottled up in a Norwegian port was to deny her access to the drydock facilities at St. Nazaire in occupied France by destroying them. This would be no easy task since the heavily defended drydock was several miles up the river Loire from its mouth. To accomplish this, a daring commando and Royal Navy raid—Operation Chariot—was concocted, with the aging *Campbeltown* selected to be the star player.

Her silhouette altered to look like that of a German Mowe-class destroyer, the *Campbeltown* led a flotilla of twenty vessels, fifteen of them speedy motor launches, into the estuary of the Loire during the night of March 28, 1942—"the only day a force could approach the dock through the shallow waters . . . because of the spring high tide," according to the Royal Navy's Web site devoted to the St. Nazaire raid. They proceeded upriver to within a mile of the drydock facilities before German defenders realized they were enemy interlopers and opened fire.

The plan was to ram the dock gate with the large ship while commandos would jump ashore and "destroy the dock's winding and pumping facilities, then wreck the dockyard infrastructure." As the online history of the mission notes, "Daring and against all the odds, the plan was accepted by the Admiralty and HMS *Campbeltown* was nominated as the ship to carry out the task of destroying the dock."

After leaving port from Falmouth, England, with her flotilla on the afternoon of March 26, the old destroyer reached the dock gate at 1:34 a.m. on March 28, exactly four minutes later than planned. But no great matter. "The Commandos disembarked under heavy fire and set about their demolitions," says the Royal Navy Web site. The destroyer did its part by ramming the gate according to the plan. In the ensuing firefight with the Germans and other moments in the raid, 169 of the 611 men taking part in the operation were killed and 215 were captured, but 222 safely returned. Another 5 escaped capture then traveled on foot and by bicycle through France and Spain to reach the British base at Gibraltar.

At St. Nazaire, meanwhile, in the late morning of March 28, the fighting long since ended, scores of Germans were poking around the badly damaged

Campbeltown, convinced the raid had failed. At 11:35 a.m., however, the old warship did her worst damage of all. As plotted by the British, she blew up. The ship had been packed with explosives hidden behind a false bulkhead. Three hundred sixty Germans were killed, and the dry-dock facility was destroyed. "Even later, 2 torpedoes that had been fired at, and were lodged in, the inner dock also exploded. This caused great confusion amongst the now jittery German defenders and a fierce firefight ensued amongst German forces, which suffered even greater casualties as a result."

Overall, "the raid was so successful that the *Tirpitz* never ventured into the Atlantic again." (The ship eventually was destroyed in port by British bombers.) The dry dock wouldn't be reopened until 1948. Meanwhile, the heroism displayed at St. Nazaire produced five Victoria Crosses and eighty other decorations for gallantry among the participants. And the sacrificial *Buchanan-Campbeltown* still is commemorated in the form of a current Royal Navy frigate named *Campbeltown*.

Driving with FDR

For his second wartime visit to Washington, Winston crossed the Atlantic aboard a Boeing flying boat, sleeping "soundly" en route in the seaplane's commodious "bridal suite" and landing safely on the Potomac River. No worries there . . . but perhaps a few when driven around Franklin D. Roosevelt's Hyde Park estate in New York by the polio-crippled president himself.

"He welcomed me with the greatest cordiality and, driving the car himself, took me to the majestic bluffs over the Hudson River on which Hyde Park, his family home, stands," Winston wrote in *The Hinge of Fate*, the fourth volume of his history of World War II. Noting that FDR drove him "all over the estate, showing me its splendid views," Winston added, "In this drive I had some thoughtful moments."

Apparently the "thoughtful moments" had something to do with FDR's special driving equipment. "Mr. Roosevelt's infirmity prevented him from using his feet on the brake, clutch, or accelerator. An ingenious arrangement enabled him to do everything with his arms, which were amazingly strong and muscular. He invited me to feel his biceps, saying that a famous prize-fighter had envied them. This was reassuring; but I confess that when on several occasions the car poised and backed on the grass verges of the precipices over the Hudson I hoped the mechanical devices and brakes would show no defects."

As a result, Winston was "careful not to take his attention off the driving," but they nonetheless made "more progress than we might have done in formal conference." Among the items on the agenda for this mid-1942 conference was discussion of the progress being made both in England and the United States on development of "Tube Alloys"—code word for the atomic bomb. The moment had arrived, Winston wrote, "when a decision must be made whether or not to proceed with the construction of large scale production plants."

Winston's talk with Roosevelt and aide Harry Hopkins on the bomb's development took place, it seems, the day after the automobile tour in a tiny ground-floor room heavily shaded against the summer sun. Even so, Winston made note of the "intense heat" that his "two American friends did not seem to mind."

Meanwhile, they decided against large-scale research and production plants in Britain because of its exposure to bombing and German aerial reconnaissance. Canada was ruled out as an alternate possibility when FDR volunteered that "he thought the United States would have to do it." At the same time, a worrisome thought was the fact that Nazi Germany was working along similar lines and doing its best to obtain "heavy water," which Winston described as "a sinister term, eerie, unnatural, which had begun to creep into our secret papers."

He speculated: "What if the enemy should get an atomic bomb before we did! However skeptical one might feel about the assertions of scientists, much disputed among themselves and expressed in jargon incomprehensible to laymen, we could not run the mortal risk of being outstripped in this awful sphere."

After returning to Washington and the White House itself, Winston was given what he called "the very large air-conditioned room, in which I dwelt in comfort at about thirty degrees below the temperature of most of the rest of the building." After the "Presidential train" from Hyde Park had arrived about eight o'clock on the morning of June 21, 1942, Winston kept busy in his air-conditioned splendor, first by reading newspapers and telegrams, then with breakfast. He looked up Harry Hopkins in his office across the corridor "and then went to see the President in his study."

But now came a terrible shock. "Presently a telegram was put into the President's hands. He passed it to me without a word." The British had just lost the Tobruk stronghold on the coast of Libya, North Africa, to Erwin Rommel's Afrika Korps, with thirty-three thousand men taken prisoner. "This was so surprising that I could not believe it," Winston recounted. It not only was true but also "was one of the heaviest blows I can recall during the war."

For the reputation of the British armies, the loss of Tobruk was embarrassing. "At Singapore 85,000 men had surrendered to inferior numbers of Japanese," Winston noted. "Now in Tobruk a garrison of 25,000 (actually 33,000) seasoned soldiers had laid down their arms to perhaps one half of their number." At the White House, Winston made no attempt to hide his shock. "It was a bitter moment. Defeat is one thing; disgrace is another," he commented.

Roosevelt and Hopkins responded to his obvious distress with "sympathy and chivalry." Added Winston, "There were no reproaches; not an unkind word was spoken." When FDR asked, "What can we do to help?" Winston immediately said, "Give us as many Sherman tanks as you can spare, and ship them to the Middle East as quickly as possible."

That request brought forth Gen. George C. Marshall, the U.S. Army chief of staff, who reported the Shermans were "just coming into production" and the first few hundred had been assigned to U.S. armored forces. "It is a terrible thing to take the weapons out of a soldier's hands," Marshall told the small group. "Nevertheless if the British need is so great they must have them; and we could let them have a hundred 105-mm. self-propelled guns in addition."

The result of this conversation was one of the most meaningful gifts the Americans made to the British during the war. "To complete the story, it must be stated that the Americans were better than their word," Winston observed. "Three hundred Sherman tanks and a hundred self-propelled guns were put into six of their fastest ships and sent off to the Suez Canal. One of these ships was sunk by a submarine off Bermuda. Without a single word from us the President and Marshall put a further seventy tanks into another fast ship and dispatched it to overtake the convoy. 'A friend in need is a friend indeed.'"

☆ ☆ ☆

Additional note: Before Winston returned to England a few days later, Harry Hopkins said, "There are a couple of American officers the President would like you to meet, as they are very highly thought of in the Army, by Marshall, and by him." As a result, Winston was introduced to Maj. Gen. Dwight D. Eisenhower, who would go down in history as commander of the Allied armies invading Normandy, France, on June 6, 1944, and Maj. Gen. Mark Clark, who would lead the American forces invading North Africa later in 1942.

Although Winston safely flew home at the end of this visit, there was a minor last-minute incident, it seems. Just before boarding his flying boat in Baltimore harbor, he noticed that "the narrow, closed-in gangway which led to the water was heavily guarded by armed American police." That was to be expected perhaps, but "there seemed to be an air of excitement, and the officers looked serious."

Reason: "One of the plainclothes men on duty had been caught fingering a pistol and heard muttering that he would 'do me in,' with some other expressions of an unappreciative character."

Result: "He had been pounced upon and arrested. Afterwards he turned out to be a lunatic."

Final observation: "Crackpots are a special danger to public men, as they do not have to worry about the 'getaway.'"

Not the End, But...

Good news at last! From the deserts of North Africa came the welcome word that Field Marshall Erwin Rommel, the "Desert Fox," and his Afrika Korps were in retreat. This after nearly two years of fighting between thousands of infantrymen and hundreds of mechanical monsters, with each ponderous force clinging to long, long supply lines. The numbers game by this time overwhelmingly favored the British, who had amassed 1,100 tanks and 200,000 troops in the area, to Rommel's 500 tanks and 96,000 troops, including 43,000 Italian soldiers. In the meantime, the British also had gained air superiority.

For many months, though, the initiative had been with Rommel as he drove eastward from Libya into Egypt, to within sixty miles of the Nile Valley . . . and beyond that lay the Suez Canal, that vital artery of supply and commerce linking Britain and its allies to the Far East. But now, midsummer of 1942, came the first of two major battles named for El Alamein, an Egyptian coastal village.

In this instance, Gen. Sir Claude Auchinleck's Eighth Army blocked and repeatedly counterattacked the advancing Axis tanks and infantry throughout the month of July, with both sides finally retiring to regroup—thus falling briefly into a stalemate that bothered Winston Churchill no end.

"The first battle of El Alamein is seldom accorded the recognition it deserves," observed historian David Eggenberger. "The successful British attack from this position four months later is often called one of the most decisive battles of World War II. But it was the first El Alamein that broke the back of Rommel's offensive 60 miles short of the Nile River, doomed his last attack at Alam Halfa and gave [Gens. Sir Harold] Alexander and [Bernard] Montgomery breathing time to rebuild the Eighth Army." Meanwhile, "as bitter reward for halting the fearsome Axis advance," Churchill relieved Auchinleck of command . . . in person and on the scene.

Winston then flew from Cairo to Moscow for a conference with Joseph Stalin and Averell Harriman (who stood in for FDR), thus missing the second battle of El Alamein, which didn't begin until late October. Now, with both sides at their peak strength, noted Eggenberger, the British opened with a barrage by 800 artillery pieces on the night of October 23 and then struck westward from El Alamein with armor. This was the start of seven days of fighting, during which at least two counterattacks by Rommel's panzers were "beaten back." Montgomery renewed the battle with a fresh offensive the night of October 30, and "on November 2 and again on November 4 [his tanks] punched wide holes in the Axis line."

As a result, "British armor broke out into the open desert, squeezing Rommel out of his defensive position. . . . The Axis withdrawal, begun the night of November 4–5, continued without letup for 1,500 miles, with Montgomery cautiously but relentlessly in pursuit." Thus there was no more threat to the Nile Valley, and with the American-led invasion of western North Africa days later (Operation Torch, which began on November 8), "Allied success in this theater was assured."

So encouraged was Winston Churchill, and yet so cautious at the same time, that when he spoke at the Lord Mayor's luncheon at Mansion House in London on November 10, he said: "The Germans have received back again that measure of fire and steel which they have so often meted out to others. Now this is not the end. It is not even the beginning of the end. But it is, perhaps, the end of the beginning."

Anything to Avoid Those Shots

In order to travel to Cairo in early August 1942 for conferences with British commanders in the Middle East and then to Moscow for a meeting with Stalin, Winston was told he needed "a whole series of protective injections." And they would be more than a mere nuisance. Some would take ten days to provide immunity; some could in the interim result in "considerable discomfort and even inactivity."

As usual, Winston was in a hurry. "The doubts I had about the High Command in the Middle East were fed continually by the reports which I received from many quarters," he wrote in his multivolume history of World War II. "It became urgently necessary for me to go there and settle the decisive questions on the spot." Furthermore, Stalin invited him to Moscow to discuss "the urgent questions of war against Hitler." It would be their first face-to-face meeting.

The troubling problem for Winston (and the reason for all those shots) was that the initial flight plan called for a five- or six-day journey from Gibraltar to Takoradi and across Central Africa up to Cairo. This would take Winston "through tropical and malarious regions," which required immunizing shots. It was a quandary for Winston and his advisers, but only until U.S. pilot Bill Vanderkloot appeared with *Commando*, a specially fitted B-24 Liberator with "some sort of passenger accommodation" in place of the original bomb racks. "This machine was certainly capable of flying along the route prescribed with good margins in hand at all stages," Winston wrote. And "Vanderkloot, who had already flown a million miles as a civilian pilot, asked why it was necessary to fly all round by Takoradi, Kano, Fort Lamy, El Obeid, etc. He said he could make one bound from Gibraltar to Cairo, flying from Gibraltar eastward in the afternoon, coming sharply south across Spanish or Vichy territory as dusk fell, and then proceeding eastward until he struck the Nile about Aissout, when a turn to the northward would bring us in another hour or so to the Cairo landing-ground northwest of the pyramids."

The confident Vanderkloot's proposal changed everything. "I could be in Cairo in two days without any trouble about Central African bugs and the inoculations against them." He left England after midnight on Sunday, August 2, and reached the Nile at dawn on the morning of August 4.

Commando, though, didn't offer the comforts of the big flying boat that had carried Winston to and from the United States. "The bomber was at this time unheated, and razor-edged draughts cut in through many chinks," Winston recalled. "There were no beds, but two shelves in the after cabin enabled me and Sir Charles Wilson, my doctor, to lie down." Thankfully, there were "plenty of blankets for all."

Possible dangers of course lay along the route. After spending the day of August 3 "looking round" the old British fortress of Gibraltar at the entrance to the Mediterranean Sea, Winston and his party took off at 6:00 p.m. for Cairo, "a hop of two thousand miles or more, as the detours necessary to avoid hostile aircraft around the Desert battle were considerable." In fact, to make his fuel last, Vanderkloot "flew straight across the Spanish zone and the Vichy quasi-hostile territory," Winston noted. "Therefore, as we had an armed escort till nightfall of four Beaufighters, we in fact openly violated the neutrality of both these regions. No one molested us in the air, and we did not come within cannon-shot of any important town. All the same I was glad when darkness cast her shroud over the harsh landscape and we could retire to such sleeping accommodation as 'Commando' could offer."

Winston slept "sound," he said, and at daybreak hurried to the copilot's seat, just in time to see "in the pale, glimmering dawn the winding silver ribbon of the Nile stretched joyously before us." Soon after, they landed, and Winston began his rounds of talks with his military commanders, along with visits to the various scenes of action, including El Alamein itself. As a result, instead of himself hearing from the front, he frequently reported back to and sought decisions from his War Cabinet in London. "Now for a short spell I became 'the man on the spot.' Instead of sitting at home waiting for the news from the front I could send it myself. This was exhilarating."

Additional note: On the other hand, far from "exhilarating," there would be difficult moments for Winston on his Mideast trip, such as removing Auchinleck from command there and then learning that Gen. William H. E. "Strafer" Gott, just appointed commander of the Eighth Army, had been shot down and killed by German aircraft—"killed by the enemy in almost the very air spaces through which I . . . flew [two days earlier]." Ironically, Bernard Montgomery then took Gott's place at the head of the Eighth Army, and so it was Montgomery instead of the unfortunate Gott who reaped the glory of routing Rommel in North Africa.

Meanwhile, Winston again made use of *Commando* in a visit to North Africa for his Casablanca conference with Roosevelt in early 1943 then flew safely home on February 7: "This was my last flight in 'Commando,' which later perished with all hands, though with a different pilot and crew." Such are the unhappy fortunes of war.

Flying the Great Man

"It was a mighty peculiar feeling," the young American acknowledged. "There was the prime minister getting into the plane after being escorted every foot of the way from 10 Downing Street to the airport. But when the door slammed shut, all those guards got back in their cars and left! It was now our responsibility. You could go crazy thinking about it, so I decided not to think about it, any more than I had to."

Bill Vanderkloot, the pilot who flew Winston into Cairo, Egypt, in a specially fitted B-24 Liberator in midsummer 1942, would try not to think too much about it while remaining Winston Churchill's pilot for three long, wartime years. Their relationship began in 1942, reported *Today's Officer* magazine six decades later, when Vanderkloot "was driven to a backstreet in an RAF car and told to walk down a dark street to a dimly lighted door and knock."

He thought his days as an RAF ferry pilot "were numbered," wrote Verna Gates in the magazine's October 2004 issue. But no, the young American from Lake Bluff, Illinois, was greeted inside by "a man with a familiar round face, wearing a brightly colored dressing gown and blue velvet slippers initialed 'P.M.'" After offering Vanderkloot a scotch and soda, "Churchill simply smiled at his befuddled guest and said, 'I understand we are going to Cairo.'"

"It took about two minutes to pick up my jaw when it dropped to the floor," Vanderkloot recounted. "Here was the greatest man in the world, and I was going to be associating with him as his pilot. It's enough to scare you to death."

Well, actually, the twenty-six-year-old Vanderkloot really wasn't scared off all that easily. After all, he had voluntarily signed up in January 1941 to ferry bombers across the Atlantic to eagerly awaiting British hands for the then-vast sum of $1,000 a month—tax free. "It was a great risk," noted the pilot's son, William Vanderkloot Jr., in the article. "If you got shot down, there was no protection for you. That was it. Nothing coming to the family, unlike the military, with pensions and death benefits. It was a big chance for civilian pilots to take."

Then, too, at the time, "everyone thought Europe was going to fall. Almost all of it had, except England. That's the reason my father volunteered for the [RAF] Ferry Command."

Adding to the obvious danger of running into enemy aircraft at the far end of the transatlantic flights were the risks posed by geography and weather for the Ferry Command crews. "The tempestuous ocean was equaled by its temperamental weather," noted Gates. "Few dared to forecast aviation meteorology for the North Atlantic; the techniques of the time were regarded as only slightly more reliable than fortune-telling."

Originally trained at the Parks Air College in East St. Louis, Illinois, Vanderkloot was a commercial airline pilot by the time World War II erupted—he had flown DC-2s and DC-3s, both multiengine planes like the big bombers coming down the line for wartime service. Approaching his job with the Ferry Command, he steeped himself in all the lore available on celestial navigation . . . in fact, his navigation skills became so "renowned," wrote Gates, "that he was tapped to map out several routes to England. He also taught navigation in the training school and later wrote a textbook."

When it came time to choose a steady, competent pilot for Winston, it was both the navigation expertise and "superior piloting" that recommended Vanderkloot to the RAF. As a result, he not only flew the PM to Cairo in the summer of 1942 for a close look and change of command at El Alamein, but then on to Moscow for Winston's first meeting with Stalin. As for the big matte-black Liberator dubbed *Commando* and its crew of one American copilot and three Canadian engineers, all were Vanderkloot's choices.

"That was some airplane, the Liberator," he said. "A fine airplane, built nicely. And the crew was the best; they knew that airplane inside and out."

On that first flight together, Winston's new pilot had to land at Gibraltar, a huge rock rising from the sea, with a tiny airfield at its base. "It looked very dangerous," Winston wrote. "One could not see a hundred yards ahead, and we were not flying more than 30 feet above the sea." Then up rose, quite suddenly, the "great precipice of Gibraltar." After three hours of flying in a mist, Vanderkloot had been so exact, "we passed the grim rock face a few hundred yards away, without having to alter course, and made a perfect landing." Vanderkloot himself said the five-thousand-foot runway was "like landing on an aircraft carrier."

Actually, until they reached Cairo, Vanderkloot didn't know about the Moscow leg of the trip. "I had mixed feelings. I didn't know if the airplane could go that far and into such a foreign country." But that leg, with a stop en route at Tehran, Iran, went well also. "After a three-week trip," wrote Gates in *Today's Officer*, "Vanderkloot returned his passengers safely to London. It had been a journey of 15,000 miles with the entire Luftwaffe on alert for Churchill, a treasured trophy."

After three years and two hundred thousand miles, Gates reported, Vanderkloot's *Commando* and crew flew "more high-ranking officials than any other aircraft in the British service." However, the limits of luck were beginning to be tested. Every plane in the Luftwaffe was gunning for *Commando*.

In fact, the night the Germans shot down a normally safe airliner flying the Lisbon-to-London route, killing actor Leslie Howard in the process, "the Germans had heard *Commando* was flying and were shooting everything down that night," said Vanderklooot's son. And years after the war, the elder Vanderkloot encountered a German visitor at a small airport in Oklahoma. "Weren't you the man who flew Churchill?" the foreigner asked.

When Vanderkloot acknowledged that he was, the German said, "I was in charge of a Luftwaffe wing assigned to shoot you down."

As it was, Vanderkloot, toward the end of the war, was becoming too well known as Winston's pilot. His son said their home was watched day and night. "People were following him in Montreal. He felt it was only a matter of time before the worst happened. It was too risky. . . . He felt it was time to stop."

Vanderkloot hated to give up his job as Winston's air chauffeur, but he did, and "reluctantly the British command transferred Vanderkloot and his crew to safer missions," recounted Gates. Unfortunately, *Commando* with a different crew was lost in March 1945.

Meanwhile, Vanderkloot returned home after the war to become a corporate pilot. He remained in contact with Winston, however, "meeting him for lunch in New York after the war." He lived until 2000, and he always remembered his days as the PM's pilot. "Churchill. What a man! He had everything!" Vanderkloot said shortly before his death. "I was his friend and his greatest admirer, still am and always will be."

Overview

With the Americans fighting the Japanese in the Pacific and, toward the end of 1942, landing in North Africa and now also committed to development of the atomic bomb, Winston couldn't exactly rest easy, but he could rest somewhat assured that his beloved Britain would survive. Difficult times still lay ahead, terrible tragedies still were to unfold, great policy and strategy issues were yet to be debated and resolved . . . but overall, as he observed, with Rommel retreating across the African desert, it wasn't the end, it wasn't even the beginning of the end, but it perhaps was the end of the beginning.

True, the British, the Canadians, and a few U.S. Rangers had taken a beating in a raid on Dieppe, France, in August 1942. The Americans also suffered in the battle of Savo Island off Guadalcanal, but the scorecard, worldwide, improved steadily after that. The Japanese had been halted in their drive on Port Moresby, New Guinea, and in February 1943, the Germans gave up their epic struggle against the Red Army at Stalingrad.

Meeting at Casablanca in January 1943, Winston and Roosevelt agreed that Germany and Japan must ultimately bow to unconditional surrender, a decision that some critics say actually stiffened German resistance in the final months of the war. Meanwhile, in February 1943, the Japanese gave up their six-month battle for control of Guadalcanal.

In April and May, the Warsaw ghetto uprising horrified the world, except for the Germans stamping out the heroic revolt by half-starved Jews . . . excepting also the Russian commissars who held their nearby forces in abeyance rather than make any effort to help.

In July and August, however, better news came, as the Anglo-American Allies successfully invaded Sicily, with Mussolini deposed shortly afterward and the Italian army surrendering in toto. The Anglo-American armies then, in September 1943, invaded Italy proper, first with the British landing at Reggio Calabria at the very bottom of the Italian "boot," soon followed by a major Allied landing at Salerno. But the Germans countered by occupying northern Italy and Rome. By October, Italy officially (but ineffectually) was at war with her former ally, Nazi Germany.

The dominoes were falling, but still the Allies had many, many difficult miles to go. Their principals would meet to plot the final strategy, and all—friend and foe—knew that meant occupied Western Europe must be invaded at some point, obviously at great cost. Invaded and occupied before Nazi Germany could be defeated. Important also, the Russians were demanding a second front in the west to relieve the pressure on their homeland. The war was far from over.

Winston and Roosevelt, plus China's Chiang Kai-shek, met at Cairo in late November 1943, followed by the first of the Big Three wartime conferences (Churchill, Roosevelt, and Stalin), held at Tehran from November 28 to December 1.

In the far-off Pacific, the Americans were beginning to recapture islands that had fallen earlier to the rampaging Japanese. The British kept the Japanese from rolling into India. In January 1944, the Italian campaign intensified with the Anglo-American landings at Anzio on the west coast of Italy. In that same month, Dwight D. Eisenhower was chosen to be supreme commander of Allied forces in Europe, meaning he would be the general overseeing Operation Overlord, the invasion of occupied France.

In the next few weeks of 1944, the longstanding German siege of Leningrad was broken, the Soviets advanced against their Nazi invaders across a broad front, the Americans staged their first daytime bombing raid on Berlin, and in the Pacific, Douglas MacArthur's island-hopping campaign was well under way. In Italy, the Germans withdrew from Rome early in June.

The major event of the spring and summer, though, was the invasion of

Normandy on June 6, the greatest amphibious military operation in history. Within weeks, after initial difficulties, the Allies were rolling across France. Paris was liberated on August 25. By autumn, the Red Army was driving into Eastern Europe and the Balkans, the Anglo-American Allies were approaching Germany's borders from the west, and on the other side of the world, MacArthur had returned to the Philippines, as he had pledged to do back in early 1942. In that part of the world, too, the Americans came away the victors in the spectacular naval battle of Leyte Gulf.

Meanwhile, Hitler had survived an assassination attempt by his own officers. In November, a weak and ailing Roosevelt won election for an unprecedented fourth term as U.S. president. The year ended, though, on a frightening note for the Allies—the costly Battle of the Bulge, a last-gasp effort by Germany to stop the Allied advance begun at Normandy. Gen. George S. Patton's Christmastime relief of Bastogne and clearing weather (which allowed Allied planes to fly again) combined to spell defeat for the German offensive in the Ardennes. Meanwhile, London and other parts of England were undergoing a renewed blitz from Hitler's latest weapons: the self-propelled V-1 buzz bombs and V-2 rockets.

With the war's end clearly in sight after the Battle of the Bulge, the Big Three met again at Yalta in the recently liberated Crimea . . . a controversial meeting in which Roosevelt, clearly weak and not well, parted company with Winston in responding to Stalin's demands on the shape of postwar Europe. Still ahead for the Americans in the Pacific were the invasions of Iwo Jima and Okinawa.

In the weeks ahead, FDR died, Hitler committed suicide, Germany surrendered, and the Red Army marched into Eastern Europe to consolidate Stalin's Yalta demands. As Winston observed in May, an iron curtain then fell across the entire region. In the Far East, the atomic bomb, dropped first on Hiroshima and then on Nagasaki, both in the Japanese homeland, brought about another surrender and final victory for the Allies over the Axis powers that had begun the war in the first place.

All this time, naturally, Winston, though visibly tiring himself, symbolized the determination of his island nation. Interestingly, as British historian Alistair Horne noted in the London *Times* on the fiftieth anniversary of V-E Day:

> On May 3 [1945], the first German peace emissaries arrived at Field Marshall Sir Bernard Montgomery's tactical headquarters on windswept Luneburg heath, southeast of Hamburg. They were gray men in gray uniforms, with gray faces that bore all the signs of the total breakdown and defeat of Hitler's once seemingly invincible Wehrmacht. It was ironic and yet, in historical terms, singularly

appropriate that they came to offer the surrender of all the surviving German forces, numbering [one million] not to the vastly stronger American and Soviet armies closing in on Berlin, but to a British commander.

For of all the allied combatants, only Britain had fought the arduous war from its first day in September 1939 [except for downtrodden Poland].

Horne added, "Britain had no possibility of winning the war against even Germany alone, until the resources of first the Soviet Union and then America, entered the balance." On the other hand, "as in the Napoleonic wars, a British victory could only be achieved by coalition warfare—with all its accompanying headaches and consequences for the postwar world. But, equally, without the base of Britain's 'unsinkable aircraft carrier,' American forces could never have invaded Europe; the Soviet Union, would almost certainly have been defeated; or, alternatively, the atomic bomb would have been used on Germany, not Japan, in 1945."

Beyond the what-ifs, though, hard facts remained. Fifty million to sixty million persons killed worldwide, including 67,635 British civilians. In gross totals, the Soviet Union suffered the most: 25.6 million perished. Germany and Japan did not escape punishing losses either, with 6.5 million and 2.4 million killed, respectively. Next worst-case scenario (after the Soviet Union) among the victims of German aggression: Poland lost six million. In the Holocaust perpetrated by Nazi Germany, an estimated 5.9 million Jews were killed.

Forty-Foot Waves

The crew of HMS *Matchless*, "a destroyer usually occupied with merchant-ship convoys in northern waters," found themselves one time late in the war on escort duty in the North Atlantic for the speedy ocean liner *Queen Mary* . . . and her special passenger, Winston Churchill, on his way for talks with President Roosevelt in the United States. (All told, they met nine times during the Second World War.) Because of the U-boat menace, speed was of the essence. "The escort," recalled crew member Eric Cowham for the BBC's "WW2 People's War" Web site, "was organized like a relay race with six destroyers positioned in pairs across the Atlantic. The *Queen Mary* was a very fast ship and could carry enough fuel to see her all the way across the Atlantic to New York. Although we were faster ships, we couldn't carry enough fuel for the distance involved, so each pair of destroyers escorted the *Queen Mary* several hundred miles to the next pair of waiting ships. . . . In this way, the *Queen Mary* could maintain her speed without having to wait for her escort to refuel."

HMS *Matchless* awaited the *Queen* at the last pickup point for the final dash to safety, but now all ships ran into "hurricane weather and the *Queen Mary* was forced to reduce her speed to avoid structural damage." The seas were so rough that the destroyer's engine room personnel "were on duty to shut down the ship's engines as the screws came up out of the waves, as to let them run free could have caused major damage through vibration."

Through it all, Churchill apparently became a bit restless. "With the *Queen Mary* now traveling at a slow rate of knots, Churchill must have felt becalmed and at one point we circled her towing a drogue behind us so that Winnie could shoot at it with an anti-aircraft gun."

How did he do?

"As we were registering forty-foot waves at the time I don't think he had many hits." Meanwhile, all ships reached port safely.

Never the Same Again

If the major plot of the Winston Churchill story for World War II was his inspiring leadership, then the subplots were his constant travels and many illnesses . . . often coming together as one. The chief perils of his travels were accident or discovery by the enemy. Of his many illnesses, pneumonia was the great fear. It, in fact, once almost did him in—while he was traveling—at the end of 1943 in North Africa.

Fortunately, as usually was the case during the war, his close friend and doctor, Lord Moran, was with him. The pneumonia struck while Winston's party was staying at General Eisenhower's villa at Carthage after conferences in Tehran and Cairo in November–December 1943. To make matters worse, Winston also experienced fibrillation of the heart. Moran recounted, "As I sat by his bedside listening to his quick breathing, I knew that we were at last right up against things."

It was a difficult and long moment for them both. "It was four hours before the heart resumed its normal rhythm, and I was relieved to count a regular pulse of 120," Moran wrote. "A man feels pretty rotten, I imagine, when he fibrillates during pneumonia, but the P.M. was very good about it."

Apparently resigned to suffer through his discomfort, Winston once asked, "Can't you do anything to stop this?"

"But when I told him that digitalis was a specific for this condition, like quinine for malaria, and that when he was under its influence the fibrillation would probably stop, he seemed comforted."

The fibrillation did suddenly stop, but three days later, even though the pneumonia was clearing under treatment with "M&B" medication (short for an antibiotic sulphonamide made by the firm of May and Baker), it came back for an hour and a half. This time, "it did not distress him as it did the first time."

Meanwhile, Winston's illness briefly had looked so serious that Clementine flew out from London in an unheated bomber to be with him. As Winston steadily improved, the party moved two days after Christmas to Marrakech, Morocco, a spot below the Atlas Mountains that Winston had loved from the time of his prewar visits. During his recuperation, he and others picnicked in or below the mountains at lunchtime almost every day, but Winston typically one day insisted on climbing down a steep gorge to a mountain stream below. The problem then was climbing back up the steep rocky path. To help a still-weak Winston make the grade, his companions made a rope of the tablecloth, tied it round his waist, and tugged and pushed him up the hill.

All too soon, it was time to fly home to England and begin preparing for the really big push—Operation Overlord, the invasion of France. The war had to go on.

Additional note: While Winston struck many as some sort of energy-superman, those closest to him, Lord Moran very much among them, saw that the strain of wartime leadership was indeed wearing him down. "As, year after year, I watched the P.M. doing the work of three men, I kept saying to myself that this could not go on forever," Moran observed in his memoirs. "'Can't you do anything for this horrible feeling of exhaustion?' he demanded at Cairo [in 1943]. And then came his illness at Carthage. He never seemed to me to be the same man again."

Overcoming FDR's Secrecy

What did Franklin D. Roosevelt tell Winston Churchill? Naturally, not many people were supposed to know. But . . . not even the intimates of FDR's official family? Not even, in the case of military matters, his own army chief of staff, George C. Marshall?

"He didn't want a record of cabinet meetings," Marshall explained. "He didn't give us the messages he was sending half the time." Roosevelt's bent for secrecy extended to the all-important wartime messages he exchanged with Churchill, who liked to sign off as "Former Naval Person" in reference to his days at the British admiralty. Himself a one-time assistant secretary of the U.S. Navy, FDR liked to address his transatlantic messages to "My Naval Friend."

But that still left Marshall, among others, out of the loop. And Marshall, as head of the U.S. armed forces, had a discernable need to know what information his chief was sharing with the British allies. "He would communicate with Churchill, he would receive a message from Churchill, and I would be wholly unaware of it, though it directly affected the affairs of the army and the air and maybe the navy," Marshall told biographer Forrest C. Pogue. But Marshall found a way to circumvent FDR's predilection for secrecy without directly challenging his commander in chief, although going around the president took some doing.

Marshal utilized the good offices of highly placed contacts in a foreign government—that is, he used British sources to find out what FDR and Winston might be planning. Marshall realized that Roosevelt's messages to Churchill would be distributed to very senior personnel in the British government, including chiefs of staff. They would notify the head of the British Joint Staff Mission to the United States, Field Marshal Sir John Dill, a good friend of Marshall's. The circuitous route of the secret messages thus went from FDR to Churchill and staff to the British chiefs of staff. "Then Dill should know it in Washington, so Dill would get a copy of it," Marshall explained to Pogue in 1957. "Then Dill would come over to my office, and I would get Roosevelt's message through Field Marshal Sir John Dill. Otherwise, I wouldn't know what it was."

Naturally, Marshall was forced to keep his personal conduit of high-level war messages a secret. "I had to be very careful that nobody knew this—no one in the War Department—and certainly not the [British] chiefs of staff, because Dill would be destroyed in a minute if this was discovered. But he knew I had to have it, and he just brought it to me and read it to me. He sat opposite me at my desk and went over this." Dill was sympathetic to Marshall's predicament. "Why should the British chief of staff have it—it was from our President—and the American chiefs of staff not have it?" was Marshall's question years after World War II.

Roosevelt's secrecy was a two-way street, of course. Not only did FDR decline to share the messages he sent to Churchill, he also did not share communications he received from Churchill. And once again Dill came to the rescue of his American "cousins" by keeping the future secretary of state and proponent of the postwar Marshall Plan au courant. Marshall, for his part, never told his fellow chiefs of staff, never told FDR . . . never told anyone—until 1957 and his interview with Pogue.

In Pogue's *George C. Marshall: Interviews and Reminiscences*, Marshall also revealed that he and his wartime "conspirator" took an additional cooperative step that suited their very special situation. "Dill would frequently get messages from Mr. Churchill . . . [asking] him to ascertain General Marshall's possible view of this. Dill would come over and read me Mr. Churchill's communication. Then he and I would make up the reply. And very often, when I wouldn't agree with it at all, very decidedly wouldn't agree to it, I would comment very forcibly and very freely to Dill in a way I wouldn't possibly comment to the Prime Minister. Then Dill would report that to Mr. Churchill. That's what I said to Dill, and that way my own feeling got across to Mr. Churchill."

Battle of the Beaches

Try as he would, Winston wasn't allowed to watch the Normandy invasion from a warship in the English Channel. George VI vetoed the notion. No, no, and no, in fact. Repeatedly.

At first, the king and his prime minister planned to be aboard the cruiser HMS *Belfast* to witness the historic landings together. But then the king realized that risking both their lives to possible air attack, errant torpedo, or a stray mine floating in the Channel—risking either national leader alone, for that matter—was not a good idea. Not even in the midst of the greatest sea armada ever assembled.

It took some doing, including two personal letters, but he finally persuaded—even ordered, by some accounts (Winston's among them)—Winston against going. In his second appeal by letter to Winston, recalled Sarah Bradford in *George VI*, the king said:

> Please consider my own position. I am a younger man than you. I am a sailor, & as King I am the head of all three services. There is nothing I would like to do better than to go to sea but I have agreed to stop at home; is it fair that you should then do exactly what I should have liked to do myself? You said yesterday afternoon that it would be a fine thing for the King to lead his troops into battle, as in old days; if the King cannot do this, it does not seem to me right that his Prime Minister should take his place.

More sharply, meanwhile, George VI wrote in his diary: "I am very worried over the PM's seemingly selfish way of looking at the matter. He doesn't seem to care about the future, or how much depends on him."

But Winston did finally—"grumpily and ungraciously," Bradford wrote—accede to his monarch's wishes. "Since Your Majesty does me the honor to be so much concerned about my personal safety on this occasion, I must defer to Your Majesty's wishes & indeed commands," Winston replied to the king's second written appeal.

As one result, Winston's whereabouts on the eve of the great invasion were far from the center of the storm he with Dwight D. Eisenhower, Bernard Montgomery, and all their best staff minds had helped to shape and formulate from the beginning—even though Winston might have preferred the strategy of continuing to press forward in Italy and to take the fight to the Germans through the Balkans (which all too soon would be overrun by the Red Army).

Meanwhile, a digression here: in the first nine months of 1944, reported Winston's daughter Mary, her mother and father gave seventy-five luncheons and nineteen dinner parties, excluding those with strictly family members. Aside from Winston's informal Tuesday lunches with his sovereign, the king came to dine at No. 10 Downing an extraordinary six times in all of 1944.

During the same January–September period as the seventy-five luncheons, Mary reported, the weekends at Chequers offered no rest cure for Winston and Clementine. Out of a total of thirty-three weekends, Mary noted, "twenty-four of them were all, or partly, taken up with entertaining official guests from abroad, or commanders home for a short while from their theaters of operations, in addition to the many men Winston had constantly around him for the purpose of conducting affairs." Sometimes, she added, "in one weekend there would be two, and sometimes three 'shifts' of guests; some lunching, others 'dining and sleeping.'"

During those same nine months, Clementine's diary only four times noted, "Dinner alone with Winston." One of those four times, though, was the evening of June 5, 1944, the night before D-Day. While the greatest military operation in history finally was uncoiling, the Churchills apparently dined quietly. Winston then visited his Map Room "to study the final dispositions and plan of attack," Mary wrote in *Clementine Churchill*. "Already great convoys were moving in the darkness to their appointed stations off the coast of Normandy."

During the past few days, of course, Winston had visited "the camps and embarkation ports." He "earnestly longed to view at closer quarters the assault from a British warship, to watch over and in some way to share in this tremendous enterprise in whose conception and growth he had played so close a part." Earlier on Monday, June 5, 1944, Winston had paid a final visit to Eisenhower's headquarters. Everywhere everyone's nerves were taut as steel—the assault should have kicked off on June 5, but bad weather delayed everything by at least a day. Any further delay could mean a weeks-long stoppage, with the secret of the destination then getting out. Now, on the night of June 5, with Operation Overlord ready to roll, Clementine joined Winston in the Map Room just before going to bed.

That was when he rather famously, and of course gravely, said to her: "Do you realize that by the time you wake up in the morning twenty thousand men may have been killed?"

☆   ☆   ☆

Additional note: For the greatest amphibious assault in history, the Allies had gathered 800,000 combat troops, 47 divisions, in the British Isles. They launched their assault on the fifty-mile stretch of Normandy beaches with the support of 4,000 ships, 4,900 fighter planes, and 5,800 bombers. Rather than Winston's 20,000, their D-Day casualties came to 11,000 total, including 2,500 killed—far less than had been expected. But then it unexpectedly took a month to clear the Normandy hedgerows and stubborn German resistance and begin the summer-long dash across France to the borders of Germany itself. The first seven weeks of fighting cost the Allies 122,000 in casualties, to the Germans' 117,000.

With Montgomery declaring, "We have won the battle of the beaches," Winston finally was able to visit Sir Bernard's beachhead six days after D-Day, June 12, Bradford noted in her biography of George VI. "The next day he reported to the King at their Tuesday luncheon, later giving the King formal permission to visit the beaches, which the King did on 16 June, driving ashore in a DKW amphibian to be met by a 'very enthusiastic' Montgomery, with whom he lunched in his caravan at his tactical HQ."

Meanwhile, no one back in London had reason to feel left out—just a week after D-Day, Germany renewed its blitz of civilian homes and centers, this time by buzz bomb, the V-1 flying bomb, and then by V-2 rocket. "Over 500 civilians were killed during the first week, sixty of them in the Guards Chapel within yards of Buckingham Palace," noted Bradford. "At the Palace windows were regularly blown out by the blast. . . . For the next few weeks the King's Tuesday luncheons with Churchill were held in the basement air-raid shelter."

Christmas Under the Gun

It was two days before Christmas in 1944, with the long, tedious war years at last winding down to a foreseeable end . . . and upstairs at Chequers, the official country residence, Clementine Churchill was in the bedroom "in floods of tears." That was the way her sister Nellie Romilly found her that December 23. And downstairs, moments before, Nellie had come across Winston in the great hall, concerned and helpless.

"It was so rare for Clementine to give way," daughter Mary wrote in her biography of her mother. "She was accustomed to sudden changes of plan and had, in these last years especially, developed a strict sense of priorities."

But Winston's announcement of changed plans this time was a blow. This time, Clementine had taken "infinite" pains to assure the family "a glowing Christmas-tide." This Christmas, after all, "seemed to have a special atmosphere." By late 1944, after all, the Battle of the Bulge aside, "the dark war years were drawing to their end like a long and bitter winter; even the least optimistic could reasonably feel that this, the sixth, was the last wartime Christmas. Everywhere families were making their arrangements, despite gaps in the family, despite the black-out and despite rationing." And among them had been Clementine herself.

But now, as Winston told Nellie, "under the seal of secrecy," he must be off the very next day, on Christmas Eve, for embattled Athens, Greece. "He begged her to go and find Clementine, who was upstairs and 'very upset.'"

The trouble in Athens by this stage of the war was not the invading Germans but communist insurgents embarked on a spree of street violence—"including the murder of many policemen, and the seizing of police stations," noted Churchill biographer Martin Gilbert. Early in the month, Winston had ordered Lt. Gen. Sir Ronald Scobie, the senior British officer on the scene: "Do not hesitate to fire at any armed male in Athens who assails the British authority or Greek authority with which we are working. . . . Do not hesitate to act as if you were in a conquered city where a local rebellion is in progress."

As the violence continued, and the British toughened their stance, Winston sent in military reinforcements from Italy and Gen. Sir Harold Alexander as the man in charge. Negotiations focused on the possibility of a temporary regency under Greek Orthodox Archbishop Damaskinos. The idea was to push the communists into a coalition cabinet led by the archbishop, although Churchill at the same time feared the inclinations of the archbishop might lead to a "dictatorship" of the Left. If Greece fell to the "powers of evil," he declared on December 22, "we must look forward to a quasi-Bolshevised Russian-led Balkan Peninsula and this may spread to Hungary and Italy."

A somewhat unwilling witness to the events of the tumultuous next few days was Churchill's personal physician, Charles Wilson (Lord Moran). He was sitting at home by the fire after taking his morning tea on December 24, just thinking how to make Christmas "amusing" for his wife, Dorothy, when the telephone rang. It was his first notification that Churchill would be off to "G" that very evening. As the PM's doctor, Moran would be tagging along with him.

But what was "G"? It could be Gibraltar, the British base and rather pleasant "Rock" guarding the entrance to the Mediterranean Sea. Moran had to know so he could take the right clothing. To find out, he and his wife drove the short distance to Chequers, happy with the recent lifting of the wartime restriction on full headlights. "So we joyfully stripped the black paper from the lamps of the car," he wrote in *Churchill at War, 1940–45*. "We had forgotten what it felt like to sweep along a road thrown up by a searchlight instead of groping our way anxiously along the dark lanes."

The news at Chequers was less cheerful. "G. is Greece," Moran wrote in his diarylike account of the war years with Churchill. Greece obviously meant cold-weather clothing . . . and troublesome conditions.

It was 11:30 that night when Churchill actually left Chequers for the Northolt airfield and the flight to Greece aboard a newly outfitted American C-54 Skymaster transport. He was awakened during the night to don an oxygen mask while the plane climbed above a snowstorm pelting the French countryside below.

By midmorning Christmas Day, the plane was on the ground at Naples, Italy, for refueling. Churchill took the opportunity to wire Clementine: "Love and many thoughts for you all at luncheon today. I am sorry indeed not to see the tree."

And next, Moran recorded: "Our aircraft landed in the failing light [biographer Gilbert reported it was 2:00 p.m.] at an airfield near Athens; from this we went in an armored car by a coast road to a jetty, where a launch was waiting to bring us to HMS *Ajax*, a small cruiser which had been in the river Plate engagement [the 1939 action in South America that resulted in the scuttling of the German pocket battleship *Graf Spee*]." The dinner guests aboard the warship that Christmas night included future prime ministers Harold Macmillan and Anthony Eden.

The house-to-house fighting in Athens had been difficult, Winston and his companions were told. Whatever the difficulties, however, he distinctly was not happy with the progress being made. "We were, he said, faced with two very forbidding alternatives: either to take on most of Greece with the growing disapprobation of the world [including that of the Roosevelt administration], or to abandon our friends to be massacred."

That night, too, Winston's language was "pretty violent." Indeed, the next day, when shells exploded near the ship while Winston was dictating to a secretary in his cabin, according to Gilbert, Winston cried: "There, you bloody well missed us! Come on—try again!"

That same day after Christmas the entire party came under unfriendly fire not once but repeatedly. After lunch aboard the cruiser, Winston's entourage prepared to go ashore to visit the British Embassy and for a conference at the Greek Foreign Office. A shell or light mortar round fell nearby, "perhaps sixty yards astern," Lord Moran reported. Then, "as we stepped aboard a launch another shell came over, hitting a landing craft by the water's edge."

After alighting on a jetty, Churchill's entourage traveled via two armored cars to the British Embassy. There, a "fussed" British officer wanted to get Winston into the embassy as quickly as possible. By Lord Moran's account, "a woman had been shot dead a few yards down the street, just before we arrived. But the P.M. stood gazing up at the windows of the house opposite, giving the V sign to the Greeks looking out." Gilbert cited a notation by Winston's private secretary John Colville that a woman had been killed on the nearby street . . . but not until the next day, December 27, when Winston returned to the embassy for a second visit.

Inside the unheated public rooms of the embassy on December 26, meanwhile, Winston made what his doctor called "a graceful little speech to the staff

. . . thanking them for their cheerfulness and fortitude." But first came a few moments of further exposure to possible danger. "The back of the house was less safe from snipers than the front, and a small garden there was said to be particularly exposed. Into it the P.M. now went with the Archbishop to pose before the photographers, whereupon an officer spoke to two soldiers, who proceeded to cover the upper windows of the adjoining buildings with their tommy guns."

Next, the group was off to the foreign ministry for the conference with the archbishop, Greek prime minister M. Papandreou, and members of ELAS (the National Popular Liberation Army, the military arm of the EAM—the Communist National Liberation Front).

The tall archbishop, his high ceremonial hat adding to his great height in the flickering light from hurricane lamps, began the meeting without the ELAS representatives, who were late. He said he was willing to form a government with or without the communists, according to Gilbert.

As Winston then was responding to the prelate's words of greeting, a commotion outside and a knock on the door signaled that the three ELAS representatives had arrived, led by M. Partsalides. "He had a gray waterproof and brown muffler over his British battledress," wrote Moran. "In the dim light I could not see how the other two were dressed, but they were muffled to the ears, like pilots coming into the mess from a winter flight. Without further greeting they took the chairs nearest to the door." Colville described them as "shabby desperadoes."

The meeting then started over. Papandreou looked ill at ease around the rebellious communists, thought Moran, whereas the communists radiated a "suppressed vitality."

Winston resumed his little speech of greeting, saying the British wanted nothing from Greece, "not an inch of her territory," except acceptance of General Scobie's terms and restoration of Greece to the ranks of the Allies. By Gilbert's summation, he added: "Mr. Eden [the foreign secretary] and I have come all this way, although great battles are raging in Belgium and on the German Frontier [the Battle of the Bulge], to make this effort to rescue Greece from a miserable fate and raise her to a point of great fame and repute."

He also assured the Greeks in the room that he and Eden would remain available for consultation at any time, added Gilbert. "He wished them well. Whether Greece remained a monarchy or became a republic 'is a matter for Greeks and Greeks alone to decide.' As he was speaking, the sound of gunfire could be heard outside. At one point, Colville noted, 'the roar of descending rockets' fired by the British fighters at a nearby Communist position 'almost drowned his words.'"

The archbishop asked if there were any questions. By Moran's account, the

ELAS members whispered among themselves, then their leader rose and thanked Winston for taking the initiative behind the meeting but added, "Inasmuch as it is a conference of our political parties, we feel that the party of EAM should also have been called. EAM, which commands the living forces of the nation, which was the first to rise in support of the great struggle which the British people waged alone."

Eden, as foreign secretary, noted the conferees could invite anyone they wished. The discussion among the Greeks then became "heated," Gilbert reported, and "Churchill rose to his feet and declared: 'I should like to go now. We have begun the work. See that you finish it.'"

On the way out, he shook hands with all but the three communists. He paused as he approached them. "He had vowed that he would not shake hands with these villains," recalled Moran. "What was he going to do?"

But Winston merely asked, "Who will introduce these gentlemen to me?"

Obviously pleased and a bit animated for the first time, the three communist representatives "wrung Mr Churchill's hand with slight, stiff bows."

Watching the entire tableau without comment or contribution was Stalin's representative, Col. Grigori Popov from the Russian Military Mission.

It all had been "intensely dramatic," Winston reported to Clementine. "All those haggard Greek faces round the table and the Archbishop with his enormous hat, making him, I should think, seven feet high."

He later suggested that if the three communist delegates to the meeting could be brought to the dinner table with him and his companions, "all difficulties might vanish." Others in his party were skeptical, however, and as the situation stood, the street fighting in Athens, for the moment, continued. That afternoon, on returning to the *Ajax*, Winston found the warship had moved a mile farther offshore to avoid communist mortar rounds. When further shells fell around the ship anyway, the captain asked if he should return fire, Gilbert reported. To which the pugnacious PM responded: "I have come to Greece on a mission of peace, Captain. I bear the olive branch between my teeth. But far be it for me to intervene with military necessity. RETURN FIRE!"

Later, while Winston slept aboard the cruiser, depth chargers were exploded around the ship periodically throughout the night "as a precaution against underwater attack."

Meanwhile, after dinner aboard the *Ajax* that evening, General Alexander pleaded for patience. Street fighting was a slow and tedious process. The ELAS fighters, dressed in civilian clothes, he explained, continually slipped behind the lines. "Of course," Lord Moran observed, "Germans or Russians would soon have liquidated the affair, blowing up houses and exterminating those who resisted, but we could not do that."

Meanwhile, Churchill warned that if the fighting dragged on, there could be difficulties both with the Americans and Stalin, although Colonel Popov's restraint at the meeting indicated a hands-off attitude on the part of Stalin. Winston nonetheless urged a quick resolution to the military situation. As events unfolded, the fighting did soon come to an end, but not before Churchill came under considerable fire, even from elements of the British press, for his dangerous personal intervention.

Summing up how her father spent Christmas 1944 away from home and family, daughter Mary wrote: "For two days [more, actually] meetings took place under conditions of siege. Churchill established his headquarters in the British cruiser *Ajax*; and while he was ashore, conferring in the British Embassy, the building was shelled and machine-gunned. He met leaders of all parties, including the Communists, and persuaded them to agree to the establishment of a Regency pending a plebiscite on the maintenance of the monarchy. His personal intervention on the spot was undoubtedly the only way in which agreement could have been reached so quickly."

---------------------------------- ----------------------------------

Wartime Glimpses

---------------------------------- ----------------------------------

Then a seven-year-old at boarding school, Chris Adams heard the "crump, crump" of the bombs falling on Coventry. "Not long after that we were taken to the village near the Dun Cow Hotel, where we saw Winston Churchill stop in his car on the way to visit Coventry. He was offered a bottle of champagne, but no one had a corkscrew to open it. He was smoking his cigar and made a 'V' [for Victory] sign to the crowd, who cheered him."

During the Battle of Britain, a land mine dropped from above exploded on Betty Macleod's south London street—"and my house was one of the many that was affected." She and her neighbors did their best to clean up the damage. "It was hard going, working amongst the dust and rubble, and we were all getting tired, down-hearted and very grubby." Just then, who should appear, walking down the street, but Winston Churchill! "He stopped to speak to us, explaining that he had heard about the land mine and had come to offer his moral support and see the damage for himself. You can imagine how our spirits were lifted by his visit."

On another occasion, Olwen George, a torpedoman from the HMS *Hardy*, a frigate lost in the early—and unsuccessful—battle for Norway, was among a dozen sailors from the *Hardy* honored at the Horse Guards Parade in London soon after their rescue and return home. They were inspected by Winston him-self, "black homber hat clamped on his head and wearing a dark coat." Not yet prime minister, he was Britain's first lord of the admiralty, and in that role he wel-comed back the sailors from an essentially disastrous Norway campaign. "He did not seem to be looking at us but at the ground," George recalled. "Part of his speech was—'When you lost your ship you did not hesitate but took up arms, leapt ashore and became the first British Expeditionary force to land in Norway!'" Not quite the case, it seems. "I remember thinking—'Some force'—we were more like drowning rats abandoning a sinking ship!" Still, "remembering the pressmen [newsmen], photographers and the propaganda of the occasion, I think it was a good demonstration to boost up the country's morale."

Not everybody was happy with Winston Churchill as Britain's wartime leader. "Only seven years old in 1945, Wendy Bylis recalled "going in friends' houses and being told 'never mention Winston Churchill in the house.' It was like swearing he was so hated, rightly or wrongly. I do remember men saying while Churchill was in England he was sending men to unnecessary deaths. These men wanted a new Britain and got Churchill out of power at the end of the war."

And yet Grace and Bill Wilson remember going to the theater with friends one night after the war, after Winston was deposed as prime minister, to see a Gilbert and Sullivan production. They arrived late, the house lights were down, and as they entered, the spotlights suddenly shone on them . . . they thought. Indeed, the audience rose for a standing ovation. But then . . . "We turned around and there was a grinning Winston Churchill and family." Afterward, a nice touch . . . while the audience again stood, Churchill walked slowly down the theater aisle until he spotted the same late-comers. "He squeezed down between the rows of seats until he reached us and he shook hands with each of us. He apologized for any embarrassment he might have caused us."

Winston's "Gestapo" Speech

For the electoral process of a modern nation, the returns had been slow to wend their way home—on the order of three weeks since the voting took place. But then, so many soldiers, sailors, and airmen were scattered so far away from Winston Churchill's sceptered isle. And their votes had to be counted too.

The countdown for the parliamentary elections of 1945 found the erstwhile leader himself abroad . . . at Postdam, Germany, for the last of the major summit meetings of World War II. As British historian Geoffrey Best wrote in *Churchill: A Study in Greatness*, "It was a strange general election, unlike any other in the history of the British Parliament."

The general election of 1945 not only produced a "long count," it followed a "long Parliament," which had been in place for the duration of the war and then some. Churchill, the wartime leader of Great Britain and nowadays a Conservative Party member, had been in charge of the government ever since his elevation to prime minister in May 1940, but it was only a coalition government, with the Conservatives dominating.

Explained Best: "The Conservatives who had acclaimed him as leader in 1940 had no objection to being in a government labeled 'National' or 'Coalition' so long as they dominated it, but Labor unsurprisingly thought differently." Quite differently at that, now that the war in Europe had been won.

"[Labor] had long been looking forward to the return of peacetime politics and wanted to get on with them. The latter days of May therefore witnessed the resignation of the Labor ministers. Hugh Dalton [minister of economic warfare] recalled how, at a farewell party at Number Ten, Churchill inimitably told them, with tears streaming down his cheeks, that the light of history would shine on all their helmets. Then came the formation of a caretaker government, without Labor content, and the announcement of 5 July as the date for the general election."

The two heavyweight contenders, of course, would be the Socialist-hued Labor Party and the Conservatives. To those closely attuned it appeared Labor might be the better prepared. "This was not because they had been less than properly supportive of the national war effort. On the contrary, they had been prominent and efficient in the front lines of government."

During the war, with Labor gaining valuable experience in domestic affairs, Winston himself, typically, had focused his energies on leading his nation through the war while leaving domestic matters to others. He had been glad back in 1940, noted Best, to embrace the Labor ministers "as co-governors for the same reasons and with the same single-mindedness as, twelve months later, he embraced the Russians as co-belligerents." For Churchill "in those dark days," the goal had been "to survive and, that once assured, sooner or later to conquer."

Thus, "the details of planning for postwar Britain had no firm lodging in his mind until the early summer of 1945. He had more important things to think about." Thus, too, the "logic of total war" had led to "a tide of collectivist organization and communitarian experience," in Best's words. The "loosely laissez-faire Britain of the 1930s had, in not much more than the twinkling of an historical eye, turned (in effect) into a showpiece of war socialism." While Winston Churchill as a young Parliamentarian had helped David Lloyd George put together key elements of the British welfare state, he now disliked "the idea of needless or excessive controls." He hoped for a postwar Britain "liberated with all prudent speed from the bondage of a militarized command economy." But he apparently overstepped himself when he warned that "no Socialist system can be established without a political police," when he even suggested a Socialist government in Britain "would have to fall back on some form of Gestapo."

According to Best, Clementine warned him against using that particular language in a nationwide broadcast, but he did anyway. As also noted by Winston's biographer Martin Gilbert in *Churchill: A Life*, "Widespread criticism met the 'Gestapo speech,' as it quickly became known." At the same time, he did promise "wartime expedients" to assure housing for all and, unknown to the public, he asked his caretaker cabinet to "prepare legislation both for a National Insurance scheme and a National Health Service," reported Gilbert.

No matter what the offsetting factors, pro-Labor or pro-Conservative, a key to all that transpired in the curious election of 1945 was timing. With the end of the war in Europe, senior Labor men in Churchill's coalition government actually were willing to see the coalition continued until the defeat of Japan. But no, the rank and file of their party, meeting at Blackpool in late May, ruled in favor of an immediate return to "the cut and thrust of Party politics," as Gilbert termed it.

Not only had it been ten years since the last general election, Gilbert noted, but "many Labor politicians had held Government office under Churchill, had gained great experience and wished, above all, to put their Socialist ideals into practice."

Told of the party's decision to seek installation of a Labor government, "Churchill realized that nothing could now save the Coalition," wrote Gilbert. "At noon on May 23 he went to Buckingham Palace to tender his resignation to the King. He had been leader of an all-Party Government, the 'Grand Coalition' as he sometimes called it, for five years and thirteen days. The King asked him to form a Caretaker Government until elections could be held and the votes of the soldiers overseas counted; this would take at least two months."

In the campaign that followed, Winston's incumbency was just as much a burden as an advantage. As his nation's wartime leader and chief officeholder, he still had other things to think about . . . such as the continuing war against Japan, such as the Soviet-sponsored iron curtain already descending in Eastern Europe, such as his still uncertain relations with a new American leader, the late FDR's successor, Harry S. Truman. Winston, in fact, was supposed to meet with Truman and Stalin at Potsdam on July 17 for a few days, rush home for the vote count on July 27, and then, if all went well, rush back to Germany for further meetings on behalf of Britain as the major powers made final plans for the postwar peace.

All that, plus a make-or-break political campaign, was a good deal for any man to bear, even for Winston Churchill. His enormous popularity aside, would this burden be especially so for a war-weary prime minister at age seventy? Meanwhile, it wasn't merely socialism that Winston feared as a result of a Labor victory, but the specter of the party's unelected executive—its leadership group—telling its cabinet ministers what to do. Winston once said that these "unrepresented persons" would "share the secrets and give the orders to the so-called Ministers of the Crown."

Was this a reasonable fear? Well, hadn't Labor executive chairman Harold Laski said that even if party leader Clement Attlee went with Churchill to Potsdam, Labor wouldn't feel committed to decisions made there without debate by the party executive?

Also a threat to Winston's continuation as prime minister was the Liberal Party, led these days by his old friend—and Churchill's second in command of the 6th Royal Scots Fusiliers during World War I—Sir Archibald Sinclair, who originally entered Parliament after the Great War with Winston's encouragement. Sinclair's party had fielded three hundred contenders for the 1945 parliamentary sweepstakes.

In any case, with a break at his disposal between the voting on July 5 and his scheduled arrival at Potsdam ten days later, Churchill took time for a brief holiday in Bordeaux by the sea. There, at the Chateau de Bordaberry, said his daughter Mary later, the "magic of painting soon laid hold of him, absorbing him for hours on end, and banishing disturbing thoughts of either the present or the future."

Confronting Stalin

Even as Winston Churchill faced the home-front crisis posed by the 1945 elections in England, events underscoring his fears of aggressive, Soviet-style communism already were under way in Continental Europe. As if to prove exactly what he feared, fourteen underground leaders from Poland were arrested while under a promise of safe conduct near Warsaw and now were to be brought to trial in Moscow, noted biographer Martin Gilbert. At the same time, much to Winston's disapproval and despite his own personal appeal to Gen. Dwight D. Eisenhower, the Americans already were pulling back troops from "a broad swathe of land in central Germany and Czechoslovakia"—as agreed earlier with the USSR, to be sure, but now in actual fact creating a void to be taken over by the Soviets.

Winston naturally wasn't happy with such developments, but he also felt, added Gilbert, "that conflict with Russia must be avoided," even if he did call the gulf between Britain and the USSR "unbridgeable except by friendly diplomatic relations." Meanwhile, Winston, at his own volition, decided he would be taking Labor leader Clement Attlee with him to the Potsdam summit, just in case the pending general election resulted in a changed premiership.

Then, with just a month to go before the meeting with Stalin and U.S. President Harry S. Truman, the fourteen political leaders from Poland went on trial in Moscow. That was on June 18, and on June 21, came word that twelve of them had been sentenced to up to eight years in prison. "For Churchill, who had fought long and hard on behalf of a Polish democratic future," wrote Gilbert, "the news was final confirmation of his fears that tyranny would be imposed wherever Communism held sway."

The fact is, for Winston, the end of the war against Nazi Germany had come as both a good news–bad news event, and predictably so, with the Potsdam meeting a necessary sequel. As early as May 11, Winston bleakly warned his foreign secretary, Anthony Eden, of a period of appeasement to come, followed by a third world war.

He regarded the "Russian peril" as "enormous," he said, while warning that it "could be better faced if we remain united." But, added Gilbert, he saw no means of halting the intense Soviet pressure, "especially amid the euphoria of victory." The seizure of the fourteen Polish underground leaders while under safe conduct and their reappearance in Moscow certainly wasn't reassuring. But what could be done to help them? "I do not see what we can do now in this interlude of joymaking," Churchill said.

May 1945 also was the time when Winston first began warning of an iron curtain coming down across what soon would become the Eastern Bloc. Unhappy to hear that half the American troops in Europe would be withdrawn and reassigned to the war in the Pacific, he warned Truman by telegram on May 12 that the Russians would be able to keep "very large armies in the field for a long time." Added Gilbert's account: "He felt 'deep anxiety' because of the Russian 'misinterpretation' of the Yalta decisions, their attitude to Poland, their overwhelming influence in the Balkans, the combination of Russian power and territories under their control or occupied, coupled with Communist techniques in so many other countries, and above all their power to maintain very large armies in the field for a long time."

In just a year or two, Winston predicted, the British and American armies would have "melted," and the French would not yet have been formed "on any major scale," with the result that only a handful of divisions, "mostly French," would be on hand in Europe to face possibly two or three hundred Russian divisions.

With an "iron curtain" being "drawn down upon their front," Winston said, "we do not know what is going on behind. There seems little doubt that the whole of the region Lubeck-Trieste-Corfu will soon be completely in their hands."

Then, too, with the projected American withdrawal from central Germany, "a broad band of many hundreds of miles of Russian-occupied territory will isolate us from Poland." With the Western Allies busy imposing penalties on Germany for her wartime sins, "it would be open to the Russians in a very short time to advance if they chose, to the waters of the North Sea and the Atlantic."

Thus, Winston asked Truman, wouldn't it be wise to come together in seeking an understanding with Russia, to "see where we are with her?" In short, to meet with Stalin. "This issue of a settlement with Russia before our strength has gone," said Winston, "seems to me to dwarf all others."

Truman agreed. Thus was born the Potsdam conference, the final summit meeting of World War II.

Reluctant Ally

Winston kept pressing Truman to agree to their Big Three meeting as soon as possible. "I am sure you understand the reason why I am anxious for an earlier date (say the 3rd or 4th of July)," Winston telegraphed on June 4. "I view with profound misgivings the retreat of the American army to our line of occupation in the central sector, thus bringing Soviet power into the heart of Western Europe and the descent of an iron curtain between us and everything to the eastward."

There it was again. That term *iron curtain*.

Truman of course had agreed to the Potsdam meeting, although he wasn't a bit anxious just then to take part in such high-level summitry. "I am getting ready to go see Stalin and Churchill and it is a chore," he soon wrote to his mother. "I have to take my tuxedo, tails . . . high hat, top hat, and hard hat as well as sundry other things." And on the serious side: "I have a brief case all filled up with information on past conferences and suggestions on what I'm to do and say. Wish I didn't have to go but I do and it can't be stopped now."

Truly, from Truman's viewpoint, the timing wasn't good. At the moment, it wasn't yet known if the highly secret atomic bomb would work. If it did, a late Russian entry in the war against Japan might not be a critical need. So far as the world knew, however, the Allies, led by American manpower, would have to invade and subdue a fanatically defended Japanese homeland to bring the war to a close. If that were the case, a horrific prospect in terms of the casualties to be expected on both sides, a Russian "distraction" would be vital in tying down Japanese forces in China and Manchuria that otherwise would be rushed back to the defense of the home islands.

In short, Truman would rather deal with Stalin from a position of strength rather than in need of any favors. Or, as his daughter Margaret stated in her biography of her father, *Harry S. Truman*, "If the bomb was a success, there would probably be no need for Russia to enter the war against Japan—and no need to make any more concessions to the Soviets in Europe for their promise to help in the Far East."

At the moment, though, progress on the atomic bomb was stymied by problems in finding a reliable detonator . . . so the Russians might be needed after all. Meanwhile, the U.S. joint chiefs had developed plans for a two-stage invasion of Japan beginning on November 1 on Kyushu, to be followed the next spring with landings on the main island of Honshu. American casualties alone could come to a staggering half million dead, estimated Gen. George C. Marshall, the army chief of staff.

"Behind these problems," Margaret Truman wrote, "loomed another specter, mentioned again and again in cables from Prime Minister Churchill: the possibility that with the Allies heavily involved in the Pacific, there would be nothing to prevent Russia from taking over most of war-ravaged, prostrate Europe."

With the atomic bomb as yet untested, its reliability still wouldn't be known until Churchill, Stalin, Truman, and their respective staffs gathered at Potsdam . . . and perhaps not even then, so far as anyone really knew.

"Colonel Warden" and Friends

They didn't all arrive on schedule—Stalin, code-named "Uncle Joe," was delayed for a day, reportedly by a mild heart attack. This gave Harry Truman, "the Other Admiral," and Winston Churchill, "Colonel Warden," time to settle in, explore a bit, and get to know one another.

"Friendship was instant between Mr. Churchill and Dad," wrote Margaret Truman. "Their talk ranged over a wide variety of topics, from the Pacific war to their tastes in music. They found themselves in hearty agreement on everything but music. Mr. Churchill loved martial music and just about nothing else in that department." Winston was surprised to learn that Truman, the haberdasher from mid-America, favored Chopin, Liszt, and Mozart.

Regardless of musical tastes, the two leaders apparently clicked from the start.

According to Winston's physician, Lord Moran, the prime minister was impressed by Truman's "immense determination." And further, Winston told Moran, "He seems a man of exceptional charm and ability. . . . He has direct methods of speech and a great deal of self confidence and resolution." In short, Lord Moran noted in his diary: "Winston has fallen for the President."

The formal meetings, or plenary sessions, of the Big Three would be taking place at a large round table beneath two wrought-iron chandeliers in the three-hundred-year-old Cecilienhof Palace. Potsdam, an old city of a hundred thousand-plus on the Havel River just sixteen miles outside of Berlin, had been heavily bombed in April, but it was chosen for the meeting because it was less heavily damaged than Berlin. The leaders themselves stayed in "palatial houses" nearby, Margaret Truman reported. Her father's yellow stucco house in Babelsberg "was on a lake swarming with mosquitoes," while Winston "had another large house only a few blocks away, and Stalin was also nearby."

Winston's residence, designed by architect Mies van de Rohe, was just four hundred yards from Truman's residence, by biographer Martin Gilbert's estimate. Lord Moran later described it as a "substantial stone house," also lakeside. When they arrived, they walked through two "bleak" rooms with large chandeliers to a room on the far side of the empty house with uncleaned french windows that opened on a balcony overlooking the lake. "And there, without removing his hat, Winston flopped into a garden chair, flanked by two great tubs of hydrangeas, blue, pink and white. He appeared too weary to move."

Churchill called for a whiskey, and they sat in silence for a time, "looking at the lawn that sloped to a lake, into which, so it was said, the Russians had thrown some German soldiers who could not walk because of their wounds." Everywhere along their way from an airfield outside Berlin there had been Russian soldiers "lining the road, behind the bushes, knee deep in the corn." The next day, after a two-hour meeting with Truman, Winston ventured into Berlin, the largely destroyed German capital (Truman did also, but separately). Accompanied by Lord Moran, Winston stopped at the Reichstag . . . that is, what was left of it. They found "a good many people" standing around the onetime home of the German legislature. "Some of the crowd looked away, others glanced at him with expressionless faces, one old man shook his fist, a few smiled," said Moran. Winston did not seem all that interested, the doctor noted. But Winston, in his own account, said that all but one old man in the crowd gathered at the chancellery "began to cheer." Further, "my hate had died with their surrender and I was much moved by their demonstrations, and also by their haggard looks and threadbare clothes."

Led across a courtyard in front of the chancellery where Hitler once held

sway, Winston was shown the steps leading to the bunker where the Führer supposedly took his own life.

Winston followed his guide, a Russian soldier, down one flight of stairs, "but
hearing there were two more flights, he gave up the idea of exploring the depths
and slowly remounted the stairs." At the top, he sat down on a "gilt chair,"
mopped his brow, and said, "Hitler must have come out here to get some air, and
heard the guns getting nearer and nearer."

On the way back to his residence, he was silent. "His thoughts were elsewhere."

At bedtime, he revealed that his reelection prospects were on his mind. "The
Socialists say I shall have a majority over all other parties of thirty-two," he remarked. But what did he think of Berlin? "He answered with a smile: 'There was
a reasonable amount of destruction.'"

Lord Moran told him he had picked up two discarded Iron Crosses, and
Churchill asked to see them. "All he said was, 'Poor devils.' Berlin did not seem to
touch his imagination."

He did offer further comment when, Moran said, he had gone through "vast,
grandiose" rooms at the chancellery. "It was from here that Hitler planned to gov-
ern the world," Winston mused. "A good many have tried that; all failed. That is
why England is where she is. I'll tell Stalin about this."

He then remarked that the children they had seen appeared well fed. But he
also "spoke of Germany as a decomposing carcass and . . . looked with terror at
the coming winter." As a long-standing government insider, he understood the
difficulties ahead in providing jobs and food for the German people.

Another highlight of Winston's nonplenary activities at Potsdam apparently
was a dinner with George C. Marshall, the U.S. Army chief of staff. "That is the
noblest Roman of them all," said Churchill afterward. "Congress always did what
he advised. His work in training the American armies has been wonderful. I will
pay tribute to it one day when occasion offers."

Still ahead, though, were the individual, head-to-head meetings of the leaders
and the all-important, full-blown plenary sessions for all three and their staffs.

Additional note: Ironically, both the Truman and Churchill residences would
spend the cold war years behind the same iron curtain that Churchill had warned
about. Truman's Babelsberg house, given the address of No. 2 Karl Marx Strasse,
actually had a section of the Berlin Wall running through its garden, according to
the Expatica ("News and Information for Expats in Germany") Web site,

www.expatica.com. The names successively given to the same street closely re-flected Germany's twentieth-century history—it once was Kaiser Strasse and then, during the Hitler era, "Street of the Brownshirts." For Truman's Potsdam stay, the house itself briefly became the "Little White House." Churchill's large, neoclassic villa had been the onetime home of German banker Franz Urbig. "During the communist era the East German government turned it into a film academy," reported the Expatica Web site. Truman's residence in more recent years has been the home of the Friedrich Naumann Foundation and a center for international seminars, "attended by foreign academics and students from many parts of the world."

Election Hovering

Winston was in a good mood after a lunch with Harry Truman and the first ple-nary session of the Big Three, held at five o'clock in the afternoon of July 17, re-ported Lord Moran. Winston had found Stalin to be "amiable" in this meeting and was impressed with Truman's "immense determination." Churchill observed, "He takes no notice of delicate ground, he just plants his foot down firmly on it."

Newcomer Truman was made chairman of the conference sessions. At this first formal meeting, Winston pressed for early, free, and meaningful elections in Poland, as agreed at Yalta. At the same time, Lord Moran also noted in his mem-oirs, *Churchill at War, 1940–45,* Winston's aides complained their man wasn't re-ally reading his briefing papers, he wasn't "mastering his stuff," and "has to be fed."

Then, too, all through the days (and nights) of the conference there was the specter of the election results hanging over the British contingent, especially over Winston. As he noted on July 20: "I shall be glad when this election business is over. It hovers over me like a vulture of uncertainty in the sky."

At a five-hour dinner meeting with Stalin, head to head, a couple of nights before, Winston had learned how well informed the Soviet leader seemed to be on the British political scene. Stalin had suggested Churchill and his Conservative Party would win by a majority of 80 seats, it seems. He predicted Labor would have 220 to 230 seats in the new Parliament. When Winston commented that he wasn't sure how the far-flung British soldiery would vote, Stalin speculated that military men preferred a strong government and therefore would vote for the Conservatives.

By contrast, Lord Moran noted, the British had no idea even who Stalin's second in command might be.

Meanwhile, Winston reported that Stalin "gave me his word there will be free elections in the countries set free by his armies." That of course turned out to be untrue. Overall, Churchill also commented after the dinner (according to Lord Moran): "I think that Stalin is trying to be as helpful as it is in him to be."

Returning from the plenary conference held on July 19, however, Winston reported, "We had a good wrangle for three hours." Even so, Churchill still sounded upbeat, saying, "I don't think Stalin was offended at what I said. He doesn't mind straight speaking. I felt reassured. Stalin, at the end of the meeting, said he saw our difficulties."

According to Moran, Churchill secretary Leslie Rowan said that Winston had "rebuked" Truman "for not supporting him" in one argument. And further, "Truman said he was not quick and apologized to the P.M. Afterwards the P.M. said that the President was all right if he had had time to consider a question, but when something came up which he had not thought about he was rather at a loss. After all, he had little experience of these conferences."

At a banquet given that night by Truman, Winston was "evidently stung" when Stalin proposed a toast to the American navy, then still fighting the Japanese in the Pacific. Winston took the Stalin toast as a critical "pinprick," since in the Atlantic warfare, it had been England's own Royal Navy that accounted for the great majority of the six hundred German U-boats sunk.

The next morning Winston was far less optimistic about Stalin. "The Russians are being very difficult," he volunteered. "They talk about the same things as we do, freedom and justice and that sort of thing, but prominent people are removed and are not seen again. We are not even allowed to enter Vienna."

Moran commented: "For three days the P.M. has been certain that Truman's firmness has changed everything. Stalin has been very fair and reasonable. Now Winston is less certain about things." To make matters a bit worse, Churchill aide John Peck later noted, Clement Attlee generated a far more "vociferous" cheer than Winston from the troops lined up for a British victory parade in Berlin on July 21.

That afternoon, the principles argued at length over the western boundary of Poland, with Stalin insisting that at Yalta no boundary agreement had been reached. Truman, Attlee, and Churchill all pressed Stalin on the issue. That night, after a dinner party given by Stalin, Winston still was dour, saying, "I thought the Russians were silent and not very forthcoming."

The next morning, July 22, Winston again brought up the election. This time it was a "bloody election" that hung "like a veil" over the future, Moran reported. Obviously irritated when Moran questioned the latest predictions, Winston hotly declared that both Conservatives and Labor people expected he would wind up with a winning majority.

He was a bit happier later in the day after an hour's meeting with Truman. "We not only talk the same language, we think the same thoughts," he said. But he still was bleak on other scores. The Russians, he said, were stripping their zone of occupied Germany of all useful items—"and want a rake off from the British and American sectors as well." Worse, "they will grind their zone, there will be unimaginable cruelties." He then voiced the undeniable reality underlying the entire Potsdam conference: "It is indefensible, except on one ground: that there is no alternative."

One reason: "I prayed the Americans on my knees not to hand over to the Russians such a great chunk of Germany, at least until after the Conference. It would have been a bargaining counter. But they would not listen. The President [a possible reference to Roosevelt] dug in. I shall ask Stalin, does he want the whole world?"

Meanwhile, Lord Moran was concerned about his patient's health. It "has so far deteriorated," he recorded, "that he has no energy left to seize his opportunities." Winston's private secretary Rowan still complained that his boss "is not mastering his brief." He seems "too tired to prepare anything," added Moran. "He just deals with things as they come up."

But then, Moran added, Winston had "quite a respectable excuse for dodging decisions." As he himself had said before traveling to Potsdam, "he would be only half a man until he knew the result of the election." He specifically had said "he intends to shelve the really big decisions until he knows what has happened at the poll."

And so it went for the British and Churchill at Potsdam—up one minute, down the next, and hanging over all the proceedings, both the uncertainty posed by the British elections and the certainty that when it came to the future of Eastern Europe, the Soviets already were in the driver's seat.

But a new factor suddenly did come into play—the atomic bomb.

On the morning of July 23, while breakfasting in his room, Winston turned to Lord Moran and spoke "with great solemnity." He had news, he said, that "you must not tell to any human being." The Americans had succeeded in splitting the atom. Their atomic bomb test had worked. It had taken place "in some wild spot in New Mexico."

Developed in great secrecy, but with the knowledge of the British, "It gives the Americans the power to mold the world." It would be used against Japan, and the Russians were to be told that very day. "It has just come in time to save the world."

Moran "was deeply shocked by this ruthless decision to use the bomb on Japan." At the same time, he said, "I knew I was hopelessly illogical."

That night it was the turn of the British to be the hosts of a Big Three banquet, and things went so well among them and their staffs that Stalin used his menu to collect signatures. The others followed suit. "There was a shortage of fountain pens and the consequent borrowing and general movement seemed to break the ice of formality and to generate a very friendly spirit."

The next day, though, Winston started out in a sour mood. He wanted nothing to do with a Polish leadership backed by the Russians. Let Foreign Secretary Eden deal with them, he said. "If I have to see them," he warned, "I shall tell them there is no support in Western Europe for a puppet Polish state, the tool of Russia." He was also irritated at the lack of water in the house, due to a broken water main. "Two very stiff whiskeys and a brandy dispersed the black clouds, and at the end of luncheon he was all quips and smiles," noted Moran.

A short nap also helped prepare him for the day's plenary session at five o'-clock and the evening to follow . . . and fortunately so, it seems. Rowan told Moran there had been a tussle with Stalin, a real "set to," and in it, Winston had been "superb." Truman, too, had been firm against Stalin. "The Russians could not introduce their particular form of government into countries liberated directly or indirectly by all the Allies and then expect America and Britain to recognize those governments. This was his view today. It would be his view tomorrow."

Overall, Moran commented, the atmosphere at Potsdam was quite different from that of the Tehran and Yalta conferences . . . and much more helpful to Churchill and his aims. "There, Stalin was at pains to secure Roosevelt's backing. The President, without a word to the Prime Minister, would declare that the Russian case was most reasonable, and that it would have his support. What could Churchill do? But here at Potsdam, it was soon plain that Roosevelt's death had changed everything. Truman is very blunt; he means business . . . and when Stalin gets tough, Truman at once makes it plain that he, too, can hand out the rough stuff."

Winston of course was appreciative. When all was said and done, though, the reality still underlying the Potsdam conference was a grim one. "If only this had happened at Yalta," he lamented that night. "It is too late now." The reality, as entered in his diary at the time by Lord Moran, "He knows that the time to settle frontiers has gone. The Red Army is spreading over Europe. It will remain."

And now, on July 25, it was time for a quick return to England to receive and digest the election news. Expecting to return later to Potsdam with his patient of the last six years, Moran left his luggage in Berlin.

Additional note: The three leaders at Potsdam indulged in a small war of one-upmanships in the form of the musical performances accompanying each of their formal dinners for the others. As stated in a letter by Truman, he offered a sergeant, Eugene List of Philadelphia, who played the piano, and "a boy from the Metropolitan Orchestra [who] played the violin." He called them "the best we have" and said, "They are very good." List played Chopin at the piano for Stalin and Churchill while Truman himself turned the pages of the score. Meanwhile, "Stalin sent to Moscow and brought on his two best pianists and two feminine violinists. They were excellent. Played Chopin, Liszt, Tchaikovsky. I congratulated him and them on their ability. They had dirty faces though and the gals were rather fat."

None of this left Churchill very happy, it seems. "Mr. Churchill was bored by all this classical music," Margaret Truman wrote in her biography of her father, "and he retaliated at his dinner by having the Royal Air Force band play a series of ear-shattering military marches."

The Unthinkable Occurs

She to him: "It may well be a blessing in disguise."

He to her: "At the moment it seems quite effectively disguised."

Clementine and Winston, even as the returns made the dreadful outcome clear. It had been a rout.

Lord Moran would be sending for the luggage he left back in Berlin. Clement

Attlee now would be representing Great Britain and her interests at Potsdam. Winston and Clementine would be vacating No. 10 Downing Street and Chequers, the official weekend retreat in the country. After six years at the helm, all was changed.

Overnight.

He could have listened to his subconscious, because it apparently saw, or at least feared, what was coming. In a troubling dream, apparently on his last night at Potsdam (July 24), he saw himself stretched out, dead, under a white sheet on a table in an empty room. Then, the morning after his return on July 25 to London from Potsdam, he suddenly awoke just before dawn "with a sharp stab of almost physical pain."

In his own words: "A hitherto subconscious conviction that we were beaten broke forth and dominated my mind. All the pressure of great events, on and against which I had mentally so long maintained my 'flying speed,' would cease and I should fall. The power to shape the future would be denied me. The knowledge and experience I had gathered, the authority and good will I had gained in so many countries, would vanish."

Winston managed to resume sleep before awakening again about 9:00 a.m. By ten o'clock, the first election returns had come into the Map Room at the underground War Cabinet Rooms complex in London: the Conservatives already had lost ten seats to Labor.

Capt. Richard Pim, head of the Map Room, was the first to convey the bad news, Martin Gilbert reported in *Churchill: A Life*. "The Prime Minister was in his bath and certainly appeared surprised, if not shocked," Pim recalled. "He asked me to get him a towel, and in a few minutes, clad in his blue siren suit and with cigar he was in his chair in the Map Room—where he remained all day."

Well, not every minute of that day, since he did take a lunch break, and it was at that luncheon that Clementine offered her blessing-in-disguise remark (which may have been heartfelt) and he his quick rejoinder about its effective disguise.

By noon, added Gilbert, "it was clear that there would be a Labor landslide." As one rebuke followed another, both Winston's son Randolph and his son-in-law Duncan Sandys had lost their parliamentary seats, although Winston retained his Woodford constituency—by a landslide. Overall and countrywide, the Conservatives lost 190 parliamentary seats, thus falling from their 1935 high of 585 to a new low of 213, while Labor gained 239 seats in the election to give them a total of 393 and control of Parliament.

Still, when Lord Moran commented that the results displayed the "ingratitude" of the British people, Winston mildly replied: "I wouldn't call it that. They have had a very hard time."

To all appearances, he bore up surprisingly well. "I shall never forget the courage and forbearance you showed at that most unhappy luncheon after defeat was known," his longtime parliamentary colleague David Margesson recalled years later. "It was a terrific example of how to take it on the chin without flinching."

Meanwhile, Winston wasted no time in resigning as prime minister. Under the British Constitution, wrote Gilbert, "Churchill could have returned to Potsdam as Prime Minister and resigned only when Parliament reassembled a few days later." Instead, "determined to accept the verdict of the electorate without delay," he went to Buckingham Palace at seven o'clock that evening to tender his resignation to the king.

"He was now Leader of the Opposition. Two hours later, a statement which he had dictated on his return from the Palace was read out over the radio. 'Immense responsibilities abroad and at home fall upon the new Government,' he said, 'and we must all hope they will be successful in bearing them.'"

All well and good, but the election results obviously did not merely sting, they bruised. While Attlee flew back to Potsdam the day after the election results came in, Winston, no longer the PM, spent the day in a round of farewells—to his military chiefs, his cabinet, his private secretaries. First came the chiefs of staff. "It was a very sad and very moving little meeting at which I found myself unable to say much for fear of breaking down," wrote Gen. Sir Alan Brooke.

Winston, on the other hand, "was standing the blow wonderfully well."

But not according to Winston's close friend and Foreign Secretary Anthony Eden, himself a future prime minister. In a diary entry jotted down some time after the farewell cabinet meeting, Eden said that Winston called him back. "He was pretty wretched, poor old boy. He didn't feel any more reconciled this morning, on the contrary it hurt more, like a wound which becomes more painful after the first shock."

Then, too, Captain Pim recalled, from late the same day and again dealing with Winston in his bath: "He turned quite gray in his bath. I thought he would faint. Then he turned to me and said: 'They are perfectly entitled to vote as they please. This is democracy. This is what we've been fighting for.'"

Nor was that the end of the tumble from power and personal pain. That weekend Winston and family members traveled to Chequers for a final weekend visit at the official country retreat—"no boxes of telegrams to keep Churchill's mind on the pressures and events of the day," noted Gilbert. And that Saturday night, July 28, daughter Mary recalled, "We saw with near desperation a cloud of black gloom descend."

Still, Winston was able to articulate some of his feelings. "I must confess I found the event of Thursday rather odd and queer, especially after the wonderful [public] welcomes I had from all classes," he wrote to Hugh Cecil, the political associate who had been best man at his wedding. "There was something pent up in the British people after twenty years which required relief. . . . My faith in the flexibility of our Constitution and in the qualities of the British people remains unaltered."

No matter, philosophic about his defeat or not, Winston still faced "the pain and shock of transition from the old life to the new," noted biographer Geoffrey Best. Winston now could have simply faded away. He could have spent his time writing memoirs, painting, and fixing up his beloved Chartwell after its months of wartime vacancy. He could visit a legion of friends and admirers worldwide. But no, noted Best, "He did not retire. He would not, he could not leave the stage upon which for so long he had played a leading part. When the new Parliament met six days later he would be in place as leader of the chastened Opposition. National and world affairs would continue to claim him."

Meanwhile, daughter Mary recounted, the family signed the Chequers visitors book before going to bed their last night there. "My father signed last of all, and beneath his signature he wrote: 'Finis.' . . . That is how he and my mother and all of us felt then."

☆   ☆   ☆

Additional note: Both at No. 10 Downing Street and at Potsdam, Winston Churchill's absence was felt immediately. As early as August 1, Marian Holmes, Winston's wartime secretary, was noting the change at No. 10 in her diary—she had stayed on under the new PM, Clement Attlee. Working for the new prime minister, she noted, was "very different." He called in his secretaries only when he had dictation for them. "No conversation or pleasantries, wit or capricious behavior," she wrote. "Just staccato orders. Perfectly polite, and I'm sure he is a good Christian gentleman. But the difference is between champagne and water."

At Potsdam, meanwhile, "Truman accepted Stalin's insistence that the Western Neisse [River] become Poland's western border," wrote biographer Martin Gilbert. "Attlee deferred to the Americans. Churchill commented a year later, 'I would never have agreed to the Western Neisse and was saving it up for a final "show down."'"

But Margaret Truman saw the effect of Winston's absence differently. "Stalin was used to Mr. Churchill's opposition, and was also used to ignoring it," she wrote. "He knew that Britain no longer had the strength to enforce its wishes. The Americans were the ones he wanted to cajole into giving him what he wanted— because they alone had the power to stop him. He was sorely disappointed when he discovered that Dad was equally tough in his own quiet way, without Mr. Churchill around."

Truman was personally "sorry for Mr. Churchill" but not sorry to see him leave Potsdam! He obviously "thought he would have a better chance of reaching an agreement with Stalin without Mr. Churchill in the way," daughter Margaret observed while also conceding, "Dad was wrong, but it shows how eager he was to agree." He, in fact, was visibly angered in the final plenary session of the conference when Stalin rejected a Truman proposal to internationalize the world's inland waterways, Europe's major rivers included. "Nyet!" the Russian dictator snapped, according to Margaret Truman. "To make sure Dad understood what he was saying, he added in English, "No. I say no!" His face flushed with anger, Truman turned to the American delegation behind him and actually "exclaimed," his daughter wrote, "I cannot understand that man!" And then, to his secretary of state, James Byrnes, but in low voice: "Jimmy, do you realize that we have been here seventeen whole days? Why, in seventeen days you can decide anything!"

Driving for Winston

Late in the war, Cecil Robinson, a drapery manager, was one of the "handpicked" drivers for Winston's four-and-a-half-ton armored car with inch-thick bulletproof glass, according to Robinson's wife, Edna. Thus he drove Winston to all sorts of places—the Houses of Parliament on most weekdays, Chequers on weekends, even at the Yalta Conference in the Crimea during the closing months of the war. He had joined the Royal Army Service Corps for the duration and became one of Churchill's select drivers in 1945.

"Cecil had a range of duties to carry out for Sir Winston," said Edna Robinson on the BBC's "WW2 People's War" Web site. "One was connected with newspapers. The Prime Minister always wanted to see the papers as soon as they were off the press. Cecil would fetch the first editions and bring them to Sir Winston early in the morning. The Prime Minister was often in his famous 'siren suit.'"

As for the Yalta Conference with Roosevelt and Stalin, Cecil Robinson noted that four Soviet warships escorted Churchill's ship for the last part of the journey by way of the Black Sea to Sebastopol at the tip of the Crimean peninsula, which recently had been the scene of heavy fighting between Russians and Germans. "It does not look very inviting, you can see the result of the battle which has now passed," he observed. And after going ashore for the short trip to nearby Yalta on February 3, 1945, he added, "It has certainly been knocked about."

Even after the hostilities in Europe ended, Cecil still drove for Churchill. "Later that year, on 21st July 1945, Cecil drove Sir Winston at the British Victory Parade in Berlin. It was a great celebration but there was a lot of concern for the Prime Minister's safety, as he wanted to meet the [German] people and kept getting out of the car and shaking their hands."

On the same trip—the Potsdam Conference at Berlin with Truman and Stalin—Cecil Robinson had one of his "strangest" experiences. Driving into the German capital from the airport and then back again, he had the prime minister of England as his passenger . . . but it wasn't always Winston Churchill. As explained by Edna Robinson, "While they were there, the election was held at home and his passenger on the return trip was Mr. [Clement] Attlee." Churchill had lost his office to the Labor Party during the 1945 parliamentary election.

Winston's Special American

He was there the very moment Churchill learned about the Japanese attack at Pearl Harbor. He refused to leave London when it came under the blitz. Like Winston, he became a familiar figure on the city's bombed streets, walking through the neighborhoods and offering consolation. Later, he was included in the small disheartened group of family and friends during the last weekend with Winston at Chequers after the shocking electoral defeat. A quiet, notably tongue-tied, and now totally forgotten hero of the war, he was an American . . . the U.S. ambassador to beleaguered England for most of World War II, Gil Winant.

A prominent Republican "blueblood," yet an early figurehead for Franklin Delano Roosevelt's New Deal, John Gilbert Winant had been born to a wealthy aristocratic family in New York City's fashionable Upper East Side, had done his schooling at St. Paul's in Concord, New Hampshire, and at Princeton, then had fought in World War I with Eddie Rickenbacker's Hat-in-the-Ring Squadron. Before going to war or serving FDR, Winant had been a teacher, though he never was a great student himself. He graduated from St. Paul's a year late, thanks to repeated failing grades in final exams. He had to drop out of Princeton at one point, also due to failing grades, it seems. He then reappeared at St. Paul's as a master who was notably eccentric in style and appearance.

According to a 1942 issue of *Time* magazine, Winant was "a bachelor whose arms always seemed to be coming out of his sleeves, who groped painfully for the right word, hooked his hands in his pants-top like a Midwestern farmer, always looked funny in a hat, lived in a single room so littered with books that there was no place to sit." And "when he talked to his classes, in a soft, throaty whisper, he was hard to hear, sometimes hard to understand." Yet he was revered by his students. "No master at St. Paul's had such an influence as Gil Winant," asserted *Time*. "His shaggy, out-thrust head, his dark burning eyes made those who saw him think of Lincoln [one of his heroes]. His young pupils . . . were convinced he would be President some day."

Ambassador to England at a time of world crisis was not a bad alternative. But that day was far off in the future. First, he would play a hero's role in the first of the century's two world wars. Quitting his job as a teacher in 1917, he left a "sheaf of unpaid bills [and] all his money and stocks to meet them" on the desk of the prep school's business manager. "Nine tenths of the bills were for milk sent to neighboring poor people." From there, Winant was off to a Virginia center to cram "twenty-five hours of air training into three days" before heading to France—and the air war raging over the western front.

Flying with Rickenbacker's squadron, he was notably absent-minded but led a charmed life. "The day before a big drive he came back from reconnaissance duty with 90 bullet holes in a wing and the motor half torn off," *Time* reported. "He took up another plane, had it shot from under him, [and] spent the rest of the day in a third plane." All told, he "cracked up seven planes" but survived the war.

Soon after his return home, he married Constance Rivington Russell, whose father was a law partner to Eleanor Roosevelt's father. Living in Concord again, Winant entered politics as a member of the New Hampshire state legislature, then was elected in 1925 to the first of three terms as governor. He tested out his own "Little New Deal" on the state level before FDR came to power in the 1930s and introduced his national New Deal. Winant in the early 1930s "was often mentioned as a possible 1936 Republican candidate for President," added *Time*.

But the architects of Roosevelt's New Deal had "noticed" Winant's efforts to ease the impact of the Depression in New Hampshire—they grabbed him up as the first chairman of the brand-new Social Security Board. And there, even though his tenure with the board was brief, he contributed materially in shaping its administrative policies for years to come. More important at the time, his background as a "progressive" Republican symbolized the Roosevelt administration's hopes to give the board wide public acceptance as politically nonpartisan. The fact is that Gil Winant was a liberal Republican . . . so much so that he shortly left the board to become a director of the International Labor Organization (ILO) based in Geneva, Switzerland.

While already impressive, his still-developing résumé wouldn't have mentioned more personal asides, such as penchants for honesty, acts of kindness, and absent-mindedness. In Washington, he wouldn't accept payment for his first two days on the Social Security Board because he had spent parts of those days doing private business. On another day he was supposed to visit the White House, reported *Time*, and "he arrived at his office with muddy shoes, rolled-up pant legs, two ties hitched together in place of a belt. He had been on a stroll in muddy Rock Creek Park [and] had forgotten to change." At another time, he boarded a ship for Europe on ILO business with just twelve cents in his pocket. In addition, "assistants who arranged Pullmans [luxury accommodations on trains] for him on trips discovered that he sat up all night in coaches talking to people."

This was the man who succeeded Joseph Kennedy, father of the future president, as ambassador to England . . . to the highly formal, protocol-minded Court of St. James. "He arrived in an England that had grown tired of ruddy Ambassador . . . Kennedy's cheerful salesmanship," alleged *Time* just weeks after the Pearl Harbor attack had thrust America into the war. Earlier, "Kennedy had slept out the bombings safely in the country [and] had returned to the U.S. to talk a sort of anti-British isolationism. Winant's modesty, his sincerity, washed the bad taste out of England's mouth."

It didn't escape notice that Winant and his wife "took a modest four-room flat in London [and] stood on the roof watching the brutal bombing attacks of 1941's spring." Or that "often he walked all night through the streets when bombers were overhead, talking to the people." He apparently remained the same unkempt, unworldly Gil Winant. "He arrived with one gray suit, which promptly fell into baggy-kneed disrepair. His conversations are brief sentences between long, groping pauses [and] long minutes staring at the floor."

Indeed, once when he was asked spontaneously to speak at a luncheon, "he stood up, shifted his weight from long leg to the other through four straight minutes of agonizing silence, finally said softly: 'The worst mistake I ever made was in getting up in the first place.'"

Awkward as Winant may have been in formal situations, he soon became a close friend to the Churchills. It wasn't totally surprising that, as ambassador, he happened to be having dinner with Winston at Chequers when they first heard about the Japanese attack on Pearl Harbor. But still, a self-conscious, tongue-tied American as part of the inner Churchill circle? Yet there he was on occasion after intimate occasion.

For Winston's return from the historic Newfoundland meeting with FDR, Gil Winant was among the greeters. For a cozy party at Chequers while Winston was representing England in conference with Stalin in Moscow, Gil Winant was with the Churchill family. At Chartwell for the day after Christmas (Boxing Day) in 1944, during Winston's absence at Athens, Winant was invited. Winant also joined the Churchill family and other intimates for that last weekend at Chequers on the heels of Winston's defeat in 1945. "The tide of war," Mary Churchill Soames observed in her biography of her mother, "brought to Winston and Clementine—and indeed to all our family—one very special friend: Gil Winant, the American Ambassador."

Describing him as "a man of quiet, intensely concentrated charm," Mary added, "Gil very quickly became a dear friend of us all, entering into our joys and sorrows, jokes and rows (in these last, always as a peace-maker). He was particularly fond of Clementine, and understood intuitively her character, and the strains and difficulties in her life." Noting his arrival as ambassador in the spring of 1941, when England still was fighting the Nazi conquerors of Western Europe alone, Winston's daughter called Winant "a brilliant choice for the job." During his five-year ambassadorship, Mary added, "he made friends with people in every walk of life." Notably, too, "he was especially beloved in the East End of London, where he was often to be seen in the thick of the air raids."

Winant favorably impressed Winston's constant companion and wartime doctor, Lord Moran, as well. "Gil Winant breaks pleasantly our ordered lives," wrote Moran in his memoirs. "Other men have to win the confidence of those they meet. Winant is allowed to skip that stag. Before he utters a syllable, people want to see more of him. He has the rapt gaze of a monk; the big dark eyes, buried in his head, look beyond you."

Meanwhile, Winant was wrong early in the war when he predicted the Soviet Union couldn't hold out for more than six weeks against the Nazi juggernaut, but he was entirely astute later when he noticed, and wrote to Harry Hopkins, that Winston's extensive wartime journeys were taking such a toll on the PM that the intervals between his illnesses have "been constantly shortened."

Like Winston himself, Winant also was preoccupied with the shape of the world to come after the war. "The mass of common men . . . want a friendly, civilized world of free peoples in which Christian virtues and moral values are not spurned as decadent and outmoded, a world where honest work is recognized and a man can own himself," he postulated. The postwar world, he added, should be guided by a political philosophy reaching "beyond selfish nationalism to a plan of prosperous political and economic collaboration."

It was to Britain's leaders that he was sent, noted *Time* magazine. "It was to them that he plugged away at his theme of a democratic postwar world." Thus, "he had long talks with Winston Churchill; met [Foreign Secretary] Anthony Eden several times a week; consulted labor leader Ernest Bevin; became fast friends with such Britons as Author-Professor Harold J. Laski [and] Sir Stafford Cripps."

Sadly, with the war over but Roosevelt no longer alive, Winant was cast adrift. "He had tied his career to that of Roosevelt," wrote historian Larry DeWitt. "With the President gone, Winant, who was not close to President Truman, suddenly found himself being nudged away from the center of American political affairs."

Allegedly $750,000 in debt, Winant retired from public life to write a three-volume memoir of his war years in London . . . but like pubic speaking, DeWitt observed, he found the task of writing "a struggle." After producing the first volume, he despaired at the prospect of turning out the next two, "which he had promised publishers." On November 3, 1947, the very day a bound copy of the completed book, titled *A Letter from Grosvenor Square*, was to be delivered to his post office box in Concord, he shot and killed himself. He never saw the book.

Phone Call from Winston

It was days after the 1945 election, and Lord Mountbatten, commander of Allied forces in Southeast Asia, was at an official lunch in London given by the Chinese ambassador when a butler approached Mountbatten and told him he had a phone call.

"I can't talk on the telephone during an official lunch," Mountbatten told the butler.

"He is very insistent, sir," said the butler. "It is a Mr. Churchill, sir."

"I don't know a Mr. Churchill."

"He said, you must come—it is very urgent."

It apparently didn't occur to Mountbatten that it could be his father's old friend, his own old friend and former boss, Winston Churchill, so recently deposed as prime minister.

Perhaps it was the butler's use of the title "Mr." that threw him off.

In any case, Mountbatten went to the telephone and said, "Yes, who is that?"

By his own account, "A voice replied: 'Is that you, Dickie? It's Winston here. Now, we must be quick, I'm calling you from a public telephone box. You've heard the bomb dropped?"

That was August 6, 1945, the day the Americans dropped their first atomic bomb on Hiroshima, Japan. The further fact is that Mountbatten had known about the highly secret atomic bomb project for the past few days—since the Potsdam Conference in late July. He once, in March 1970, told the story in a lecture he gave at the University of Berne (available on the Churchill Centre Web site, www.winstonchurchill.org).

"I was summoned to come back to the Potsdam Conference, and here I was let into the greatest secret of the war. General [George C.] Marshall told me about the American atomic bomb, which I didn't know anything about. This was the end of July and it was to be dropped in August."

Both Truman and Churchill also told Mountbatten about the bomb, but then, to go with the dramatic news, Winston had strict instructions for Mountbatten. "When the bomb is dropped they will surrender and when they surrender you must take over immediately. What are your plans for doing this?"

Mountbatten was taken aback. "Good Lord," he said. "You've only just told me—how can I have a plan?"

Well, he must make immediate plans, Churchill told him.

"When I told him I had a big invasion plan for Malaya—with about a quarter of a million soldiers and big fleet with which I proposed to land in Malaysia about the beginning of September, he replied: 'Too late, too late. You must load at once and be ready to go and to expect no opposition." He went on to tell Mountbatten he should send out the order by telegram without giving a hint as to why—"It's much too secret."

Mountbatten protested that his deputy, an American, would think him crazy "if I tell him to load the ships a fortnight earlier and to send them out on the assumption that the Japanese won't resist." But the preparations were made, as *Prime Minister* Churchill specified. The forces involved "were ready to sail as soon as I gave the word after the bomb dropped."

And now, on the day the bomb was dropped, here was *citizen* Churchill calling, and it was all about the same orders he earlier had given Mountbatten at Potsdam.

"Have you given the order, have you told your fleet to sail," Winston asked, with no further preliminaries.

Now, Mountbatten really was taken aback.

"No sir," he replied.

"Why not?" Winston snapped.

"I'm waiting to confirm the order with my new boss."

"And who is your new boss?"

"It is Mr. Attlee."

"Good God, you're not going to wait for him, are you!"

Additional note: As events turned out, it took until August 14—after an atomic bomb was dropped on Nagasaki on August 9—for the Japanese to surrender. The formal surrender ceremony ending the war took place on the USS *Missouri* in Tokyo Bay on September 2; Mountbatten accepted the surrender of the Japanese in Malaysia in Singapore on September 12. Sadly, he is the same Earl Mountbatten of Burma, former viceroy and governor-general of India, who was assassinated by Irish extremists who planted a bomb aboard his yacht in 1979.

★ PART 5 ★
Final Glimpses

Until Now IV

"My dear Winston," wrote this correspondent on July 31, 1945, "I am writing to tell you how very sad I am that you are no longer my Prime Minister." Like so many in England, the same correspondent quite honestly could say, "Your breadth of vision & your grasp of the essential things were of great comfort to me in the darkest days of the War, & I like to think we never disagreed on any really important matter."

As legions also would agree: "For all those things I thank you most sincerely."

Further, "I feel that your conduct as Prime Minister & Minister of Defense has never been surpassed." Thousands, indeed probably millions, surely would have joined in the feeling that "you have had many difficulties to deal with both as a politician & as a strategist of war but you have always surmounted them with supreme courage."

But *this* correspondent felt he alone could add: "For myself personally, I regret what has happened more than perhaps anyone else." Could truthfully lament, "I shall miss your counsel to me more than I can say." Could promise, "But please remember that as a friend I hope we shall be able to meet at intervals." Could sign off not only "very sincerely," but also "gratefully."

Until now—that is, during the five years that Winston had served as prime minister—the same correspondent had had a very special relationship with Winston. Thus, as very few others in England could claim, "During the last 5 years of war we have met on dozens, I may say on hundreds, of occasions, when we have discussed the most vital questions concerning the security & welfare of this country & the British Empire in their hours of trial."

It was a very personal, albeit official, relationship. "I shall always remember our talks with pleasure & only wish they could have continued longer." On a personal level also: "You often told me what you thought of people & matters of real interest which I could never have learnt from anyone else."

Such was the extent of this friend and admirer's feelings that he actually wrote Winston not once but twice on July 31 to express his regrets over the election results, both times in his own hand.

In the first of the two letters that George VI—Winston's fourth king of England—wrote on July 31, he said, "My heart was too full to say much at our last meeting." Indeed, the king added, he had been "shocked at the [election] result & I thought it most ungrateful to you personally after all your hard work for the people."

In response to both letters, an obviously touched Winston wrote back—by hand and in his own inimitable shorthand: "It was always a relief to me to lay before my Sovereign all the dread secrets and perils wh. oppressed my mind, & the plans wh. I was forming, & to receive on crucial occasions much encouragement. Yr. Majesty's grasp of all matters of State & war was always based upon the most thorough & attentive study of the whole mass of current documents." On a more personal level, matching the king's own, Winston said that the friendship mentioned by the king "is indeed a vy. strong sentiment with me, an honor which I cherish."

As reported by Sarah Bradford in her biography of George VI, Winston also told the king he had read his letter (apparently the second one) "with emotion."

Their relationship of course would be "one of the things which Churchill, too, regretted with his loss of power," Bradford added. "While waiting for the results of the election he had, [Lord] Moran recorded, comforted himself with his recollections of this. In three years, he said, he had lunched more than 200 times with the king. No servant had been present and they had waited on themselves. If Churchill got up to get something for the king, the king would in turn fetch something for Churchill. 'No subject had ever been so honored,' Churchill said; he wanted no other reward."

Actually, Winston would have loved the honor of the Order of the Garter, the highest order of knighthood that a British monarch can confer upon a subject. According to Bradford, George VI offered Winston that high honor, but he declined on grounds "it would not be suitable," since he now was leading the Opposition in the House of Commons. While declining for the moment, though, Winston apparently expressed hope he could accept the honor later. But, added Bradford, "It was to be eight years before he did so, on the occasion of Queen Elizabeth II's coronation in 1953"—an event brought about by the death of her father, George VI.

☆ ☆ ☆

Additional note: George VI was the same king, not so incidentally, who back on May 10, 1940, had viewed the possibility of Churchill as prime minister with definite misgivings. Noted Bradford: "In May 1940 . . . Churchill was very much the King's second choice. He had suggested [Lord] Halifax to Chamberlain as his successor, but having been told that Halifax was not enthusiastic over the prospect principally because, being a peer [Lord], he would have found it difficult to carry on business in the House of Commons, the King conceded, as he wrote in his diary, 'that there was only one person whom I could send for who had the confidence of the country & that was Winston.'"

Celebrating Victory

Winston was still in power when Britain at last could celebrate victory over Nazi Germany . . . which, when it finally came, had been predictable for months but wound up as a confusing tug-of-war among the Allies. "Events are moving very fast now," George VI had written in his diary on April 30, the day Hitler committed suicide in his Berlin bunker, noted biographer Sarah Bradford.

And so they had been. The Allies had crossed the Rhine just days before, and, wrote Bradford, "the last V-2 silo had been bombed by the RAF after 1,050 of the ballistic rockets had hit targets in England." Then, in quick succession, Berlin fell to the Red Army on May 2, and, "on 4 May Montgomery reported to Eisenhower that all enemy forces in Holland, north-west Germany and Denmark had capitulated with effect from eight o'clock the following morning." That would be May 5. Then, at 2:41 a.m. on May 7, Col. Gen. Alfred Jodl, representing the German High Command, signed the official instrument of unconditional surrender of German forces to the Western Allies and the Soviet Union, but "the actual moment for the end of the war in Europe was to be one minute after midnight on 8/9 May." Bradford observed, "A last-minute muddle between the Powers as to the timing of the announcement of the end of the war made it all something of an anti-climax."

Winston wished the announcement to be made May 7, but Harry Truman and Joseph Stalin opted for May 8 instead, and even that timing briefly was in doubt, due to "further attempts to delay by Moscow." Thus, Winston couldn't make *his* formal announcement of V-E Day until 3:00 p.m. on May 8. Bradford noted, "Appropriately, 8 May was a Tuesday, and the King and Churchill lunched together as usual. The King wrote: 'We congratulated each other on the end of the European War. The day we had been longing for has arrived at last & we can look back with thankfulness to God that our tribulation is over. No more fear of being bombed at home & no more living in air raid shelters. But there still is Japan to be defeated & the restoration of our country to be dealt with, which will give us many headaches & hard work in the coming years.'" Bradford added, "Preparations for V-E Day had been going on for months." King George, in fact, had recorded and filmed his victory speech in advance.

Well aware that the official end was coming, the British citizenry still waited with surprising discipline. "Even though we knew the Germans had surrendered, we waited patiently for the official declaration of V-E Day and for permission to celebrate," wrote Russell Miller, author of *Ten Days in May: The People's Story of V-E Day*, in the London *Times* on May 7, 1995. "When it came, there was an outpouring of rejoicing and relief and patriotism the like of which the world will never see again." For the thousands of people jamming the streets of London it would be an unforgettable experience, "one of the happiest days of their lives." Indeed, "strangers linked arms in the comradeship of their happiness, kissing and hugging were the order of the night, and there was dancing on the streets whenever and wherever space could be found. When the crowd was not singing, it was cheering; when it was not cheering it was laughing. The pubs ran dry, but who cared? This was a celebration driven by communal joy; no other stimulants were needed."

Until the last minute, nobody knew exactly when V-E Day would fall. "The problem was that the Allies had agreed the announcement would be made simultaneously in London, Washington and Moscow, and the Russians were insisting the news should not be made public until the surrender had been formally ratified in Berlin," wrote Miller. Finally, the BBC read "a bald statement from the Ministry of Information" saying that Tuesday, May 8, would be "treated as Victory in Europe Day and will be regarded as a holiday."

One result was an outpouring of rejoicing in London that very night and more or less organized celebrating the next day, complete with "an army of entrepreneurs" selling paper hats, flags, and other items in patriotic red, white, and blue. "At three o'clock, huge crowds jammed Parliament square and Whitehall to listen to Churchill's speech in the House of Commons, which was relayed over loudspeakers." The crowds naturally cheered wildly when Winston said that hostilities officially were about to end, and, "The German war is therefore at an end."

Late that afternoon, the king and queen and their two daughters appeared on a red-and-gold draped balcony at Buckingham Palace, joined minutes later by a beaming, bareheaded Winston Churchill. As Churchill's grandson (also Winston Churchill) recalled years later: "At about 5:30 there was a momentary hush as the French windows were opened and my grandfather stepped on to the balcony with the royal family. . . . I don't remember being in the least surprised to see my grandfather in such company. Every small boy believes his grandfather to be the most important person in the world." But maybe he was at that.

Meanwhile, just a short while later, at dusk, the streetlights in London came on. No big deal . . . except it was for the first time in six years!

Amid the relief, there were regrets for those lost, especially in recent days and thus, with the war effectively won, seemingly to no apparent good purpose. There still were the shock, the horror, the revulsion over the growing revelations emerging from the newly liberated Nazi death camps . . . instruments of what would become known as the Holocaust.

On May 4, with the shooting in Europe all but over, photographer Cecil Beaton in Wiltshire wrote in his diary: "Now good news, like the blossom and flowers, is pouring from every source. 'Berlin falling!' Goebbels dead!' 'Germans surrender!' The worst of the nightmare is past: the terrible casualty lists, the ghastly deaths of so many unquestioning young people, the gassing of Jews, the butcheries in German-occupied territories. Yet one is conscious of so much continued suffering throughout the world that it is hard to celebrate."

And still looming—unresolved, but at least portending victory, albeit a difficult one—was the Japanese war with countless more deaths and even more devastation yet to come. That difficult victory, however, came much more quickly than most people expected, thanks to the two atomic bombs that the United States dropped on Hiroshima and Nagasaki in early August. Thus, in London, George VI would be back on the palace balcony on V-J Day, on August 15, again to receive the cheers of a crowd celebrating an enemy's surrender . . . but he missed having Winston by his side. "I wish he could have been given a proper reception by the people," the king lamented in his diary that night.

Additional note: Even while out of office, Winston did have a minor impact on another victory observance. In his enforced "retirement," Winston was unhappy to read in the newspapers that the late Erwin Rommel's white stallion, nicknamed "Rommel" by the British troops who captured it, was to be exhibited in a victory parade. The horse had been presented to the king by Field Marshal Sir Bernard

Montgomery on behalf of his 21st Army Group. Field Marshal Rommel, suspected of involvement in the July 1944 assassination attempt on Hitler, had committed suicide. Now, in June 1946, Winston wrote to the king, "I was rather upset by the idea of this poor creature being led in triumph through the streets." And so, the plan to display Rommel's horse was canceled.

No Longer PM

For Winston, those first days without portfolio were a vast readjustment. Quite suddenly, the bottom had dropped out of his professional life . . . to which, of course, he was more than ordinarily devoted. More than devoted to it for the past five years, you could say he had been absolutely welded to it. And now he was separated from the overarching structure that had been his for so long.

That first night after the election count came in, family and close friends gathered to wonder and commiserate at dinner, daughter Mary recalled. Among them were Winston's brother Jack, "still looking thin and ill" from a recent heart attack. Another, ironically, was Venetia Montagu, the young woman who had so beguiled Prime Minister Asquith at the time of Winston's first real downfall, during the First World War. Long since widowed, she now was "battered by the course of a mortal illness but stalwart to the end."

Others at this subdued, "first night after the count" dinner ranged from good friends and longtime political associates Anthony Eden and Brendan Bracken to daughters Sarah, Mary, and Diana, the latter accompanied by her husband, Duncan Sandys, who in the election count that same day had lost his parliamentary seat. Said Mary: "Dinner was a somewhat muted affair, understandably so; with everyone trying to help and say the right thing." Through it, "My father still maintained his courageous spirit."

In the days ahead, though, reality hit hard. "The next few days were, if anything, worse than that dreadful Thursday. After years of intense activity, for Winston now there was a yawning hiatus. The whole focus of power, action and news had been transferred to the new Prime Minister. The Map Room was deserted; the Private Office empty; no official telegrams; no 'red boxes.' True, letters and messages from friends and from countless members of the general public started pouring in, sweet and consoling, expressing love, indignation and loyalty. But nothing and nobody could really soften the bitter blow."

Even so, there were the many rounds of good-byes to tend to, the packing and the moving out of No. 10 Downing Street to make room for the incoming Attlees, the house hunting for new London quarters, and the beginning of a long refurbishment for Chartwell, its upkeep only minimally maintained during the war years. The London quarters issue was quickly settled by the choice of No. 28 Hyde Park Gate in Kensington, while Chartwell was to be approached a bit cautiously. "Realizing that it would be extremely difficult to get domestic help, Clementine decided not to use the ground floor and basement rooms at all, but to organize their life on the top two floors," wrote Mary. "But at this moment, the work entailed in carrying out this sensible plan had only just begun."

On the plus side of the war's aftermath, of course, all of the immediate family had survived. Winston, with all his travels and illnesses, many times had been at risk. Randolph had parachuted into Yugoslavia to work with Tito's partisans against the occupying Germans. The entire family as mere residents primarily of London had escaped the death and destruction brought to so many others by the bombings, buzz bombs, and V-2 rockets (67,635 civilians in the United Kingdom were killed during the war).

Then, too, seemingly at odds with the election results, it was clear from public reaction to Winston's appearances anywhere that he had emerged as a treasured icon to the British people and nation. When he first appeared in Parliament less than a week after his Conservative Party's shellacking at the polls was announced, the Conservatives in the House greeted him by singing, "For he's a jolly good fellow." Two days after V-J Day, Prime Minister Attlee rose in the House to say: "In the darkest and most dangerous hour of our history this nation found in my Right Honorable friend the man who expressed supremely the courage and determination never to yield which animated all the men and women of this country. In undying phrases he crystallized the unspoken feeling of all. . . . His place in history is secure."

In addition, Clementine wrote to Mary that on V-J Day, Winston "got mobbed in Whitehall by a frenzied crowd" and "many people gathered round this block of flats [where they temporarily were staying before moving to 28 Hyde Park Gate] to see Papa & cheer him." At the opening of Parliament on August 16, the same day that Attlee spoke, Clementine reported: "Papa made a brilliant moving gallant speech. . . . He was right back in his 1940–41 caliber. The new house full of rather awestruck shy nervous members was riveted & fascinated." Clementine added, "These friendly manifestations have reassured & comforted him a little. He says all he misses is the Work & being able to give orders." Cheers and comforts, yes, but who could forget the down side? "The crowds shout 'Churchill for ever' & 'We want Churchill.' But all the King's horses & all the King's men can't put Humpty Dumpty together again."

Still another unhappy (apparently temporary) effect was the new strain, after all the wartime strains, on the Churchills' marriage. "I cannot explain how it is," Clementine wrote to Mary, "but in our misery we seem, instead of clinging to each other to be always having scenes. I'm sure it's all my fault, but I'm finding life more than I can bear. He is so unhappy & that makes him very difficult."

As another aspect of the postwar readjustment for both Winston and Clementine, they now joined an entire nation on short rations and economic hard times. Just as peace in the wake of devastating war was no panacea for the general public, neither was it for Winston and Clementine. Perhaps even less so, since they weren't used to all the deprivations visited upon the public in general. Explained Mary: "Although they had lived for over five years on an exhaustingly heroic level, they had not suffered the physical shortages and domestic difficulties which had been the lot of ordinary people. Because they had to entertain so many people officially, they received 'Diplomatic Rations'; Chequers was staffed by the Women's Services, and civilian staff had been available for London; cars and petrol were always at hand. Now, of course, all these comforts and facilities disappeared."

Setbacks or no, domestic life and public affairs both had to go on. Thus Winston soon enjoyed holidays abroad, resumed his painting, began gathering his thoughts for his epic history of the war, and applied finishing touches to his history of the English-speaking peoples, a book nearly two decades in the making. Politically, he was leader of the opposition Conservative Party, true, but he never was a party animal. On the other hand, he certainly didn't care for Labor's leadership on social issues and granting independence to Burma and India. Primarily interested in foreign affairs, he did make his presence felt in that arena at least.

And he did have a new-old cause. Two causes, in fact. The second of the two, which he would urge at Zurich University on September 19, 1946, was creation of a "council of Europe," a first step toward European union. His other great concern, already pungently expressed to Harry Truman back in May 1945, would require a trip to the United States in January 1946 to enunciate before the world . . . but at a small college town in Truman's home state of Missouri.

The Chiastic Churchill

When John F. Kennedy uttered his famous inaugural line, "Ask not what your country can do for you, ask what you can do for your country," he committed a chiasmus, but Winston Churchill was the real master of the oratorical device. Here's just one example, stated in the House of Commons on the heels of Prime Minister Neville Chamberlain's "peace in our time" visit with Hitler in Munich:

> You were given the choice between war and dishonor.
> You chose dishonor and you will have war.

As might be evident from the two quotes, to use a chiasmus in the spoken or written word is to reverse the order of words in two otherwise parallel phrases. Another example would be Samuel Coleridge's "Each throat / Was parched, and glazed each eye."

Chiasmus and Winston Churchill's mastery thereof—news to most of us, true—are noted by psychologist Mardy Grothe of Raleigh, North Carolina, proprietor of the Web site chiasmus.com and a student of the chiastic phenomenon among men of letters, especially Churchill as the leading chiastic practitioner of them all. "Given his love of language and linguistic skill, " says Grothe, "it's not surprising to discover that Churchill was fond of chiasmus. In fact, no other political leader rivals him in the use of the technique (JFK comes in a very distant second)."

Grothe offers thirty examples of Winston's chiastic turn of phrase, many of them among the most famous of his statements, whether uttered verbally or stated in print. For instance, from 1942, just after the great British victory at El Alamein:

> Now this is not the end.
> It is not even the beginning of the end.
> But it is, perhaps, the end of the beginning.

Not quite so well known is Winston's further observation, recalled by Grothe and stated in Winston's later writings: "Before Alamein we never had a victory. After Alamein we never had a defeat."

Actually, notes Grothe, Winston might have "borrowed" part of his "beginning of the end" quote from Talleyrand's "It's the beginning of the end" prediction after a French defeat during Napoleon's disastrous 1812 invasion of Russia. "There is also evidence that the entire thought was in Churchill's mind decades before WWII," adds Grothe. "British writer John Campbell reported Churchill saying virtually the same thing about the Battle of the Marne in 1914. According to Campbell, Churchill 'remembered and tucked [it] away for use again twenty-seven years later.'"

Still another pungent Churchillian chiasmus during World War II, this time in reference to Hitler:

> Our defeats are but stepping-stones to victory,
> and his victories are but stepping-stones to ruin.

To be sure, over the years there were so many other subjects upon which Winston spoke . . . and often with the use of couplet-like chiasmus:

> All I can say that I have taken more out of alcohol
> than alcohol has taken out of me.

and:

> I am ready to meet my Maker.
> Whether my Maker is prepared for the ordeal of meeting me is
> another matter.

Often cited as Winston's last words, but wrongly so, this presumably facetious statement came, actually, on his seventy-fifth birthday, as the reply when a reporter asked if he had any fear of death. "Churchill was in rare form that day. . . . One awestruck photographer said to him: 'I hope, sir, that I will shoot your picture on your hundredth birthday.' Churchill looked the young man over and, to the great amusement of those assembled, replied, 'I don't see why not, young man. You look reasonably fit and healthy.'"

Employing the chiastic approach again, he once said:

> I hope I shall never see the day when the Force of Right
> is deprived of the Right of Force.

and another time:

> In finance everything that is agreeable is unsound
> and everything that is sound is disagreeable.

(The same could be said, just as chiastically, about *diet* instead of *finance*.) Also in the area of economics and finance:

> Solvency is valueless without security,
> and security is impossible to achieve without solvency.

He did have a high regard for scientists, engineers, and technocrats, especially since so many of that ilk contributed significantly to Allied weapons development during the two world wars. Still, that didn't stop him from issuing this warning during a speech given at the University of Copenhagen in 1950:

> We want a lot of engineers in the modern world,
> but we do not want a world of engineers.

Or, on politics, an interesting observation in view of his own political background:

> Some men change their party for the sake of their principles;
> others their principles for the sake of their party.

Since Winston himself changed political parties not once but twice, even his best friends might see "mild" but forgivable hypocrisy in the quote, suggests Grothe, who, not so incidentally, wrote a book on language called *Never Let a Fool Kiss You, or a Kiss Fool You.* "Both times, he said he was motivated by principle, but many observers—and all of his opponents—saw him motivated as much by political opportunism."

Meanwhile, one of the earliest chiastic statements Winston ever made in public came up in his maiden speech to Parliament back in 1901 when the up-and-coming Welsh MP David Lloyd George decided against moving an expected amendment. "For Churchill, who had prepared every word of his speech with painstaking care, Lloyd George's failure to move his amendment was an unexpected reverse," wrote Randolph Churchill in his father's official biography. Winston's planned opening words no longer applied.

Seeing his hesitation, Thomas Gibson Bowles quickly suggested what amounted to a chiasmus. Why not say, he suggested:

> Instead of making his violent speech without moving his moderate
>   amendment,
> he [Lloyd George] had better have moved his moderate amendment
>   without making his violent speech.

Seizing upon this "manna" from heaven, Winston repeated the suggested words, but without the term *violent* and in somewhat more moderate language overall. Thus:

> It has been suggested to me that it might perhaps have been better
>   on the whole,
> if the honorable member instead of making his speech without
>   moving his amendment,
> had moved his amendment without making his speech.

And there we have it . . . one of the very few times that Winston Churchill, master and frequent user of the chiasmus, used an unplanned chiasmus.

Poker Pals

One of the most famous speeches in history can be traced in large part to a scribbled note from a U.S. president to a former prime minister of England. "Dear Winnie," Harry S. Truman scribbled on the bottom of an acquaintance's letter, "This is a fine old school out in my state. If you come and make a speech there, I'll take you out and introduce you." That suited Winston very well, and there he was, on the afternoon of an early March day in 1946, boarding a train to Missouri with Truman, various aides, and "the usual entourage of Secret Service men," reported Margaret Truman.

Actually, it was Winston who first thought of traveling to America to impart some of his deepest thoughts. "I think I can be of some use over there; they will take things from me," he told Lord Moran. Thus, in late 1945, it was announced that he would be visiting America. About that time, too, Frank Lewis "Bullet" McClure, president of Westminster College in Fulton, Missouri, was looking for an eminent speaker for the small Presbyterian school's annual Green Foundation lecture, recalled Robert Pilpel in *Churchill in America*.

McClure told Westminster alumnus Brig. Gen. Harry Vaughan, a White House military aide, that the school would like to land Churchill as its speaker. In no time, McClure found himself at the White House closeted with Vaughan's boss, Harry Truman, who then promised to forward the invitation to Chartwell "under aegis of the Presidential Seal," Pilpel wrote. That was when Truman scribbled his "Dear Winnie" note of encouragement on the bottom of the letter.

"Thus the stage was set for what was to become 'Fulton's Finest hour,'" added Pilpel, also noting that Winston decided to make a holiday out of the speaking engagement as well. "I want sun, solitude, serenity, and something to eat, and perhaps something to drink," he told Moran. "On January 14 [1946], accordingly, he and Clementine arrived in New York aboard the *Queen Elizabeth* en route to the Miami Beach estate of . . . Colonel Frank Clark [a Canadian wood-pulp magnate]." After restful days painting, indulging in nonrationed foods for a change (eggs were a welcome novelty), and beginning to work on his speech, Winston turned up in Washington, ready for the sojourn to Truman's home state of Missouri.

The speech ahead would be serious, but for the moment it was a lighthearted, convivial group boarding the ten-car presidential special. "Dad assigned General Vaughan to keep Mr. Churchill liberally supplied with his favorite liquid refreshment," Margaret Truman recounted. This decision prompted a Churchillian pronouncement on his drinking habit: "When the General delivered the first drink," Margaret noted, "Mr. Churchill held it up to the light, and said, 'When I was a young subaltern in the South African [Boer] war, the water was not fit to drink. To make it palatable we had to add whiskey. By diligent effort I learned to like it.'"

As Winston soon found out, too, a hand or two of poker were in the offing for the long hours ahead on the overnight train. Margaret recounted: "Dad proposed to teach Mr. Churchill the intricacies of poker, about which he claimed to know nothing. He soon had the poker-playing Missourians doubled up with comments such as, 'I think I'll risk a few shillings on a pair of knaves.' But their laughter dwindled as he displayed a startling knowledge of the game, plus some sly remarks that he had played something like it during the Boer War."

According to the late White House Counsel Clark Clifford's autobiography *Counsel to the President*, however, it was Winston who, at dinner on the train, proposed: "Harry, I understand from the press that you like to play poker." To which Truman allowed, "I have played a great deal of poker in my life." In Clifford's version of the story, it was Winston, playing in his blue, one-piece zippered "siren suit," who then turned out to be the lamb among wolves.

At an early point, it seems, Truman enjoined his aides: "This man is cagey and is probably an excellent player. The reputation of American poker is at stake and I expect every man to do his duty." Later, when Winston clearly wasn't doing very well, Truman warned, "I don't want him to think we're pushovers, but at the same time, let's not treat him badly." In the end, Clifford wrote, Winston probably lost a total of about $250—"just enough so that he could not go back to London and brag that he had beaten the Americans at poker."

Meanwhile, after arriving at Fulton the next day, according to Margaret, "Mr. Churchill's desire for liquid refreshment became something of a problem. Fulton was a dry town. Dad ordered General Vaughan to spare no effort or expense to find their speaker a drink. After some frantic scouting, the General produced the wherewithal and arrived in Mr. Churchill's room, liquor and ice water in hand.

"'Well, General,' said the guest of honor. 'I didn't know whether I was in Fulton, Missouri, or Fulton, Sahara.'"

Less than a hour later, Truman introduced the distinguished visitor to the Westminster College audience.

Iron Curtain Speech

After seeing Winston stumble a bit as a poker player on the overnight train to Fulton, Missouri, White House counsel Clark Clifford was then treated to a stunning display of Winston's strong suit—his oratory. First, though, the presidential party led by Harry Truman and including Winston Churchill as honored guest arrived in Jefferson City, the state's capital, about 11:20 a.m. on March 5, 1946. A motorcade took them through the town, Robert Pilpel reported in *Churchill in America*, and then accompanied them on the twenty-five mile drive to Fulton, home of Westminster College. There, with Winston's liquid needs presumably tended to, they lunched at college president Bullet McClure's home, and then it was on to the speech making in the school's crowded gymnasium.

Truman's introduction, typically, was brief. Noting that he had met both Winston and Joseph Stalin at Potsdam ("a conference," he said, without naming it), Truman said he became "very fond of both of them." As for the day's occasion,

Truman said, "I understand that Mr. Churchill is going to talk about the sinews of peace. I know he will have something constructive to say to the world."

Presidential counselor Clifford, for one, would never forget what came next. "From the point of view of high rhetoric," he recalled, "I had never heard anything like it before. As a demonstration of the power of ideas, it was an astonishing tour de force." The tour de force was Churchill's Iron Curtain speech, which was instantly famous and controversial all at once. The reaction was a "furor," Margaret Truman wrote.

What Winston said that day in 1946 strikes us today as simple fact, but he was the first major Western figure to point out the aims and results of Soviet aggression in no uncertain terms: "From Stettin in the Baltic to Trieste in the Adriatic, an iron curtain has descended across the Continent. Behind that line lie all the capitals of the ancient states of Central and Eastern Europe. Warsaw, Berlin, Prague, Vienna, Budapest, Belgrade, Bucharest, and Sofia, all these famous cities and the populations around them lie in what I must call the Soviet sphere, and all are subject, in one form or another, not only to Soviet influence but to a very high and in some cases increasing measure of control from Moscow."

It basically was what Winston already had written to Truman back in May 1945, even before Potsdam. Also true was a second observation from Winston's speech at Fulton: "From what I have seen of our Russian friends and allies during the war, I am convinced that there is nothing they admire so much as strength and there is nothing for which they have less respect than for military weakness." Thus, Margaret Truman observed, Winston "urged an Anglo-American 'fraternal association' to stop Russia's persistent aggression."

Simple truths stated or not, the outcry was immediate. Stalin of course reacted "with grim evidence of his paranoia," Margaret Truman noted in her biography of her father. "He accused the United States of allying itself with Great Britain to thwart Russia. He declared Churchill's speech at Fulton was an unfriendly act. 'Such a speech if directed against the United States would never have been permitted in Russia.' Never was there more tragic evidence of the Russian dictator's complete inability to understand a free society."

But there also was critical reaction in the West, the United States and Britain included. Among other American critics, Senator Claude Pepper (D-FL) not only denounced the speech but warned against becoming "a guarantor of British imperialism." James Roosevelt, son of the late president, said Winston's statement at Fulton represented only "the British point of view."

On a related theme, many in the American press, wrote Margaret Truman, echoed the *New York Herald Tribune*'s Bert Andrews in saying Truman "went along largely with what Mr. Churchill had to say, if not entirely." This was not true, Margaret insisted. She, unlike her father's critics, was able to cite his personal letter to his mother and sister, dated only days after the speech, in which he said: "I'm glad you enjoyed Fulton. So did I. And I think it did some good, although I'm not yet ready to endorse Mr. Churchill's speech."

Just a year later, however, Truman was quite ready to declare his anticommunist Truman Doctrine, by which it would be the official policy of the United States to provide moral and financial assistance to "free peoples" resisting takeover by "armed minorities or by outside pressures" (that is, by communist subversion, insurgency, or overt aggression). "With this declaration," noted Pilpel, "the United States assumed responsibility for backing the existing regimes in Greece and Turkey against Communist insurgency, thereby relieving the British, who were financially unable to bear the burden any longer." Then, too, "exactly fifteen months after Fulton, the new American Secretary of State, George Marshall, proposed a plan for European recovery"—the Marshall Plan.

Still, at the time of Winston's Fulton speech, Margaret Truman insisted, "Dad did not have the slightest idea what Mr. Churchill was going to say at Fulton until they met at the White House before boarding the train to Missouri. He approved of *Mr. Churchill* saying it, because he was not a head of state. In fact the ex-prime minister made a point of reminding his audience that he represented no one but himself. My father in no sense considered the speech a break with Russia, nor did he want one. In fact, he later invited Marshal Stalin to come to Missouri and deliver a speech, stating Russia's point of view on the various disputes that were imperiling the peace."

Stalin never came and instead the cold war succeeded World War II.

Additional note: If Winston in the meantime had to weather one storm over his iron curtain remarks, he also, before finishing his 1946 visit to the United States, had to confront another stormy but old issue as well, Pilpel points out in his book on Winston in America. Traveling to New York City after further visits to Washington, two stops in Virginia, and a visit to FDR's grave at Hyde Park, Winston ran afoul, quite separately, of complaining Irish and communist protesters. The communists naturally didn't care for his iron curtain remarks, while the Irish still remembered Winston's "link to the Black-and-Tans."

The irony here "was that Churchill had been one of the most instrumental factors in bringing about an Irish settlement in the years before and after World War I," wrote Pilpel. "As a Liberal he had been a staunch advocate of Irish independence since 1905, and as Secretary of State for the Colonies in 1922 he had helped negotiate the Ulster compromise which made that independence possible."

Who First Said It?

Here's a historical footnote to ponder. Rather than Winston Churchill, could it have been the leadership of Nazi Germany that came up with the term "iron curtain"? On the other hand, could it have been an Englishwoman who was a socialist member of Parliament visiting Bolshevik Russia in 1920? Or even a German admiral talking about submarines during World War I, with no reference to the Russians in mind at all? All three, and perhaps more, are distinct possibilities . . . and somewhere along the line Winston picked up on the phrase himself.

Peter Millar, writing in the London *Sunday Times* of May 7, 1995—on the eve of the fiftieth anniversary of V-E Day—seems (among others) to have opted for the Nazi leadership as Churchill's inspiration. "In the closing days of the war the analyses in London and Berlin were uncannily identical," Millar wrote. He then cited a statement by Nazi chief propagandist Josef Goebbels that appeared in the weekly *Das Reich* in February 1945 as the Red Army closed in on Berlin from the east, while the Western Allies advanced from the west.

As reported by Millar, and perhaps coming to Winston's attention at the time, Goebbels had written: " If the German people lay down their arms, the Soviets—even after the agreements between Churchill, Roosevelt and Stalin— would immediately occupy all of east and southeast Europe, including large parts of the Reich. Before this vast territory, including the Soviet Union, an iron curtain would descend." Surmised Millar: "Churchill, with his expert eye for a good line, was to make it his own later."

Nor was the Goebbels reference a chance and isolated remark, it seems. As Millar goes on to explain, the iron curtain reference was to be "a keynote phrase in German diplomacy" during the fateful springtime of 1945. "Even with Hitler dead and Germany in ruins it resurfaced when Count Schwerin von Krosigk, the rump Reich government's new foreign minister, made a broadcast to the nation for the ears of Western leaders on May 2." In the east, von Schwerin said, "the iron curtain, behind which, unseen by the eyes of the world, the work of destruction goes on, is moving steadily forward."

Note, by this time, the term appears to have achieved such accepted status as to qualify for the definite article *the*. Note, too, how similar to a worried Winston's own statement in his telegram of May 12, ten days later, to Harry S. Truman: "An iron curtain is drawn down upon their front. We do not know what is going on behind." And, finally, the key lines in his famous iron curtain speech at Fulton, Missouri, on March 5, 1946: "From Stettin in the Baltic to Trieste in the Adriatic, an iron curtain has descended across the Continent. Behind that line lie all the capitals of the ancient states of Central and Eastern Europe. Warsaw, Berlin, Prague, Vienna, Budapest, Belgrade, Bucharest, and Sofia."

Often forgotten or ignored is the fact that a presumably still-unwinding, vacationing Winston wrote his wife, Clementine, from the south of France in late 1945, weeks before Fulton, to say, in part, that little was known "behind the Russian iron curtain, but [he added] evidently the Poles and Czecho-Slovakians are being as badly treated as one could have expected." This letter reflected the same overall theme that was to be heard at Fulton: "The Bolshevization of Europe proceeds apace and all the Cabinets of Central, Eastern and Southern Europe are in Soviet control, excepting only Athens."

The term *iron curtain* by itself cannot be considered unique to the postwar events in Europe, not when, for one thing, it literally meant the curtain sometimes used to close off the stage in a theater or any other closing off or fencing in. For instance, at another time when Winston himself might have been paying close attention, German Adm. Alfred von Tirpitz during the First World War apparently used the term in quite an unrelated context. As recalled by neurosurgeon Jules C. Ladenheim of Teaneck, New Jersey, in a letter to the editor of the *New York Times*, von Tirpitz in 1916 told an American interviewer, "We shall envelop England within an iron curtain." Explained Ladenheim, "He was referring to an impending German submarine blockade." Ladenheim added, "Churchill, who was first lord of the Admiralty, tucked away the phrase in the recesses of memory and drew it out three decades later, when the generation that could recognize it was dead and forgotten."

Or, again at a time and place when the decidedly anti-Bolshevik Winston Churchill could have been listening, in 1920 socialist MP Ethel Snowden visited the Soviet Union with a British delegation and came away with a decidedly negative impression. She described the Soviet Union's western border area as an iron curtain in her book *Through Bolshevik Russia*, but it appears she really meant the border controls imposed by the countries adjoining Russia, rather than Russian border monitoring.

No Breakfast, Thanks

It would have been nice, but . . .

A visit to Virginia and an address to the General Assembly were on the itinerary for Winston after the iron curtain speech at Fulton, Missouri, and he thought it would be fitting for him to deliver that address in the old colonial capital of Williamsburg rather than in the capitol at Richmond. He had turned down similar invitations from Kentucky and South Carolina, but he acceded to the Virginia legislature's invitation, supplemented personally by Governor William M. Tuck, because, he said, of his readings of history. The Virginia legislature, dating back to colonial days at Jamestown, was (and is) the oldest in North America. Since he already had agreed to visit Williamsburg on March 8 with his old comrade in arms, Dwight D. Eisenhower, now U.S. Army chief of staff, Winston thought he perhaps could address the lawmakers that day and in the same locale—itself quite historic.

But Tuck replied that scheme posed problems. Before World War II, he wrote, the Virginia Assembly had made it a practice early in its biennial sessions to meet at least once in the old capitol building still standing in the restored part of town known as Colonial Williamsburg. That tradition had been dropped during the war, though, and now Winston was proposing to have the lawmakers travel to Williamsburg for a day very late in their session. In fact, it would be just one day before the assembly's scheduled adjournment. "Many of the leaders of the Assembly believe that much of the important and necessary work may be neglected, or acted upon without proper consideration, if the General Assembly should leave Richmond for the day on March 8," Tuck wrote on February 19 to Winston, who was still enjoying a restful interlude at Miami Beach.

Instead, Tuck invited Winston, Clementine, and party to breakfast at the executive mansion, where Winston had stayed with Gov. Harry F. Byrd Sr. and his family two decades before. And so, it was agreed and so it took place . . . making front-page news in the local newspapers. Winston addressed the Virginia legislature in Thomas Jefferson's Capitol at Richmond, which, as Governor Tuck said, "is itself quite old and historic."

As for the speech itself, Robert Pilpel noted in *Churchill in America*: "Smarting a bit from the furious controversy his Westminster speech had stirred up, he rhetorically inquired of the legislators: 'Do you not think you are running some risk in inviting me to give you my faithful counsel on this occasion? You have not asked to see what I am going to say. I might easily, for instance, blurt out a lot of things people know in their hearts are true but are a bit shy of saying in public, and this might cause a regular commotion and get you all into trouble.'"

When the Virginians obligingly laughed at this, Winston went on to make it clear, from his speech anyway, that "he did not repent of a single syllable he had uttered at Westminster College." He warned: "Peace will not be preserved by pious sentiments. It will not be preserved by casting aside in dangerous times the panoply of warlike strength." And then, with all that said, he continued on to Williamsburg with Eisenhower.

And breakfast in the governor's mansion that morning? Did it go well? Not exactly, since Winston turned down the invitation, saying it would be better for him to have his usual breakfast in bed aboard the train from Washington and then go straight to the Capitol for his address to the General Assembly.

And that's exactly what he did. "The 72-year-old [but not until November 30] Briton came sleeping into the city aboard a five-car train from Washington at 5:45 a.m.," reported James Jackson "Jack" Kilpatrick for Richmond's afternoon *News Leader*. "He stayed snoozing peacefully until about 8:30 o'clock and then breakfasted alone on grapefruit, bacon and eggs and coffee," wrote the reporter, later to become the newspaper's editor and then a nationally syndicated columnist. "He was to be greeted by State officials at 10 o'clock and shortly thereafter was to leave for the Capitol."

Winston, Eisenhower, and Tuck then rode the mile-plus distance from Broad Street Station to the Capitol in an open car, despite falling rain that "drenched" crowds of onlookers, the morning *Times-Dispatch*'s James B. Gibson reported. "Mr. Churchill acknowledged the plaudits of the multitude, gesturing with his big, black cigar and now and then saluting the crowd with his famous 'V' salute." Awaiting him and his address at Jefferson's capitol, Gibson noted, was "a joint assembly of the oldest parliament on the mainland of the Western Hemisphere."

☆ ☆ ☆

Additional note: In Williamsburg later that day there was a brief flurry of fright among the onlookers when the horses hooked up to an open eighteenth-century carriage shied "violently" with Winston and Eisenhower aboard. Explained Pilpel, the two men had just climbed into the carriage "for a tour of the town when photographers' flashbulbs caused the horses pulling it to rear violently in their traces."

Eisenhower grabbed Winston's arm protectively, "while Winston himself settled his hat more firmly on his head and clamped down on his cigar." Once the horses settled down, it seems, the tour continued on—but on foot.

Additional note two: For the record, this writer, as a staff member at the late *Washington Star*, interviewed the late Governor Tuck during the 1970s and came away with the impression that Churchill originally planned his iron curtain speech for Williamsburg instead of Fulton, until told the Virginia Assembly was too busy for the one-day diversion in Williamsburg. Whether this writer misunderstood, or the governor three decades after the fact misremembered the true scenario, is unclear. However, the governor, at another time, also told political reporter James Latimer of the *Richmond Times-Dispatch*: "He decided to come. And sometime afterwards—after he had come and gone—it occurred to me he had in mind delivering that Iron Curtain speech to us at Williamsburg."

"Loved That Man"

Before leaving America in 1946, Winston Churchill paid tribute to his wartime ally Franklin Delano Roosevelt by visiting his gravesite eleven months to the day of FDR's death in Warm Springs, Georgia, on April 12, 1945. Thus, it was on March 12, 1946, that Winston, accompanied by Eleanor Roosevelt, placed a wreath of carnations and rhododendron leaves by the late president's grave at the Roosevelt estate on the Hudson River above New York City. At the site, "he stood apart, bareheaded and silent, lost in memories of his departed friend," wrote Robert Pipel in *Churchill in America*. "Bright sunshine played on the simple stone of white marble, and a sharp breeze ruffled the pine boughs surrounding it."

When Winston finally turned away, his eyes were brimming, and he was heard to sigh, "Lord, how I loved that man."

Additional note: Pilpel also cites evidence that Winston and FDR were related—as seventh cousins once removed. "Their common ancestors being Henry and Helena Glover, seventeenth-century residents of New Haven, Connecticut."

Overview

The year that World War II ended, Winston turned seventy-one. After all he had done for his country, the Allies, and Western civilization itself, he certainly could go off and rest easy somewhere, couldn't he? His accomplishments were legendary, his résumé unrivaled. And now, as he approached the age of seventy-two in 1946, he had added his "iron curtain" warning of the Soviet monolith's intentions, and he had given the concept of a European Union a boost as well. What more could await a statesman of his age, experience, and worldwide standing, other than graceful retirement and perhaps a comfortable series of well-paying lectures and commencement speeches?

In Winston's case, what still lay ahead was more than most men or women could possibly achieve in a lifetime. For he again would be prime minister of England; he would produce another ten volumes of historical prose, including his six-volume history of World War II; he would be honored with knighthood; and he would win the Nobel Prize for Literature. Both of the latter two events came in 1953, when he was seventy-eight.

His second tenure as PM was the product of the second of two general elections held in Britain in 1950 and 1951 (and came about despite a minor stroke he suffered in 1949). The first of the two elections retained but weakened Labor's hold on the government reins, and the second gave the Conservatives a narrow majority of twenty-six parliamentary seats, enough, barely, to install Opposition leader Winston Churchill as prime minister for a second time. Anthony Eden became his foreign secretary, and his longtime scientific "guru," Frederick Lindemann (now Lord Cherwell), became paymaster general with the charge of advising on scientific matters, especially nuclear research.

Once again, domestic issues were not Winston's chief interest, not de-rationing or other "de-controlling" measures, not even the controversies over the return of nationalized steel production and railroad transportation to private ownership. Still determined to do all he could to strengthen Anglo-American ties, Winston almost immediately (in January 1952) went to Washington and Ottawa, Canada, to bolster relations with the New World cousins. Among other issues, he assured Washington that the British would stick it out with the Americans in the Korean War.

In 1953 he was knighted and awarded the Nobel Prize for Literature, but he suffered a partially paralyzing stroke in June, forcing him to postpone a meeting with President Dwight Eisenhower, in which he hoped to talk his WWII compatriot into agreeing to a summit meeting with the Russians. They did meet in Bermuda that December for a four-day conference, which also included France, regarding the exchange of nuclear information. This was immediately followed by Eisenhower's suggestion before the United Nations of an "Atoms for Peace" program. In early 1955, visibly failing at age eighty but still seeking that summit session, Winston gave the green light to British development of a hydrogen bomb.

Winston resigned as PM in April 1955 but continued on in the House of Commons (soon becoming "father of the house") while Anthony Eden took his place as prime minister. Just weeks later, Eden announced there indeed would be a four-power conference at Geneva. Meanwhile, Sir Winston's long simmering, four-volume *A History of the English-Speaking Peoples* at last appeared in book form, starting in 1956 . . . year also of the abortive and bloody Hungarian revolution against Soviet domination and the Suez Crisis, in which the United States refused to back Britain's armed intervention.

Final Winston milestones: in 1959 he won his last opposed election to Parliament, and in 1963, by Act of Congress, he was made an honorary U.S. citizen. There would be one more milestone, on January 24, 1965, but first . . .

"Poor England"

As PM once again, Winston was eager to pay another visit upon his American "cousins," since, in his view, "the key to preserving Britain's greatness lay in close collaboration with the United States," noted Robert Pilpel in *Churchill in America*. In the few years since Winston first took the reins of power in an England at war, however, "the biggest, though conspicuously not the strongest, of the victorious Big Three powers [England] had shrunk from nearly a quarter of the world's territory and a third of the world's population to a fiftieth and a twentieth respectively of its former size." By now, in late 1951, "India was gone, Burma was gone, and the last vestiges of control in the Middle East were going fast. . . . All that was left of the glory of Great Britain was a lingering memory and a small island off the coast of Western Europe, a small island whose economic viability without its empire was very much open to doubt."

It was New Year's Eve when Winston set sail aboard the *Queen Mary* for his twelfth visit to the land of his mother's birth. "Although the two countries were cooperating in Korea, they had fallen out of step on the issue of recognizing the People's Republic of China. In Iran, moreover, the seizure of British oil companies by the government . . . had found Washington unwilling to associate itself with London's official protests, and much bad feeling had been the result."

By a quick revisit with Harry Truman and company in Washington, Winston obviously hoped to reignite the "special relationship" between Great Britain and the United States that he always cherished so much. For the Truman administration, though, Winston's timing wasn't ideal. In early January, the president would be busy preparing both a State of the Union address and a budget message to Congress. A Churchillian visit, experience had proven, could be very demanding of official Washington's time and energy. And further, there were the expectations of pleas and demands for American help. "Hardly a day goes by without one department or another providing a little about something it expects Mr. Churchill to demand and which he is not going to get, about some stiff questions he is going to be asked, or some policy that is going to be thrust down his throat," said the London *Times* in an advance report cited by Pilpel.

So thick were the rumors of a hostile reception awaiting Winston this time, Truman "felt obliged to repudiate them publicly." He did so in a press conference by saying that such reports were "foolish" and by promising "as warm a reception [for Winston] as possible."

Aboard his mighty ocean liner plowing westward across the Atlantic, Winston sadly but accurately told Lord Moran, "When I have come to America before it has been as an equal. [But now,] they have become so great and we are now so small. Poor England!"

Actually, the visit went well for Winston on a personal level, since he indeed was popular and welcome in his mother's home country. He enjoyed a diversion to New York for a stay with old friend Bernard Baruch, made another diversion to Canada and its "even more wildly affectionate" people, and finally triumphed in a once-again dreaded address to a joint session of Congress, Winston's third such foray. He also was inducted into the exclusive ranks of the Society of the Cincinnati, its membership restricted to those whose ancestors fought the British in the American Revolution. Winston, though half British, qualified, Pilpel noted, "thanks to his great-great-grandfather Lieutenant Reuben Murray of Connecticut, who had marched with General Washington."

Additional note: Also on the American theme, Pilpel recalled the moment when Lord Hastings "Pug" Ismay, Winston's wartime chief of staff at the Defense Ministry, now secretary of state for commonwealth affairs, was discussing NATO's need for a common rifle for all its armies. At issue was a choice between the American .303 Garand and the British .280. Ismay somewhat woefully asked, "Isn't there some bastard Anglo-American type of fitting that could be adapted?" Responded Winston, in jest of course: "Oh, Lord Ismay, I must ask you to guard your language. I am an Anglo-American type, you know."

About the Bomb

After New Year's Day of 1953, "Prime Minister Churchill arrived for another visit and enlivened our spirits immensely, as he always did," Margaret Truman noted in her biography of her father. While many still differ on the decision to use the atomic bomb to end the war with Japan, there is no doubt where Winston stood on the issue. The alternative, he noted, would have been horrendous casualties, including Japanese suicides like "the many thousands" of suicides that greeted the Allies at Okinawa. "Now all this nightmare picture had vanished," he wrote. "In its place is a vision—fair and bright, indeed it seemed—of the end of the whole war in one or two violent shocks." But Margaret cited a little known postscript.

As vice president of the United States, Truman didn't know anything about the highly secret Manhattan Project that developed the atomic bomb until the evening of the fateful day in April 1945 he succeeded Franklin D. Roosevelt as president. Once Truman knew about the program, and once two operational bombs were ready, he approved their use. Years later, in early 1953, the last days of the Truman administration, Churchill was present for a dinner attended by Secretary of State Dean Acheson, Gen. Omar Bradley, Ambassador Averell Harriman, and Defense Secretary Robert Lovett. All well and good, but imagine the shock of those present when Winston turned to Truman and said quite aloud: "Mr. President, I hope you have your answer ready for that hour when you and I stand before Saint Peter and he says, 'I understand you two are responsible for putting off those atomic bombs. What have you got to say for yourselves?'"

We'll never know what Truman might have replied, because Lovett quickly salvaged the awkward moment by asking, "Are you sure, Prime Minister, that you are going to be in the same place as the President for that interrogation?"

Winston replied, "Lovett, my vast respect for the creator of this universe and countless others gives me assurance that he would not condemn a man without a hearing."

"True," answered Lovett, "but your hearing would not be likely to start in the Supreme Court, or, necessarily, in the same court as the President's. It could be in another court far away."

According to Margaret Truman's biography, Winston "rumbled" back, "I don't know about that, but wherever it is, it will be in accordance with the principles of the English Common Law."

Not one to be left out, Dean Acheson chimed in, "Is it altogether consistent with your respect for the creator of this and other universes to limit his imagination and judicial procedure to the accomplishments of a minute island, in a tiny world, in one of the smaller of the universes?"

"Well," said Churchill, "there will be a trial by a jury of my peers, that's certain."

"Oyez! Oyez!" cried Acheson in imitation of a court bailiff. "In the matter of the immigration of Winston Spencer Churchill. Mr. Bailiff will you empanel a jury?"

And from there silliness took over these men of international stature. "Everyone eagerly accepted historical roles," recounted Margaret. "General Bradley decided he was Alexander the Great. Others played Julius Caesar, Socrates and Aristotle. The Prime Minister declined to permit Voltaire on his jury—he was an atheist—or Oliver Cromwell, because he did not believe in the rule of law." And so on.

The light mood still prevailed later in the evening as Winston was asked to sit in judgment for a comparison of Truman's "merits as a statesman" versus his "demerits as a pianist." Winston found for Truman's statesmanship.

On a more serious note, added Margaret, Winston had nothing but praise for Truman's statesmanship. Confessing he had been very pessimistic when the one-time haberdasher (and former U.S. Senator) succeeded FDR, Churchill now told Truman: "I misjudged you badly. Since that time you, more than any other man, have saved Western civilization."

Margaret did not indicate if her father ever responded to Churchill's question about meeting St. Peter at the Pearly Gates.

Additional note: Before saying his farewells to the outgoing president on this 1953 visit, Winston again spent a few days in New York . . . and a few hours with President-elect Dwight Eisenhower, who disappointed and indeed angered the aging apostle of Anglo-American cooperation by telling Winston's private secretary and aide Jock Colville that the "special relationship" Winston touted so highly shouldn't be pressed too hard publicly for fear of offending other nations. Meanwhile, Winston visited the house in Brooklyn in which his mother, Jennie Jerome, was thought to have been born. Thus, he visited the home of Mr. and Mrs. Joseph Romeo at 426 Henry Street . . . only later it turned out that his mother had been born at nearby 8 Amity Street.

Caught Off Guard

Then there was the time a visiting Margaret Truman had just finished lunch with Winston at Chartwell, and he asked her to take one of his famous paintings back to her mother and father in America. "I'll be glad to," came the bold and surprising reply, "if you put my name on it so that eventually it will be mine." Caught off guard, the great man, "harrumphed," Margaret recounted, then wondered aloud if she oughtn't to ask her father first. "Just put my name on it," she pertly replied. "I can handle him."

Two of Winston's daughters also were present for the lunch, Margaret wrote—Sarah, whom Margaret counted as a friend, and Mary and her husband, Christopher Soames. "They watched open-mouthed while he capitulated and put my name on the painting, which was a lovely view of his favorite North African landscape, around Marrakech." Later, Sarah confided to Margaret "that I was the first person who had accomplished the feat of extracting one of his paintings from him."

Additional note: When time came for the Truman estate to sell the painting at Sotheby's in 2007, the record price paid for a Churchill painting was $2.06 million.

Prize for Oratory Too

They had had their eye on him for a few years. His name had been advanced before. And now, against the usual rules of the game, even though he was in government at the time, he would be named the prize winner of 1953 while holding the position of prime minister of England.

"Churchill's name was first thought of in connection with the Prize by the Swedish," wrote Kjell Stromberg in a publication for the Nobel Prize Library. "In later years, this candidacy, which quickly became popular, was proposed again and again, almost exclusively by Swedish writers and historians. Several of these were members of the [Swedish] Academy, and they were quick to settle on this name, which by mid-century was illustrious above all others. Even so, it was passed through a fine critical sieve by two reporting Academicians."

In one case, Stromberg wrote, the "aged" former permanent secretary of the academy, Per Hallstrom, found "no literary merit" in Winston's early (and only) novel, *Savrola*, "which a youthful Lieutenant Churchill had written to relieve the boredom of garrison life in India when there was no enemy to fight." The same Nobel investigator "dismissed *The World Crisis*, Churchill's highly praised account of the First World War, as history." Hallstrom had found the autobiographical *My Early Life* "not entirely lacking in charm, or in artistic quality," but still, in his view, only Winston's four-volume biography of the Duke of Marlborough could serve as a measure of Churchill the historian.

Those were Hallstrom's findings in 1946, but in 1948 along came a second investigator for the Swedish Academy, Nils Ahnlund, who went beyond his own opinions of Winston's historical works. He, in fact, cited Cambridge University professor George Trevelyan, a "great admirer of Churchill's work," who had been "the first to propose Churchill for the Nobel Prize in spite of the violent abuse which Churchill had heaped upon the celebrated historian Macaulay, who was Trevelyan's great-uncle and the first biographer of Marlborough."

Ahnlund also was impressed by the great documentary value of Churchill's magnificent work on World War I, said Stromberg. "At no place in the exceptionally rich historical literature on that war, he observed, was the true pulse of the age to be sensed so well or the direct breath of the great events to be felt so clearly." And Ahnlund felt further that "Churchill was the incomparable painter of the history of our time."

Incomparable or not, Ahnlund concluded, "perhaps his historical work could not, by itself, justify the award of a Nobel Prize." Add Winston's "activity as an orator," however, and, "there would be no doubt that he would fulfill the conditions of the Prize, for Churchill was an orator without a peer in his century." Commented Ahnlund: "No man has better known how to awaken such an echo by his eloquence, or to reach so vast a public. It is, then, basically for his oratory that Churchill deserves the Prize; but his art as an orator is well framed by the rest of his production."

Still, that favorable report wasn't enough to persuade the Swedish Academy to award Winston its Nobel Prize for Literature . . . not for another five years, that is. Not until 1953 did the academy yield "to the appeals which came with ever greater urgency from all corners of the globe" and give him the prize "for his mastery of historical and biographical descriptions as well as for brilliant oratory in defending exalted human values."

Winston hoped to attend the presentation in Stockholm, "the only European capital which, to his regret, he had never visited," but he was to be held up by Dwight D. Eisenhower's international conference in Bermuda, held to discuss nuclear research and the mutual defense of Europe in the aftermath of Joseph Stalin's recent death. Thus, Clementine and their youngest daughter, Mary Soames, attended the Nobel banquet in Winston's place. There, Clementine read "her husband's acceptance speech—a charming address in which Churchill's delightful humor counter-pointed his graver statements, which were often moving." The nearly one thousand in the audience listened "in a deep silence" and responded "with a veritable thunder of applause" for the brilliant orator who wasn't there.

Runt Would Do

Sometimes known to be a bit parsimonious, Sir Winston no doubt had the best of intentions in mind when he ordered his animal doctor to find a nice puppy for his spinster secretary Grace Hamblin. It was to be a black poodle to take the place of Winston's own black poodle Rufus, who rather markedly had attached himself to Hamblin in the years before the dog died at Chartwell.

"Rufus, I'm sorry to say, took rather a liking to me," Hamblin once explained in a talk on her Chartwell memories. "Poodles are very one-man dogs, you know. And this made Sir Winston rather cross. He'd say, with his head down, 'You've stolen my dog's affection.' I didn't, really. It was just that I was there, and I took him on walks which nobody else did. No wonder the dog liked me. He was a good dog, because after Sir Winston had been away, he would always welcome him back—which was very decent of him."

When Rufus at last died, the elderly Churchill happened to be in a London hospital recovering from a broken hip. Back at Chartwell, Hamblin wondered how to convey the bad news, "because," she noted, "Rufus was quite a big thing in our lives." She telephoned Lady Churchill for guidance. "She said, 'You'd better write him a little note and I'd take it along to him.'" When he read the note, "the tears came to his eyes." But he also had immediate concern for his secretary. "Poor Miss," he apparently said, "she must have a puppy." Added Grace Hamblin: "So you see, I was forgiven."

But that was not the end of the story. Winston indeed procured a black poodle for her to take the place of Rufus in her affections. According to Hamblin, the veterinarian later revealed that Winston's instruction to him was a bit parsimonious in tone. "Would you find a little puppy for Miss," Churchill told the vet. "I think she'd like a black poodle. You know, she lives alone so it's for company. A runt will do." Said the forgiving secretary: "He wasn't really mean—he just thought it a pity to spend too much money."

Lion's Roar

Still prime minister, second go-round, Winston responded to celebrations and plaudits on his eightieth birthday, November 30, 1954, with a simple and humble statement: "It was the nation and the race dwelling all round the globe that had the lion's heart. I had the luck to be called upon to give the roar."

The official observances, with presentations of gifts by both houses of Parliament, were held in Westminster Hall before an audience of twenty-five hundred. To mark Winston's entrance, with Clementine by his side, a drummer beat out a V in Morse code, in remembrance of Winston's famous two-fingered "V for victory" trademark salute during World War II.

Clement Attlee—who had been Winston's deputy from 1940 to 1945 and succeeded him as prime minister in 1945 and now served as leader of the Opposition—called Winston "the last of the great orators who can touch the heights."

Aside from declaring he merely was the roar of the lion, Winston acknowledged on the spot, "I am now nearing the end of my journey." Then he added: "I hope I still have some service to render. However that may be, whatever may befall, I am sure I shall never forget the emotions of this day."

Harkening back to World War II, he said, "I have never accepted what many people have kindly said—namely, that I inspired the nation." The citizenry's will, he added, "was resolute and remorseless, and as it proved, unconquerable."

Meanwhile, tributes and gifts poured in from all over the world. Parliament presented Winston a portrait of himself by the artist Graham Sutherland. (Two years later, Clementine destroyed the portrait, explaining later that Winston always had disliked it and it had preyed on his mind. The unhappy artist responded that this was "an act of vandalism.")

In the meantime, because of his declining health, Winston stepped down as prime minister in 1955.

Additional note: Just two years earlier, in June 1953, Winston had suffered such a serious stroke, his doctor, Lord Moran, did not believe he would survive. Instead, John Keegan noted, Churchill "refused to give in to his symptoms . . . and, over the next four months dragged himself back to health by sheer determination."

Personal Glimpse

In Winston's final years, the great engine that had powered him for so long was visibly wearing down. At the same time, a busy world was moving on without him. But there still was his beloved retreat in Kent. "Chartwell never failed him, in good times or bad," wrote daughter Mary in her biography of Clementine. "Not even in the last sad years when, silent and remote from us all, he would sit for hours in the golden sunshine of the summer days, gazing out over his enchanted valley and lakes; down over the lushly green and tufted Wealden landscape beyond, which melts at last into the faint blue-gray line of the South Downs."

Winston and Randolph

Sadly, the same Winston Churchill who once had his problems relating to an aloof father also, many years later, had problems with a difficult son, and it's hard to say why. A chip off the old block to some degree, Randolph grew up to become a journalist, a combat veteran of World War II (for the exclusive, commando-like Special Air Service—SAS), and a politician—even, briefly, a Member of Parliament. Like his father, he enjoyed his toddy . . . but he very publicly didn't handle it nearly as well.

Notably, in the eyes of British historian Geoffrey Best, Randolph "managed to commit no faux pas" when standing in at the Kennedy White House for his ailing and aging father for the ceremony conferring honorary U.S. citizenship on Sir Winston in 1963. At the same time, Randolph "no doubt enjoyed delivering an acceptance speech that included a defiant affirmation of the sovereign equality with the United States of Great Britain," wrote Best in *Churchill: A Study in Greatness*.

Best also noted that Randolph was a "successful" journalist, even "clever," but he also was "combative and controversial and an unsuccessful politician." (A narrow loss in 1950 marked his fourth unsuccessful bid for a seat in Parliament; however, he did win an uncontested seat in a by- election in 1940.) Not the "ideal as his father's deputy," said Best, Randolph was "willful, explosive, capable of being very rude, and much given to drink."

While his eminent father "never doubted" Randolph's loyalty or literary ability and thus welcomed the son as "official" biographer telling Sir Winston's remarkable life story, their relationship, observed Best, "can be summed up as a series of rows, which neither could prevent happening and which both immediately regretted."

As a sad case in point, historian Sir Anthony Montague Brown, a private secretary to Sir Winston from 1952 to 1965, once witnessed an excruciating scene between the two on Aristotle "Ari" Onassis's yacht, the *Christina*. Introduced to the Greek shipping magnate by Randolph, Winston was treated in his declining years to a number of cruises aboard the *Christina*, beginning in 1958. For the most part, they were a great pleasure for the great statesman of the twentieth century. Best noted: "Between 1958 and 1963 Churchill sailed on the *Christina* no less then eight times, not only in the Mediterranean but also around the Caribbean and once even up to New York. Churchill found life on the *Christina*, and in Onassis's Monte Carlo hotel, entirely to his liking. He could have with him his whole entourage and as many of his family as were free to come. He could play bezique, his favorite, and other card games for hours on end. He was fussed over, rested, and as securely protected from intrusive eyes and unsympathetic strangers as he could desire."

On Sir Winston's last *Christina* voyage, in June 1963, Randolph and grandson Winston were included in the party. At first, private secretary Brown recounted (in *Long Sunset: Memoirs of Winston Churchill's Last Private Secretary*), Randolph had "behaved well, treating his father with respect and affection, and I was congratulating myself for having pushed for his inclusion." But all that changed one night at dinner after the yacht passed through the Straits of Medina and turned into the Adriatic Sea. Quite suddenly, Randolph "erupted like Stromboli," Brown recalled. "For no apparent reason his rage was directed at his father, but then he began to particularize with violent reproaches relating to his wartime marriage. What he said was unseemly in any circumstances, but in front of comparative strangers it was ghastly."

Both Brown and Onassis tried to divert him, but to no avail. "Short of hitting him on the head with a bottle, nothing could have stopped him. . . . It was one of the most painful scenes I have witnessed. I had previously discounted the tales I had heard of Randolph. Now I believed them all."

As for Sir Winston, he "made no reply at all, but stared at his son with an expression of brooding rage." He, in fact, soon went to his cabin. "I followed him and found him shaking all over. I feared that he would suffer another stroke, and sat drinking whiskey and soda with him until he was calmer."

In the aftermath of the ugly scene, Brown and Onassis decided they must find a way to remove Randolph from the ship as soon as possible. Onassis quickly made arrangements by setting up an exclusive interview for Randolph with the king or queen of Greece "at their palace on the eastern Greek mainland." This would entail putting into Corfu with the *Christina* the next evening and disembarking Randolph for a flight to Athens.

After "a harmonious but silent dinner" that day, it was done. Randolph departed humming "Get Me to the Church on Time," but the humming was somewhat disingenuous. "I accompanied him in the launch to the harbor," Brown reported. "After a while he fell silent and I saw he was weeping. 'Anthony,' he said, 'you didn't think that I was taken in by that plan of Ari's and yours, do you? I do so very much love that man [his father] but something always goes wrong between us.'" Well aware of the decline in Sir Winston's physical strength, Brown "could only hope that there would be enough time for Randolph to demonstrate his love and WSC [Winston] his."

As events turned out, Winston Churchill, age ninety, died less than two years later, on January 24, 1965, after even further physical weakening. Randolph never progressed farther than 1914 in his biography of his father, thanks to an "intemperate lifestyle bringing about his death in 1968, " noted Geoffrey Best.

Additional note: Winston and Clementine Churchill paid a painful price in grief over four of their five children. Their firstborn, Diana, born in 1909, was subject to depression, drank heavily, and died a suicide in 1963. Sarah, born in 1914, was an actress also troubled by drinking. She died young, in 1982. Randolph, born in 1914, had his problems, some of which are described above. Marigold, born in 1918, died in 1921. And Mary, born in 1922 and still living at this writing, "alone seemed to be happily normal," noted Best. Meanwhile, Mary once said in an interview with Graham Turner for the London *Daily Telegraph*, "Mama and Randolph never got on, which was partly because my beloved papa spoiled him something rotten. . . . That was really a reaction from the cold way his father had treated him, so he over-indulged Randolph dreadfully." Unfortunately, too, that "threw Mama into being the 'No' factor."

Last U.S. Visits

Among Churchill's postwar visits to the United States, one highlight was his 1954 get-together with Dwight D. Eisenhower, now president of the United States. These were tough cold war days, but Churchill was still eager to promote a summit meeting with the Russians, saying at one point, "Meeting jaw to jaw is better than war."

In fact, Winston's biographer Martin Gilbert once said—in a talk before the Royal Automobile Club, London, on March 18, 1991—Winston himself coined the word *summit* for a meeting of Soviet and Western leaders. "Churchill knew how to protect the West against an aggressive Soviet Union, hence his support for the Truman Doctrine, and for the North Atlantic Treaty Organization," Gilbert said. "But he also believed in trying to bring the Soviet Union to the negotiating table."

The fact is, a previously reluctant Eisenhower was about to go to Moscow for exactly such a meeting in 1960. But a U-2 incident (in which the Soviets shot down a U.S. spy plane over Russia, one of a series of such flights personally approved by Ike) aborted that plan, and the cold war then turned absolutely icy.

Meanwhile, Churchill had come to visit Ike again—in 1959, this time to stay at the White House and go with Ike to his farm at Gettysburg. Later, leaving from Andrews Air Force Base, Churchill looked down from the steps of his plane and said, "Farewell to the land . . ." He paused, then added, "of my mother. God bless you all."

He was back one last time, for his sixteenth visit to the United States, in April 1961, now eighty-six years old and traveling up the East Coast in easy stages— but also through a storm—from a stop in Palm Beach, Florida, to New York City aboard Aristotle Onassis's yacht, the ocean-going *Christina*.

John F. Kennedy was now president, and he invited Churchill to visit Washington via *Air Force One*, but Winston simply wasn't up to it. He did see his old friend Bernard Baruch before flying home from New York on April 14, 1961. Two years later son Randolph had to accept his honorary U.S. citizenship for him, because Winston, the great apostle of close Anglo-American ties, was too feeble to fly. In addition to Randolph, the ninety-two-year-old Bernard Baruch was among those who attended the White House ceremony.

Personals Potpourri

He called his bouts with depression "Black Dog." He insisted his future grave in Woodstock, England, should have a view of the window in the ground-floor cloakroom in Blenheim Palace where he was born. As a child, he rode a pony called Rob Roy (named after the Scottish rebel leader). His favorite music was Victorian music hall songs. And he loved Noel Coward's "Mad Dogs and Englishmen."

For his part, Noel Coward, while having dinner with Winston in May 1945, the European War just ending, "felt an upsurge of gratitude that melted into hero worship," he wrote in his memoir *Future Indefinite*. Suddenly "submerged" in emotion, he and dinner companions Venetia Montagu and Juliet Duff, "without exchanging a word, as simultaneously as though we had carefully rehearsed it, the three of us rose to our feet and drank Mr. Churchill's health."

Speaking of his health, his longtime friend Brendan Bracken wrote to fellow Churchill confidante Lord Beaverbrook (Max Aitken) in April 1958, when Winston was eighty-three: "Our friend Winston is, of course, a medical marvel. He had disregarded all the normal life-lengthening rules and has witnessed, doubtless with regret, but with some complacence, the burial of most of his doctors, save Charles [Wilson, Lord Moran]."

Bracken's observation came just after Winston turned down an invitation from President Eisenhower for a visit to the United States that spring. In March, he had been ill while on holiday in France.

Naturally, Winston's best subject in school was history. His favorite authors included Rudyard Kipling, Sir Walter Scott, and Robert Louis Stevenson. He once had tea with German chancellor Otto von Bismarck, he attended German war maneuvers with the Kaiser . . . and he exulted at the British sinking of the German battleship *Bismarck* in World War II but empathized for the sailors who went down with their fighting ship.

In his lifetime, he lived in more than thirty places—owned, borrowed, loaned, leased, or made available as official government residences. His nickname at Harrow was "Copperknob," for his red hair. His longest serving butler was Inches. His grandfather Leonard Jerome gave his name to the well-known thoroughfare Jerome Avenue in the Bronx, New York, hard by Yankee Stadium. Winston apparently once, if briefly, thought of buying a farm and settling down in Canada. His great-great-grandmother may have been an American Indian.

His favorite whiskey was Johnny Walker Red, and his pet champagne was Pol Roger, especially the 1947 vintage.

He didn't stutter, but he did lisp. "All his life," Dr. John Mather notes on the Churchill Centre Web site (www.winstonchurchill.org), "Churchill had an impediment of his speech, not unlike his father's speech defect, in which he also had difficulty in pronouncing the letter 's.'" Told by a specialist that he had no physical defect, Winston practiced and practiced at his speechmaking, "rehearsing such phrases as, 'The Spanish ships I cannot see for they are not in sight.'" He tended to avoid words beginning or ending with an S, and there was one word he always did absolutely mutilate. "To his great advantage," noted Mather, president of the Washington (D.C.) Society for Churchill. That word, in Winston's rendition, was something very much like "Narzees" for "Nazis."

John Mather has written extensively in refutation of easy acceptance of the theory that Winston's father, Lord Randolph, suffered from and died as a result of syphilis. "While syphilis may have been a reasonable diagnosis in the absence of modern techniques," Dr. Mather wrote, "the patient's temperament, combined with his speech and articulation problems and absence of dementia, is more consistent with a tumor deep in the left side of his brain."

Kings, princes, dukes, lords, and only three other commoners came before Winston in this ancient and honored post, ceremonially bestowed upon him with bells pealing and bands amarching after the war, but announced, actually, by the Royal Court on September 23, 1941. Supposedly reluctant on May 10, 1940, to appoint Winston, rather than Lord Halifax, as prime minister, George VI now rewarded Winston's remarkable leadership during Britain's greatest trial by fire by appointing him lord warden and admiral of the Cinque Ports.

For Winston, who loved history and tradition, along with all things naval or military, it was an honor to savor. The oldest of England's military honors, it harkens back to the days, even before William the Conqueror's appearance in 1066, when the authorities of five ports—Dover, Hastings, Hythe, Romney, and Sandwich—formed a common naval force for their mutual defense. Even William treated the confederacy gingerly, giving it certain tax exemptions in return for its maintenance of a protective fleet. The Cinque Ports held considerable power and had their own members in Parliament until later kings finally took the steps needed to create a national, or Royal, navy. As the London *Times* said on September 24, 1941, "to this august tradition of Keeper of the Gates of England and Watcher of the English Seas, Mr. Churchill now succeeds." Only upon Winston's death in 1965, was he succeeded by the obvious: Queen Elizabeth II.

Franklin D. Roosevelt once set up his good friend Winston for a good joke at lunch by seating him next to a woman who was a zealous crusader for an independent India. Sure enough, at her first opportunity, she said, "Mr. Prime Minister, what do you intend to do about those wretched Indians?" Unperturbed, Winston shot back: "Madam, to which Indians do you refer? Do you by chance refer to the second greatest nation on earth which under benign and beneficent British rule has multiplied and prospered exceedingly or do you mean those unfortunate Indians of the North American continent which under your administration are practically extinct?"

He did not subsist on just a few hours of sleep, as his late-night working schedule for most of his adult life might suggest. Winston once told Walter Greabner, *Time-Life* representative in London, after the war: "You must sleep some time between lunch and dinner, and no half-way measures. Take off your clothes and get into bed. That's what I always do. Don't think you will be doing less work because you sleep during the day." During the war, he also said, he often was "obliged" to work far into the night. "I had to see reports, take decisions and issue instructions that could not wait until the next day. And at night I'd also dictate minutes requesting information which my staff could assemble for me in the morning—and place before me when I woke up."

But there was another reason to sleep during the day. "Sleep enables you to be at your best in the evening when you join your wife, family and friends for dinner. That is the time to be at your best—a good dinner, with good wines . . . champagne is very good . . . then some brandy—that is the great moment of the day."

Winston at Chartwell (and presumably elsewhere also) always was, Lord Hailes told biographer Martin Gilbert, "a meticulous host. He would watch everyone all the time to see whether they wanted anything. He was a tremendous gent in his own house. He was very quick to see anything that might hurt someone. He got very upset if someone told a story that might be embarrassing to somebody else in the room. He had a delicacy about other people's feelings. In the house and to his guests he was the perfection of thoughtfulness."

On a somewhat related point, Churchill scholars have their doubts about the story that Winston told a female guest met in Virginia Gov. Harry F. Byrd's executive mansion in 1929 that she should pin a corsage on her "white meat" (for "breast"), since he always and notably was a gentleman around the ladies.

In *Churchill: A Life*, biographer Martin Gilbert told London's Royal Automobile Club in 1991 that he tried:

> to show Churchill's enormous resilience, humor, joie de vivre, strength of mind, strength of character, and strength of purpose, despite the terrible and long periods of adversity. He was always brimming over with ideas to serve his country in every possible sphere. You will see that in his very first speech at Bath in 1897 the young, the very young, soldier returned from the North-West Frontier of India and proposed to a Conservative audience that the Government should introduce a system of profit-sharing so that a worker would, in a good year for the enterprise in which he worked, have some benefit, and therefore some reason for looking forward and working for success; a proposal which Churchill repeated at [the] Conservative Conference at Blackpool fifty years later, in 1948.

What did Winston tell Lady Mary Astor, born Nancy Langhorne of Albemarle County, Virginia, and later married to Englishman Waldorf Astor and herself a Member of Parliament, when she allegedly said (at a weekend house party at Blenheim Palace in the 1930s): "Winston, if I were married to you, I'd put poison in your coffee?" His alleged riposte: "Nancy, if I were married to you, I'd drink it." The authoritative Churchill Centre Web site reports: "The famous exchange between them is apparently not apocryphal, as we had previously believed."

Winston and Clementine occasionally had their squalls. "Mummy could be very freezing and cutting if she was angry," daughter Mary once told London *Daily Telegraph* interviewer Graham Turner. "Yet she wasn't at all a cold figure. Underneath, she was really boiling with passion. She once threw a dish of spinach at my father, though she wasn't a bad-tempered woman and recovered very quickly. Father, on the other hand, was frightfully noisy when he lost his temper. . . . I don't remember long periods of chill at Chartwell. There were blow-ups and boo-hoo and banging doors and then it was over and they were reconciled. Summer storms!"

Meanwhile, whatever happened to Chartwell itself? Gradually, the old Churchill lifestyle at the country retreat reasserted itself after the war, but, wrote daughter

Mary, "never on the pre-war scale." She noted in the foreword to a National Trust booklet on Chartwell, "In 1946 a group of Winston's friends and admirers bought Chartwell and presented it to the National Trust [Britain's historical preservation organization], with the proviso that Winston and Clementine should live there for their lifetimes." As a result, their wonderful and historic country home is open to the public today, as are Blenheim Palace and the War Cabinet Rooms/Churchill Museum in London. All three, plus the Imperial War Museum in London, are must-see stops for anyone remotely interested in Winston Churchill and/or the history of World War II.

As for Winston's brother, Jack, his London home was blown up during the war, and he briefly lived with Winston and Clementine at No. 10 Downing Street or its wartime annex. He died on February 23, 1947, hardly two years after the war in Europe ended. "He had no fear & little pain," Winston wrote to Lord Hugh Cecil, best man at his wedding. "The only thing Jack worried about was England. I told him it would be all right." The timing had been a sad sequel to the joyful day, February 11, 1947, when Mary married Christopher Soames.

Man for the Ages

Who, at the end of 1999, should have been regarded or even titled Man of the First Millennium . . . that is, of the first thousand years since the birth and life of Christ? Shakespeare? Napoleon or Leonardo da Vinci? Einstein? No, no, and no, on all counts, repeatedly argued writer, lecturer, and twenty-seven-year parliamentary veteran Winston S. Churchill. No, it should be his grandfather, Sir Winston S. Churchill, father of the younger Winston's father, Randolph.

"His was a remarkable life to which none can hold a candle," this chip off the old block argued in a speech he repeatedly made during a promotional tour of the United States toward the end of the millennium for his book *The Great Republic*, a collection of his grandfather's writings about America. "When I call him 'Man of the Millennium,' I do so with deliberation and conviction."

And why so? First and foremost, clearly, "in the greatest war in history, no single individual made a greater contribution to turning the tide of victory and securing a favorable outcome than Winston Churchill." And this despite the fact that just weeks after Winston's ascension to prime minister, only a resolute Britain remained, quite alone, in the path of the Nazi onslaught across Western Europe.

"Viewed objectively, Britain's position was hopeless," summarized his grandson. "Hitler had amassed a huge war-machine which was out-producing Britain in almost every field of military production by a factor of two or even three to one. Europe was at his mercy. Soviet Russia was his ally. Only 21 miles of English Channel stood between him and his next intended conquest. The mood at home was divided." That is, many members of Parliament, even some government ministers, favored a negotiated settlement with Hitler, which would have meant Nazi rule—"concentration camps and death camps would have been established in England's green and pleasant land."

But Sir Winston wouldn't allow it. His "strength as a war leader rested in his burning conviction, in the teeth of all the odds, that in our Island, we were unconquerable." Then, too, there was "his ability to communicate that spirit of resolution to the British nation."

As stated during the war by the American broadcaster Edward R. Murrow, and echoed by John F. Kennedy, "Churchill mobilized the English language and sent it into battle." Added to his memorable wartime speeches was his own sense of destiny, his grandson recalled. He cited Sir Winston's recollection of the night he became prime minister: "I was conscious of a profound sense of relief. . . . I felt as if I were walking with destiny and that all my past life had been but a preparation for this hour and for this trial."

Emboldened by that same sense of destiny, he, as a young man, "seems to have concluded that he was bullet proof and, after graduating from Harrow to Sandhurst, he proceeded to launch himself into a military career with an almost complete lack of regard for his personal safety." In that regard, he made it his business, using all influences at his command, his mother included, "to seek out wars wherever they were to be found with the aim of earning a reputation for bravery."

On top of dangerous exploits in the battle zones of Cuba, northwest India, the Sudan, and South Africa, he then survived the wreck of an airplane in the earliest days of aviation, served in the front-line trenches of Flanders during World War I, and endured a painful collision with a taxicab in New York City. "One cannot but help reflect that his preservation through all these hazards was nothing short of miraculous," the younger Winston noted.

But then, "as remarkable as his firm belief in his own destiny, was the incredible roller coaster of his political career, which spanned 55 years from his election to Parliament in 1900, aged 26 in the reign of Queen Victoria, to the reign of Queen Elizabeth and the thermonuclear age." Amazingly, too, "on no fewer than four occasions his political career hit rock bottom and was judged by many to be finished. But each time he climbed from the abyss."

The first such fall came, of course, when he was made "the scapegoat" for the failure of "the Dardanelles landings." Within two years, though, he was "back again under Lloyd George, first as Minister of Munitions and then Colonial Sec-retary." Out again with the fall of the Liberals in 1922, the senior Winston once again bounced back as both a member of Parliament and as chancellor of the ex-chequer. "But then in 1929, following the defeat of the Tories, he found himself cast into the wilderness this time for fully ten years, during which he became in-creasingly alienated from his party over the rearmament of Germany." These ten years "were undoubtedly the toughest period of his life." Regardless, "he saw with the utmost clarity the looming danger and tried, desperately, to warn the world before it was too late—but all in vain."

Still, redemption lay ahead yet again, as war broke out in 1939, and the elder Winston once more was appointed first lord of the admiralty. "There it fell to him for the second time in a quarter-century to prepare the Fleet for war." But this was not yet the end of the remarkable Winston Churchill story . . .

"When he became Prime Minister the following year he was already 65 years of age and qualified to draw the old-age pension." Next, after his inspiring wartime leadership came his final and fourth fall. "After six long years of war, dur-ing which he led Britain and the world to victory over Hitler, he was abruptly cast aside by the British electorate." And finally, another resurgence: "Against all the odds, in 1951 at the age of 76, he made his fourth and final comeback from the politically dead, becoming Prime Minister again and remaining in office until just past his eightieth birthday."

But there was so much more to his life story than political service and leader-ship. "By the time of his death at the age of 90, he had published some fifty vol-umes of history, biography and speeches [to say nothing of his Nobel prize for literature]. At his beloved home of Chartwell in Kent there were nearly 500 can-vasses that he had painted, some of remarkable quality. In addition, he built, largely with his own hands, three cottages and a high [brick] wall round his exten-sive vegetable garden. And to think that, in between, he managed to find the time to beat the daylights out of Hitler."

And so, from a grandson and namesake who was admittedly "biased," a summing-up that was more than fair in any case.

Additional note: On a related point of greatest this or greatest that, Sir Winston was voted "greatest Briton of all time" in a 2002 BBC poll that generated more than a million votes. "Participants in the survey voted the Second World War leader top of the list of the country's 100 most significant individuals with 447,423 votes," the BBC announced. Thus, he received almost half the vote . . . his nearest rival, engineer Isambard Kingdom Brunel, lagged behind by 56,000 votes. By contrast, Oliver Cromwell came in tenth, and last on the list: Adm. Lord Horatio Nelson, ninth, and Queen Elizabeth I, eighth. Princess Di was third in the polling, Charles Darwin fourth, and William Shakespeare fifth, followed by Isaac Newton and John Lennon (of the Beatles). Voted second on the month-long survey was Brunel, for whom Brunel University was named. The BBC asserted that it "identified people trying to rig the voting" and "eliminated" their choices, but the BBC also noted that students from Brunel "were behind a 'legitimate' campaign to get their institution's namesake out in front."

Final Days

The decline was long, grim days interspersed with bright ones, but always downhill . . . and naturally none too easy on all those involved. The beginning of the end perhaps was signaled by Winston's fall at their Hyde Park Gate London home in mid-November 1960. He broke a small bone high in his neck but made "an astonishingly good recovery," daughter Mary wrote in her biography of her mother.

Even so, the vicissitudes of old age had set in. He made his last visit to the United States the following April, that strictly private visit aboard the *Christina*, and he managed to visit the French Riviera four times in 1961. There, he was a "habitual" visitor at the Hotel de Paris in Monte Carlo . . . but in the summer of 1962 he fell at the hotel and broke a hip, "necessitating two operations and a prolonged recovery period."

During Winston's convalescence at Middlesex Hospital, a visibly worn Clementine set about turning his former office at 28 Hyde Park Gate into a bedroom so he could avoid stairs. She also had a lift installed from the ground floor to the dining room on the lower ground floor, "so that Winston could still come down to meals, and also have easy access to the garden, where he so loved to sit."

After this most recent accident, though, it would be "a whole year before he went to Chartwell again." For Clementine, always by his side, it was "a long vigil." Exhausted, she had spent weeks recovering in a hospital while he was visiting the United States in the spring of 1961. Meanwhile, Christmas of 1962 was spent in London instead of at Chartwell. After that, Mary noted: "Now not only was Winston physically less strong, but mentally he had become more lethargic. Gradually the silences became longer, and he was content to sit gazing into the fire. . . . He rarely initiated a subject, and his deafness was an added and most daunting barrier to communication."

In mid-August 1963, he suffered a "vascular stoppage" above his left ankle, sending him to bed for a time, even though he recovered. Meanwhile, suffering "nervous exhaustion and mental anxiety," Clementine, ten years younger than Winston, was hospitalized again for three weeks. In this same sad year, daughter Sarah suddenly lost the husband she had married just the year before, to a massive coronary, and Diana, estranged from former husband Duncan Sandys (who had remarried), took an overdose of sleeping pills and died.

During the same year, Winston had been forced to face up to his frailties and decide against running again for his Woodford seat in Parliament. Thus he was present in the House of Commons for a last time on July 28, 1964. "He had been a Member almost continuously for over half a century."

The next day, a House contingent led by Prime Minister Sir Alec Douglas-Home called upon Winston and immediate family members at Hyde Park Gate to present him with a House resolution acknowledging his pending retirement and, more important, thanking him for "his services to Parliament, to the nation and to the world." The same resolution also cited, "above all, his inspiration of the British people when they stood alone, and his leadership until victory was won."

After 1963, Winston never left England again . . . but he and Clementine spent "the better part of three months" in the summer and early fall of 1964 at Chartwell. Clementine's health was improved, "but she felt Winston needed her more than ever, as slowly but perceptibly his health and spirits declined," wrote Mary. "Clementine, like all of us, was conscious that the sands were gently running out." During that year, a highlight for both of Mary's parents, Clementine had represented Winston at the formal opening of Churchill College at Cambridge University, founded by Winston in 1958.

This, of course, was Winston's ninetieth year, and his birthday on November

30 "brought an avalanche of good wishes." The queen sent flowers, and the prime minister, Harold Wilson, visited. Close family members gathered for the birthday dinner party, but "in our hearts we knew the end could not be far off."

Indeed, on January 11, 1965, just weeks later, they learned that Winston experienced a heart "spasm" and a stroke . . . in the days following he gradually became paralyzed on his left side. Lord Moran, his longtime physician, said Winston would be gravely impaired, if he survived.

Mary's husband, Christopher, on January 12 offered a silent and remote Winston a glass of champagne. "Winston looked at him vaguely. 'I'm so bored with it all," he said. These were, I think the last coherent words he spoke to any member of the family."

In the days following, he fell into semi-sleep, semi-consciousness, slipping always, it seemed, farther and farther away. His marmalade cat "curled up at his feet."

He once, allegedly, had predicted he would die on the anniversary of his father's death on January 24, 1895.

Mary now moved into the house at Hyde Park Gate to be with Clementine and Winston full time, since it was quite clear what was happening. "My mother said she would like a priest to come, and I telephoned Philip Hayllar, the vicar at Eridge. . . . He slipped into the house, unremarked [by the press]. . . . My mother and I knelt on either side of my father's bed while Philip Hayllar said some simple prayers and blessed him."

Others in the family were constantly in and out as Winston now lay quietly in his bedroom at Hyde Park Gate. "It was such a peaceful scene—the gently lighted room full of flowers; the quiet form in the big bed, with the beautiful hands spread on the quilt," observed daughter Mary.

"For fourteen days he was not seen to move," wrote Lord Moran. "His strength left him slowly as if he were loathe to give up life." Finally, during the night of January 23–24, "it appeared that a crisis was at hand." His breathing was shallow and labored, and by eight the next morning it ceased. "Mary, sitting by his side, looked up at me. I got up and bent over the bed, but he had gone."

On January 24, 1965, seventy years to the day after his father Randolph's death, Winston was gone. He would join his father, his American-born mother Jennie, and his brother Jack in the little churchyard at the Bladon parish church, where they all lay, with a view of Blenheim Palace where Winston himself was so suddenly born little more than ninety years before.

☆　☆　☆

Additional note: Winston Churchill lay in state at Westminster Hall, where some three hundred thousand people slowly shuffled past his coffin to pay their parting respects. Winston then began his last travel on this earth, borne by gun carriage to St. Paul's Cathedral in London for England's first state funeral for a commoner since that of the Duke of Wellington more than a century earlier. Fifteen heads of state and six sovereigns were among the six thousand able to cram inside the cathedral. A barge then carried his remains on the Thames River to Waterloo Station, from which Winston was carried by train on the long-familiar trip to Woodstock and the Bladon churchyard adjoining Blenheim Palace.

⎯ ⭑ **PART 6** ⭑ ⎯
His American Mother
Jennie

by Ingrid Smyer

SHE WAS TERRIBLY BEAUTIFUL. She was terribly intelligent. She was terribly able. She was terribly resourceful. She was terribly courageous. She was terribly daring.

All of these attributes she used to the fullest while living a terribly exciting life.

A life so vivid that it could have leaped right out of a breathtaking novel.

Born into an America still in its frontier stage, Jeanette Jerome was the second of four daughters born to Leonard Jerome and Clarissa Hall Jerome. The year was 1854.

It was January 9, a cold and blustery winter day, when she was born in a modest three-story red-brick house on Amity Street in the Cobble Hill section of Brooklyn, New York.

But such modest surroundings would not be hers for very long.

It was a time in America when industries were growing like mushrooms across the land, a boom time often accompanied by unrestrained corruption at the financial centers and even at the seat of government in Washington.

Thus it was the perfect environment for the dashing Leonard Jerome and his favorite younger brother, Lawrence, to stake their claims at every chance to win a quick fortune. And so they did.

In addition to his background as a lawyer, Leonard was a newspaper editor in Rochester (NY), the U.S. Consul at Trieste, an art collector; part-owner of the *New York Times*, and a stock speculator . . . or, you might say, stock manipulator.

Newspapers called him the "King of Wall Street," because he was a famous speculator who could make and lose millions of dollars and then make them again. He was also known as the "Father of American Turf," for an influence on organized thoroughbred horse racing that contributed to its social acceptance in the United States.

The Jerome brothers came from a family of soldiers and farmers. Early forefather Timothy Jerome arrived at Meriden, Connecticut, in America's colonial days with a royal grant in his pocket that led to a monopoly on salt making in the area—needless to say, he died a rich man. During the American Revolution, Timothy's son Samuel fought the British alongside his own five sons. One of them, Aaron, married a cousin of George Washington. Since Washington had no lineal descendant, Jennie's father, a descendant of Aaron, liked to claim that he was of the closest kin to the Founding Father.

Aaron and his wife had many sons, among them Isaac, a farmer and Bible-toting, quiet man who began and ended every day with prayer. He married a dynamic Scotswoman named Aurora, whose father, Reuben Murray, also had fought in the American Revolution. Much like her dynamic father, Aurora had a reputation of being ambitious, smart, and witty, but the better part of her energy was spent bearing and raising a brood of twelve children. She and Isaac had nine sons and three daughters; the fifth son born to them was Leonard . . . Leonard Jerome.

The Jeromes lived on a farm in the hill country of Pompey, New York. Here, Isaac expected his sons to farm the family land, but Aurora had bigger ideas. She wanted her sons educated and then sent out into the world to seek their fortunes.

That is exactly what Leonard did, after seeing two of his older brothers packed off to the College of New Jersey (Princeton today). He followed suit in 1836 but stressed family finances dictated that he transfer into Union College in Schenectady, New York.

Surprising fact: One of his cousins, James Roosevelt, father of Franklin Delano Roosevelt, attended Union College several years later.

By one account, meanwhile, Leonard was graduated because an influential uncle, Judge Hiram Jerome (allegedly a former law partner of Abraham Lincoln) may have pulled a few strings allowing his young nephew Leonard to receive his bachelor's degree. Other accounts say that Leonard graduated at the top of his class. Whatever the case, by all accounts, the handsome and popular young man was involved in several college pranks—one of which took place on a July 3 at the College of New Jersey and became legendary.

On the eve of that Fourth of July, it seems, Leonard decided a cannon the British once had removed to New Brunswick should be returned to its rightful place. He organized a group of patriotic students, and together they began moving the cannon by horse-drawn cart, but the immense weight of the big gun was too much for the cart, which fell apart and dumped the cannon in a field. Undaunted, the college boys found a more substantial cart and continued on to their destination, finally returning the cannon to its original place—where it still proudly stands today on the campus of Princeton University.

Meanwhile, after his graduation, Leonard and favorite brother Lawrence were invited to join Uncle Hiram's staff in Palmyra, New York, then a thriving town on the Erie Canal amid the brightly painted packet boats passing by with all sorts of people and goods. When these two tall, handsome, and athletic young men with bushy moustaches arrived in town, they soon met two attractive sisters, Catherine and Clarissa Hall. The lovely sisters came from an entirely different background from the dashing brothers, but no matter . . . the Jerome brothers married the Hall sisters, although several years apart. Lawrence married Catherine quite soon, but it took five years for Leonard to propose to Clarissa.

The Halls were gentlefolk, and Clarissa, who later shortened her name to Clara, never let anyone forget it. Her parents had died when she was only two, and she and her siblings were split up among several couples. She and Catherine were living with an aunt when the Jerome brothers met them. Their father, Ambrose Hall, himself strikingly tall and handsome, had been a wealthy landowner and a prominent member of the New York State Assembly. Their mother, also a Clarissa (Willcox), came from a Massachusetts family of early settlers. The Hall women were known for their black hair, dark features, and high cheekbones, which they referred to as HALL-marks.

Ralph Martin takes note in *Jennie: The Life of Lady Randolph Churchill* of the family's whispered legend that these features came through a grandmother who was raped by an Iroquois. But other accounts say that Jennie's grandmother Anna Baker and her mother came from Nova Scotia, and there were no Iroquois living there at that time.

Whatever the real story, many years later Clarissa Hall Jerome's son-in-law Moreton Frewen referred to her as "Sitting Bull" and her sister Catherine as "Hatchet Face." Five years before his death, grandson Winston Churchill allegedly told one of his doctors, "You may not know it, but I am descended from a Seneca Indian squaw who was an ancestor of my mother."

Uncle Hiram put a bit of distance between Clarissa and her beau, Leonard, when he moved his law practice to Rochester, taking his nephews with him. The handsome Jerome brothers were soon swept up in Rochester's social scene. According to biographer Martin, one local socialite remembered the brothers as "screamingly funny . . . very popular with the ladies owing to the dashing manner in which they rode high-spirited horses." Distance or no, Leonard and Clarissa were married in 1849.

The brothers soon were thriving in various enterprises, including publishing a newspaper, the *Daily American*, through which they offered political support to like-thinking Whig Millard Fillmore, U.S. vice president at the time. For championing the vice president and his ideas, Leonard was rewarded by Fillmore—when he became president upon the death of Zachary Taylor—with an appointment to the consulship of the independent state of Trieste. Moving to this center of culture on the Adriatic Sea, the Jeromes took along both their daughter Clarita and her seven-year-old friend Lillie Greenough, later to become one of Jennie Jerome's closest companions. Leonard loved the fine art and music Trieste offered, while Clarissa thrilled to the cosmopolitan European atmosphere. Called back to the United States upon Franklin Pierce's election to the presidency, Leonard was sorry on one level but happy on another to resume his many business ventures.

Back in Brooklyn, Clarissa became pregnant, and here, Jeanette, forever to be known as Jennie, was born—at what is now 167 Amity Street, even though a plaque on a home at 426 Henry Street for many years incorrectly stated she was born there (the Jeromes had moved just before Jennie's birth). By this time, the Leonard Jeromes were quite affluent; little Jennie thus was assured of an upbring-ing in comfort and privilege. As a young lady of such circumstance, she was ex-pected to master the French language, study voice and piano, and read the classics, along with such American fare as *Uncle Tom's Cabin*, *The Scarlet Letter*, and the McGuffey readers for children. Learning the art of needlework was yet another requirement, as was the socially important issue of correct deportment. The girls were expected to curtsey and the boys to bow on greeting adults; young-sters of either gender were to remain standing until given permission to sit.

In addition, young ladies like Jennie were expected to know the correct order of a household. That order, as recalled in biographer Charles Higham's *Dark Lady: Winston Churchill's Mother and Her World*: "butler came first, followed by the housekeeper and the maids, from ladies' maid to kitchen hand, down to the humblest drudge."

By the age of eight, Jennie was sent off to Miss Lucy Green's exclusive school for girls on Fifth Avenue in Manhattan. This dreary red-brick building stood on what was once an execution site, where prisoners were hanged in public, a back-ground only adding to the gloomy atmosphere of the establishment. Lucy Green, dressed in grim gray, reflected the harsh program she expected the young girls to undertake. Not only was each girl to carry heavy chairs to and from the dining table, they were to set the places, remove, wash, dry, and return the dishes to the kitchen. They also had to attend chapel and memorize the fire-and-brimstone ser-mons preached by bleak old theologian Dr. George B. Cheever.

Leonard, on the other hand, thought that girls should have every opportunity in all fields of endeavor, and Jennie soon excelled in pony riding, ice-skating, and other outdoor activities. In terms of personality, Higham wrote: "She was strong-willed, sharp, single-minded and passionately in love with life. She adored her laughing Blackbeard the Pirate of a father far more than she cared for her still, chaste and humorless mother, and she and her sister Clarita were very close."

Jennie had two other sisters, Camille and Leonie. Their father had recently acquired the Bathgate estate at Fordham in Westchester County, a property that held an old racetrack. Here, the sisters loved to romp and play, and Jennie could ride her horse to her heart's content. Here, too, they were free as the wind and enjoying life to the fullest. But in 1863, tragedy struck when six-year-old Camille died of a fever. Jennie was devastated. More than ever she valued her sisters, five-year-old Leonie and twelve-year-old Clarita.

It was a time when death seemed to be everywhere, with the Civil War raging at high pitch, but Jennie later reminisced that all she remembered was that "every little Southerner she met at dancing school was 'a wicked rebel,' to be pinched if possible." Her father was strongly committed to the Union. After the assassination of President Lincoln, Jennie, then twelve, always carried the memories of gloom and doom. "I remember our house in Madison Square [they had moved into Manhattan] draped from top to bottom in white and black and the whole of New York looking like one gigantic mausoleum."

In no time, Jennie's "pirate" father became a lion on Wall Street, a stockjobber, and manipulator. One day he would make a killing in stocks, the next he was almost ruined. Jennie understood even as a child that playing the stock market was like a high-stakes poker game. The years after the Civil War were daring times for Northern businessmen, Leonard very much included. In fact, he reputedly used the crafty ploy of having a friend at the *New York Herald* announce in the paper that a certain stock was in trouble. He would bide his time until the price went down, then he would buy the stock at its bottom price. Next, he would turn around and have a friend at the *New York Times* write a story refuting the *Herald*'s original story. Leonard would then jump in with a sell order when the stock went up in price again, making a killing on the transaction.

With the Civil War years passed, America was entering its Gilded Age. But making money, and not always in ethical manner, was just one of Jerome's interests. These days, too, Jennie's father turned his attention to art, music, yachting, thoroughbred horse racing, and a bit of womanizing. But mostly he focused on horses. He and financier August Belmont formed the Coaching Club, a fashionable four-in-hand carriage-driving club. Jerome's horses were trained to rear up and prance entertainingly for "the gay and laughing ladies in gorgeous costumes," a reporter noted.

But that was only a beginning. With their joint sponsorship of thoroughbred horse racing, Jerome and Belmont together changed the way society viewed the sport. As one such contribution, Jerome built an elaborate track on his Bathgait estate with grandstand seating for eight thousand, along with a magnificent clubhouse and additional facilities for polo, sleighing, and ice-skating. With his help, horse racing was becoming the "Sport of Kings."

The starry-eyed Jennie was thrilled on opening day at the Jerome Park Racetrack on September 25, 1866, an extravaganza described by the *New York Tribune* as "the social event of all time . . . a new era in horse-racing." Indeed, one of the special guests in attendance was none other than Civil War hero Ulysses S. Grant.

Before all was said and done, Leonard Jerome also would be an organizer of the American Jockey Club and creator of the Sheepshead Bay Racetrack, which served the Coney Island Jockey Club. The first Belmont Stakes, named for his friend August Belmont and today best known as one of horse racing's Triple Crown events, was run at the Jerome racetrack in 1867. Just for good measure, if a bit unrelated, Jerome also established the American Academy of Music. The same wheeling and dealing entrepreneur, who often did his yachting with William Kissam Vanderbilt, still is remembered by place names in the city that was his home for many years: Jerome Avenue and the Jerome Park Reservoir in the Bronx were named for him, as was Jerome Avenue in Brooklyn.

If the opening of Jerome Park was a thrill for young Jennie Jerome, meanwhile, her adoring father would be offering even more thrills to come. On December 1, 1866, Jennie, her mother, and sisters were at Sandy Hook near New York to see him off on a daring race across the Atlantic in James Gordon Bennett's yacht *Henrietta* for a sixty-thousand-dollar prize against competitors Pierre Lorillard in the *Vesta* and the wealthy Osgood brothers in the *Fleetwing*.

It was to be another triumph for Leonard the risk-taker as he and his crew rounded the shores of the coast of England to a wild reception. Queen Victoria, among others, sent congratulations, and the Royal Yacht Squadron at Cowes on the Isle of Wight gave an elaborate reception. What irony, too, for Cowes would play a pivotal role in Jennie's life a few years later.

While her father was celebrating on the Isle of Wight, though, Jennie was sad to know he would miss her thirteenth birthday. But on December 30, one day before the new year and just ten days before Jennie's birthday, the take-charge Leonard was devising a way to return for his daughter's special day.

Brother Lawrence, who had been a member of the winning yacht's crew, could double in England as his brother Leonard, for they resembled each other very much. Who would know, other than the other sailing contestants, and they wouldn't tell.

Thus, while the real Leonard was making his way to Liverpool to catch the *City of Baltimore*, Lawrence, acting as Leonard, gave a brilliant acceptance speech with lots of humor that had everyone in stitches, according to biographer Higham. All the while Jerome was speeding across the Atlantic—on this crossing he again was competing with time and again he won, with his ship arriving on January 9.

Jennie was at Jerome Park for her birthday celebrations and the opening of a brand-new ice-skating rink, when who should appear after all—in a donkey cart—but her loving father! A happy and successful surprise that, of course, was duly reported in the *New York Times*.

Indeed, newspapers and magazines were constantly full of Jerome family happenings, but the gossip columnists soon were citing Leonard's reputed affairs. It was titillating reading—not only the excitement of racing yachts and horses, but Leonard's womanizing. Jennie, along with the general public, was reading these accounts. But to her, according to biographer Martin, all the notoriety only made her father even more of a dashing figure. And Leonard always seemed to find time to take favorite daughter Jennie to the opera or a concert or a matinee. Jennie appreciated his efforts to "improve my mind," whereas older sister Clarita's interests, like their mother's, were more attuned to clothes, fashions, and the latest hair styles. Youngest sister Leonie still was barely ten.

The Jerome lifestyle might have seemed all glamour to the casual reader, but there was a downside . . . the family was distressed, indeed quite embarrassed, when Leonard's offer of five thousand dollars as an annual prize for senior classmen at his alma mater, the College of New Jersey, was turned down. Perhaps his prankster days at the college, plus his shady business dealings, were the reasons. In any case, Clarissa about this time felt unable to compete in the social world of New York against the likes of August Belmont's wife, daughter of Commo. Matthew Perry, whose high style, jewels, and French manner were the envy of society. Also stung by the notoriety of her husband's blatant affairs, Clarissa announced she was moving to Paris with the children. Leonard, it turned out, was happy to leave the New York scene and join them for the time being as well.

With the family soon settled in an apartment on the Rue Malesherbes, in "Gay Paree," and her father soon traveling back and forth to America on business, Jennie was thrilled to be living in the City of Lights. Here, too, she and Clarita could renew their childhood friendship with Lillie Greenough, who had married American expatriate banker Charles Moulton and lived at the Chateau de La Petit Val, a magnificent setting just outside of Paris, complete with a moat, drawbridge, and formal gardens.

The year was 1867, an exciting time to be in the French capital, with dangerously turbulent events soon to follow. Leading the excitements for Leonard Jerome's teenaged girls was the Paris Universal Exposition, which attracted important royalty and nobility from all over Europe. The Prince of Wales, along with French Emperor Napoleon III and his glamorous wife Eugenie, attended from time to time, as well as the czar of Russia and emperor of Austria-Hungary.

But more excitement was in store. Clarita was presented to the imperial court. Now a fifteen-year-old romantic, Jennie glowed with pride at the vision of big-sister Clarita in her low-cut gown of billowing white tulle. Jennie was not envious, just impatient to have her teen years hurry by so she, too, could be free of chaperons, little-girl clothes, and bedtime curfews.

The fast-blossoming Jennie was full of vitality . . . and she put it to constructive use. Her love of music and innate self-discipline led to hours of practice at the piano. Then, too, when her father was in town, he would escort her to the theater, opera, and concerts. Obviously enjoying the family move to Paris himself, he also took her on picnics or on afternoon horseback rides in the Bois de Boulogne. A handsome sophisticated man of the world, he was the perfect squire to introduce her to the adult society of Paris.

His adored Jennie was turning into a beautiful little woman. Dark hair bounced into little curls atop her head, eyes full of daring and set in a perfectly sculptured face, she was ready to taste life on her own terms. Not only her natural beauty and maturing figure, but her personal magnetism soon had her surrounded by young swains waiting in line to be her escort. But her older sister's complicated romances, in which Jennie played the proverbial role of messenger, discouraged any thoughts Jennie might have had of marriage for herself. "I'm never going to marry," she once told her father. "I'm going to be a musician." But life plays its little tricks, and though Jennie would become quite accomplished as a pianist she would also most certainly become the marrying type.

In the meantime, at age fifteen in 1869 and living in the most glamorous city in Europe, Jennie was too young to attend royal court events, while around her and her family, Europe's political situation rapidly was deteriorating—France and Prussia were at loggerheads and war was imminent. On the personal level, the young Jennie bemoaned the thought that she might never be presented to the emperor and empress. For the adults making up her world, however, fears of revolution stirred memories of the terrors that wracked late eighteenth-century France and brought down the Bourbons. Indeed, violence was breaking out. Supporters of Emperor Napoleon III were the target, and swirling crowds of students and laborers invaded wealthy districts to hurl sticks and bricks through windows. Even so, Madam Jerome, apparently hoping things would calm down, made no immediate effort to leave Paris.

But the day after Jennie's sixteenth birthday, January 10, 1870, real riots erupted, houses on the street where they lived were set afire, hundreds were killed in Paris, and many more seriously injured. The Jeromes, staying home under curfew, probably escaped injury because they displayed an American flag from their front window. Leonard, at the time back in New York, sent cables instructing them to flee to England.

A bit late to be sure, Clara (as she now called herself) gathered her children, hurriedly packed their trunks, and set out by train and coach for Deauville on the northwest coast, from which they took the ferry to Dover, England. Here they at least would be safe, even though England at the time was pro-German, and the hated name of Napoleon stuck in every Englishman's throat. Back on the Continent, the Franco-Prussian War would in fact bring about Napoleon III's final downfall (and result in the unification of Germany). In London, meanwhile, a grim foggy winter, torrential rains, noisy and flooded streets, and the ever-present soot from hundreds of chimneys greeted the tired travelers. Still, sleeping quarters were found, routines soon established, and Jennie soon was at a piano as usual for long hours of practice.

Meanwhile, Leonard rushed to France from America and found that Civil War hero Gen. Philip H. Sheridan was in charge of U.S. interests in France. Sheridan was able to assist Leonard in retrieving his family's possessions and especially his art collection, which miraculously had evaded pillagers.

With the peace treaty of May 10, 1871, ending the Franco-Prussian War, the Jerome family's dreary stay in London ended. The following January the Jeromes again were in their beloved Paris, greeted by sunny skies and unseasonably warm breezes. The Place de la Concorde was bustling again with happy promenaders strolling among the brilliantly striped stalls offering once again all the goods anyone could desire. Clara Jerome one afternoon found herself in an open-air auction of imperial-family possessions; she made her bid and proudly won a set of china monogrammed with gold crowns and the unmistakable N. This prize would eventually pass to her grandson Winston Churchill, who used it with much amusement at Chartwell.

Just as things were looking up for Clara and her daughters in Paris, however, bad news struck Leonard in New York. The stock-manipulating Jay Gould, who had a large holdings in Pacific Mail, dumped his stock on the open market, worsening an already precarious position for Leonard. In addition, Congress was threatening an investigation that could be embarrassing to Leonard, who now set sail once again for Europe. Meanwhile, Paris had changed—it seemed too quiet even for the staid Clara. Thus, Leonard's wife and daughters were delighted when he suggested a move to England's Isle of Wight, more specifically to the posh regatta town of Cowes. Here, in the summer of 1871, the girls could become part of a larger and more important social circle revolving around the Prince of Wales, the future king of England. Leonard himself felt a certain nostalgia for the Isle of

Wight, since it was from here that his forebears had sailed for the New World in the eighteenth century. Helpfully, too, Leonard previously had befriended Frances Bertie, future British ambassador to France and at the moment an undersecretary in the Benjamin Disraeli government—more pointedly, he was a contact who was well known to the aristocrats who flocked to Cowes in the summer and who had the ear of the Prince of Wales.

At Cowes they all moved into a charming seaside villa, Rosetta Cottage—in reality a small mansion—with a lovely garden overlooking the sea and roses arching over the front door. Jennie and Clarita (sister Leonie was at school in Weisbaden) were delighted with their flowery abode—and with the ambiance of the social whirl. Leonard, though, soon would be away, once again shoring up his business interests in the United States.

Once the favorite retreat for Henry VIII, Cowes by this late in the nineteenth century had overtaken rival Brighton as a retreat for the rich, for the aristocrats, the kings and queens. Victoria loved the island, a source of happy memories from her childhood—she even wished to die there. Since 1815, for that matter, Cowes had been home to the Royal Yacht Club. By the time the Jeromes arrived in 1873, Cowes was famous for its yachts, its sailing races, and the accompanying spectacle of the yacht club members in their dashing blue jackets and white trousers strolling the decks of their floating palaces.

A major event that particular August at Cowes was a royal party aboard the guard ship *Ariadne*, honoring Grand Duke Alexander and his wife the Grand Duchess, heirs to the Russian throne who were in town for the annual races. Leonard and Clara Jerome, along with their daughters, beautiful dark Jennie and beautiful blonde Clarita, were among those invited to the gala event.

Jennie, making her debut in English society at the age of nineteen, was dressed in an off-the-shoulder white gown that cascaded down about her lovely ankles. Trimmed in fresh flowers, both she and Clara had the dance cards dangling from their dainty wrists fully filled. One can only imagine the excitement felt by the two young American beauties as they strolled the decks of the royal guard ship to the music of a marine band as the British and Russian flags snapped overhead.

For a moment, Jennie, the story goes, stood alone. Just then Leonard's contact Bertie, who seemed to know everyone, appeared and said, "Miss Jerome may I present an old friend of mine who has just arrived in Cowes, Lord Randolph Churchill." It was a fateful moment. Next to Bertie, she saw a pale and slender youth with narrow shoulders, heroic mustache turned up at the ends, and slightly bulging blue eyes. The rings and jeweled studs he wore gave hint of the dandy, an impression immediately corrected by a deep, commanding voice marked by an attractive lisp. As Jennie's dark eyes looked straight into his, he seemed to drink in the American beauty standing so straightforward before him. By all accounts, it was one of those "love at first sight" meetings.

He asked her to dance, though he soon confessed that he was having trouble keeping up with the intricate steps of the quadrille and asked if they could sit this one out. Despite his apparent lack of rhythm, she was intrigued with this young aristocrat and his intense way of speaking rapidly about things and places she was interested in. They found that they had traveled to many of the same places, that they could both drop names of the rich and famous around the world, and that they both loved horses.

As dance after dance was forgotten by the young Englishman and the lovely American girl, time seemed to stand still . . . until Jennie's mother came searching for her. The ambitious Clara did not wish for her daughter to be monopolized by one young man, so Jennie reluctantly left the intriguing young aristocrat's side. Before the evening was over, however, she had persuaded her mother to invite Randolph and a friend for dinner the next evening.

The next day Jennie spent much time with Clarita rehearsing a piano duet they would play for the gentlemen that evening. With Jennie wearing her prettiest dress, it turned out to be a delightful evening for the young people. After they happily chatted for a time, the harbor lights twinkling in the near distance, the sisters played their duet. When Randolph's friend commented in an aside on the sisters' musical performance, Randolph allegedly replied in a whisper that he admired them both, "and if I can, I mean to make the dark one my wife."

Later, Jennie asked her sister what she thought of Lord Randolph, younger son of the Duke of Marlborough. Clarita was not very impressed, but Jennie assured her that she could grow to like him, and please try, because, "I have the strangest feeling that he is going to ask me to marry him."

The next day Clarita couldn't keep the secret to herself and told her mother what Jennie had said. Clara was startled and not a bit pleased. She had much grander plans for her daughter than a duke's second son who was not even in line for the dukedom. Meanwhile, Jennie had already made plans to meet her young aristocrat along a path she walked each afternoon. Awaiting her at the appointed time and place, he told her he must leave the next day but that he wanted to see her again that evening. She again persuaded her mother to invite the young lord.

And after dinner that night, her mother somewhat unhappily excused herself with a headache, while Clarita, with a smile and a simple good night, disappeared also.

Alone, they strolled into the garden. Jennie recalled, "When finding ourselves alone for a moment, he asked me if I would marry him and I said yes."

And there it was . . . the epochal moment of their young lives! But they agreed not to tell Jennie's mother, who would not understand the suddenness of it all. And they were so right. Randolph did arrange to stay on a few more days before returning to Blenheim Palace, and together they went one day to break the news to Clara, who indeed was so upset that she not only said no, she at once forbade her daughter even to write the young man at Blenheim Palace. Nor was anyone at the palace happy to hear this astonishing news from the second son. First son and older brother George Charles, the Marquess of Blandford, who was in Scotland with his father the Duke of Marlborough, wrote to Randolph a scathing letter that revealed his sordid nature. An affair with a married woman would be acceptable, he wrote; he could even understand marriage for money, but a love match to this young American girl? Never!

JENNIE AS WIFE AND MOTHER

Lord Randolph Churchill's father, the Seventh Duke of Marlborough, not only was firmly opposed to the marriage, he immediately began inquiries as to who were these Jeromes. According to Winston's official biographer, Sir Martin Gilbert, the duke then warned Randolph: "It is evident that he [Leonard] is of the class of speculators, he has been declared bankrupt once [not true]; and may be so again."

Leonard, on the other hand, exuded confidence that the Duke would only learn that "our family is entirely respectable—which is all that can be said for any American family." Thus the duke should be entirely pleased with his son's choice of a bride. Leonard also wrote Jennie with reassurances that financial provision could be made for her, saying in passing, "I always thought if you ever did fall in love it would be a very dangerous affair." For his part, Leonard was most confident that the scent of money would give the duke second thoughts.

In truth, Jennie's father, completely parting company with his wife on the issue, was thrilled with the imminent marriage, saying that it would be the "greatest match any American has made since the Duchess of Leeds." His reference was to the marriage of the daughter of a wealthy Baltimore family who had married the Marquess of Carmarthen, who ten years later succeeded his father as Seventh Duke of Leeds. Clara still had other ideas for Jennie, who as wife of a second son probably would never become a duchess herself.

All reservations aside, and as events turned out, the two fathers and their lawyers soon ironed out an agreement by which a handsome annuity would be divided between Jennie and Lord Randolph. This agreement certainly smoothed the way for the two young lovers, but it didn't hurt, on the British side of the equation, that the Prince of Wales, thoroughly impressed by the lovely Jennie's charms, expressed his own delight with the match.

After all the ups and downs and final agreement by both families, the Duke of Marlborough had one more chip to call in from his fairly idle son—a promise to run for Parliament from little Woodstock. It would not be an easy campaign, even though Woodstock was the seat of the family's own Blenheim Palace. A political neophyte, Randolph would have to campaign against an Oxford don already accusing the Marlboroughs of buying the parliamentary seat.

Not yet married to Jennie, Randolph ran as promised and won. Meanwhile, it often has been suggested that the two passionate lovers could hardly wait for the wedding to take place . . . and in fact didn't. At any rate, Jennie Jerome and Lord Randolph Churchill were married on April 15, 1874, in a surprisingly small and simple wedding, considering the social prominence of both families, along with Clara's grand ambitions for her daughter and the aristocratic history of the Marlboroughs. Lord Randolph's best man was Francis Knolly, secretary to the Prince of Wales, and Jennie chose her sister Clarita as her maid of honor.

The bride wore a gown of white satin with a long train, all trimmed with Alencon lace. Ralph Martin noted: "She wore white silk stockings, white satin slippers, and long white kid gloves. There was a knot of white flowers at her breast and a fine tulle veil covering her from head to foot. Her only jewelry was a string of pearls, a wedding gift from her father." The newlyweds left for a honeymoon at the Chateau de la Petit Val, the glorious estate of Jennie's American friends Lillie Greenough and her wealthy husband, Charles Moulton, outside Paris. The honeymooning horse lovers were offered magnificent stables housing two dozen prize horses, with thirty-five stable hands and grooms in around-the-clock attendance. But they had to cut short their French honeymoon for the opening of Parliament.

When Winston Churchill wrote years later that the marriage of his mother and father was a love match if ever there was one, he added that they had so very little money, they had to live on a less grand scale in London than everyone else in their social circle. Perhaps so in some ways, but not when it came to housing. For Randolph's father had given them a thirty-seven-year lease on a lovely house on Charles Street, complete with flower boxes on the balconies. Since it was not available when they returned from their honeymoon, they made arrangements to rent a house on Curzon Street, but that, too, was not ready, so the young couple decided to go to Blenheim Palace.

Passing through little Woodstock on the edge of the Cotswolds, as Jennie now found out, the road to Blenheim, a street at this point, takes the visitor across a quadrangle and through a triumphal arch to reveal, quite suddenly and all at once, a view guaranteed to stun newcomers. Even the sophisticated Jennie was impressed. "As we passed through the entrance archway and the lovely scenery burst upon me," she recounted, "Randolph said with pardonable pride, 'This is the finest view in England.' Looking at the lake, the bridge, the miles of magnificent park studded with old oaks . . . and the huge and stately palace, I confess I felt awed. But my American pride forbade the admission."

But living in the awesome structure with the Marlboroughs was another proposition. The very first duchess, Sarah, had referred to Blenheim as "a wild and unmerciful house." Much later Jennie's nephew Hugh Frewen called it "a bastard of a building." He also remembered it had "a palace smell . . . rather like the weighty smell of locked-in history . . . with hints of decaying velvet." At the time Jennie arrived, there was only one bathroom in the enormous edifice—no trivial fact to the lowly chambermaids kept busy emptying the chamber pots.

Biographer Ralph Martin noted the formality and tradition that ruled at Blenheim. Randolph's mother, the current duchess, dictated everything to her guests, including the arrival train they must take and the time of their departure. Jennie remarked later that when the family was in residence without guests: "Everything went on with the regularity of clockwork. So assiduously did I practice my piano, read and paint, that I began to imagine myself back in the schoolroom."

A morning hour was devoted to reading the newspapers in order to be informed and make intelligent conversation about the issues of the day at dinner, when conversation invariably turned to politics. "After dinner, which was a rather solemn full dress affair, we all repaired to what was called the Vandyke room." There one could read a book, or play a game of whist, or simply watch the clock. Sometimes the clock had been advanced half an hour by some anonymous sleepy sneak, since no one would dare to venture a good night until the clock chimed the sacred hour of eleven. "Then," added Jennie, "we would all troop out into a small anteroom, and lighting our candles, each in turn would kiss the duke and duchess and depart to our rooms."

Breakfast was formal—with the women dressed in silk or velvet. No one would dare eat until everyone else had arrived and been seated and served. Luncheon, too, was a formality, with "the duke and duchess carving joints of meat for the whole company, including governesses, tutors, and children." After lunch the children filled baskets of leftover food for ailing or impoverished villagers.

Jennie had little time to take it all in before she was expected to attend her royal debut at Queen Victoria's drawing-room reception at Buckingham Palace, at which the queen would appear in person. Since tradition dictated a lady of distinction was to present a newcomer to the court, Randolph's mother, the Duchess of Marlborough, would be more than fitting as Jennie's sponsor. Guests were expected at the noon hour and were to approach the queen as she sat in the throne room. Far from intimate, though, Jennie's presentation came on an afternoon with three thousand guests waiting in line to pass through the narrow doorway for their individual presentations. It was a slow process for the heavily bejeweled ladies in cumbersome dresses, but, nevertheless, Jennie was now accepted at the royal court.

Jennie and Randolph soon settled into their rented house on Curzon Street in London's fashionable Mayfair section, a stone's throw from Piccadilly and Marlborough House on Pall Mall, where the Prince of Wales lived. Jennie's mother-in-law was quick to instruct her in the ways of high society—for instance, she must pay a formal call upon certain society leaders. Further, young married couples were expected to hibernate for a few months before appearing at social functions . . . but Jennie and Randolph violated that rule by appearing at a ball after only one month of marriage.

Already having caught the eye of the Prince of Wales, Jennie next attended a costume ball dressed as the Queen of Clubs at his request. Like so many others, the future king saw more than beauty in Jennie—he enjoyed her freshness, her wit, and her intelligence. Indeed, the young Churchills were the center of attention wherever they appeared in London. Free at last from her mother's watchful eye, somewhat removed also from the strictures of Randolph's own stern mother, Jennie was ready to spread her wings and fly. Randolph, totally intrigued with his beautiful butterfly, was enjoying the flight.

For Jennie, life now was a never-ending round of garden parties, the races at Ascot, the regatta at Henley, pigeon shoots at Hurlingham, visits to the Princess Cricket and Skating Club, the opera and the theater, or evening parties that wouldn't break up until dawn. Unexpectedly, the fast, glittering pace of life in London took a backseat, however briefly, one weekend in late November while they were visiting Blenheim.

Quite pregnant by now but still indulging in constant activity, a restless Jennie joined a shooting party at the grand estate one blustery afternoon. Walking along a rough path, she fell and hurt her ankle. Undaunted, she then rode in a bouncing pony cart while the servants beat the bushes for game. Next, she thought nothing of attending the annual St. Andrews Ball at Blenheim Palace that Saturday night as a highlight of the otherwise quiet moment in the social scene. Pregnant or not, Lady Churchill was seen dancing at the ball—before a sudden departure.

Thanks perhaps to her vigorous activities, her recent fall, or both, she was struck with such pain that she was unable to make it up the steep steps to her room. A quick decision was made to lay her on a bed in a ground-floor room being used as a ladies cloak room that evening. Just minutes before, the bed had been covered with velvet, silk, and fur wraps.

The pains continued into the first minutes of the next day, Sunday, November 30, 1874, with Jennie unable to leave her sudden sanctuary. The couple's London physician was notified, but he couldn't come right away because of the limited weekend train schedules, so a local Woodstock doctor, Frederic Taylor, hurried to Jennie's bedside. It was 1:30 a.m. when he assisted in a delivery that was to become history making. Jennie's baby boy, the first of her two children, of course, was Winston Spencer Churchill.

Lord Churchill, writing to his mother-in-law in Paris, gave her a reassuring picture of the blessed event, "She suffered a good deal poor darling, but was very plucky and had no chloroform," he informed Clara Jerome. "The boy is wonderfully pretty so everybody says, dark eyes and hair and very healthy considering its prematureness." That prematurity, naturally, has been questioned through the years, but its veracity was reinforced, more or less, by the item soon appearing among the birth notices in the *Times* of London: "On the 30th of Nov., at Blenheim Palace, the Lady Randolph Churchill, prematurely, of a son. The happy family spent Christmas at Blenheim and the baby was Christened in Blenheim Chapel by the Duke's chaplain."

Historic birth notwithstanding, and of course not yet comprehended, after the brief interlude at Blenheim, the young family soon was back in London, just in time for the beginning of the social season. At their Mayfair home on Curzon Street the young Churchills were surrounded by the most elegant, brilliant, and socially important people of their times. Jennie not only found herself the most popular young matron in London but was often hosting American friends such as Fanny Ronalds, an attractive divorcee traveling abroad—some say "scouting" for a lord or duke to share her wealth. Still, British society tended to view Anglo-American marriages with considerable skepticism. The Prince of Wales, for one, though, was impressed with American women—and he had been smitten with Jennie from the first time he had met her at Cowes. He especially liked the freshness she and her American friends brought to his salons. He allegedly found them less squeamish than their English sisters, more outspoken, and better able to take care of themselves.

Jennie certainly could handle herself well in her role as a social leader; it was not only her gift of wit and banter but her ability to take constant flattery from men with a lilt, a quip, and an infectious laugh that made her so popular with both men and women. Indeed, her warmth was quite a contrast to her husband's coldness. But she gave Randolph a calm sureness and resilience that he badly needed, even as he gave her access to his social class, consisting at that time of England's most important people, many of them political leaders as well as lions of society.

Among her admirers was the opposition leader of the Liberal Party, William Ewart Gladstone, who enjoyed the couple's dinner parties from time to time. In fact, he and Randolph secretly maintained a mutual respect that would have given pause to parliamentary newcomer Randolph's Tory colleagues. Jennie warmed also to the famous Disraeli, who had become prime minister the same year the young Churchills married, but a year after his wife had died. The widowed PM apparently enjoyed the company of the far younger Lord and Lady Churchill. And certainly, she did his. She recalled: "When I left the dining room after sitting next to Gladstone, I thought he was the cleverest man in England. But when I sat next to Disraeli, I left feeling that I was the cleverest woman!"

Meanwhile, the Prince of Wales's interest in Jennie became more and more obvious . . . and perhaps troubling, since he was well known for his culinary and sexual appetites. "His eyes almost bursting from his head, his cheeks plump and flushed, his voice loud and commanding, the prince resembled some monstrous chuckling baby," biographer Higham wrote. All this, plus a personality that was "cheerful, defiantly hedonistic, all-embracing," exerted, for Jennie, "an unsettling appeal." But at that particular time she and Randolph were totally caught up in the social whirl around them, the demands of a new baby or future king notwithstanding.

There did come a time when Randolph had to buckle down and work on his maiden speech in the House of Commons. Jennie put her talents and energies into helping him write the speech, which by most accounts made a strong impression.

As a young mother, according to one school of biography, Jennie pretty much ignored Winston until he was old enough to be interesting. In some ways that is true, but it is also true that Jennie as Lady Churchill had adapted to the normal way of life for the British upper class of the era: a fixture in every home with children was the proverbial "nanny."

Nannies were, to a large extent, substitute mothers who came into the home when the child was born and stayed until the youth went off to school or even longer. Little Winston Churchill's nanny was Elizabeth Ann Everest. And it was she, Winston later wrote, who was his "confidante," who "looked after me and tended to my wants." It was to her, rather than his mother, to whom "I poured out my many troubles." His mother, by contrast, shone for him "like the evening star." He "loved her dearly—but at a distance."

Visiting sister Clarita (or Clara, as she now called herself) about this time found Jennie in a frantic social whirl. Clara's letters to their mother in Paris provide a glimpse of Jennie's activities: "Lord Hartington took me to lunch in a private room with the royalties, the Prince himself giving his arm to Jennie. . . . Jennie took her Sir William Cumming all to herself, he being the swell of the party and does not let anyone else talk to him. . . . Sir Cumming . . . began *tres serieusement a faire la coeur* to Jennie last night. . . . There was a party for the Prince [later Emperor Frederick] and Princess of Prussia. . . . We came away about three o'clock . . . escorted by a whole troop of men!"

Where was Randolph during all the parties, dances, and outings at the races that Clara felt so comfortable writing about? One has to wonder. Meanwhile, Clara also was the typical gushing aunt in writing about her precocious nephew Winston. "The baby is too lovely. He is so knowing. I wish you could see him on the piano stool, playing the piano!"

Jennie's parents made several trips to see their grandson, Leonard coming from New York and Clara from Paris. After one particular visit, Clara, still a handsome woman, "returned to her salon on Rue de Roi de Rome, catering mostly to minor royalty, faded diplomats, unappreciated artists, and unpublished poets," according to biographer Martin. Leonard stayed a while longer, probably to see his former mistress Fanny Ronalds, who had set up her own London salon where occasionally the Duke of Edinburgh played the violin, the Prince of Wales the piano, and Fanny sang the songs of Sir Arthur Sullivan, of Gilbert and Sullivan fame, with whom she was having an affair. Jennie and Fanny became close friends, even though the sophisticated woman of the world had had a long relationship with Jennie's father in competition with Jennie's mother. The fact is, Fanny offered the friendship of someone older and wiser at a time when Jennie apparently was trying to handle some extramarital affairs of her own.

Leonard also enjoyed time with his two daughters, taking them to the races and splurging on hats and gowns for them both. During this visit also, he met the Duke and Duchess of Marlborough for the first time. There is no written record of Leonard Jerome's opinion of Randolph's titled parents, but the all-seeing Clara wrote her mother that there was a growing tension between the duchess and Jennie. "I can't tell you how jealous Randolph says the Duchess is of Jennie and I," Clara wrote. A real and open rift was about to come.

To make matters worse, Randolph's older brother, Lord Blandford, the heir to the Marlborough dukedom who had tried to stop the marriage between his brother and Jennie, now became more captivated with his beautiful American sister-in-law. Married to Lady Albertha Hamilton, herself related to half the great peerages of England, Blandford had long since lost interest in her, and he now became so smitten with Jennie that he gave her a ring. Jennie made the mistake of showing the ring to her mother-in-law.

This infuriated the duchess, to put it mildly, and soon the feathers were flying. She turned on Jennie, then her sons, first Blandford, then Randolph. Hurtful letters flew back and forth between the parties. Jennie returned the ring, hoping this would be the end of it, but the duchess still blamed her daughter-in-law for causing all the trouble.

In London, His Royal Highness, the Prince of Wales, was the key to social success. Because his mother, Queen Victoria, had withdrawn from public and private social gatherings after the death of her husband, Albert, the royal social duties had fallen to the willing prince and his wife as the royal standard-bearers for London society. Great prestige therefore accompanied acceptance in the prince's entourage, widely known as the Marlborough House Set. Basically, it merely was a clique of his friends and their wives or, in several instances, his mistresses and their husbands. Lord and Lady Churchill were privileged to be a part of this vigorous, if inane, social whirl. For a time, everywhere the Prince of Wales went, there were Jennie and often Randolph too . . . at the fancy dress and masquerade balls, at the shooting parties, at the derby, the races at Ascot, and simply at an unending round of dinners, balls, and parties. Jennie later recalled the only serious moment for them all was the "sudden illness of the greatest hairdresser of his day."

With many of the royal revelries being reported by the newspapers, Prime Minister Disraeli suggested to the queen that she might send her son and heir to Ireland, where he could hunt and socialize out of sight and might even learn something about governing. But the prince decided on a trip to India instead. As he gathered his entourage for the trip, Jennie and Randolph were invited but declined—some say for financial reasons, others suspect that Randolph was beginning to resent the prince's obvious attentions to his wife.

Even so, the prince's trip to India, begun October 11, 1875, was destined to have an unexpected impact on Jennie and Randolph. As the prince set sail, on board was Lord Heneage, Earl of Aylesford, while his wife, Edith, Countess of Aylesford, moved to Packingham, the family seat, with their two daughters. Taking up residence in an inn conveniently nearby was Randolph's brother Lord Blandford, who as heir to the Marlborough dukedom, lived pretty much as he pleased. As later revealed, Blandford's nearby presence was so convenient, he discreetly could enter an unused wing of Edith's large mansion each evening with a key she had given him and spend the night with her.

All of this might have been of little consequence, since it was accepted practice that some lords and ladies of the land visited one another's beds during the night. Indeed, discreet hostesses holding a weekend party at their country house were known to assign nearby rooms for those known to be having affairs. Thus, all apparently was going smoothly for the illicit lovers at Packingham until, in February 1876, they decided to elope. Edith then rather thoughtlessly informed her husband, still in India, and he hurried home. Meanwhile, the Duke of Marlborough sent one of his sons-in-law to try to discourage son George in this folly, though he himself felt it was a hopeless gesture.

To complicate matters further, Edith's brother then challenged Blandford to a duel, a threat that now precipitated Randolph's entry into the situation . . . which by now was playing out like a French farce. Randolph told all interested parties that only Lord Aylesford himself could challenge George to a duel. Randolph even hired a detective to watch both George and his challenger, "to prevent a breach of peace."

This should have been the end to the brouhaha. But no. Randolph now discovered that his brother's predecessor in Edith's bed was none other than the Prince of Wales himself, and he had carelessly written her love letters that Edith had saved. As summed up by Winston's biographer William Manchester, "the breakdown in decorum was complete" when Randolph now took the further step of calling upon the future king's wife, Alexandra, and asking her to use her influence with the prince to persuade Lord Aylesford against divorcing his "erring wife." Randolph thought he thus could put an end to the matter, but he only sealed his own social doom by waving the love letters and boasting, "I have the Crown of England in my pocket."

The queen, hearing of Lord Randolph's behavior, wrote her son in India, calling the fracas "a dreadful disgraceful business." The prince returned in a rage—and denied everything, even writing Prime Minister Disraeli that Lords Randolph and Blandford were spreading lies about him, and that "it is a pity that there is no desert island to which these young gentlemen could be banished." Short of that, he made it clear that the two brothers henceforth were to be in a social Coventry—banished from the scene.

Jennie of course was stricken. Not only would she miss the prince, but along with Randolph and George, she was a social outcast, no longer to be included in the Marlborough House Set in London, no longer to be invited to country estates for shootings, balls, and races. Realizing that he had gone too far, Randolph surrendered the letters to a royal intermediary, Lord Hartington, later the Duke of Devonshire. Hartington—who had been sleeping with another duke's duchess for thirty years—burned them in Randolph's presence. But it was too late, the couple's ostracization was complete . . . the prince had announced that he no longer would attend any event in which the Churchills were included. The whole Marlborough dukedom now had a gloom cloud hanging over it.

Randolph made every attempt to ingratiate himself and his family and finally wrote to Disraeli for advice. Dizzy, as he was affectionately know, suggested to Randolph's mother, the Duchess Fanny, "My dear Lady, there is but one way: make your husband take the Lord Lieutenancy of Ireland and take Lord Randolph with him. It will put an end to it all."

And so it would be, but before this solution was devised, Jennie and Randolph made a quick trip to America. But there, even more gloom awaited Jennie. The weather in her hometown of New York City was wretched—hot and rainy, the streets crowded and noisy. The construction din from the Third Avenue elevated train seemed never ending. Her father, who had always been her jaunty pirate and prince charming, was older, wiser, but a bit bowed after recent financial setbacks. Leonard for some time had barely been able to pay Randolph and Jennie's shared allowances. This caused some conflicts, but most painful for Jennie was having to face a New York society all too aware of the Churchills' disgrace in London society.

Back home in England, meanwhile, Jennie, along with the duke and other members of their family, long had considered nearby Ireland as some sort of distant and lowly outpost of the empire, but they had no options at this juncture but to jump at Disraeli's suggestion. They all may well have felt they were being exiled to a desert island, but perhaps there was some balm as the duke was greeted in Dublin by a ceremonial salute of twenty-one guns, invested with the collar and insignia of the Order of Saint Patrick, and installed in the vice regal lodge. The Randolph Churchills moved into the neighboring Little Lodge.

Politically, Ireland at the time was experiencing a period of relative calm from the rebel Fenians, giving Randolph, acting as secretary to his father, a chance to mature, perhaps also to learn something of governing. In the meantime, he still held his seat in Parliament and did attend sessions of the House of Commons.

Jennie, for her part, found not a rocky island in Dublin but a lush green setting—and an Anglo-Irish aristocracy ready to receive and delight her. Once again, in fact, she plunged into a whirl of balls, theater and dinner parties, steeplechases, and fox hunts. Now in her early twenties, Jennie was at the height of her beauty.

Her son Winston, whose first real memories came from Ireland, recalled often seeing his mother those days in Ireland "in a riding habit, fitted like a skin and often beautifully spotted with mud."

Another picture of Winston's mother once was evoked by Viscount D'Abernon, statesman, banker, former ambassador to Berlin, and considered by many to be the handsomest man in England. He first saw Jennie at the vice regal lodge, standing alone at one end of the room while her father-in-law the duke sat on a raised dais at the other end. Wrote D'Abernon: "Eyes were turned not on him or on his consort, but on a dark lithe figure, standing somewhat apart and appearing to be of another texture of those around her, radiant, translucent, intense. A diamond star in her hair, her favorite ornament—its luster dimmed by the flashing glory of her eyes. More of the panther than of the woman in her look, but with a cultivated intelligence unknown to the jungle."

Later, Margot Asquith, wife of Prime Minister Herbert H. Asquith, upon meeting Jennie at a racecourse, added her own description with animal overtones: "She had a forehead like a panther's and great wild eyes that looked through you."

When the young couple left for Ireland, little Winston was only two—he would be six when they returned. In the interim, all those formative years, Elizabeth Everest was Winston's constant companion as well as his nanny. She liked to dress her little redheaded, freckled-faced charge in a sailor suit and take him on excursions. But she complained to Winston's mother that the youngster, always in perpetual motion, needed clothes, that those he had were shabby, and it was a disgrace how few he had.

Jennie, in the meantime, was so busy with her many commitments that little Winston one time threatened to run after a train she was taking. Apparently he said, "I can't have my Mama go and if she does I will run after the train and jump in."

One early memory for Winston of course would be of a milestone family event, taking place in Dublin—the birth of his brother, John Strange Churchill, or simply Jack. Despite all her riding to the hounds, shooting parties and balls, Jennie had found time to produce another healthy Churchill heir, born February 4, 1880, and named for John Strange, the future Fifth Earl of Roden, a longtime friend of the Duke and Duchess of Marlborough. As events turned out, Jack would be the "good boy" of the two, would do all the right things, would give his mother and Nanny Everest little trouble. Winston himself always would adore his little brother—and they remained friends and confidantes throughout their lives.

If Jennie and Randolph had lost most of the fire of their earlier life, meanwhile, they had been drawn together by their social exile, which also gave them both fresh political interests. Even at social events during this maturing period in

Ireland for the young Churchills, Jennie found herself included in serious conversations about Irish Home Rule with such Irish leaders as Charles Stewart Parnell, Isaac Butt, and Lord Justice Gerald FitzGibbon.

Though he was unconverted to Home Rule, the new familiarity with the crucial issue, according to biographer Martin, "not only made Lord Randolph strongly sympathetic to Irish problems but served as a springboard for his future." With the failure of the potato crop in 1877, Ireland experienced two years of hunger, terror, and ruin. Realizing the need for much more than the monies officially available to meet the crisis, Randolph's mother began a relief fund. Jennie and Randolph joined in the drive and traveled around the country to drum up support. Jennie recalled, "In our walks, we had many opportunities of seeing the heart-rending poverty of the peasantry who lived . . . more like animals than human beings." Jennie wrote letters to friends in positions to help and raised £135,000, a fortune by anyone's standards, but too little to go far in assuaging the outright starvation stalking the land. As one predictable outgrowth of Ireland's misery, ten thousand small landholders and Fenians met in County Mayo to call for revolution.

Turbulent times lay ahead for the Irish when, in 1880, the duke's term as viceroy ended. As he and his wife returned to their beloved Blenheim, Jennie and Randolph took their little family home to a rented house at 29 St. James Place in London.

Having taken part in political discussions almost as an equal in Ireland, Jennie became deeply committed to politics once they were settled back in London. Using all her charm and energy, she joined her husband in the effort to unseat the old regime of the Conservative Party. Throughout the campaign, according to Higham, "Jennie was at Blenheim and on local hustings, bringing glamour to every meeting." In London the Churchills were still socially out of favor with the prince and his clique, but this freed Jennie to have more time for their political battles. With Gladstone in as Liberal prime minister, Jennie and Randolph hoped to form a "splinter group to build a fire" under the old men whom they thought were ruining the Conservative Party. Oddly enough, the men they chose for their so-called Fourth Party were maverick figures and scarcely young themselves.

Be that as it may, with their Fourth Party established, Randolph realized that he was poised at the start of a serious political career. He once admitted to a friend that, before this, he really knew nothing, that all he had learned at Eton and Oxford had long since vanished and that only now was he reading the Roman classics, which he credited to Jennie's persuasion. In fact, many biographers of Randolph and Jennie agree that Jennie turned her dilettante husband into a serious and dedicated politician. And it indeed could be argued that by the spring of 1881, Jennie had used her strength, her determination, and her intelligence to help her husband acquire a supreme self-confidence he had not known before.

On June 2 of that same year, Higham's biography recalls in somewhat stringent terms: "Jennie's sister Clarita had been married—without the Churchills present—to the adventurous foolish international speculator Moreton Frewen at Grace Church in New York, where both were visiting. He was good looking, of decent family, but a brainless and indigent pipsqueak, always coming up with absurd money-making schemes that drained what little income he had. He was emphatically a cad; he hated Jennie and her mother, whom he rudely dubbed Sitting Bull, in reference to her imaginary native American origins."

Almost a year later, Jennie and Randolph set out for New York, ostensibly for a family visit, but in truth they were concerned because Leonard was again negligent in making the payments he had guaranteed as part of Jennie's dowry. The matter was left unresolved, since he apparently had lied about selling his Madison Square mansion—he had only leased it and mortgaged it. Returning to London, Jennie and Randolph had to give up their house on St. James and settle into a small cottage in suburban Wimbledon.

Winston, now age seven, by all accounts was a handful—biographer Higham stated that he was "noisy, bumptious, a tiny egomaniac." When his parents were away on political or social outings, Winston and Jack, together with the faithful Everest, were sent to Blenheim. Here, the boys had the run of the magnificent parks and servants at their disposal to answer every wish. But all good things must come to an end, and for Winston that meant going away to boarding school for the first time, in November 1882.

In Victorian England, harsh treatment was to be expected for the young boys sent away to "public" school. Jennie recalled her own first school experience at Lucy Green's in New York, which she attributed to the steel in her soul, and she wanted her sons to be strong too. At the time also, Jennie had more on her mind than coddling her young sons. For one thing, she was basking in the glory of her now famous husband.

But Jennie also began an affair that would take her heart. She may have first met the handsome Count Charles Rudolf Ferdinand Andreas Kinsky in London in 1881, but it's more likely that they had met in Ireland earlier, when he was visiting with Empress Elizabeth of Austria. Born in Vienna, Kinsky was four years younger than Jennie—at five foot seven he was slight in figure, but extraordinarily handsome, with compelling blue eyes. He would become the talk of the town as the first amateur to win England's Grand National Steeplechase on his own chestnut mare Zoedone, and eighteen years later he would inherit the title Prince Carl Kinsky. Since he was a fiery young man, impulsive and romantic, he and Jennie were emotionally made for each other.

Jennie now had a life crowded with politics, a home to manage, two children to raise, her affair with Kinsky, and quite suddenly a resumed and intense social whirl, since she and Randolph no longer were excluded by the Prince of Wales and his entourage. At the same time, she was concerned with young Winston's health—he was often ill, and he complained bitterly about his truly harsh treatment at his first boarding school, St. George's at Ascot. She found him a smaller, more forgiving school in Brighton near their family doctor, Robson Roose.

That summer, Jennie and Randolph took Winston on a vacation to the Austrian Alps. Here, in Gastein, a well-known "watering hole," the nobility and aristocracy of Europe came to enjoy the simple life. Here, too, Jennie and Randolph were the frequent guests of Otto von Bismarck (the "Iron Chancellor") and the German emperor William I. Jennie, as usual, had captivated these leaders and had the ear of the reticent Bismarck. Blandford joined the holiday group for some mountain climbing. By now, the duke had died, an event that brought the two brothers closer.

Back home in England, the Fourth Party was barely teetering along. In 1883, one of its members, Sir Henry Wolff, proposed an idea. The primrose had been Disraeli's favorite flower, and on the anniversary of his recent death, many members were wearing the flower in their buttonholes. Why not form an organization and call it the Primrose League? Randolph was excited about the idea and quickly involved Jennie in its formation. The Primrose League that resulted was a political-social organization in which men and women of conservative leaning could meet and discuss issues of the day. An elaborate organization, it gave its officers romantic titles—male officers were knights and women officers were dames, and the various clubs were called habitations. Randolph made his mother, the duchess, president of the Ladies Grand Council, while Jennie was a dame. To be sure, in some quarters the league was ridiculed, but it was a successful innovation that brought women into politics.

Jennie found it tremendously stimulating and was eager to persuade women to join with her. She later wrote: "I became Dame President of many Habitations and used to go all over the country inaugurating them. The opening speeches were often quaint in their conceptions, a mixture of grave and gay, serious and frivolous—speeches from members of Parliament, interspersed with songs and even recitations, sometimes of a comical nature. The meetings would end with the enrollment of converts. A strange medley, the laborer and the local magnate, the county lady and the grocer's wife, would troop up to sign the roll. Politics, like charity, are great levelers."

More and more these days, Jennie was in the limelight—she even became a so-called PB, a reference to the "Professional Beauties," an elite group of England's most beautiful women, whose photographs were sold in shops all over the country. She, of course, was censured by her friends, but she did nothing to stop the persistent publicity, interviews, and magazine articles about the PBs and/or herself.

Sisters Clara and Leonie undoubtedly would have been included in the PBs, but as biographer Martin pointed out: "Clara and her French maid and Moreton Frewen were far distant in their log house at Big Horn, Wyoming, with few visitors except bears, buffalo and such friends as Lord Queensberry and Buffalo Bill." Leonie was busy planning her upcoming wedding to Lt. John Leslie of the British Guards. Soon after the posh wedding, however, Ritzman's of London added the two sisters to their window display of PBs, only to have *Town Topics* write, "Pretty as these two heads are, neither can compare in beauty with the second sister, Jennie."

Meanwhile, in 1885, with the Conservatives swept into power, the new prime minister, Lord Salisbury, appointed Randolph secretary of state for India. He then authorized a military expedition against Burma as punishment for its failure to stop attacks on British merchant ships and for its fine imposed on a British trading firm, with the result that on January 1, 1886, Burma was annexed to the British Empire outright. Randolph called it a "New Year's present to the Queen." Twenty-five days later, in another election, the Conservatives were thrown out; the Liberals were back in, although Randolph held on to his seat in Parliament. That same spring the family was alarmed by eleven-year-old Winston's severe bout of pneumonia, but he recovered, if slowly.

Another crisis, political in nature, also struck. Prime Minister Gladstone wanted Home Rule for Ireland, giving the Irish a parliament able to decide on Irish issues. Taking up for the Irish Protestants afraid of Catholic rule, Randolph predicted in a letter made public that "Ulster will fight, Ulster will be right," words that quickly became a slogan for the Protestants in the north of Ireland.

Then, with the help of breakaway Liberals calling themselves Liberal Unionists and opposed to Gladstone's Home Rule policy, the Conservatives regained control later the same year. Lord Salisbury, back as PM, now named Randolph, just thirty-seven years old, chancellor of the exchequer. This was to be a short-lived pinnacle of Randolph's career, however. Later that year, in his zeal to cut government spending, he made the mistake of warning he might leave his new post if certain of his budget proposals were not accepted. Rightly or wrongly, Salisbury interpreted Randolph's warning as a letter of resignation, accepted it, and that was that.

All this was a political disaster from which Randolph never recovered, not even as an opposition leader when Gladstone and the Liberals returned to power in 1892, although as one high-water mark for Winston, personally, that summer he had one of the "three or four long intimate conversations with him [his father] which are all I can boast." As Winston's official biographer Martin Gilbert wrote in *Churchill: A Life*, "Lord Randolph explained to his son that older people, absorbed in their own affairs, were not always considerate toward the young 'and might speak roughly in sudden annoyance.'"

By this time, too, Jennie had to devote more and more time in her crowded life to the hidden illness that had struck her husband. At the same time, Winston, always needy, it seemed, always was writing her and making demands. As he well knew by now, his mother would "come through" some of the time . . . and she indeed did write him regularly. His father, though, once again was diffident and unreachable. Winston's grandmother, the duchess, did love and spoil him as a baby and seemed to maintain a warm relationship with him throughout her life. But it was Winston's grandfather Jerome who gave him love freely and openly.

Leonard Jerome had paid a visit to London in 1885, just in time to observe his favorite daughter take to the political trail on her husband's behalf. With the general election coming up, Randolph offered an alternative he termed "Tory Democracy," but he felt his own parliamentary seat was so secure that he need not bother to campaign. Once again, Jennie took charge. This time even his mother, the duchess, joined in campaigning for him. In fact, she and Jennie drew closer, and she actually defended Jennie to her social friends.

Still a boy, Winston nonetheless was following the campaign with deep interest, not only because he had become interested in politics, but there were his glamorous and socially prominent mother and his grandmother, the dowager duchess, ringing doorbells and soliciting votes for his father, who was busy preparing for his expected role as secretary of state for India. Jennie, now here, now there, riding in a carriage drawn by pink-ribboned horses, became the surrogate candidate, making Randolph's election that year a triumph at the polls carried out by women. It wasn't long before the remarkably young Randolph then was appointed chancellor of the exchequer for a fatefully short time.

At this time, too, serious financial problems hovered over the Churchills—for one thing, members of Parliament received no salary until 1911. Regardless of this or that adversity, however, through thick and thin, the three sisters and their families supported each other, even when it meant they themselves had conflicting interests. This sense of strong family ties, a mutual defense against outside criticism and loyalty to kin, would be a support system, learned from his mother and his aunts, that Winston would carry throughout his life.

Winston's father, meanwhile, had recently turned his attention to horse racing. He began buying yearlings and putting them out for training with the idea of enjoyment while making money. Love of horses was something he and Jennie had always shared, and at this time they rented a country house, Banstead Manor on Chievely, just outside Newmarket. It just so happened that Count Kinsky also had a country house nearby, and Jennie later would cite these months as pleasant times. "We would ride out in the early morning from six to seven to see the horses do their gallops," she recounted, adding with possibly unconscious irony, "It was a most healthy and invigorating life."

About this time, too, young Winston was about to enter a more vigorous life at a new school. When it was decided that he would attend Harrow, the lad leaving home had to ask his father where he had gone to school—Eton or Harrow? This may seem unfathomable by the norms of today's father-son relations, but Randolph was so remote as a father that when, in the fall of 1887, Winston wrote to his father, "I wish you could come to the distribution of prizes at the end of this term," he felt compelled to add, "but I suppose it's impossible."

Even more heartrending was his request to his mother that she be home when he returned for the Christmas holidays. Jennie would perhaps have honored this simple request, but she and Randolph were soon leaving on a semi-official trip to Russia. The two of them were accompanied by friends Tommy Trafford and the Marquis de Breteuil, the latter perhaps because he was descended from an ancestor who had been ambassador to the court of Catherine the Great. Jennie was reluctant to leave at this time for more reasons than one—the boys' holidays and the expense of the trip. Also, according to biographer Anna Sebba's *American Jennie: The Remarkable Life of Lady Randolph Churchill,* Jennie was well aware that earlier that year an attempt had been made on the life of Czar Alexander III. It was not the first time the czar had been a target, although it led this time to the arrest and execution of Alexander Ulianov, brother of Vladimir I. Lenin, for his connection to the plot. On the other hand, Jennie may also have reasoned, they would pass through Berlin on their way, both coming and going, and that's where Count Kinsky was posted. Plus, going to mysterious Russia would be a great adventure.

"Jennie was lionized during this trip," wrote Sebba. "Several Russian princes were struck by her unusual black hair and smoldering eyes." In fact, the Russian aristocracy dubbed her "Dark Jennie." She was, of course, her usual stunning self at the many balls and grand events held in their honor, and by contrast relatively few paid much attention to Randolph.

Sebba notes that Jennie devoted thirty pages to these six weeks in her *Reminiscences*. She described the Russian people as "charming and hospitable and full of *bonhomie*, and [said] we saw no signs of that grinding despotism and tyranny which supposed to be synonymous with Russian life." But then she and her party spent their time at the opera, ballet, and theater. Sebba commented, "They were indulged with lavish entertaining and lots of sleighing and skating," all activities in which Jennie "excelled." A week before they were to depart, a grand ball was given at the British Embassy, for which eight hundred invitations had been sent out. According to the London *Times*, "The *elite* of St. Petersburg society . . . crowded into the State apartments of the Embassy, where Lord and Lady Randolph Churchill formed the center of attention."

On the return trip, the Churchills arrived in Berlin on January 23, 1888, and were the guests of British ambassador Sir Edward and Lady Malet. In top form after her grand reception in Russia, Jennie was even more elated to have time with Kinsky. While Randolph was in political meetings, she was out with her favorite riding companion.

Once they were back home, Randolph was increasingly restless—he spent more and more time traveling, gambling, and at health spas. His growing expenditures did not deter him from writing Jennie letters warning her not to go into debt. In one such message, he added the biting comment, "You seem rather like Winston about money." Still, they rented a house in Egham for the next summer, with Randolph apparently unable or unwilling to see the contradiction with his own warnings.

Jennie did not need any warnings about finances, since they already had been a constant worry. But she did have the happy memories of all the sights seen in Russia, to say nothing of the charm and hospitality of the people they had met. Perhaps—invigorating thought!—she could benefit from their recent trip in a tangible way by writing about it. Here, in addition to her skills at the piano, would be another way to be an accepted part of the artistic and intellectual world. And, also important, possibly a way to make a little money.

The article she wrote about society in Russia sold to the *New Review* as probably her first moneymaking piece of writing ever. Others would follow, and she took her writing seriously . . . but the occasional published article, as much as she enjoyed the act of writing, did not put very much bread on her fancy table. Instead, the couple's money continued to flow out, rather than in, thanks to their unceasingly peripatetic lifestyle. That lifestyle seemed to mean spending a few weeks in London, followed by a few days at Blenheim, then a day two at San-dringham, Wimborne, Norwich, or Newmarket, and thence to Paris, where the Jeromes still felt at home.

One attraction in Paris were younger sister Leonie and husband Jack Leslie. As of late 1888, they had taken an apartment on the Rue Tilsitt, close to the Arch de Triomphe. Jack was studying at the prestigious Juliens Academy, so Leonie and Jennie could spend time together in their favorite city and shop to their heart's content.

There was always such excitement when Jennie was around, Leonie wrote to Clara, that she dreaded it when Jennie left. Jennie knew all the little out-of-the-way shops, where they could find bargain laces and such things, and of course Jennie returned home with stacks of boxes of wonderful finds. Oddly or not, Count Kinsky often seemed to be in Paris about the same time, to wine and dine Jennie and take her to the theater. Randolph, meanwhile, still was traveling from one spa to another in Europe, seeking a cure for a mysterious ailment. One minute he might also be off to Egypt and another to the Riviera and Monte Carlo. He and Jennie kept in touch by frequent letters.

She, for her part, had another worrisome distraction nowadays: her father wasn't well. He came to visit with Clara and Moreton in their home on London's Alford Street. "The beautiful paneled dining room on the ground floor was given over to the invalid," wrote his grandson Shane years later. He sat "in a big-backed red velvet chair while timid grandchildren peeped at him." Because of the London fog and damp weather, the sisters moved Leonard to coastal Brighton, where the family hoped the sea air would help him to improve. But on May 3, 1891, Jennie's handsome and charming pirate died. He had lived seventy-three fast and exciting years.

Among those at the funeral in Grosvenor Chapel were the U.S. Minister, Robert Todd Lincoln, President Lincoln's son, and the German ambassador. Moreton Frewen, Clara's husband, agreed to take the body back to the family mausoleum in Greenwood Cemetery, Brooklyn.

That summer of 1891, Jennie invited her mother and two sisters, together with children, to join her at the Churchill home at Banstead. Count Kinsky was at his estate nearby, and all the husbands were away. Randolph was in South Africa searching for gold—the magic word was out that it had been discovered there. Jack Leslie was with his family at their estate in Ireland, and Moreton Frewen was on his way to Australia.

The scenario hardly suggests a family with financial problems, but the unwelcome news was that Leonard Jerome, who had made life so pleasant and easy for them, had died in debt. Still, the three sisters would continue to live well . . . somehow.

Tough Times Ahead

Jennie missed her father terribly, but she bravely kept up appearances and continued to live well, even though he no longer was there to hand his girls the frequent envelope stuffed with cash or checks. He always had been Jennie's dashing pirate, full of enthusiasm and positive support. Now, more than ever, she needed such a stalwart as she faced a future fraught with more problems than financial insecurity . . . but that too.

While Randolph's growing lack of interest in politics alarmed Jennie, sister Clara still believed in her husband Moreton, who talked a good show and acted as if he would strike it rich with one of his—what some called "harebrained"— schemes. From the beginning she thought he was truly visionary, but after spending their honeymoon and many months thereafter at his ranch in Wyoming, even losing a baby there, she rushed back to New York, never to seek out the ranching life again. Then, just before her father's death, Frewen introduced his latest and most amazing scheme yet, a "Gold-Crusher" that would extract gold from old mine tailings. Asking Clara to entertain friends who could invest in his project, he was sure it would produce a fortune for all.

Meanwhile Randolph desperately needed to make some money—he believed the South African gold might be the answer. His growing health problem made his travels in Africa more and more difficult, but he persisted for the better part of a year anyway. In the end, brushing aside brother-in-law Frewen's gold-crusher scheme, he persuaded his sisters, his mother, and friends to invest in a gold-seeking syndicate with a total capital investment of £15, 994. And it did give him fresh income, whereas Frewen's gold-crusher never proved feasible. Meanwhile, on the strength of the syndicate's gold discoveries, Randolph sent Jennie diamonds, one of which weighed seven carats before she sent it to Amsterdam to be cut.

"How dear of you to send it to me," Jennie wrote. Happily, she had a glittering pin made from some of the diamonds, but more important in the long run, the syndicate Randolph had joined became so successful that it would pay her £70,000 after his death, even though he had sold off some of his shares beforehand. Sadly, much of this went to pay off debts.

But for now Jennie and Randolph had no money, and Clara and Moreton had even less. Again, this little problem didn't seem to stop the Jerome sisters.

While Randolph continued to travel, Clara went to Paris to visit sister Leonie, and Jennie gave up her London house to double-up with brother-in-law Moreton on Alford Street. Jennie wrote to Clara, "We make a very good ménage." Adding that she saw little of Moreton, "as I lunch and dine out," Jennie didn't point out that Count Kinsky was staying at his club nearby. As Anne Sebba noted, "The Churchills might not have enough money for a house, but Jennie begged her sisters in Paris to choose her a chic little black hat for Newmarket, 'something in the sailor line, all black or white and black.'"

Jennie escaped London whenever she could. Together with sister Leonie, she made a trip to Bayreuth, the hometown of Wagner, just then the rage of Europe. Loving music as she did, and a Wagner fan to boot, she previously had engaged a German musician to come to London and give a series of lectures on Wagner. In Bayreuth, Jennie was struck with a severe toothache, but acceding to another fan's offer of some cocaine to ease the pain, she managed to attend all the performances.

Meanwhile, when Randolph returned after spending the better part of 1891 in Africa, he sported a full beard that did little to disguise the marked change in his appearance. If he was hoping it would hide his gauntness, it in fact only emphasized the stark change. Even worse, Randolph's decline was not limited to appearances only. While he was traveling in Africa, his rudeness and sudden mood changes had been well covered in the newspapers back home. His attacks on the Boers embarrassed Cecil Rhodes, the British-born financier and prime minister of the Cape Colony who established De Beers Consolidated Mines, which in 1891 owned 90 percent of the world's diamond mines. Randolph's sometimes inexplicable behavior kept him in the limelight and gave credence to Boer accusations of British high-handedness—the same Boers, ironically, who in a few short years would be contributing, however unintended, to his son Winston's sudden fame.

Punch magazine was one of many publications that lampooned the gold-hunting Lord Randolph, calling him "Grandolph," while the *Clarion* could not resist a catty reference to Jennie in its suggestion that the keyhole shield of their London house was much scratched in his absence.

There is still much speculation as to the physical and mental problems of Lord Randolph Churchill. In the absence of modern technology such as brain scans or sophisticated blood testing, it is impossible today to determine whether he had contracted syphilis, as the doctors of the day thought. Certainly, he thought so, if we are to accept the historical allegation that from 1885 onward, following medical advice, he and Jennie did not share a bed.

In examining Randolph's reported symptoms, including a marked change in personality, problems with speech and additional evidence of neurological and other deterioration, Dr. John H. Mather, medical historian to the International Churchill Society, considered the conclusions of Lord Churchill's doctor, Dr. Robson Roose, that Randolph showed the effects of excessive smoking, too much alcohol, tea, and coffee, overwork, and sleeplessness. Thus, wrote Mather in the Churchill Centre's *Finest Hour* publication, "Much of Randolph's behavior during his last five years seems to be no more than an accentuation of his prior personality, associated with real medical problems."

Randolph, to Jennie's chagrin, always had been a heavy smoker. Even before their marriage she often would end her love letters with the postscript, "please don't smoke so much." Noting the smoking among other factors, Mather added that Randolph might have suffered from epilepsy or a brain tumor, among other possibilities. "It is not possible to say with certainty what killed Lord Randolph," Mather concluded, "but it is no longer possible to say he died of syphilis."

Whatever we may think today, noted biographer Sebba, "Randolph, himself, seems to have believed, from about 1886 onward, he had a severe degenerative neurological condition which was possibly syphilis." Whatever the cause, his many days of 1892 spent in the spas of Austria and Germany in hopes of finding a cure did little to stop the deterioration.

For a time Jennie was not well. Family physician Roose at least twice wrote to the traveling Randolph of the severity of her condition. After returning home and seeing that Jennie's life apparently hung in the balance, he wrote to Winston and Jack, telling them that though their mother had been extremely ill the day before, "thank God today there is an improvement and the doctors are vy hopeful."

Whatever Jennie's illness—some have suggested pelvic peritonitis, an ovarian cyst, a uterine fibroid, or an inflamed appendix—removal of the problem was not an option. Indeed, the first known appendix operation took place ten years later on Edward VII (the family's old friend the Prince of Wales). Fortunately for Jennie, her mysterious swelling went down of its own accord. She recovered her strength within a few months, but it took longer for her usual vitality to return.

By 1893, Randolph at least felt able to make a few speeches in Parliament, but falteringly so. A speech against Home Rule for Ireland was especially tremulous. After one such speech, brother-in-law Moreton told Clara, "He was very nervous, almost inaudible, but when he found his voice, I hear, it was admirable." By the end of that year his speeches were hardly reported, a stark contrast to the days when his name was in the papers all the time.

Meanwhile, Randolph's brother Blandford, having left his paramour and divorced his wife, traveled to America to find himself an attractive heiress. Lily Hammersley, a wealthy widow would do instead. Though she was overweight, dressed badly, and was prone to facial hair, her annual income of $150,000 and a personal fortune of some $5 million, plus her sweet face and good nature, made her more than acceptable. Still, the British press had a field day on this Anglo-American marriage, suggesting, among other remarks, that "ready cash buys Norman blood."

Undeterred, Jennie tapped all her connections and used all her talent to ease her new sister-in-law into society. First, she persuaded Lily to lose twenty pounds, then get rid of the facial hair. Also she had the "determined help of her other five sisters-in-law—Lady Wimborne, Lady De Ramsey, Lady Majoribanks, Lady Curzon, and the Duchess of Roxburgh—as well as the Dowager Duchess," according to biographer Ralph Martin, "all of whom pressured their friends to accept the new Duchess of Marlborough." As events unexpectedly turned out, Randolph's brother suddenly died in November 1892 at the age of forty-eight—his son, Winston's cousin "Sunny," became the ninth Duke of Marlborough.

It had been Lily's kindness and good nature that won over the family and its support. A few years later, in fact, young Winston formed a warm relationship with Blandford's widow, Duchess Lily, when he spent the Easter holidays with her at Blenheim while recuperating from injuries he suffered playfully jumping off a bridge for a tree limb. Then just nineteen, Winston, together with Jack and their mother, had been visiting Lady Wimborme near Bournemouth, when Winston, as usual playing the daredevil, took his dangerous leap. Jennie was by his side almost at once with "energetic aid and inopportune brandy," Winston recalled.

His injuries were diagnosed as a ruptured kidney, deep shock, and concussion (a fractured thighbone went undetected). But even more painful for the future world leader was the report about the same time that he had failed in his second entrance exam for Sandhurst Military College. Now, he must attend a cram course in London for a third try. Happily, by August of that year, while touring Switzerland, Winston could write to his mother and father, who were both at a spa in Germany, that the extra effort finally had brought the happy results of acceptance at Sandhurst.

When Randolph responded to Winston's success with criticism for a "slovenly happy-go- lucky harum-scarum style of work," Winston, as increasingly was the case these days, looked to his mother as a go-between. He wrote begging her to ask his father to set up an allowance for him. He was now old enough to say, quite frankly, how unhappy he was with his father's attitude toward him and that he felt Randolph treated him as a child.

At this time he was especially hurt when his grandmother the duchess fired poor "Woomany," Elizabeth Everest, by now a devoted family servant of twenty years' standing. The duchess had never liked the nanny and, finding her of no further use, had simply sent her packing. Winston wrote his mother a long letter asking her to intercede, but despite his good intentions, Everest was dismissed. She continued to correspond with her two young men, Winston and Jack, and they in turn visited her and sent her money from time to time.

Because of money problems Jennie and Randolph were now living with the duchess at Grosvenor Square, and yet they spent more time apart than together. The letters they exchanged were full of health complaints, with even Jennie confessing to being tired. Randolph's condition continued to deteriorate even while he was claiming that his doctors were satisfied with his progress. To the contrary, on visiting Doctors Roose and Thomas Buzzard, Jennie learned how seriously ill he was. Randolph of course was furious to hear she had discussed such matters with his doctors.

Traveling to Paris to relieve the stress, exactly twenty years after beginning what she thought was to be her story-book life with a charming young lord as her husband, she now was receiving letters from a much older, desperately ailing lord and husband . . . but at least he was pleading loneliness without her and saying he would be glad when she returned to Grosvenor Square. But back in London, Jennie recognized that her husband's mood swings and unpredictable behavior threatened ruin. Friends such as Randolph's childhood friend Lord Rosebery (later a prime minister) pleaded with Jennie to keep her husband from attending the House of Commons and making nonsensical speeches, as he was embarrassing himself and the party. Thus, Jennie went along with Randolph's desire to embark upon a round-the-world trip. Dr. Thomas Keith, a prominent surgeon who specialized in treating the genital and ovarian areas, accompanied them. In addition to two menservants and the doctor, they took with them a lead-lined coffin.

On June 27, 1894, the party sailed from England with a first stop in Jennie's hometown of New York, but instead of indulging in visits to happy childhood haunts, for fear of somehow stirring Randolph's anxieties, they soon embarked on a train for Bar Harbor, Maine, which Jennie likened to a second Newport, Rhode Island. Much like Newport, it was a summer resort for the wealthy seeking to escape the heat of the cities. Rusticators, as they were known, built huge shingle "cottages" here furnished with every amenity.

For the moment, Bar Harbor was a welcome reprieve from the long ocean voyage, and Jennie was in her element. They were entertained by George Vanderbilt in his house facing the sea, complete with a swimming pool "open to the sky, [and] through which fresh sea water constantly flowed," according to Elisabeth

Kehoe's *Fortune's Daughters: The Extravagant Lives of the Jerome Sisters: Jennie Churchill, Clara Frewen and Leonie Leslie*. Jennie danced the popular "Boston" at a local country club. Kehoe noted that Jennie still thought of herself as American and had not lost her American accent. Indeed, she was happy to meet "some delightful women, with whom I found myself in that perfect sympathy which can only be felt between compatriots."

Such happy moments were not to last—Randolph's health and temper became worse, causing scenes. One ugly argument sent one manservant back to England.

Randolph was often ill because he insisted that they keep moving. His irritability or mood set the pace of the day; he showered abuse on Jennie when he was out of sorts. In this manner the small party staggered across Canada to Banff Springs, then on to Vancouver and San Francisco. All along the way in Canada, the irascible patient only grew worse.

Jennie kept in touch with her two sisters—in one especially sad letter she wrote to Leonie from Banff: "As soon as he gets a little better from having a rest and being quiet he will be put back by this traveling—and *nothing* will deter him from doing what he likes."

In the same letter, cited in Peregrine Churchill and Julian Mitchell's *Jennie, Lady Randolph Churchill, A Portrait with Letters*, Jennie added, "He is very kind and considerate when he feels well—but absolutely *impossible* when he gets excited—and he gets like that 20 times a day—you may imagine my life is not an easy one. . . . I try to make the best of it."

"Making the best of things," whatever happened, was Jennie's way of dealing with unpleasantries, and she often added such sayings in her letters to friends and family. Especially to Winston, ignorant of her true situation, she added such homilies when she wanted to encourage him or reply to his pleading letters.

From San Francisco, Jennie and Randolph, Dr. Keith, and the remaining manservant set off next for Japan. Randolph only became visibly more ill, more difficult to deal with. More angry scenes . . . and the second servant was sent home. After Japan, Randolph insisted that they visit Burma, which he had been so instrumental in annexing for the British Empire years before. And to top off all of Jennie's other miseries, she received a telegram from Count Kinsky announcing his engagement to Countess Elizabeth Wolff Metternich zur e Gacht. Jennie was devastated, and her subsequent letter to Clara shows it: "I HATE IT. I shall return without a friend in the world & too old to make any more now." And then to Leonie, while steaming to Egypt from India: "I suppose Charles [Count Kinsky] has written to you about his engagement he wired it to me—and from his last letter I wasn't expecting it. . . . Oh, Leonie darling, do you think it is too late to stop it? Nothing is impossible."

Actually, the always-resolute Jennie for once was reduced to pleading: "Can't you help me—for Heaven sake write to him. Don't be astonished at me writing this. . . . But I am frightened of the future all alone—& Charles is the only person on earth that I cd start life afresh with." She added: "The future looks too black and lonely—without him—don't let him marry until he has seen me—It is only a month to wait."

Thus, her journey from hell continued as they visited Cairo and Alexandria, Egypt, where they joined a ship to Marseilles. Jennie then gave in to Randolph's insistence that they go to Monte Carlo before they could return to England.

Christmas back home in London was a sad affair. Even though Randolph seemed a bit better physically, mentally he was "1000 times worse," Jennie wrote to Leonie. As her husband now lay dying, she added, "Up to now the General Public and even Society does not know the real truth & after all my sacrifices and the misery of these 6 months, it would be hard if it got out."

On January 9, 1895, Kinsky was married. Two weeks later, on January 24, Randolph died. He left substantial debts—his Rand gold mining shares, which would have made his children millionaires, had to be sold to cover the debts. Jennie was left with very little financial security, and in this grim January 1895 she had lost the two men she had loved the most.

Still, these blows did not keep Jennie down for long. She indeed believed in making the best of things—no weeping and wailing for this beautiful lady. She felt that she deserved a little fun and, as Peregrine and Julian noted, she now took her parental duties ever more seriously. Historians naturally have devoted much more attention to Winston, but his younger brother Jack also benefited from Jennie's greater interest in their affairs. While Jennie spent so much time on the more demanding and at times "difficult" son, she in fact was equally involved with her younger son, albeit less visibly.

In addition, Jennie soon left behind the coldness of the duchess and the restraints of formal mourning—she was expected to wear black and refrain from attending social events—to visit her familiar open and Gay Paree. Here Leonie and her young son Seymour, who was confined in a body cast in hopes it would cure his tubercular hip, joined her. Not able to romp and play with other children, Seymour spent most days lounging on the sofa watching the grown-ups. Little "Chou Chou," as Jennie called him, would later remember the elegant little salon where his mother and aunt—they were so different, so complementary—would entertain "*le tout Paris*." Visitors such as the Prince of Wales, Ignace Paderewski, and perhaps Marcel Proust were among them. But the one who captured the youngster's imagination was the "friendly Irish ogre," William Bourke Cockran.

The recently widowed Cockran was an Irish-born American lawyer and politician, a self-made man who had left Ireland at the age of seventeen, had clerked in a New York department store, taught Latin and French, been a principal in a public school, and worked as a foreign correspondent. By now a member of Congress, he was a man of eloquence and enormous charm. Clearly, as if they emerged from a Hollywood script, the charismatic Jennie and Bourke were made for each other.

Soon Jennie and Bourke were seen everywhere together. They had so much in common—horses, theater, music—and they both loved conversation, in which each was a prolific master. Jennie wrote home to her sons that Paris was "charming." She went bicycling—daringly wearing black bloomers, the latest fashion for active ladies. And on the pond at the *Palais de Glace*, she was happy to report, she still could perform the figures that usually were the province of really accomplished skaters.

Most important, though, she was sharing these joys with a dynamic Irish American who also had just lost a spouse. Here, it appeared so tantalizingly, was a man she could find love with again. But then the charming spell was broken—Jennie was summoned back to England, to her seventy-year-old mother's bedside. On April 2, 1895, Clara Hall Jerome died with her three surviving daughters by her side. The sisters had agreed to escort their mother's body to Brooklyn for burial next to their father in Greenwood Cemetery, but Jennie decided instead to return to Paris, even though her affair with Cockran had ended. They would remain friends throughout their lives, and just months later, on Winston's first trip to America, the great orator would be an enormous influence on the young future leader and coach him in the art of public speaking.

Again at loose ends, Jennie jumped into the familiar breathless, if a bit mindless, social whirl of country-house parties, dinners, and balls but began wondering, as she later wrote, "if indeed this was all that the remainder of my life held for me." With all her vitality and joi de vivre, Jennie must have known that there was much more in store for her.

She already realized that her contacts were invaluable to Winston in seeking his journalistic outlets and military postings. When he wrote an article for the *Saturday Review* about the fighting between the Spaniards and rebels in Cuba in 1895, Jennie wasted no time in sending copies to influential friends. Later Jennie arranged for him to cover the action on the northwest frontier of India for the *Daily Telegraph*, and when he had his book on that experience ready, she helped obtain Longman as the publisher for *The Story of the Malakand Field Force*. She, more than anybody else, helped Winston, himself always short of money, turn his writing skills and journalistic bent into a moneymaking enterprise.

In June 1898, meanwhile, Jennie was invited to a country-house party at Warwick Castle by Daisy Warwick, who had had a long reign as the Prince of Wales's favorite mistress. Among the guests was a handsome young officer in the Scots Guards, George Cornwallis-West, a twenty-four-year-old with upper-class credentials: Eton College, Sandhurst, and now his posting with the Guards. All in all, it was a background similar to that of Jennie's son Winston. Even their ages were close—Cornwallis-West was exactly sixteen days older than Winston. The only son of an ancient family, he was heir to Ruthin Castle in Denbighshire, a property of ten thousand acres. With little real money to his name, however, he was expected to marry an heiress. His two sisters had done very well in that regard—one had married the wealthy Prince of Pless, and the youngest was engaged to the very rich Duke of Westminster.

Warwick Castle, one of the most splendid places in England, stands on a bluff above the river Avon. In this magnificent setting, George at once noticed the lady guest whose striking beauty and zest for life made her seem ageless. In no time, he was totally smitten by her charms. Before their fellow guests were aware, the two were out boating on the river together. And he had fallen desperately in love. Soon they were writing each other twice a day; their relationship quickly progressed to the point that he was addressing her as his "Darling little Missus" or "Dear Angel."

At first his family had welcomed the intelligent and talented Jennie, hoping some of her culture would rub off on their unintellectual heir. Daisy Warwick was enthusiastic over the match, saying, "A nice, clever woman will only influence him for the good." Others were not so sure, and when his mother realized the seriousness of the attraction, she was appalled. After all, and sad to say, Jennie's reputation for financial extravagance and sexually charged affairs was well known. In addition to those negative factors, Jennie's age provided no hope for her to give George an heir. Understandably, his mother made it as difficult as possible for the two to get together and hoped the attraction would wear off. The fact is, Jennie's friends also tried to keep the two lovers apart. As a result, Jennie and George resorted to clandestine meeting—perhaps adding unexpected zest to their relationship.

But there always was the financial worry for Jennie. And having seen Winston begin living by the pen, she mused over ways she also could find a niche in the literary world. After all, this was the age of the New Woman. Women were beginning to work outside the home, and several had become well-known journalists and editors. Biographer Sebba observed that Jennie had so many of the right attributes: "She was bold, enterprising, highly educated and unconventional, but with one great advantage—she was enormously well connected." After much thought, Jennie decided to start a literary review.

Winston encouraged his mother in one breath, as an enthusiastic young son would, but in the next breath he rather thoughtlessly said that the project would make up for all her silly social amusements. Most important, though, it could be profitable.

She discussed the project with many people, but Bourke Cockran was the adviser she valued the most. He was in London that winter; they had continued seeing each other on and off during 1896 and 1897, but Jennie was never going to leave England, and Bourke felt compelled to go back to New York and his seat in Congress.

Jennie's *Anglo-Saxon Review* was at last launched—to mixed reviews, as the saying goes. But the friend who now became her staunchest supporter was fellow American Pearl Craigie. Contributing to the review under her pen name (John Oliver Hobbes), she was always at Jennie's disposal. Without her help, Jennie declared, the review would never have got off the ground.

While Jennie was terribly busy putting this new venture together, George hovered in the background, nervous and constantly feeling inferior to the energetic Jennie. His letters from this time suggest that his interests did not go beyond horses, steeplechases, and shooting. Jennie, for her part, wrote a friend: "I suppose you think I am foolish. But I don't care. I'm having such fun."

After the first issue of the review was out, Jennie and George escaped to Paris for a few delightful days. Later George wrote, "I did so enjoy my two days and nights!! in Paris, my love, and trust that they were only a foretaste of what is to come."

Paradoxically, Jennie was trying to cool down their romance . . . but not trying very hard. Another person who was trying to change the course of their romance was the Prince of Wales himself. That August, in Cowes, he ordered the young lieutenant to confer with him aboard the *Britannia* and explained that he should not marry Jennie. He also warned that after years of negotiations with the Boer Republic in South Africa, war was now imminent. As summer melted into autumn, the Prince of Wales was proven right on the war issue. George then learned the prince had arranged his appointment as a general's aide-de-camp, and he would be serving in South Africa, far from Jennie's side.

Jennie was furious with the prince for having George sent off to war. But a more pressing issue held her attention. She had been asked to preside over a committee of prominent American women in London to raise funds to refurbish a hospital ship, to be christened the *Maine*, bound for Cape Town. Other members included the two duchesses of Marlborough—the widowed Lily and Sunny's wife, Consuelo Vanderbilt—and her father's old mistress Fanny Ronald. At once it was obvious that Jennie, with her limitless energy, would be the guiding light and inspiration. A program of musical concerts was organized, and a chalk drawing of Jennie by John Singer Sargent was commissioned for the program cover—the same drawing still hangs in Winston's study at Chartwell. Overall, Jennie's committee raised almost £45,000 for the hospital ship.

Jennie later wrote that those weeks were perhaps the most absorbing of her life. Secretly she planned to accompany the hospital ship to South Africa, scene of the raging Boer War, on the chance that she might get to see George and Winston, both on the scene with the British army (although her bold Winston, typically, would be a reporter part of the time and an army officer at other times).

On December 16, 1899, Leonie's good friend (and brother to the Prince of Wales), the Duke of Connaught, visited the *Maine* to present the ship's company a Union Jack in the name of the queen and commented that never before had a ship sailed under the combined flags of Great Britain and the United States. This was thanks to Jennie, who obtained an American flag herself when President William McKinley refused to send one, since the United States was largely anti-British and pro-Boer in its sentiments. On the eve of their departure, the Prince of Wales sent Jennie a note to wish her a safe return and added, "I admire your courage."

Jennie of course handled her role dramatically and dressed the part. As the ship left the English coast, she wore a starched white nurse's uniform with lace frills on the blouse and a red cross on her arm, an outfit she had designed. While at sea she wrote on the ship's notepaper depicting three flags—American, British, and Red Cross—also her design. As she knew, Winston had signed a contract as a war correspondent with the *Morning Post*. He then set off for South Africa with eighteen bottles of ten-year-old Scotch whiskey and six of very old *eau de vie*, as well as twelve bottles of Rose's lime juice cordial. She did not know, however, that son Jack had enlisted and he, too, would be in South Africa when the hospital ship arrived. In fact, Winston had helped to obtain Jack's commission in the South African Light Horse.

Just before sailing, meanwhile, another disappointment for Jennie—she was informed that George had suffered a severe sunstroke that endangered his heart, and he was being sent home from the war. She was committed, however, to the hospital ship's cruise to South Africa, no easy voyage as it turned out. She wrote to

Leonie with complaints about the cold and wet conditions aboard the ship, which had been forced to set sail before everything was ready. A highlight had been the celebration of her birthday as the *Maine* crossed the equator, but she bemoaned the difficulty of trying to play the piano on the high seas.

Jennie later reported her version of the trip in the form of a series of letters to be published in her *Anglo-Saxon Review* in June. Here she describes passing through a terrible storm on the way to Cape Town and passing through hailstones the size of "small plums."

She held some hope of catching up with George in South Africa before he was sent home to England, but it seems that their ships may have passed in the night as he steamed toward England and she to South Africa.

The *Maine* arrived at Cape Town on January 22 with much ado both aboard and at a reception ashore. But the British high commissioner and other officials boarding the ship said it must sail immediately to Durban, fill up with patients, and return to England with them. This was not at all what Jennie understood was to be the *Maine's* purpose. The ship was equipped with X-ray equipment and a qualified medical staff. Rather than merely transport the sick and wounded, the *Maine* was designed to treat them aboard.

Lady Churchill was not one to accede meekly, and as she spent a few happy hours reunited with both of her sons, she was determined to keep her ship on course as a treating facility. After all the trouble she had gone to, the *Maine* was not to be regarded as a mere troopship. Unsurprisingly, Jennie would have her way; she later reported turning aside three attempts to send her right back home.

In the meantime, writing to Leonie on February 3, Jennie said she had seen both Jack and Winston off to the front. Jack's presence of course had been a surprise, and the reunion with Winston was especially poignant since it was their first sight of each other since his sensational escape from a Boer prison just before Christmas. While they were the only two in the world she really cared about, as if an afterthought, she mentioned George and wondered if his family and others were "making mischief between us."

Jennie was preparing to receive the sick and wounded as they arrived at the hospital ship a few days later by train. Many of the casualties were survivors of the terrible battle of Spion Kop, which Winston covered in his correspondent's role. And Jennie herself was mentioned in the *Central News* of Durban: "Lady Randolph Churchill superintended their reception, personally directed berthing and flitted among the injured as an 'angel of mercy.'" A week later, on February 13, Jack was brought aboard as a patient, having been wounded in the leg. Not seriously hurt, Jack was soon literally back in the saddle with the Light Horse.

Once Jennie was satisfied that the ship was running smoothly, she was off to visit the front lines herself. Naturally, she was given all the proper passes and permissions, even the use of an official's private railway car. Thus she soon saw the big cannon named the "Lady Randolph Churchill" in her honor and the site where Winston had been captured in mid-November of the previous year. A guard pointed out the wreck of his armored train, and she saw the graves of those killed in the incident. Like any mother, Jennie thanked God that her son had been spared the same fate. With Winston by her side, she also saw the "desolation and misery" of war at Ladysmith, recently liberated after a long siege. In a tent overlooking the town, Jennie was given a shell from the gun named for her.

After two weeks in South Africa, the ship set sail for home filled with wounded men. After a brief stop was made at gloomy St. Helena, site of Napoleon Bonaparte's final exile and death, to take on fresh water, the hospital ship *Maine* arrived at Southampton on April 23, having been away for four months.

Back home she found that George still was ill with complications from his sunstroke and feeling sorry for himself. They hadn't seen each other for six months, and the long absence that everyone hoped would draw them apart had in fact only made their hearts grow fonder. Now it seemed they simply must get married.

While plans went forward, friends, and even the Prince of Wales, who had arranged for George to be sent to war and out of Jennie's orbit, began to come around to their obvious determination to wed. Winston, it seems would be able to attend the wedding on June 30, but Jack still would be on duty in South Africa. When he wrote that he felt like the prodigal son "sent away to these horrible colonies with instructions never to be seen or heard of again," she wrote back to assure him the wedding would be small in scale. "It will be very quiet—no breakfast—except for the family—but I won't do it in a 'hole & corner' fashion as tho' I was ashamed of it—I pray from the bottom of my heart that it won't make you unhappy—You know how dearly I love you both—& the thought that it may hurt you—is the one cloud on my happiness. But you won't grudge me the latter?" Jennie may have revealed a bit of her own doubts when she added, "Nothing could exceed George's goodness & devotion—& I think we shall be very happy."

The wedding took place at St. Paul's Knightbridge, with Winston in attendance, but none of the Cornwallis-Wests. Winston reported on the wedding to Jack the next day in simple, matter-of-fact terms: "Mamma was married to George West on Saturday and everything went off very well. The whole of the Churchill family from Sunny [now the Ninth Duke of Marlborough] downward was drawn in solid phalanx and their approval ratified the business. The wedding was very pretty and George looked supremely happy in having at length obtained his heart's desire." But Winston tellingly added: "As we already know each other's views on the subject, I need not pursue it."

The newly wed "odd couple" went off to Paris, Belgium, then Scotland—a honeymoon that lasted four months. But then reality set in, and Jennie left George to campaign for Winston, who was seeking a parliamentary seat from Oldham again. She also faced financial problems at her recently neglected *Anglo-Saxon Review*. While Jennie was dealing with these pursuits, George went fishing and reported how excited he was over an eight-pound salmon he had caught, "the first in my life!"

George later would write in his memoirs that it was a glorious time when the cost of living was low and money was very much in evidence. The wealth was "possessed by the nicest people, who entertained both in London and in the country." Unfortunately the wealth so much in evidence to the new groom was not in his bank. After paying Jennie's many debts and coming to terms firsthand with her extravagances, there was not much left out of his small income to live on.

Unable to afford a country place of their own, the Cornwallis-Wests were grateful to be invited by such wealthy friends as Alfred Rothschild at Holton, his estate in Herefordshire. Here they were included with his many eclectic friends—Alfred himself was somewhat eccentric and often entertained guests with a small private circus or his own orchestra. Also, almost as an aside, Jennie was not above using those close to Alfred, such as Lord Kitchener, to further her son Winston's career.

The end of a truly historic era came on February 2, 1901, with the funeral of Queen Victoria, whose reign had seen the British Empire grow to the point that the sun never set over one or another of its many lands. Jennie's relationship with her good friend, admirer, and, some say, onetime lover, the Prince of Wales, now Edward VII, would change. For his coronation, she and sister Leonie were given seats in the king's box—a favor to his women friends. Leonie was included because of her close relationship with the king's brother, the Duke of Connaught. The new king had cooled a bit on Jennie after she went against his wishes and married George, but he had now forgiven her and, in fact, dubbed her Lady of Grace of St. John of Jerusalem and presented her with the Order of the Royal Red Cross for her services on the *Maine*.

Meanwhile, George, try as he might, could not seem to add to their small finances. While tolerating the childish antics of her new husband, Jennie turned more and more to Winston for intellectual stimulation. Her *Anglo-Saxon Review*, which was not a financial success, was no longer published. Seeing she was restless and looking for another project, Winston suggested she go through all the correspondence she had saved over the years. Surely it was valuable material . . . perhaps she should go through the letters and sort out her thoughts about her life with Randolph.

But this was not enough for the energetic Jennie—she instead would write a play. And yet, no, she wouldn't. She now turned to her memoir, *Reminiscences*. And when this was well received—as a best seller, actually—she then set out to write her play, titled *His Borrowed Plumes*. The plot, not so surprisingly, would almost follow the real-life happenings of Jennie and George. According to George, it was Jennie who asked the most celebrated actress of their day, Mrs. Patrick Campbell, to play the lead. Thus—fatefully, it would turn out—entered "Mrs. Pat," as she was called, into their lives.

A huge party was given before opening night . . . and that was just as well, since the play unfortunately folded after a few performances, but the star performer, Mrs. Pat, remained in the picture in an unexpected way.

Jennie once again was on a social whirl of parties, dinners, concerts, and balls, but this time to help cover up the cracks forming in her marriage. More and more she was realizing what everyone else had known all along: she and George had nothing in common. She tried to spend time with her sons, but they were busy getting on with their own lives. Both sons would be married in 1908, and both brought into her life daughters-in-law whom she was pleased with and indeed liked. Jack's Gwendeline Bertie, daughter of the Earl of Abingdon, and Winston's Clementine Hozier.

Faced, as always, with the constant need for money, Jennie now turned, with Winston's encouragement, to a business of spending money, which she certainly enjoyed, and making money as a result—by buying attractive run-down houses and redecorating them with style and reselling them for a profit. Then, with the birth of Jack and Goonie's son and, six weeks later, the baby girl born to Winston and Clemmie, Jennie had come full circle. Her happiness at becoming a grandmother only made it clear in her own mind that her marriage was coming apart, thanks, but only in part, to George's infatuation with none other than Mrs. Pat.

On the occasion of their divorce on July 15, 1913, she wrote a long and still-loving letter to George: "Thank God I have the physical and mental strength and courage enough to fight my own battle in life." And this was true, even though she was now a fifty-nine-year-old grandmother who had gained weight over the years and had let her hair go gray. She still was a beautiful woman with dark sparkling eyes and not yet ready to end her incredible story.

In 1913, at the wedding of her nephew Hugh Frewen, held in Rome, she met young Montagu Phippen Porch, who quickly became her newest admirer. After the wedding parties were over, she spent a few delightful days showing her new friend her favorite Italian sights. Twenty-three years younger than Jennie, he was immediately struck with love, it seems. They would marry in London on June 1, 1918, with World War I still tearing Europe apart.

Three years into this marriage, as her husband went off to Nigeria in search of investment opportunities, Jennie went to visit her old friend Vittoria Colonna in Rome, and here she shopped to her heart's content, spending money from the recent sale of her house. She was especially pleased with a fancy pair of elegant shoes she found in one of the many boutiques ready to serve her. When she returned to England, she visited her friend Lady Frances Horner at Mells, an Elizabethan manor in Somerset. Part of Jennie's charm was her thrill in spending money and having things to show for it. Rushing down the oak stairs one evening, wearing dainty Italian shoes, perhaps the ones she had recently bought in Rome, she tripped and fell, fracturing her left leg near the ankle.

She remained at Mells for a few days, but the pain continued, and it was decided she should return to London by ambulance. Two weeks later her doctors discovered that a portion of the skin around the ankle had blackened. Diagnosing it as gangrene, they decided that amputation was the only way to save her life.

It was a blistering hot summer, which only added to the anguish of everyone around her, especially Jennie's two sisters, who with "jagged nerves," according to nephew Oswald Frewen, were in constant attendance. As the weeks passed, Jennie began to recover from her amputation and agreed to see visitors. But on June 29, just after breakfast, an artery well above the point of amputation suddenly gave way, and she began hemorrhaging.

She just managed to say, "Nurse, I'm feeling faint," before she fainted, never to regain consciousness. As the family rushed to her bedside, it was too late. Winston had run in his pajamas from his house nearby, arriving at the same moment as Jack. By the time Clara was rushing through the city streets, she saw the news posters in Trafalgar Square announcing the death of Lady Randolph Churchill. It was June 29, 1921.

Winston soon after wrote to a friend, "She suffers no more pain nor will she ever know old age, decrepitude, loneliness." But still, she would be missed.

Acknowledgments
Appendix
Bibliography
Index

Acknowledgments

As always with our *Best Little Stories* historical books, we stand on the shoulders of so many who have gone before us. We owe them all, each and every one, our sincere thanks, especially in this case to Winston Churchill's daughter, Lady Mary Soames, and her magnificent biography of her mother, *Clementine Churchill*, and to Sir Winston's official biographer, Sir Martin Gilbert, and his many books, but chiefly his *Churchill: A Life*, our Churchill "Bible" and chief reference whenever a question arose.

Almost never in history, of course, has so much been written by so many about one man, we could also say with little fear of contradiction—thus, it would be well nigh impossible in a single lifetime to read all that has been written about this extraordinary man who sprang from an English aristocrat and a dazzling American beauty in the late nineteenth century and then rescued Western Civilization from disaster in the twentieth. In the bibliography, we list those other books we consulted by those who went before us, including the Nobel Prize–winning Sir Winston himself. As indicated, our sources barely scratch the surface of what's available for the truly dedicated scholar or aficionado to consult on his or her own.

Say what any of them will, however, it may be a former wartime secretary to Sir Winston, who, in a letter written in her nineties, best summed up his greatest accomplishment of all. Writing to Laurence Geller, president of the American-based Churchill Centre, in 2006, the late Elizabeth Nel said (and it is worth repeating in full):

> In assessing my former boss's achievements I have asked myself, and have frequently passed the thought on when speaking: "What did WSC actually do—what did he achieve?" I was in London before the war, though I grew up in British Columbia, and I well remember the attitude of Londoners at the time: "We mustn't have another war; we're still suffering from the pains and losses of the last one. Let's rather go along with Hitler—let's try to work with him to

avoid war. He's probably not nearly as bad as he's portrayed. We just want to live in peace."

And what was my boss's reaction? He who knew what Hitler had in mind? He raised a clenched fist and answered in powerful tones, "Get up and fight." He reminded them of Britain's beginnings, her past struggles, her establishment of Freedom and Justice. His words appealed to the latent spirit which lies deep in British hearts. And they did get up and fight, by land, sea and in the air.

No one can take that away from Winston Churchill. The British people reacted to his courage, his determination, and his absolute loyalty to Britain and all she stood for. It was that inspiration which enabled us to win the war; not money, or clever inventions, or bombs or guns. I know. I was there.

On a more personal note, we wish to thank Dr. John Mather, president of the Washington (D.C.) Society for Churchill, for sharing his extensive knowledge of the Churchills; Allen Packwood, director, and his staff at the Churchill Archives Centre, Churchill College, Cambridge University; Alexandria Searls for her invaluable help in clearing our computer jams and in her editing suggestions; John Cammell of London for his close reading of our manuscript for historical accuracy; history buff Patrick Fogarty for his many tips; Sid Elliott; Kristin and Daniel Dubrow, and their mother, Dr. Ingrid Smyer, for listening. Last but far from least, we owe a big thanks to Joan Gore, program director, University of Virginia Center, School of Continuing and Professional Studies, and her husband Luther and all her staff for allowing us to take part, as faculty, in the 2007 seminar on Winston Churchill held at Oxford University under the joint sponsorship of the adult education programs at Virginia and Oxford—indeed, that was the very stimulus for this book. As always also, many thanks and a tip of the hat to our editor at Cumberland House, Ed Curtis, and to Ron Pitkin, president of Cumberland House, and all of his staff who are so kind to publish, promote, and distribute our books worldwide.

Note: The stories "Mole Machine Abandoned" (pages 251–53) and "Overcoming FDR's Secrecy" (pages 270–71) appeared in largely the same form in the author's *Best Little Stories from World War II* (1996). The personal stories related in "Wartime Glimpses" (pages 279–81) are based on the BBC Web site "WW2 People's War," as are the stories "Personal Glimpse" (pages 225–26), "Dictation from the Bath" (pages 249–50), "Please Don't Look Up" (pages 250–51), "Forty-Foot Waves" (pages 267–68), and "Driving for Winston" (pages 298–99).

Appendix

Best-Known Quotes

People always ask, "Didn't Winston Churchill say this or say that?" Sometimes he had not, but here are a few better-known statements he did make during the course of his extraordinary life. Many of them already appear in the text of this book, but for some readers the following may serve as a handy listing. Note: Many of his quotes are also gathered in one spot herein in "The Chiastic Churchill" (pages 317–20) and in "Personals Potpourri" (pages 344–49).

NEVER GIVE IN

At the Harrow School, October 29, 1941, with Britain still greatly threatened by Nazi Germany: "This is the lesson: never give in, never give in, never, never, never—in nothing, great or small, large or petty—never give in except to convictions of honor and good sense. Never yield to force; never yield to the apparently overwhelming might of the enemy."

SOME NECK

Before the Canadian Parliament, December 30, 1941, just days after addressing a joint session of the U.S. Congress on December 26: "When I warned [the French] that Britain would fight alone, whatever they did, their Generals told their Prime Minister and his divided cabinet: 'In three weeks England will have her neck wrung like a chicken.'

"Some chicken . . . some neck!"

IF FATHER HAD BEEN AMERICAN

Before the U.S. Congress, the day after Christmas 1941: "By the way, I cannot help reflecting that if my father had been American and my mother British, instead of the other way around, I might have got here on my own!"

BUILDINGS SHAPE US

In the House of Lords, October 28, 1943, after the historic House of Commons was destroyed in a bombing raid, not to be rebuilt until 1950, and even then in its old limited capacity, so that it always would look full and busy, rather than half empty: "We shape our buildings, and afterwards our buildings shape us."

He then went to say: "Having dwelt and served for more than forty years in the late Chamber, and having derived very great pleasure and advantage therefrom, I, naturally, should like to see it restored in all essentials to its old form, convenience and dignity."

SERVED HIM COURSE BY COURSE

In the House of Commons, October 5, 1939, after Prime Minister Neville Chamberlain returned from his infamous "peace in our time" meeting with Hitler in Munich: "The German dictator, instead of snatching the victuals from the table, has been content to have them served to him course by course."

NOT MADE OF SUGAR CANDY

Before the Canadian Parliament, December 30, 1941: "We have not journeyed across the centuries, across the oceans, across the mountains, across the prairies, because we are made of sugar candy."

CANADA THE LINCHPIN

While on the Canadian theme, here's what he said at a luncheon in London, September 4, 1941, honoring Canadian prime minister Mackenzie King: "Canada is the linchpin of the English-speaking world. Canada, with those relations of friendly, affectionate intimacy with the United States on the one hand and with her unswerving fidelity to the British Commonwealth and the Motherland on the other, is the link which joins together these great branches of the human family, a link which, spanning the oceans, brings the continents into their true relation and will prevent in future generations any growth of division between the proud and happy nations of Europe and the great countries which have come into existence in the New World."

BLOOD, SWEAT, TOIL

To the House of Commons, May 13, 1940, his first speech before the chamber as the new prime minister of England: "I would say to the House, as I said to those who have joined this Government, I have nothing to offer but blood, toil, tears and sweat. . . . You ask what is our policy. I will say, it is to wage war with all our might, with all the strength that God can give us. . . . You ask what is our aim? I can answer in one word: Victory. Victory at all costs. Victory in spite of all terror. Victory however long and hard the road may be."

ON THE BEACHES, IN THE STREETS

To the House of Commons, June 4, 1940: "We shall fight in France, we shall fight on the seas. . . . We shall fight on the beaches, we shall fight on the landing-grounds, we shall fight in the fields and in the streets, we shall fight in the hills. We shall never surrender!"

FINEST HOUR

To the House of Commons, June 18, 1940, with France just joining the list of Hitler's victims in Western Europe: "I expect that the battle of Britain is about to begin. Upon this battle depends the survival of Christian civilization. Upon it depends our own British life, and the long continuity of our institutions and our empire. The whole fury and might of the enemy must very soon be turned against us. Hitler knows that he will have to break us in this island or lose the war. If we can stand up to him, all Europe may be free and the life of the world may move forward into broad, sunlit uplands. But if we fail, then the whole world, including the United States, including all that we have known and cared for, will sink into the abyss of a new Dark Age made more sinister, and perhaps more protracted, by the lights of perverted science. Let us therefore brace ourselves to our duties, and so bear ourselves that if the British Empire and its Commonwealth last for a thousand years, men will still say, 'This was their finest hour.'"

WAR FOR ALL

To the nation by way of a BBC broadcast, July 14, 1940: "This is no war of chieftains or of princes, of dynasties or national ambition; it is a war of peoples and of causes. There are vast numbers, not only in this island but in every land, who will render faithful service in this war but whose names will never be known, whose deeds will never be recorded. This is a war of the Unknown Warriors; but let all strive without failing in faith or in duty, and the dark curse of Hitler will be lifted from our age."

TRIBUTE TO "THE FEW"

Before the House of Commons, August 20, 1940, in the midst of the Battle of Britain: "The gratitude of every home in our island, in our Empire, and indeed throughout the world, except in the abodes of the guilty, goes out to the British airmen who, undaunted by odds, unwearied in their constant challenge and mortal danger, are turning the tide of the world war by their prowess and by their devotion. Never in the field of human conflict was so much owed by so many to so few."

Bibliography

Best, Geoffrey. *Churchill: A Study in Greatness*. New York and London: Hambledon and London, 2001.

———. *Churchill and War*. New York and London: Hambledon and London, 2005.

Best, Nicholas. *The Kings and Queens of England*. London: Weidenfeld and Nicolson, 1995.

Bland, Larry I., ed. *George C. Marshall: Interviews and Reminiscences for Forrest C. Pogue*. Lexington, VA: Marshall Research Foundation, 1991.

Bradford, Sarah. *George VI*. New York and London: Fontana, 1991.

Coombs, David, with Minnie Churchill. *Sir Winston Churchill: His Life and His Paintings*. Philadelphia: Running Press, 2004.

Churchill, Jennie. *The Reminiscences of Lady Randolph Churchill*. New York: Century Company, 1908.

Churchill, Peregrine, and Julian Mitchell. *Jennie, Lady Randolph Churchill: A Portrait with Letters*. New York: St. Martin's Press, 1974.

Churchill, Randolph S. *Winston S. Churchill*. Vol. 2, *Young Statesman, 1901–1914*. Boston: Houghton Mifflin, 1967.

Churchill, Winston S. *Frontiers and Wars*. New York: Harcourt, Brace & World, 1962.

———. *A Roving Commission: My Early Life*. New York: Scribner, 1930.

———. *The Second World War*. 6 vols. New York: Simon & Schuster, 1996.

Eggenberger, David. *An Encyclopedia of Battles: Accounts of over 1,560 Battles from 1479 B.C. to the Present*. 1967. Reprint, New York: Dover, 1985.

Fedden, Robin. *Churchill at Chartwell*. New York and Oxford: Pergamon Press, 1969.

Fishman, Jack. *My Darling Clementine: The Story of Lady Churchill*. New York: David McKay, 1963.

Gilbert, Martin. *Churchill: A Life*. New York: Holt, 1991.

———. *Churchill and America*. New York: Free Press, 2005.

———. *Winston S. Churchill*. Vol. 3, *The Challenge of War, 1914–1916*. Boston: Houghton Mifflin, 1971.

Hatch, Alden. *The Mountbattens: The Last Royal Success Story*. New York: Random House, 1965.

Higham, Charles. *Dark Lady: Winston Churchill's Mother and Her World*. London: Virgin
     Books, 2006.

Holmes, Richard. *In the Footsteps of Churchill: A Study in Character*. New York: Basic
     Books, 2006.

Humes, James C. *The Wit and Wisdom of Winston Churchill: A Treasury of More than
     1,000 Quotations and Anecdotes*. New York: HarperCollins, 1994.

Innes, Bill, ed. *St Valery: The Impossible Odds*. Edinburgh: Birlinn, 2004.

Jenkins, Roy. *Churchill: A Biography*. New York: Farrar, Straus and Giroux, 2001.

Keegan, John. *Winston Churchill*. New York: Viking/Penguin, 2002.

Kehoe, Elisabeth. *Fortune's Daughters: The Extravagant Lives of the Jerome Sisters*. London:
     Atlantic Books, 2005.

Lukacs, John. *Five Days in London: May 1940*. New Haven, CT: Yale University Press, 1999.

Martin, Ralph G. *Jennie: The Life of Lady Randolph Churchill*. 2 vols. New York: New
     American Library, 1970.

Olson, Lynne. *Troublesome Young Men: The Rebels Who Brought Churchill to Power and
     Helped Save England*. New York: Farrar, Straus and Giroux, 2007.

Pilpel, Robert H. *Churchill in America, 1895–1961: An Affectionate Portrait*. New York
     and London: Harcourt Brace Jovanovich, 1976.

Roberts, Keith. *Churchill*. New York and London: Longman, 1992.

Sandys, Celia. *The Young Churchill: The Early Years of Winston Church*. New York: Dutton,
     1995.

Sebba, Anne. *American Jennie: The Remarkable Life of Lady Randolph Churchill*. New York
     and London: Norton, 2007.

Shirer, William L. *Berlin Diary: The Journal of a War Correspondent, 1934–1941*. New
     York: Knopf, 1941.

Snyder, Louis L., and Richard B. Morris, eds. *A Treasury of Great Reporting: "Literature
     Under Pressure" from the Sixteenth Century to Our Own Time*. 2nd ed. New York:
     Simon & Schuster, 1962.

Soames, Mary. *Clementine Churchill*. London: Cassell, 1979.

Thompson, Lawrence. *1940*. New York: William Morrow, 1966.

Truman, Margaret. *Harry S. Truman*. New York: William Morrow, 1972.

Wilson, Charles. *Churchill at War, 1940–45*. New York: Caroll & Graf, 2002.

Ziegler, Philip. *Mountbatten*. New York: Knopf, 1985.

PERIODICALS AND OTHER SOURCES

The Churchill Centre, http://www.winstonchurchill.org.

Sunday Times, London. May 7, 1995.

Time magazine archives.

Times, London. June 6, 1995.

"WW2 Peoples' War," BBC, http://www.bbc.co.uk/ww2peopleswar.

Index